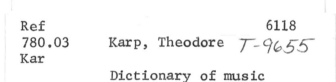

DICTIONARY
of
MUSIC

Theodore Karp

"A LAUREL ORIGINAL"

GALAHAD BOOKS · NEW YORK CITY

**Published by
Dell Publishing Co., Inc.
1 Dag Hammarskjold Plaza
New York, New York 10017**

THEODORE KARP

a graduate of the Juilliard School of Music, received his Ph.D. in Music at New York University, where he was an A. Ogden Butler Fellow. He is currently Chairman of the Department of Music at the University of California, Davis, California.

Contents

Preface

This dictionary aims to assist the music lover and the student of music toward a better understanding of the musical heritage of the Western world. It seeks to present in compact and understandable form information regarding the history of Western music, the constitution of its more important forms, biographies of the greatest composers, and accounts of compositional techniques, performance media, and acoustic phenomena, together with brief definitions of basic terms in performance and theory.

In order to preserve the advantages of a compact format and still cover all points essential to basic articles, the choice of articles reflects considerable selectivity. The reader will observe, for example, that there are no entries either for performers or for individual compositions; nor are entries provided for strictly esoteric matters. While such information is of interest, it does not contribute sufficiently to the primary purpose of this work.

Entries differ somewhat in the degree of technical language employed. In basic entries an effort has been made to keep the language as simple as possible and to relate as directly as possible to matters within the experience of the nonmusician. However, more technical terminology has been utilized for more complex subject matter. The inexperienced reader who requires information on technical matters can obtain some background by consulting the articles on Notation (excluding the section on history), Interval (and also the brief entries for specific intervals), Chord, and Scale.

The nature of the present-day concert and record repertoire has influenced the selection of biographical entries and the space accorded to each. This repertoire emphasizes music written during the period 1700–1920. Thus the reader will find that less space is devoted to the great masters of the Middle Ages and Renaissance than to comparable masters of later periods. Minor figures active before 1700 are less well represented than their more recent counterparts. On the other hand, an effort has been made to treat 20th-century composers as generously as space permits. American composers of this period are given slight preference over their European colleagues. In some instances the space accorded a particular composer reflects the importance his thoughts had for his contemporaries rather than the intrinsic merit or popularity of his music.

On the whole, the author wishes to emphasize not isolated bits of information, but the context in which specific information is to be understood. Many entries treated separately in other works are to be found under a common heading in this volume. There is, for example, a single entry for all of the common woodwind instruments. There we are able to discuss the basic techniques shared by all, together with a brief account of the history of these instruments and their repertoire. Individual entries are provided for each of the instruments, but these contain only the briefest possible definition. Names and terms given separate entries are placed in capitals when occurring elsewhere in the dictionary; capitals are used also to signal the presence of information pertinent or essential to any entry consulted. Since a consistent effort has been made to hold duplication of information between entries to a minimum, the reader is urged to make use of the cross-references provided in the text.

Major entries have been provided for each of the main historical periods. In this volume, Medieval Music covers the period c.600–1425; the Renaissance, 1425–1600; the Baroque, 1600–1750; the Classical Era, 1750–1820; the Romantic Period, 1820–1910; and the Modern Period, 1910 to the present. These dates represent a concession to convenience, for it should be obvious that no major stylistic change in any art occurs overnight or from one year to the next. Change occurs steadily and only at a comparatively slow pace. Furthermore, for any given time one may observe an intermingling of progressive, moderate, conservative, and even reactionary currents. The Baroque, for example, begins to give way to the Classical era by the 1730s in Italy, and yet Baroque traits are still observable in music written a few decades after 1750. Scholars often disagree regarding the dating of historical periods; the dates given above reflect the author's choice from alternatives advanced by eminent scholars. Since stylistic comparisons between adjacent periods are made frequently, the reader may obtain useful information by consulting additional articles in the historical series. Information concerning the Renaissance, for example, may be obtained through comparisons given in the article on the Baroque. The reader will often gain a useful historical perspective for the understanding of a biography by reading the entry for the pertinent historical period. Conversely, the reader concerned with a particular historical period will often find useful information given in the biographies of the greatest composers of that period.

The article, Bibliography, has been provided for the reader who desires to widen his horizons by consulting more specialized works of greater technical difficulty. Important abbreviations and musical symbols are treated before the main body of the work itself.

The author wishes to express his deep gratitude for the kind interest and friendly advice of several of his colleagues. Chief among these are Professors Robert Fowells, Richard Hoppin, Edward Kravitt, and Richard Swift.

THEODORE KARP

ABBREVIATIONS USED IN THIS DICTIONARY

b.	born
bapt.	baptized
Brit.	British
c.	circa
d.	died
F	French
G	German
Gr	Greek
I	Italian
L	Latin
P	Portuguese
Pr	Provençal
S	Spanish

ABBREVIATIONS OF MUSICAL TERMS

A.	Alto
Adg°, Ad°	Adagio
All°	Allegro
Allgtt°, Alltt°	Allegretto
All'8va	All'ottava
Arp°	Arpeggio
A.S.	Al segno
B.	Bass
B.c.	Basso continuo
Bl.	Blasinstrumente (wind instruments)
Br.	Bratsche (viola)
C.	Cantus, Canto
C.a.	Coll'arco or Cor anglais (English horn)
C.B.	Col basso

Cb., C.b.	Contrabass
C.d.	Colla destra
C.f., Cf.	Cantus firmus
C.i.	Corno inglese (English horn)
C. I	Canto primo
Cl.	Clarinet, cello, or clavier
Coll'ott., C. 8va, C.O.	Coll'ottava
Co. So., C.S.	Come sopra (as above)
C.P.	Colla parte
C.S.	Colla sinistra
C. voc.	Colla voce
D	Dominant
D.C.	Da Capo
Div.	Divisi
D.S.	Dal Segno
E.H.	English Horn
f	Forte
ff	Fortissimo
fff	Fortississimo
Fg., Fag.	Fagott, Fagotto (Bassoon)
Fl.	Flute, Flauto, Flöte
F.O.	Full Organ
fp	Forte-piano
fz	Forzando, forzato
Gd. Ch.	Grand Choeur (Full Organ)
G.O.	Grand Orgue, Great Organ
G.P.	General Pause or Grand Positif (Great and Choir Organs combined)
G.P.R.	Grand Positif Récit (Great, Choir, and Swell Organs combined)
G.R.	Grand Récit (Great and Swell Organs combined)
Gr. Fl.	Grosse Flöte (Flute)
Gr. Tr.	Grosse Trommel (Bass Drum)
Gsp.	Glockenspiel
Hb.	Hautbois, Hoboe (Oboe)
H.C.	Haute-contre (Alto)

Hlzbl., Hzbl.	Holzbläser (Woodwinds)
Hr., Hrn.	Horn(s), Hörner
Hrf.	Harfe (Harp)
H.W., Hptw.	Hauptwerk (Great Organ)
Kb.	Kontrabass (Double bass)
Kfg.	Kontrafagott (Double bassoon)
Kl.	Klarinette or Klavier
Kl. Fl., K.F.	Kleine Flöte (Piccolo)
Kl. Tr.	Kleine Trommel (Snare Drum)
L., L.H.	Left hand, Linke Hand
M., Maj.	Major
m., min.	Minor
M., MM.	Maelzel's Metronome
M.d.	Mano destra, Main droite (right hand)
mf	Mezzo forte
M.g.	Main gauche (left hand)
mp	Mezzo piano
MS	Manuscript
M.s.	Mano sinistra (left hand)
M.V.	Mezza voce
Obbl.	Obbligato
O.C.	Organo Corale (Choir Organ)
O.E.	Organo Expressivo (Swell Organ)
Op.	Opus
O.W., Obw.	Oberwerk (Swell Organ)
P., Pos.	Positif (Choir Organ)
p	Piano
p.f	Poco forte or Più forte
Pf., Pfte.	Pianoforte, piano
Pizz.	Pizzicato
Pk.	Pauken (Timpani)
pp	Pianissimo
ppp	Pianississimo

P.R.	Positif Récit (Choir Organ and Swell Organ combined)
Ps.	Posaune (trombone) or Psalm
R.	Récit (Swell Organ)
rf, rfz	Rinforzando
Rk	Rank
Rit.	Ritardando, Ritenuto
S.	Soprano
s.	Senza (without or remove)
SATB	Soprano, Alto, Tenor, Bass
sf, sfz	Sforzato, Sforzando
sfzp	Sforzando-piano
Sp.	Spitze (point)
Str.	Strings, Streichinstrumente
String.	Stringendo
S.W.	Schwellwerk (Swell Organ)
T.	Tenor, Tonic, Tutti, or Tempo
T.C.	Tre corde
Ten.	Tenuto
T.P., Tempo I	Tempo primo
Tr.	Trumpet or Trill
T.S.	Tasto solo
U.C.	Una corda
U.W.	Unterwerk (Choir Organ)
V.	Violin or Voice
Va.	Viola
Vc., Vcl., Vllo.	Violoncello
Vl., Vn.	Violin
V.S.	Volti subito
Vv.	Violins
WoO	Without Opus

ABBREVIATIONS USED IN BIBLIOGRAPHICAL CITATIONS OF MUSIC

BWV *Bach Werke Verzeichnis* (Schmieder's thematic catalogue of the works of J. S. Bach)

D Deutsch catalogue of the works of Schubert

DdT *Denkmäler der deutscher Tonkunst*

DTB *Denkmäler der Tonkunst in Bayern* (second series of DdT)

DTO *Denkmäler der Tonkunst in Österreich*

GMB Schering, *Geschichte der Musik im Beispielen*

H Hoboken catalogue of the works of Haydn

HAM Davison and Apel, *Historical Anthology of Music*

K, KV Köchel Verzeichnis (the standard thematic catalogue of the works of W. A. Mozart)

K Kirkpatrick's listing of keyboard works of D. Scarlatti

L Longo's edition of keywork works of D. Scarlatti

M Mandyczewski's edition of works of J. Haydn

MGG *Die Musik in Geschichte und Gegenwart*

S Schmieder's thematic catalogue of works of J. S. Bach (see BWV)

Wo Wotquenne's thematic catalogue of the works of C. P. E. Bach

WTC Well Tempered Clavier (a collection of preludes and fugues by J. S. Bach)

PITCH NAMES

Diatonic notes

ENGLISH	C	D	E	F	G	A	B
GERMAN	C	D	E	F	G	A	H
FRENCH	Ut	Re	Mi	Fa	Sol	La	Si
ITALIAN	Do	Re	Mi	Fa	Sol	La	Si

Accidentals

	♯	x	♭	♭♭	♮
ENGLISH	Sharp	Double-Sharp	Flat	Double-Flat	Natural
GERMAN	Kreuz	Doppelkreuz	Be	Doppel-be	Auflösungszeichen
FRENCH	Dièse	Double dièse	Bémol	Double bémol	Bécarre
ITALIAN	Diesis	Doppio diesis	Bemolle	Doppio bemolle	Bequadro

ENGLISH	C♯	Cx	D♯	Dx	E♯	F♯	Fx	G♯	Gx	A♯	Ax	B♯
GERMAN	Cis	Cisis	Dis	Disis	Eis	Fis	Fisis	Gis	Gisis	Ais	Aisis	His
ENGLISH	C♭	D♭	D♭♭	E♭	E♭♭	F♭	G♭	G♭♭	A♭	A♭♭	B♭	B♭♭
GERMAN	Ces	Des	Deses	Es	Eses	Fes	Ges	Geses	As	Ases	B	Bes

Octave Registers

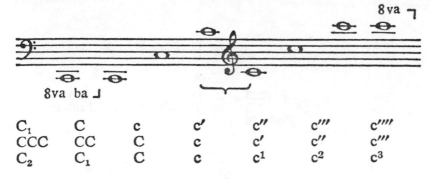

C_1	C	c	c'	c''	c'''	c''''
CCC	CC	C	c	c'	c''	c'''
C_2	C_1	C	c	c^1	c^2	c^3

MUSICAL SYMBOLS

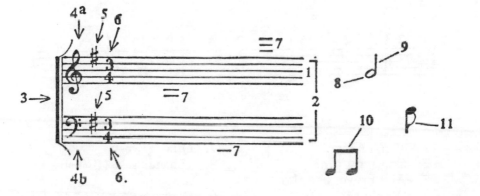

1. Staff.
2. System. If only two staves are connected, these may be termed a grand staff.
3. Brace.
4a. Clef (Treble).
4b. Clef (Bass).
5. Key Signature.
6. Time Signature.
7. Ledger lines.
8. Note-head.
9. Stem.
10. Beam.
11. Flag or hook.

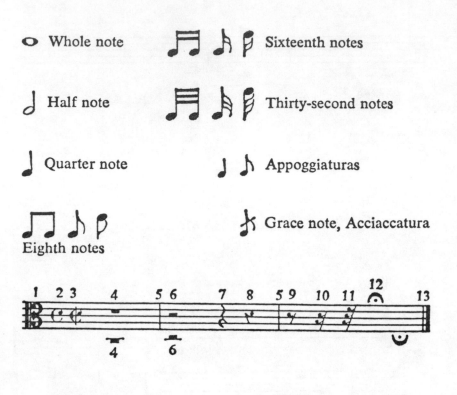

Whole note   Sixteenth notes

Half note   Thirty-second notes

Quarter note   Appoggiaturas

Eighth notes   Grace note, Acciaccatura

1. Clef (Alto).
2. Common time.
3. Alla breve, Cut time.
4. Whole rest.
5. Bar line; the space between two bar lines is a
   measure or bar.
6. Half rest.

7. Quarter rest.
8. Quarter rest (British
   usage).
9. Eighth rest.
10. Sixteenth rest.
11. Thirty-second rest.
12. Pause, hold, fermata.
13. Double bar.

#	Sharp.
x	Double sharp.
♭	Flat.
♭♭	Double flat.
♮	Natural.
✢	Trill.
∿	Mordent.
∿	Inverted mordent.
∽	Turn.
∽	Inverted turn.

1. Clef (Alto).
2. Repeat begins at this point.
3. Repeat this note as a series of eighths equalling the value of a whole note.
4. Repeat this note as a series of eighths equalling the value of a half note.
5. Repeat this note as a series of sixteenths equalling the value of a half note.
6. Crescendo.
7. Diminuendo, decrescendo.
8. Repeat the previous measure.
9. Repeat (from sign 2 if present, from the beginning, if not).
10. Alternate between these two notes in eighths until the total value equals that of a half note.
11. Alternate between these two notes in sixteenths until the

total value equals that of a half note. (See Tremolo.) Nos. 12–23 do *not* refer to the notes themselves but to the auxiliary symbols.

12. Glissando.
13. Arpeggio; 13a, a nearly obsolete form of the same symbol.
14. Slur.
15. Staccato. In present usage, the wedge represents a sharper staccato than the dot. In conjunction with fast values, the dot may also indicate the bowing technique, *sautillé*. The wedge may also indicate the bowing technique, *martelé*.
16. Accent.
17. Accent (a heavier accent than 16).
18. Accent (a less emphatic accent than 16); tenuto; the dash may also indicate the bowing technique, détaché.
19. Portato.
20. Portato; if written in conjunction with fast values, the combination of slur and dots may also indicate the bowing technique, *ricochet*.
21. Tie.
22. Dot.
23. Repeat (from 9, if present; from 2 if 9 is not present; or from the beginning if neither 9 nor 2 is present).

         ⊓   Down-bow.
         ⋁   Up-bow.

A

Absolute music: (1) music that does not openly represent specific ideas or emotions (i.e., the opposite of PROGRAM MUSIC); (2) music—such as BACH's *Art of Fugue* and much RENAISSANCE music—that is conceived independently of particular instrumental or vocal tone colors and may therefore be performed suitably by different instrumental and vocal combinations (infrequent, erroneous usage).

Absolute pitch: the ability to recognize or sing a given PITCH without reference to any previously identified sound.

Abstract music: synonym for ABSOLUTE MUSIC.

A cappella (I): choral music or choral performance without instrumental ACCOMPANIMENT.

Accelerando (I): a gradual quickening of pace.

Accent: a stress, which may result from increased loudness (dynamic accent), increased note length (agogic accent), or higher PITCH (tonic accent). Unless otherwise specified, the term implies a dynamic accent. In most familiar music there is a regular stress pattern, arising from the symmetrical organization of rhythm and a moderately steady rate of harmonic change. This may be reinforced by dynamic accents of varying degrees of subtlety. Louder than normal accents occurring at customary places in this pattern and accents occurring at unusual places may be indicated by the signs $>$, $\wedge$, $\vee$, and —; the abbreviations *sf* and *sfz*, for *sforzato* or SFORZANDO, and *rf* or *rfz*, for RINFORZANDO, also indicate dynamic stress.

Acciaccatura (I): (1) an ornament in BAROQUE keyboard music. A DISSONANCE a second below a chord note is played together with the chord and released immediately (at a slow TEMPO, all notes may be played in rapid succession, the main notes being held); (2) a short APPOGGIATURA (recent usage, not universally accepted).

Accidental: a sharp, flat, double-sharp, double-flat, or natural notated within the body of a work rather than as part of the KEY SIGNATURE (which immediately follows the CLEF at the left-hand edge of the staff).

Accompaniment: that part of the musical structure which fills a supporting role, either from the standpoint of musical content or of audience attention. From the former point of view, accompaniment tends to be associated with chordal textures or simple figurations. (A good melody usually exceeds a purely subordinate role in that it attracts some measure of attention to itself.) Similarly, accompaniment is more often in a low rather than a high register since the highest part of a musical web tends to prominence.

In many works for mixed groups, one or more performers stand out as soloists; the remaining parts are designated as accompaniments regardless of their musical importance. In works for CHORUS and KEYBOARD, for example, the chorus occupies the center of attention. Some choral accompaniments consist of little more than doublings of the vocal parts; this is done to give greater body to the sound and to help maintain proper PITCH. In most CONCERTOS, SONATAS for solo instruments and keyboard, and in ROMANTIC LIEDER, the care lavished on the accompaniment is a prime factor in determining the overall musical quality; in these works the accompaniment often has an equal rather than a subordinate role.

Accordion: a portable KEYBOARD instrument using metal REEDS. These are set into two rectangular headboards, connected by a bellows that furnishes the air pressure to make the reeds vibrate. The right-hand headboard is provided with a small keyboard on which the melody is played, while the left-hand headboard is provided with rows of studs. The first two rows control single bass notes, the others, CHORDS. *See illustration on opposite page.*

A *concertina* is a similar instrument, smaller in size and usually hexagonal in shape. It is provided with studs on both sides, each side working as its counterpart in the accordion. The concertina is preferred in England. An Argentinian favorite is the square - shaped *bandoneon*, also with studs; no single stud

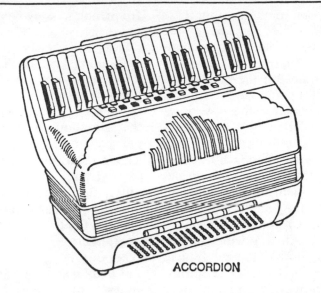

ACCORDION

on this instrument controls a full chord.

A prototype of these instruments was patented by C. F. L. Buschmann in 1822. Charles Wheatstone's Concertina was patented in 1844. **Acoustics:** (1) the science of sound; (2) in a restricted sense, the sound dispersal and absorption characteristics of a given place. Sound is produced by a series of rapid vibrations. Irregular vibrations result in sounds normally classified as noise, while regular series produce musical tones. (Certain modern composers regard all kinds of sound as potential material for artistic use and therefore blur or disregard this traditional classification.) The musician is interested primarily in three characteristics of sound: PITCH, which is governed by frequency; *loudness,* which is governed by amplitude; and TONE COLOR or timbre, which is governed by the complexity of the vibration pattern.

Pitch. The more rapidly a body vibrates, the higher the resulting pitch. The human ear can detect vibrations between 20 and nearly 20,000 cycles per second, but only the lower fifth of this range is used in vocal and instrumental composition. Frequency, the number of vibration cycles per second, is controlled by the length and diameter of the vibrating body and by the degree of tension of either the string, membrane, or, in the case of wind instruments, the player's lips. To produce a lower pitch one may either increase length, increase diameter, or decrease tension. For example, the strings serving the high notes on the right hand side of a piano are far shorter than those for the low notes on the left; under equal tension, drums with small surface area produce higher notes than those with broad surface; and, finally, a violin string may be made to sound higher by pulling it more tightly. Among wind instruments, those of low pitch have longer and wider columns than those of high pitch. Bear in mind, however, that a wind column closed at one end usually vibrates at half the frequency of an open column of the same length. If one were to produce a sound by blowing across the top of a small-mouthed bottle, then knock the bottom off and blow again, the second sound would be roughly an octave higher than the first.

Interference. If two sounds of different frequencies are produced concurrently, certain side effects, known as interference, may occur. When the two frequencies differ only slightly, there is an alternate intensification and weakening in sound. The moments of intensification are termed beats, and the number of beats per second equals the difference between the two frequencies. Slow beats are not disagreeable; they are produced deliberately in the organ stop, *vox coelestis* (or *unda maris*), by coupling two pipes very slightly out of tune with each other. However, the sensation of 5–30 beats per second may be unpleasant. The concurrent sounding of two strong and sufficiently different frequencies will often produce the sensation of additional faint tones, known as COMBINATION (or resultant) TONES.

Loudness. The ear's response to intensity varies slightly according to frequency; that is, we are less sensitive to intensity in the lowest and uppermost portions of our hearing range than in the central one. However, the sensation of loudness depends primarily on the amplitude of the vibration. Amplitude, in turn, depends upon the force with which the vibrating body is set into motion and upon the size of the vibrating area. If, for example, a tuning fork is struck with moderate force, a very soft tone will be produced; if the same fork is struck with greater force, the tone will be louder. In either event, if the fork is placed into contact with a body that vibrates readily, the loudness will suddenly increase. The vibrations of the fork will cause the second body to vibrate, increasing the area of vibration. Should the second body, when struck, produce the same frequency as that of the tuning fork, direct contact between the two is not needed; the second body will vibrate when in proximity to the fork. This is known as sympathetic vibration. The principle is employed in the construction of certain instruments, such as the VIOLA D'AMORE and the MARIMBA. The former has free strings, not touched by the player, which vibrate in sympathy with the bowed strings or their overtones; the latter has gourds or other air columns suspended beneath wooden bars which are struck by the player. If the vibrating body and the resonator have different natural frequencies, contact between the two is necessary. The sounding board of the piano and the belly and back of instruments of the violin and lute families are important examples of general resonators. The term RESONANCE may cover both sympathetic and forced vibration, or it may mean the former alone.

Harmonics. Most vibrations not generated under laboratory conditions are comparatively complex. That is, a vibrating body moves not only as a whole, but also in smaller segments. A string, for example, vibrates in its entire length, in halves, thirds, fourths, fifths, and so forth. The full-length vibration produces the fundamental tone

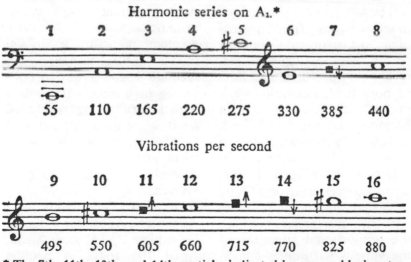

Harmonic series on A₁.*

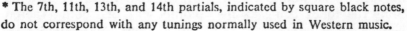

* The 7th, 11th, 13th, and 14th partials, indicated by square black notes, do not correspond with any tunings normally used in Western music.

(first harmonic), which is heard by the listener. The half-length vibration (second harmonic) has twice the frequency of the fundamental, producing a tone an octave higher than the fundamental. The frequencies of the other harmonics vary inversely to the fractions of string-length that produce them. The entire complex is known as a harmonic series; data pertaining to the first 16 members of a series founded on *A* is given herewith.

Tone color. Since the amplitude of the second and higher harmonics is only one-fifth to one-fiftieth of that of the fundamental, these tones normally pass unnoticed. They may be made audible, however, by means of special resonators.

The strength of specific harmonics varies from instrument to instrument. The second harmonic, for example, is relatively powerful in a flute or horn tone, but quite weak in an oboe tone. The fifth harmonic, on the other hand, is relatively powerful in an oboe tone, but very weak in a flute or horn tone. Differences between individual tone colors are determined in large part by differences between the proportional strengths of the various harmonics constituting the tones being examined.

Action: the mechanism of an instrument.

Adagio (I): a slow TEMPO.

Adam, Adolphe Charles: *b.* Paris, July 24, 1803; *d.* Paris, May 3, 1856. A successful composer of OPÉRA COMIQUE and BALLET, Adam studied under BOIELDIEU. He was professor of composition at the Paris Conservatoire from 1849. His ballet *Giselle* retains a place in the repertory, while his *Cantique de Noël* is the best known of his non-stage works.

Adam de la Hale: *b. c.*1240; *d.* Naples, 1287, one of the last TROUVÈRES. Best known for his dramatic pastorale, *Le Jeu de Robin et Marion,* Adam composed settings of his poems for one to three voices, cast in a variety of secular forms of his time.

Added sixth: *see* SIXTH CHORDS.

Aeolian: *see* CHURCH MODES; SCALE (natural minor).

Aeolian harp: a device consisting of a long, narrow box with several strings stretched lengthwise; these are exposed to the wind, which causes them to sound.

Aerophone: *see* INSTRUMENTS.

Affettuoso (I): warmly.

Aggazzari, Agostino: *b.* Siena, December 2, 1578; *d.* Siena, April 10, 1640. A prolific composer of both sacred music and MADRIGALS, he wrote both in the traditional style of the late RENAISSANCE and in the new monodic style of the BAROQUE. He was among the first to write concerted church music and he wrote the first treatise to deal exclusively with FIGURED BASS.

Agitato (I): agitated.

Agnus Dei (L): one of the movements of the Ordinary of the MASS.

Agréments (F): ornaments.

Agricola, Alexander: b. Flanders(?), c.1446; d. Valladolid, Spain, 1506(?). Widely traveled, Agricola held posts under Lorenzo de' Medici, Galeazzo Maria Sforza, and Philip I of Castile, among others. One of the leading composers of his generation, he wrote polyphonic CHANSONS, MOTETS, and MASSES.

Air: a song, or songlike instrumental melody. The term had a variety of applications from the 16th to the 18th centuries. *See* SONG.

Alba (Pr), **Albe, Alborado** (S), **Aubade** (F), **Tagelied** (G), **Wächterlied** (G): in the Middle Ages, a song about the morning departure of a lover; often a warning of approaching danger. Some *Tagelieder*, however, are pious morning pieces. *Alborado* and *Aubade* are now titles of rustic morning pieces.

Albéniz, Isaac: b. Campredón, Spain, May 29, 1860; d. Cambo-Bains, May 18, 1909. Now remembered for his nationalistic and impressionistic piano music, especially *Iberia,* Albéniz was a child prodigy and later a prominent pianist. His works include a number of OPERAS.

d'Albert, Eugene Francis Charles: b. Glasgow, April 10, 1864; d. Riga, March 3, 1932. A pupil of LISZT, d'Albert was highly regarded in his day both as a piano virtuoso and composer. He was particularly active in the writing of German OPERA, *Tiefland* being his best remembered work. In addition, he wrote two piano CONCERTOS and miscellaneous piano compositions, together with songs, CHAMBER MUSIC, and a few orchestral works; he was active also as an editor of piano music.

Albert, Heinrich: b. Lobenstein, Saxony, July 8, 1604; d. Königsberg, October 6, 1651. A cousin and pupil of Heinrich SCHÜTZ, Albert achieved prominence as a song composer and poet. He was organist at the Cathedral of Königsberg from 1631. His songs, written mainly for solo voice and FIGURED BASS, are distinctly different from contemporary Italian MONODIES.

Alberti bass: conventional broken-chord patterns used as ACCOMPANIMENT in 18th-century piano music. Domenico Alberti (*c.*1710–40) was among the first to use such figurations extensively. These patterns were particularly prominent in music of the late 18th century.

Albinoni, Tomaso: *b.* Venice, June 8, 1671; *d.* Venice, January 17, 1750. Active mainly in Venice, he wrote nearly four dozen OPERAS, together with CONCERTOS, solo SONATAS, and trio sonatas. He was greatly admired by J. S. BACH and was one of the first to write solo concertos for violin.

Alborado (S): *see* ALBA.

Albrechtsberger, Johann Georg: *b.* Klosterneuberg (near Vienna), February 3, 1736; *d.* Vienna, March 7, 1809. Although highly respected in his day as a composer and court organist, Albrechtsberger is remembered chiefly as a theorist and teacher. BEETHOVEN was one of his pupils for a brief period.

Albumblatt (G): Album leaf, a title employed by ROMANTIC composers for short CHARACTER PIECES.

Aleatoric music: *see* CHANCE MUSIC.

Al Fine (I): *see* FINE.

Alkan, Charles Henri Valentin (real name: Morhange): *b.* Paris, November 30, 1813; *d.* Paris, March 29, 1888. One of the brilliant piano virtuosos of his day, Alkan wrote chiefly for his own instrument. The technical challenges and musical imagination displayed in his best works make these worthy counterparts to works by CHOPIN and LISZT.

Alla breve (I): Cut time (symbol: ¢), in present usage, a direction to perform $\frac{4}{4}$ music briskly and thus treat the half note rather than the quarter as the unit of time.

Allargando (I): a broadening of TEMPO and volume.

Allegretto (I): a moderately quick TEMPO.

Allegri, Gregorio: *b.* Rome, 1582; *d.* Rome, February 17, 1652. From 1629, Allegri was a singer in the Papal Chapel. His *Miserere* for double chorus has been sung at the Sistine Chapel during Holy Week for many generations. He composed a moderate amount of other sacred music, as well as some instrumental CANZONE and SINFONIAS.

Allegro (I): a fast TEMPO.

Alleluia: a florid, jubilant CHANT, the third item of the MASS Proper except during Lent and in REQUIEM MASSES, on which occasions a TRACT is used instead. The word itself is derived from Hebrew.

Allemande (F): (1) in the late 16th and early 17th centuries, a moderately slow dance of German origin in duple METER. In the late 17th and early 18th centuries, the TEMPO of the Allemande (still in duple meter) was increased. The piece usually began with a quick upbeat and continued in steady sixteenth-note rhythm. In this guise, the Allemande was used as the first dance movement of a SUITE. (2) In the late 18th century, the term referred to a quick, waltzlike dance in triple meter.

Allentando (I): slowing down.

Alphorn: Alpine horn, a folk instrument used by European mountain herdsmen. Its wooden tube, either straight or slightly curved, has an upturned bell; the instrument may be as much as 10 feet long.

Al Segno (I): *see* SEGNO.

Alteration: the raising or lowering of a note by the addition of an ACCIDENTAL.

Alto: (1) a female VOICE of low range, or a high male voice of identical range; (2) a variety of CLEF; (3) an alternative name for the viola (*see* VIOLIN family); (4) the second or third highest of a family of instruments (e.g., alto recorder); (5) the second highest voice-part of a composition.

Ambrosian Chant: *see* MEDIEVAL MUSIC.

Anche (F): REED or reed instrument.

Andante (I): a moderate TEMPO.

Andantino (I): usually a TEMPO slightly faster than ANDANTE.

Anerio, Felice: *b.* Rome, *c.*1560; *d.* Rome, September 27, 1614. Anerio succeeded his master, PALESTRINA, as composer to the Papal Chapel in 1594. His output includes CANZONETTES, secular and sacred MADRIGALS, HYMNS, RESPONSORIES, and other sacred music.

Anglaise (F): (1) in BAROQUE music, a quick dance in duple METER without an upbeat; the Anglaise might appear as one of the optional dances of a SUITE; (2) in CLASSICAL music, any of a number of dances of English origin, including the COUNTRY DANCE and ÉCOSSAISE.

d'Anglebert, Jean-Henri: *b.* Paris, 1628(?); *d.* Paris, April 23, 1691. In 1664 d'Anglebert succeeded CHAMBONNIÈRES, his former teacher, as harpsichordist to Louis XIV. His *Pièces de clavecin* contains original works and transcriptions from operas by LULLY, together with information regarding ORNAMENTATION and FIGURED BASS.

Anglican chant: music, consisting of a set of harmonic formulas, used in the Anglican service for the performance of PSALMS and CANTICLES. The earliest chants originated in the late 16th century. In single chants, a 7-measure formula is repeated for each verse; double chants contain material for a pair of verses. The uppermost of the four voices is derived from the Psalm tones of GREGORIAN CHANT; when the number of syllables to be sung exceeds the number of notes, the first or second half of the verse opens with a recitation. Unlike Gregorian chant, Anglican chant observes a strict METER.

Answer: (1) a statement of a FUGUE subject based on the DOMINANT; (2) the second member of a pair of phrases of similar construction. The first member—the question or antecedent—has an inconclusive close, while the second—the answer or consequent—brings the same thought to a more positive ending.

Antecedent: (1) the first voice to enter in a CANON; (2) the first member of a pair of phrases of similar construction (*see* ANSWER).

Antes, John: *b*. Frederickstownship, Pa., March 24, 1740; *d*. Bristol, England, December 17, 1811. Moravian minister, watchmaker, inventor, instrument maker, and composer, Antes was the first native American to write CHAMBER MUSIC. He wrote also about 25 short ANTHEMS with instrumental accompaniment.

Antheil, George: *b*. Trenton, N.J., July 8, 1900; *d*. New York City, February 12, 1959. Antheil's use of DISSONANCE and nonmusical sounds created a brief furor in the 1920s; his later style became much more conservative. His works include the *Ballet mécanique*, six SYMPHONIES, CHAMBER MUSIC, piano SONATAS, a few OPERAS, and film scores.

Anthem: (1) a vocal or mixed setting of a sacred text, used in the Anglican service. The anthem began in the late 16th century in England as a work for chorus, similar to the MOTET, though more syllabic in style. By the end of the century, greater variety was achieved by setting certain passages for one or more soloists with instrumental accompaniment. This sort, known as a *verse anthem*, was prevalent during the 17th century; the *full anthem*, employing chorus throughout, regained favor in later periods. More elaborate anthems, often written to celebrate special occasions, were also composed during the 17th and 18th centuries (e.g., by BLOW and PURCELL); these works are similar to CANTATAS since their structures employ recitatives and instrumental interludes. (2) a patriotic song, or similar song of praise.

Anticipation: a NONHARMONIC TONE sounded immediately before the chord to which it belongs; sometimes two or more anticipations may be used simultaneously.

Antiphon: a piece of GREGORIAN CHANT, or a polyphonic work based on it, normally designed to be sung before and after a PSALM or CANTICLE. Certain processional antiphons and the four Antiphons of the Blessed Virgin Mary are independent CHANTS for special occasions.

Antiphonal: music alternating passages for different CHOIRS, either vocal or instrumental.

Antiphonal, Antiphonary, Antiphoner: a book containing GREGORIAN CHANT for the OFFICE.

A placere (I): at pleasure; the performer is to exercise his own discretion with regard to rhythmic or dynamic nuance.

Appoggiatura (I): a NONHARMONIC TONE, usually sounding together with a CHORD and resolving stepwise to a chord tone. Some writers further specify that the appoggiatura is reached by a skip; they call a similar nonharmonic tone reached by step an accented passing tone. The treatment and notation of the appoggiatura has varied over the centuries. In the BAROQUE and CLASSICAL eras, it was regarded as an ornament and was so notated. In performance, the ornamental tone usually took half or two-thirds of the value of the following main note. There were, in addition, short appoggiaturas (now sometimes wrongly called ACCIACCATURAS), played quickly. In the 19th century, the long appoggiatura was written in ordinary notation; the short appoggiatura was written as a grace note (a tiny note with a diagonal line through the stem), normally performed before the BEAT rather than on it.

Arabesque: (1) an ornate figuration, a flowing, curved line; (2) title of a ROMANTIC CHARACTER PIECE for piano, often in fanciful style.

Aragonaise: see JOTA.

Arcadelt, Jacob: b. Liège(?), c.1504; d. Paris, October 24, 1568. Arcadelt's chief posts were as member of the Papal Chapel and as musician to the duc de Guise. A prolific composer of MADRIGALS and CHANSONS, he also left a score of MOTETS and three books of MASSES.

Archlute: see LUTE.

Arco (I): bow. *Coll' arco*, with the bow—a direction to the string player to resume BOWING rather than to continue to play by plucking (PIZZICATO).

Arensky, Anton Stepanovich: *b*. Novgorod, Russia, August 11, 1861; *d*. Terijoki, Finland, February 25, 1906. A student of RIMSKY-KORSAKOV, Arensky was a harmony instructor at the Moscow Conservatory (1882–94) and director of the Imperial Chapel (1895–1901). He wrote works for one and two pianos, songs, some CHAMBER MUSIC, a BALLET, and a handful of CONCERTOS, SYMPHONIES, and OPERAS. His somewhat sentimental style loosely resembles that of TCHAIKOVSKY.

Aria (I): (1) during the 18th to 20th centuries, a fairly elaborate work for one or two voices and instrumental accompaniment, n o r m a l l y functioning as a self-contained entity within an OPERA, ORATORIO, CANTATA, or MASS. Similar, but lighter, forms are normally called ariettas or CANZONETTAS, though no consistent distinction was made much before 1700. The aria of the mid- and late 17th century, however, is not often extensive by modern standards; its main distinguishing marks are a moderately florid treatment of the text and more regular rhythm than is to be found in contrasting passages of RECITATIVE. Many mid-BAROQUE arias are simple STROPHIC songs, but if the term is used without qualification, a nonstrophic form is implied. The aria is designed to elaborate the high points of the drama and, often, to show off the vocal beauty and dexterity of the singer. Some operas consist largely of arias, connected by narrative recitatives in rapid, parlando style. A large number of conventional classes of aria were developed during the 18th century, each concerned with specific areas of vocal technique. The form employed most often is that of the *aria da capo,* which consists of an extensive opening section, a contrasting middle, and a repeat of the beginning (often the occasion—in earlier times—for the improvisation of embellishments). Obviously, this use of musical and textual repetition delays the unfolding of the narrative. (2) An instrumental work in the style of a vocal aria.

Arietta (I): *see* ARIA.

Arioso (I): (1) a melodic style more lyrical than that employed in RECITATIVE, less expansive than that in ARIA; (2) a section of music in this style.

Arne, Thomas Augustine: *b*. London, March 12, 1710; *d*. London, March 5, 1778. A leading English composer for the stage, Arne turned to music after studying law. He is best known for his settings of MASQUES (including *Comus* and *Alfred,* which contains the song *Rule Britannia*), but composed also ballad OPERAS, operas in Italian style, CATCHES and GLEES, two ORATORIOS, and some instrumental music.

Arpa (I): harp.

Arpeggio: a CHORD, played one note at a time, proceeding in order, usually from the bottom upward. The notes may be written one after the other or as a block chord, preceded by an ORNAMENT sign. The sign now customarily used is a vertical zigzag.

Arpeggione: a short-lived string instrument, invented in 1823. The arpeggione was the size of a cello and was played with a bow. However, it was shaped like a guitar and had FRETS and six strings.

Arrangement, Transcription: (1) the transfer of a work from one medium to another. A piano piece, for example, may be orchestrated, or an orchestral score reduced for piano. (2) The alteration of a work involving primarily an increase or decrease in difficulty. Such changes may be effected either to obtain a more brilliant concert display or to place a work within a student's limited ability. (3) The setting of a familiar melody. Such arrangements may vary from simple harmonizations to extended paraphrases of the tune and rich orchestrations.

Articulation, the nature of attack given to each of a series of tones. The performer may cause these to flow smoothly into one another as an uninterrupted stream (LEGATO), or he may make the listener aware of one or more fresh impulses by detaching the tones from each other to a greater or lesser extent (e.g., as in STACCATO or PORTATO). The term itself tends to emphasize the latter form of execution. Techniques of articulation vary according to the nature of the instrument or voice employed; bowed string instruments, such as the violin, command a particularly wide range of nuance.

Arriaga, Juan Crisóstomos: *b.* Rigoitia, Chile, January 27, 1806; *d.* Paris, January 17, 1826. The SYMPHONY, STRING QUARTETS, and miscellaneous works composed by Arriaga in his teens aroused high hopes for his future, left unrealized by his early death.

Ars antiqua (L): music of the late 12th and 13th centuries. *See* MEDIEVAL MUSIC.

Ars nova (L): music of the 14th century. *See* MEDIEVAL MUSIC.

Art song: a generic designation for independent works for solo voice and instrumental ACCOMPANIMENT (usually keyboard or lute). Included are German LIEDER, French CHANSONS and MÉLODIES, Italian CANZONE and ARIAS, and so forth. The term serves partly to distinguish such works from FOLK SONGS and popular BALLADS. *See* SONG.

Assai (I): very.

A tempo (I): a return to normal TEMPO following some deviation.

Atonality: (1) the absence of clearly-marked tone centers in a musical work; (2) the use of a harmonic and melodic vocabulary that proceeds beyond the confines of that of the major-minor system. In its loosest sense, atonal may describe works in any of the following styles (among others): (a) late ROMANTIC compositions in which the extensive use of chromatic harmonies results in the obscuring of tonal centers; (b) IMPRESSIONIST compositions employing novel harmonies and sometimes novel modes; (c) NEOCLASSICAL and other works employing tone centers, but using many dissonant harmonies; (d) TWELVE-TONE compositions; (e) CHANCE MUSIC; (f) ELECTRONIC MUSIC. The term has been bitterly attacked for its vagueness, subjectivity, and negative orientation. The ability to perceive tone centers in certain 20th-century works depends greatly upon training and listening habits. The negative focus on the lack of tonality tends to distort the historical perspective attaching to tonal styles, which were dominant only for the period from shortly before 1700 to shortly after 1900. *See also* TONALITY.

Attacca (I): continue from one movement to the next without pause.

Aube, Aubade (F): *see* ALBA.

Auber, Daniel Francois: *b.* Caen, January 29, 1782: *d.* Paris, May 13, 1871. One of the most prominent and prolific French composers of OPERA. He was director of the Paris Conservatoire from 1842, and imperial music director to Napoleon III from 1857. His *Masaniello, ou la Muette de Portici* produced such an effect on the audiences that it helped spark the Belgian revolution for independence. Musically, the work contributed to the establishment of the rich style of French grand opera, furthered by MEYERBEER and ROSSINI. *Fra Diavolo,* based on a romantic tale, was another outstanding success.

Augmented: a size of INTERVAL or CHORD larger than normal.

Augmentation: the restatement of a MELODY in longer time values. The most frequent form of augmentation involves the doubling of the original values.

Aulos (Gr): (1) a double-REED instrument of ancient Greece, an ancestor of the oboe. Two *auloi* were generally played by one performer at the same time. The *aulos* had a shrill sound; it was associated with Dionysian rites and with the drama. (2) A generic term, similar to the English *pipe*.

Autoharp: a portable instrument with strings parallel to the soundbox; its simple mechanism permits the strings of a chosen chord to sound when the instrument is strummed and silences all others.

Auxiliary tone (neighboring tone): a NONHARMONIC TONE a step above or below a chord tone; the melodic figure proceeds from the chord tone to the auxiliary and then back.

Ayre: old spelling of AIR.

B

Babbitt, Milton: *b.* Philadelphia, Pa., May 10, 1916. Babbitt studied at Princeton University, later teaching music and mathematics there. He is prominent a m o n g those TWELVE-TONE composers who extend serial control beyond PITCH to include RHYTHM, DYNAMICS, and INSTRUMENTATION. He has written works for various small instrumental ensembles and is prominent in the field of ELECTRONIC MUSIC.

Baborák: a Bohemian dance, alternating between duple and triple METER.

Bach, Carl Philipp Emanuel: *b.* Weimar, March 8, 1714; *d.* Hamburg, Germany, December 14, 1788. The second surviving son of JOHANN SEBASTIAN BACH, Carl Philipp Emanuel was trained by his father. He became chamber musician to King Frederick the Great and, in 1767, music director for the principal churches of Hamburg. One of the most important musicians of his day, he helped shape the expressive style of the mid-18th century and played an important role in the development of the SONATA and RONDO forms. His output is rich and varied, including SYMPHONIES, CONCERTOS, CHAMBER MUSIC, keyboard sonatas, ORATORIOS, PASSIONS and other sacred vocal music, CANTATAS, and songs. His treatise *Essay on the True Art of Playing Keyboard Instruments* is a document of great importance.

Bach, Johann (John) Christian: *b.* Leipzig, September 5, 1735; *d.* London, January 1, 1782. The youngest son of JOHANN SEBASTIAN BACH, Johann Christian studied with his brother, Carl Philipp Emanuel, and with MARTINI. Following a stay in Italy, he went to England in 1762, where he became extremely popular. He was appointed music master to the wife of King George III in 1763. A prolific composer, J. C. Bach wrote OPERAS, SYMPHONIES, CONCERTOS, CHAMBER MUSIC, songs, and piano music. His lyric style influenced the development of the classical idiom, particularly through its effect on MOZART.

Bach, Johann Sebastian: *b.* Eisenach, March 21, 1685; *d.* Leipzig, Germany, July 28, 1750; the greatest master of the German BAROQUE.

J. S. Bach was descended of a long line of musicians and received his earliest musical training from his father, Johann Ambrosius. He continued his studies with his brother, Johann Christoph, after becoming an orphan when only ten. His apprenticeship period was completed as a choirboy at St. Michael's Church in Lüneburg. Bach became organist at St. Boniface in Arnstadt (1703), and then at St. Blasius in Mühlhausen (1707). In 1708, Bach entered the service of the duke of Weimar, first as organist and later as concertmaster. From 1717 to 1723, Bach was music director for Prince Leopold of Anhalt (at Cöthen). In May 1723 Bach became cantor at St. Thomas in Leipzig, holding this post until his death. He served as organist and music director for the churches of St. Thomas and St. Nicholas and instructed the choirboys. Bach married twice. Among his twenty children, CARL PHILIPP EMANUEL, JOHANN CHRISTIAN, Johann Christoph Friedrich, and WILHELM FRIEDEMANN became prominent composers.

As was customary in his day, Bach learned much about composition by copying older composers' works, by arranging them, and by basing new works on older themes. In this way, Bach, who spent his entire life in central Germany, became thoroughly familiar with both Italian and French music, as well as with the music of his Protestant and Catholic countrymen. His own music combines German polyphonic mastery with the rhythmic drive and tonal clarity of the Italian CONCERTO and the refinements of French dance forms. Several of Bach's works have a pedagogic as well as aesthetic purpose; he wished the performers and listeners to learn how themes were to be constructed and developed. Yet, while MOZART and BEETHOVEN (a m o n g others) were influenced by their contacts with Bach's music, his influence on his contemporaries and immediate successors was limited. He was admired as a peerless organist and master improvisor. He was acknowledged as a supreme craftsman at COUNTERPOINT, but contrapuntal forms were passing out of style. The facility of TELEMANN was preferred to the intensity of Bach. Thus Bach had no true successors. Even his sons are numbered among the first masters of a new era.

Except for opera, Bach brought each of the major forms of the Baroque to its greatest height. The *Art of Fugue* and the *Well-Tempered Clavier* sum up all that had been accomplished in the realm of the instrumental FUGUE, while the techniques of VARIATION and CANON find superlative expression in the *Goldberg Variations,* the *Musical Offering,* and the *Canonic Variations on Von Himmel hoch.* The Brandenburg Concertos are among the finest examples of the CONCERTO GROSSO, while the four orchestral OVERTURES and the various PARTITAS and SUITES demonstrate Bach's command of French and Italian dance styles. Among Bach's best-known works are sacred compositions for chorus, vocal soloists, and orchestra, including the two PASSIONS—one according to St. Matthew, the other according to St. John—the *Mass in B Minor,* the *Magnificat,* and such chorale CANTATAS as *Wachet auf, Ein' feste Burg,* and *Jesu der du meine Seele.* (In all, Bach is said to have written five cycles of sacred cantatas for the church year, including many for vocal soloists and instruments, but less than 200 sacred cantatas survive.) The *Coffee Cantata* is a delightful example of Bach's lighter music.

Bach's surviving compositions number more than a

thousand, and it is difficult to estimate how many others have been lost. It is a frequent practice to identify surviving works by means of the number assigned to them in the standard catalogue of Bach's works—the *Bach Werke Verzeichnis,* abbreviated BWV. This catalogue does not follow a chronological arrangement, as do many similar works.

What Bach wrote depended heavily on the nature of his duties. For example, much of his CHAMBER MUSIC was composed when at Weimar and Cöthen. The constant demand for fresh music led Bach, like many of his contemporaries, to reuse previously composed music in new situations. Certain concertos are arrangements that employ different solo instruments, while several movements of the *Mass in B Minor* (written to gain the honorary title of court composer to the king of Poland, elector of Saxony) are derived from earlier cantatas.

Bach's sacred music draws heavily on traditional chorale melodies and on the pictorial symbolism developed by his predecessors (*see* PROGRAM MUSIC). He used both sources of material with remarkably rich imagination. Bach was intensely interested in expressing in his music the essence of the text's central emotion, although the means chosen are not always immediately apparent to the modern listener.

Bach, Wilhelm Friedemann: *b.* Weimar, November 22, 1710; *d.* Berlin, July 1, 1784. The eldest son of JOHANN SEBASTIAN BACH, Wilhelm Friedemann was trained by his father and by J. G. GRAUN. He served as organist in Dresden and Halle. Because of his restless and dissatisfied nature, W. F. Bach did not hold to these positions, and, when older, failed to obtain others. He died in poverty. He wrote an OPERA (lost), several CANTATAS, harpsichord and organ works, CONCERTOS, sinfonias, and CHAMBER MUSIC.

Bach trumpet: a small, modern trumpet, designed to facilitate the playing of BAROQUE parts with very high notes. The instrument does not correspond to those normally used during the Baroque era.

Badinage, Badinerie (F): a title used during the 18th century for playful, dancelike movements of a SUITE.

Badings, Henk: *b.* Bandoeng, Java, January 17, 1907. Badings studied mining engineering before studying composition under William Pijper. He was appointed director of the Royal Conservatory at The Hague in 1941. Badings has written in almost all traditional genres and has pioneered in the compositional use of tape recorders. Conservative and mildly modernistic elements intermingle in his music.

Bagatelle (F): a short trifle; a title used for some ROMANTIC CHARACTER PIECES for piano.

Bagpipe: a family of instruments having REEDS actuated by the wind pressure within a bag. The wind supply of the bag itself may be furnished either by a bellows action or by the player blowing into a tube entering the bag. The reeds may be either single or double. Normally a few pipes exit from the bag. The one provided with fingerholes is used for the melody and is known as the chanter. The others, generally resting on the shoulder, provide sustained notes (i.e., drones). The family includes the French *cornemuse, musette,* and *biniou,* the Spanish *gaita,* the Italian *piva* and *zampogna,* and the German *Dudelsack* or *Sackpfeife,* in addition to the well-known Scottish and Irish instruments. The bagpipe was known in ancient Rome as the *tibia utricularis.*

Baguette (F): (1) drumstick; (2) a BATON or the stick of a violin bow.

Balakirev, Mily Alexeyevich: *b.* Nizhny-Novgorod, January 2, 1837; *d.* St. Petersburg, May 29, 1910. Having had instruction from Dubuque and Eisrich, and having had access to the music library of Oulibishev, Balakirev was the best trained of the Mighty FIVE; his advice was often sought by BORODIN, MUSSORGSKY, and the others. Balakirev was a concert pianist briefly, one of the founders of the St. Petersburg Free School of Music (1862), and Director of the Court Chapel (1883–95). He collected FOLK SONGS of the Russian empire and published two groups of these in harmonized versions. His most famous works—the overture *Russia* and the piano fantasy *Islamey*—employ Russian and oriental folk melodies. Balakirev wrote also two SYMPHONIES, two piano CONCERTOS, the symphonic poem *Tamara,* a piano SONATA, miscellaneous piano pieces, and a few dozen songs.

Balalaika: a Russian instrument of the guitar family, with a triangular body and three strings. The instrument is made in several sizes.

Ballad: (1) a narrative song, dealing with romance, adventure, or contemporary events. Some are ART SONGS with new music for each stanza (sometimes with short RECITATIVES); some are FOLK SONGS; some are written in folk style. (2) A popular sentimental piece of the past century. *See* BALLADE.

Ballade (F): (1) a medieval French verse form with a refrain occurring at the end of a seven- or eight-line stanza. The earliest of these were written and set monophonically by TROUVÈRES. Polyphonic settings were composed from the 13th to the 15th centuries. (The form was particularly popular during the 14th century; the musical structure is equivalent to BAR form.) (2) The title of several extensive ROMANTIC piano pieces; some of these were apparently inspired by poems.

Ballata (I): a 14th-century Italian verse form, similar to the VIRELAI.

Ballet: a stage work in which the principal interest resides in skillful dancing, done in costume and with scenery. Many ballets have dramatic plots. Usually the music consists entirely of a continuous orchestral accompaniment. However, singing and spoken dialogue were employed in some early ballets and MASQUES (1580–1680), and singing has reappeared in a few modern scores, such as De Falla's *Three-Cornered Hat* and Stravinsky's *The Wedding*. Much ballet music is presented as concert music (often in the form of SUITES), and one can thus hear music for works no longer mounted on the stage. Several works not originally intended for dancing have been made into ballets. Short ballets may appear within OPERAS and musical comedies; ballet scenes were especially popular with 19th-century French opera audiences.

Ballet originated in France during the RENAISSANCE, employing elements with still older roots. The first work for which music survives is the *Ballet comique de la royne* (1581), directed by Balthasar de Beaujoyeulx (Baldassare de Belgioioso). Early ballets dealt with mythological and allegorical subjects. Elaborate and stereotyped forms were developed, reaching a peak in the late 17th century, with the works of LULLY. At first many dancers were members of the nobility; for example, King Louis XIV enjoyed participating in ballets. Gradually, however, professional dancers became more frequent and technical demands increased. Dance now requires a rigorous physical training and discipline. The designing of motion patterns for individual dancers and groups is termed *choreography*. Several systems of dance notation have been devised to enable choreographers to put down their ideas in fixed, schematic form. Although the range of subject matter treated in ballets broadened, and although gradual changes were effected in the dancers' repertoires of steps and body positions, traditional ballet of the 19th and 20th centuries was a somewhat conservative and conventional medium, drawing heavily on a comparatively restricted number of patterns employed in different combinations. By contrast, modern dance, which is deeply indebted to the pioneering efforts of Isadora Duncan (1878–1927), uses an almost infinite variety of expressive movements.

Although composers such as GLUCK, MOZART, BEETHOVEN, and SCHUBERT contributed music for ballets, the genre did not receive a great deal of attention from the major composers of the late 18th and early 19th centuries. There was a significant upsurge of interest in ballet in Russia during the 19th century, leading to such works as *Swan Lake, Sleeping Beauty,* and *The Nutcracker* by TCHAIKOVSKY. Many of STRAVINSKY's early masterpieces are ballets; *The Firebird, Petrouchka,* and *The Rites of Spring* were commissioned by Diaghilev for performance in Paris. Aaron COPLAND has also written several important ballets.

Balletto, Ballett (I): (1) a gay vocal composition in a dance rhythm, usually with a *fa la* refrain; such works were popular *c.*1600. (2) An optional movement of a 17th- or 18th-century SUITE.

Ballo (I): dance.

Banchieri, Adriano: *b.* Bologna, September 3, 1568; *d.* Bologna, 1634. A prominent composer and theorist, Banchieri was also a competent organist, a poet, and a priest. His output includes MASSES, MOTETS, PSALMS and other sacred works, CANZONETTE, MADRIGALS, and instrumental ensemble works. He is famed chiefly for his dramatic madrigals.

Band: (1) in strict modern usage, a large instrumental ENSEMBLE consisting mainly or entirely of wind and percussion instruments. There are several varieties of bands, the largest being the symphonic or concert band. In this group, massed clarinets often serve functions similar to those of orchestral violins. (It is not always effective to treat the clarinet as a substitute for the violin in scoring for band, however.) There is a very full complement of woodwinds, including members of the flute, oboe, bassoon, and saxophone families. The brass section includes a greater variety of instruments than are normally used in an orchestra, and the lower parts may be reinforced by string basses. All of the percussion are available. Neither oboes nor bassoons are used in marching bands, and the number of clarinets is much smaller than in a concert band. The number and variety of saxophones is reduced and the flutes are often replaced by fifes. Brass bands have a still smaller instrumentation, eliminating all woodwinds with the possible exception of the alto saxophone. The military band is midway between the symphonic and marching bands in fullness of instrumentation. The size and instrumentation of each of these bands is variable in different locales, particularly among the amateur groups that constitute a large part of the band movement in the United States. The musical traditions of bands date back to the military and other outdoor ensembles of the RENAISSANCE. Much band music has high spirit, but until recently, little was of high artistic merit.

(2) In a loose sense, the term band may designate any instrumental ensemble. The makeup of JAZZ bands is extremely flexible; the prominent instruments are likely to be the trumpet, trombone, clarinet, saxophone, string bass, piano, and drums. Large dance bands may feature violins. It is possible to speak also of balalaika bands, marimba bands, etc. This loose usage corresponds to the oldest usage of the term, which was applied to the string orchestras of the kings of France and England in the 17th century.

Bandoneon: *see* ACCORDION.

Bandurria: a Spanish instrument of the guitar family, with six pairs of strings.

Banjo: an American instrument of the guitar family. It has a circular body, consisting of a parchment-covered metal hoop, and a long neck, marked by FRETS. A six-stringed form is frequent, but the number of strings may vary.

Bar: the musical segment contained between two bar lines. *See* BAR LINE.

Barber, Samuel: *b.* West Chester, Pa., March 9, 1910. Barber completed his musical education at the Curtis Institute and taught there from 1939 to 1942. His lyrical and basically tonal style has won widespread acceptance for his works. He has composed in a wide variety of traditional genres, his most famous works including the *Adagio for Strings*, the OPERA *Vanessa*, the BALLET *Medea*, a violin CONCERTO, and the *overture to The School for Scandal*.

Barcarole, Barcarolle: a Venetian gondolier's song, or an instrumental or vocal work written in similar style. The Barcarole has a rocking motion, expressed in 6/8 or 12/8 RHYTHM.

Bard: a Celtic poet-musician belonging to a tradition dating from the Middle Ages and lasting until the early 18th century. During the 19th century, bardic gatherings, known as *eisteddfodau*, were revived, primarily as musical competitions.

Bar form: a musical form that may be represented by the schema *A A B*. In settings of MEDIEVAL and RENAISSANCE poetry, each *A* section would usually comprise two lines of verse, while the *B* section would complete the setting, comprising three or more lines of verse. In many works the endings of the *A* and *B* sections are similar or identical.

Bariolage (F): a technique used on bowed string instruments that involves a rapid alternation between notes produced on open and stopped strings (unfingered and fingered) for the sake of nuances of TONE COLOR.

Baritone: (1) a male VOICE lower than tenor, higher than bass; (2) a brass instrument of the tuba family; (3) a variety of CLEF; (4) one of the lower of a family of instruments (e.g., baritone saxophone). *See* BARYTONE.

Bar line: a vertical line used in NOTATION to mark out a musical segment containing a specified number of time units. A double bar is used to mark the end of a section, movement, or work.

Baroque music: the music of *c*.1600 to *c*.1750. During this fruitful period new forms of harmonic thinking developed, together with new harmonic means of defining and relating tone centers (*see* TONALITY). The older modal system was gradually replaced by the more tightly-organized major-minor system. Since the Baroque is the first period of a still larger cycle that includes the CLASSICAL and ROMANTIC periods, the codification of the new procedures by such late Baroque theorists as RAMEAU provides the core of the theoretical foundation for the major part of our concert repertoire. The vocal forms of OPERA, ORATORIO, and CANTATA, as well as the instrumental forms of the SUITE, TOCCATA, PRELUDE and FUGUE, CHORALE PRELUDE, trio SONATA, and CONCERTO GROSSO originated during the Baroque, and, with the possible exception of opera, found then their richest expression. Many of our present instruments acquired their basic forms during the Baroque and it was during this period that the orchestra came into being.

While the late RENAISSANCE favored equilibrium and moderation, the early Baroque was an exuberant period, favoring contrasts in range, TONE COLOR, DYNAMICS, and TEMPO. In the late Renaissance, for example, there was parity between the various voice parts of a polyphonic work. While this tradition did not die out in the Baroque, it was often overshadowed by thorough bass (FIGURED BASS) procedures, which emphasized the contrast between the outer voices and treated the inner ones as incidental fillers. This technique was developed during the late 16th century, and was championed by a group of Florentine intellectuals, known as the CAMERATA. Seeking to find the most effective musical means of representing the wide range of emotion in contemporary poetry, these men rejected earlier contrapuntal practices, holding that they obscured the text. The Camerata favored instead solo vocal melody, supported by economical harmonies realized on a keyboard instrument or lute. The resultant style was known as MONODY. Since this new style of vocal melody was often based on the PITCH and RHYTHM patterns of oratory, it was more irregular and contained more sudden contrasts than were customary in the music of the late Renaissance. Thorough bass was quickly adopted in the realm of instrumental ENSEMBLE music. Indeed, the technique, which emphasizes the strength and contrast between the outer voices, was so influential that the Baroque is sometimes known as The Era of the Thorough Bass. The development of a bass line that functions both as a harmonic support and a melodic line was also of importance in the development of new techniques of DISSONANCE treatment.

While the makeup of Renaissance performance groups was quite varied, works of that era were rarely created in terms of specific instrumental or vocal colors. The Renaissance composer might subdivide his force to obtain contrasts of texture within a piece, or employ various groups in polychoral combinations. Contrast of color naturally ensued, but this was apparently not a primary goal. During the Baroque, composers began to plan contrasts between specific vocal, instrumental, o r m i x e d CHOIRS. These contrasts are illustrated in the late works of Giovanni GABRIELI and are developed further by his pupil, Heinrich SCHÜTZ. The resultant style of composition is termed CONCERTATO.

Another result of the Baroque awareness of color was

the development of idiomatic instrumental repertoires. Interest in instrumental music, incipient in the Renaissance, burst into full bloom in the Baroque, without detracting from the richness of vocal composition.

While Renaissance music was governed by an even pulse proceeding at a moderate pace, early Baroque MADRIGALS were sometimes performed at an erratic gait designed to mirror the changing emotional qualities of the text. Contrasts of tempo were an important feature of the toccata and other rhapsodic instrumental forms. Whereas CRESCENDI and DECRESCENDI were frowned upon in the mid-Renaissance, they formed an important part of early Baroque performance practice, and the juxtaposition of loud and soft passages (terraced DYNAMICS), as in Giovanni Gabrieli's *Sonata pian e forte*, was a favorite device. Echo effects, introduced in the late Renaissance, proliferated. Because of its ability to project dynamic contrasts, the violin family gained ascendancy over the thinner-voiced viols. Refinements made in the construction of woodwinds (especially the double-reeds), and changed playing techniques permitted both more refined tone color and a greater range of dynamics.

The techniques of monody, thorough bass, and concertato, together with the changed emotional content of vocal music, entailed the creation of new forms. The main new vocal genres were opera, oratorio, and cantata. These are each composite forms with similar principles of inner organization; their respective lines of development were interrelated.

The actual performance of monody was not as stark as is suggested by the NOTATION itself. The texture was enriched not only by the realization of the thorough bass, but also by florid, improvised embellishments of the vocal line. Improvisation in general was an important and highly prized technique throughout the period. (A good part of BACH's reputation among his contemporaries rested on his extraordinary powers in that area.) A given harmonic structure may support a variety of melodic realizations, and Baroque composers often played on this possibility. STROPHIC variations, in which fresh melodies are set over a bass that remains unchanged in essence, were one of the first forms of the early cantata and were used frequently in opera. There are numerous instrumental parallels, the most important being the CHACONNE and PASSACAGLIA.

As purely musical values—apart from mere prosody—began to assert themselves, and as the pervasiveness of the recitativic style of the first operas was broken more frequently by the insertion of choruses and instrumental sections, a differentiation of melodic styles arose. The narrative sections of text were treated in more cursory fashion; these sections, resembling highly stylized speech, are known as RECITATIVE. The sections permitting lyrical or dramatic elaboration were given expanded treatment as ARIAS. This distinction apparently originated in solo cantatas, but was quickly transferred to opera, where it became a ruling principle. Set forms were developed, in particular the *aria da capo*. Individual vocal numbers became longer and more ornate as the Baroque progressed. They were more richly orchestrated, and orchestral RITORNELLI—passages appearing at the beginning and end of a vocal number and often at intermediate points —became not only unifying devices, but also effective ways of presenting the mood of the entire section. As vocal and instrumental idioms developed, they were also interchanged. The style of lyrical

arias was transferred to movements of instrumental works, while some arias imitated certain instrumental effects.

Most early Baroque instrumental music belongs to one of three categories: (a) music derived from dances; (b) music that had liturgical function; (c) music derived from older vocal models.

The Renaissance practice of grouping a slow dance in duple METER with a livelier one in triple was continued in the early Baroque, though the identity of the dances changed gradually. Occasionally a third, still faster dance was added to the group. One of the accomplishments of the mid- and late Baroque (to which FROBERGER especially contributed) was the standardization of a particular selection of four dances—ALLEMANDE, COURANTE, SABABANDE, and GIGUE—as the basic movements of the SUITE. While dance movements of the early and mid-Baroque are often brief and simple, later movements, often written after the dances themselves had gone out of fashion and not intended for actual dancing, were longer and more elaborate. Dances also served as the basis for many variation forms, which remained prominent throughout the period.

An important segment of

early Baroque ORGAN music had a liturgical function. In the Catholic service, PSALMS and MAGNIFICATS were often performed alternating verses in PLAINSONG with instrumental elaborations of the chant. This custom extended even to the MASS. An *intonazione* (prelude) might be used to establish the pitch for the celebrant, and a toccata might be played during the elevation of the Host. Sections of the Mass, such as the Gradual, that formerly were either chanted in plainsong or performed in polyphonic elaboration of the plainsong, now could be recited quietly by the celebrant while the organist or an instrumental ensemble performed an independent composition. Works employed for liturgical purposes were not restricted to such use, and the prelude and toccata developed into independent, virtuoso media. In the Protestant liturgy, the chorale occupied a central place and gave rise to a rich repertoire of chorale preludes, designed as introductions to the singing of the chorale by the congregation.

The imitative forms of Baroque instrumental music had their origins in older vocal models. Transcriptions of polyphonic CHANSONS had furnished a goodly part of the late Renaissance keyboard repertoire. These were known as CANZONAS (*canzona da sonar*), and the same title was employed for newly composed works in similar style. Other imitative forms—RICERCAR, CAPRICCIO, FANTASY (fancy)—differ from the canzona in details of treatment or in the rhythmic nature of the themes employed. Elements from various of these genres contributed to the late Baroque development of the fugue. Both an instrumental and a vocal form, the fugue reached its greatest heights among German composers, who never completely relinquished the polyphonic traditions of the Renaissance. These traditions were also observed by a small group of Italian composers of sacred music. However, Baroque POLYPHONY can be readily distinguished from earlier polyphony despite its links with the past. The harmonic thinking that grew from monody not only gave Baroque polyphony a chordal foundation, but also affected the very nature of the themes themselves, which were orientated in terms of tonality.

The orchestral music of the Baroque developed from two sources: the early *concertato* works and accompaniments to operas and oratorios. The concerto grosso (and later the solo concerto) and suite (including the French OVERTURE) are the primary independent orchestral forms. The varied assortment of instruments employed in MONTEVERDI's *Orfeo* was reduced by the mid-Baroque to a homogeneous group consisting largely or entirely of strings. Late Baroque composers often added individual wind instruments —especially oboes and flutes —to the string nucleus. Brass and percussion could be added if the occasion demanded pomp. Among late Baroque composers, HANDEL and RAMEAU show especially keen awareness of potentials of tone color.

In general, the evolution of Baroque music was one that led to the codification of diverse elements into fewer channels, to greater regularity of form and style, and to more monumental works. From the standpoint of chronology, the Baroque is often divided into two periods, the earlier encompassing roughly the 17th century, the later, the first half of the 18th. Stylistically, however, it might be preferable to distinguish between three periods. In terms of Italian music— the fountainhead of the Baroque—these periods may be dated: 1580–1630, 1630–80, 1680–1730; corresponding dates for other countries are generally one or two decades later. Among the outstanding composers of the early Baroque are Monteverdi, Giovanni GABRIELI, FRESCOBALDI, SWEELINCK, Schütz, SCHEIDT, and SCHEIN. The masters of the mid-Baroque include such men as CARISSIMI, ROSSI, STRADELLA, LULLY, CHARPENTIER, Froberger, and Purcell, while the late Baroque culminated in the work of Alessandro SCARLATTI, CORELLI, VIVALDI, COUPERIN, Rameau, and—above all—in those of J. S. Bach and Handel.

Barra (I), **Barre** (F): BAR LINE.

Barrel organ: (1) a mechanical organ with works that include interchangeable barrels with protruding pins. The lateral placement of a pin determines which of the several organ pipes that pin will strike when the barrel is rotated. The contact between pin and pipe opens the closure on the pipe, air rushes in, and a sound is produced. The order of sounds is determined by the place of the pins with regard to the circumference of the barrel. The barrel organ was popular in England during the 18th and 19th centuries, especially for the playing of HYMNS. (2) A mechanical piano operated by a similar mechanism (incorrect usage).

Bartók, Béla: *b.* Nagy Szent Miklós, March 25, 1881; *d.* New York City, September 26, 1945; one of the greatest modern composers and outstanding folklorist.

Piano lessons with László Erkel prepared Bartók for the Royal Academy of Music in Budapest, where he studied with Hans Koessler. From 1907 to 1934 Bartók was a member of the academy's piano faculty; his concert appearances were devoted mainly to performances of his own works. An abhorrence of Nazism caused· Bartók to emigrate to the United States in 1940. Until the end of 1942 he held a research grant in FOLK music from Columbia University. His last years were difficult ones; he died of leukemia.

The folk music of his native region—the Hungarian-Rumanian border—was of deep interest to Bartók. He collected several thousand folk melodies of central Europe, Turkey, and North Africa, often working jointly with KODÁLY from 1906. Bartók's publication of these tunes and his writings on folk music did much to systematize study in this area.

Bartók's music has a stark strength that derives in part from his affinity for folk music. From this source springs the strong and often asymmetric rhythmic drive of his fast movements. Many of his melodies are based on folk patterns—pentatonic, dia-

tonic, and irregular in structure. Bartók's harmony is often dissonant; he uses irregular chords and TONE CLUSTERS. Tonal centers are clearly defined, even though they are not used in accordance with earlier conventions. Percussive tone quality and novel TONE COLORS are achieved with traditional instruments. A fine sense of formal balance and a masterly handling of thematic development are to be found in Bartók's larger works.

Much of Bartók's output is for piano, including a SONATA, SONATINA, and many short pieces. Some of the latter are suited for beginners at the piano, and the *Mikrokosmos* series even constitutes a complete piano method. There are also three piano CONCERTOS, a sonata for two pianos and percussion, and a RHAPSODY for piano and orchestra. Other large works employing orchestra include two rhapsodies and a concerto for violin and orchestra, a *Concerto for Orchestra*, and *Music for strings, percussion, and celesta*. Bartók's six string quartets are the most important contribution to the genre by a 20th-century composer; he wrote also a variety of other CHAMBER MUSIC. His stage works—*Duke Bluebeard's Castle, The Wooden Prince,* and *The Miraculous Manda-*

rin—were written before 1920. His vocal music includes songs and the *Cantata profana*.

Baryton: a bowed string instrument of the late 17th to mid-19th centuries. Similar in range to a bass gamba (VIOL) or cello the baryton is furnished with as many as forty wire strings that may vibrate in sympathy with the tones produced on the six bowed strings. The former lie within a very wide, open neck and may be plucked from below with the thumb of the left hand. HAYDN composed many works for the instrument in various chamber and orchestral combinations.

Barytonhorn (G): euphonium. *See* BRASS INSTRUMENTS.

Bass: (1) the lowest part of a composition: the harmonic foundation; (2) a deep male VOICE; (3) short for double bass, the lowest instrument of the VIOLIN FAMILY; (4) short for bass tuba (infrequent); (5) a variety of CLEF; (6) the lowest or next lowest member of a family of instruments (e.g., bass clarinet).

Bass-bar: a narrow strip of wood glued to the underside of the belly of instruments of the VIOLIN (and viol) FAMILIES. Placed perpendicular to the left foot of the bridge, the bass-bar aids the spread of the vibrations over the surface of the instrument.

Basse Danse (F): a slow dance of the RENAISSANCE, executed with low, gliding steps, rather than leaps.

Basset horn: an alto clarinet with a narrow bore and thin walls, invented in the late 18th century. Originally crescent-shaped, it is now largely straight. A small but interesting CHAMBER MUSIC repertoire exists for the instrument, which is used also in a few orchestral scores.

Bass fiddle: the double bass, the lowest member of the VIOLIN FAMILY.

Bass horn: a bass instrument of the BRASS FAMILY, derived from the serpent, but shaped like a bassoon (known also as a Russian bassoon).

Basso continuo: *see* FIGURED BASS.

Basson (F): BASSOON.

Bassoon: a deep WOODWIND instrument employing a double reed.

Basso ostinato: *see* OSTINATO.

Bass viol: the double bass. *See* VIOLIN FAMILY.

Baton: a rod of wood, metal, or plastic, used by conductors to make clearer their motions governing TEMPO and DYNAMICS. The baton—which is of early 19th-century origin —is employed by most orchestral conductors; many choral conductors, however, prefer not to use one.

Battery: (1) the percussion instruments of the orchestra;

(2) a BAROQUE term for AR-
PEGGIO.

Battuta (I): BEAT. *A battuta*
requires that a passage be
played in strict time; *senza
battuta* indicates a flexible
rhythm.

Bax, Arnold Edward Trevor:
b. London, November 8,
1883; *d.* Cork, Ireland, October 3, 1953. Bax completed
his studies at the Royal Academy of Music under Tobias
Matthay and Paul Corder.
His romantic style of composition won him wide favor
in Britain; he was knighted
in 1937 and appointed Master
of the King's Music in 1942.
His numerous works include
SYMPHONIES, CONCERTOS,
SYMPHONIC POEMS, BALLETS,
CHAMBER MUSIC, songs, and
works for voice and orchestra.
He was keenly interested in
Irish folklore and set many
FOLK SONGS.

Be (G): flat.

Bearbeitung (G): arrangement.

Beat: (1) a steady measurement of time, marked off by
movements of a conductor's
hand or BATON, by tapping,
by a metronome, or by count-
ing, audibly or inaudibly. (2)
A designation used for different BAROQUE ornaments (rare).
See ACOUSTICS (*Interference*).

Bebung (G): a clavichord vibrato effected by alternate
pressure and relaxation on a
key that is being held down.

Bécarre (F): natural.

Becken (G): CYMBALS.

Beethoven, Ludwig van: *b.*
Bonn, *bapt.* December 17,
1770; *d.* Vienna, March 26,
1827; one of the greatest
masters of the CLASSICAL period.

Beethoven's musical training began at an early age,
first with his father, a singer
at the Electoral Court in
Bonn, and then with other
court musicians, including
the organist NEEFE. Mastering
the keyboard instruments as
well as violin and viola,
Beethoven entered into the
official musical activities of
the court in 1782. A trip to
Vienna in 1787 was cut short
by his mother's death. HAYDN's
praise of an early cantata per-
suaded the Elector Max Franz
to send Beethoven to Vienna
in 1792. He studied briefly
with Haydn and, seeking
sterner academic discipline,
with Johann Schenk, Johann
Georg Albrechtsberger, and
Antonio Salieri. Beethoven's
reputation as a piano virtuoso
and improvisator was rapidly
established, and his earliest
significant works were completed during the first years
of his Vienna residence. His
stipend from Bonn ceased in
1794 and Beethoven derived
his later income from concerts, teaching, the sale of his
compositions, and from the

generosity of wealthy bene-factors, including the Arch-duke Rudolf and Princes Lob-kowitz and Kinsky. He was the first master to break away successfully from the tradi-tion of service to church and state. Possessed of great per-sonal magnetism, Beethoven was able to retain the loyal friendship of many persons despite rude and erratic be-havior and an unpredictable temper. In 1800 his hearing began to fail, causing him great anguish. He was forced to give up playing in public after 1815, and total deafness set in by 1820. Before his death Beethoven was univer-sally recognized as the great-est composer of his genera-tion, notwithstanding the fact that his final works soared far beyond the comprehen-sion of most of his contem-poraries.

It is customary to classify Beethoven's music according to three styles or periods, which may be set approxi-mately as 1783–1802, 1803–14, and 1815–27. Any such designations must, however, be interpreted flexibly. Bee-thoven's early style derives from the mature works of Haydn, MOZART, and other Classical composers such as C. P. E. BACH, CHERUBINI, and CLEMENTI. However, even from the time of his three piano sonatas, Op. 2 (1795),

the differences between Bee-thoven's music and that of men about him are marked. The vigor of Haydn and Mo-zart undergoes greater com-pression and tension in Bee-thoven; their cheerfulness becomes rougher humor. One is tempted to compare the bal-anced elegance of a Raphael with the greater sweep and virility of a Michelangelo. Often in a Beethoven theme, rhythm rather than melody serves as the mainspring. This may be observed in such works as the first Rasumovsky Quartet (Op. 59, No. 1: the Allegretto) or the Waldstein Sonata (Op. 53: the opening Allegro). There is also an in-creased awareness of sonority in Beethoven, a deepening and widening in the range of his instrumental works. Most im-portant of all, there is the feeling of propulsion that de-rives from the motivic dissec-tion of the themes. Beethoven is among the supreme mas-ters of motivic development, and it is the heightened com-mand of such development that marks his middle period. This period is characterized also by the further expansion of the Classical instrumental forms: the SONATA, STRING QUARTET, and SYMPHONY. The pace of the longer move-ments is amply sustained through a keen sense of for-mal balance and astute use of tonal contrast, together with the developmental techniques mentioned. Beethoven required the extension of existing performance techniques, both instrumental and vocal. The piano works place increased demands on octave technique, use more difficult trills, require greater sheer speed; the violin works make more use of the higher register and of double stops. The demands on vocal stamina in such works as the Ninth Symphony and the *Missa Solemnis* are considerable. Beethoven's last period is characterized by a still deeper insight into thematic development and a greater freedom in the choice and handling of forms. He turned increasingly to FUGUE and fugato techniques to provide some of his most inspired moments.

Beethoven's greatness rests partly on his capacity for refining his original ideas, as is eloquently documented by surviving sketchbooks. Because he worked slowly and critically, and because he usually worked on a grand scale, the number of his compositions is smaller than that of most of his predecessors. His major works include 9 symphonies, 5 piano CONCERTOS and 1 violin concerto, several OVERTURES, 16 string quartets, a variety of other CHAMBER MUSIC including 10

sonatas for violin and piano and 5 for cello and piano, 32 piano sonatas, a song cycle (*An die ferne Geliebte*) and about 70 other songs, the *Missa Solemnis* and the Mass in C, an oratorio (*The Mount of Olives*), and the opera *Fidelio*. He was a vital influence on all realms of instrumental composition throughout the 19th century.

Begleitung (G): ACCOMPANIMENT.

Bel canto (I): a style of singing that emphasizes the sheer beauty of vocal color and technique, together with dramatic interpretation; *bel canto* is of especial importance in 18th- and 19th-century Italian operatic style.

Bell: (1) a PERCUSSION INSTRUMENT, which, in its most familiar form, is made of metal, hemispheroid in shape, and is struck either from within by a clapper, or from without by a hammer. The rim of the vessel vibrates, while the top is nearly or entirely still. Bells have been made of shell, wood, earthenware, and glass, in addition to metal. (The most frequently used metal is an alloy of copper and tin.) Bells exist in a variety of shapes: the cross-section may be round, ovoid, or rectangular. Normally the center is suspended from above, but there are also resting bells of modest size that have rims faced upward, the center being placed on a cushion. Sizes range from those of tiny hand bells to that of the Tsar Kolokol Bell, estimated to weigh upward of 350,000 pounds. Modern church bells usually weigh from 5,000 to 15,000 pounds. *See also* BELL CHIME. (2) The orchestral bell is a metal tube, suspended from the top, which is struck by a metal hammer. A full set of these bells will include one tuned to each semitone of the octave. (3) The flaring end of a wind instrument.

Bell chime: a set of BELLS, each tuned to a different pitch of the scale. A melody may be played on these, either directly or by means of a mechanism, by one musician. Bell chimes are known in both the East and West. Those employed in church towers are known as CARILLONS.

Bellini, Vincenzo: *b.* Catania, Sicily, November 3, 1801; *d.* Puteaux, France, September 23, 1835; prominent early ROMANTIC opera composer.

Descended of a musical family, Bellini studied with Nicola Antonio Zingarelli at the Naples Conservatory. Apart from miscellaneous student works, his output consists of ten OPERAS, which, for the most part, blend the traditions of the Italian *opera seria* with the developments of grand opera in France. The best of his works are *I Capuleti ed i Montecchi, La Sonnambula, Norma,* and *I Puritani e i Cavalieri.* Bellini's long, lyrical melodies for virtuoso singers are the outstanding feature of his work; these are sometimes reminiscent of the elegiac melodies of CHOPIN, who was a close friend. A second important feature is the masterly handling of the CHORUS and ENSEMBLES. Bellini's work is sometimes criticized for a lack of harmonic imagination.

Belly (Table): the upper surface of the body of a string instrument.

Bémol (F), Bemolle (I): flat.

Benedictus (L): (1) the second half of the *Sanctus* of the MASS; (2) the first word of the canticle *Benedictus Dominus Israel* and of other liturgical CHANTS.

Benevoli, Orazio: *b.* Rome, April 19, 1602; *d.* Rome, June 17, 1672. Benevoli is known for his MASSES and MOTETS for several CHOIRS (both vocal and instrumental); the most famous of these is a Mass for 52 parts with CEMBALO, written for the Salzburg cathedral. Benevoli's major post was as choir director at Santa Maria Maggiore in Rome (1646–72). His technique blends features of the Palestrina style with a Venetian flair for color.

Bequadro (I): natural.

Berceuse (F): (1) cradle song; (2) an instrumental piece in slow TEMPO with a rhythm suggestive of rocking motion (in 6/8 time).

Berg, Alban: *b*. Vienna, February 9, 1885; *d*. Vienna, December 24, 1935. Following the lead of his friend and teacher, SCHOENBERG, Berg— together with his fellow pupil, Webern—played a major role in the establishment of TWELVE-TONE composition. Berg taught privately in Vienna and wrote and lectured on modern music. His first works, a piano sonata and two groups of songs, show stylistic roots in the music of WAGNER and MAHLER. However, in keeping with Schoenberg's example, he avoided the expansiveness of these composers in favor of a more concise style. His operatic masterpiece *Wozzeck* (1921) welds together atonal and tonal elements, older instrumental forms (such as SUITE, PASSACAGLIA, SONATA FORM, FANTASY and FUGUE, SCHERZO, and RONDO) and newer structures in the service of a powerful social drama. His other outstanding works are the *Chamber Concerto for Piano, Violin, and 13 Wind Instruments*, the *Lyric Suite* (for string quartet), *Der Wein*, a setting after Baudelaire for soprano and orchestra, the *Violin Concerto*, and the unfinished opera *Lulu*. Berg's style is highly lyrical; twelve-tone elements freely intermingle with traditional tonal ones. Control of rhythmic development and structure are two of Berg's main concerns. His use of instrumental color is highly sensitive.

Bergamasca (I): (1) a 16th-century dance tune from Bergamo, Italy, that served as the basis for several works in variation form; (2) a lively 19th-century dance in 6/8 rhythm.

Berger, Arthur: *b*. New York City, May 15, 1912. Composer, critic, and teacher, Berger studied under PISTON, MILHAUD, and Nadia Boulanger. His style may be termed neoclassical. Among his important works are the *Serenade Concertante* and *Ideas of Order* (for orchestra); he has written keyboard and CHAMBER MUSIC as well as songs.

Bergerette (F): (1) a one-stanza VIRELAI of the 15th century; (2) a 16th-century dance in fast triple METER; (3) an 18th-century French pastoral song.

Bergsma, William: *b*. Oakland, Calif., April 1, 1921. Trained by HANSON and ROGERS, Bergsma is among the more prominent modern American composers writing in a romantic vein. His larger works include an OPERA, *The Wife of Martin Guerre*, two BALLETS, two SYMPHONIES, and two STRING QUARTETS.

Berlin, Irving (real name: Isidore Balin): *b.* Temun, Russia, May 11, 1888. Berlin came to the United States as a boy of five. Though unable either to read or write music, his melodic gifts were such that he contributed greatly to the development of American musical revues and comedies, both as lyricist and composer. Some of his famous shows include *Yip, Yip, Yaphank, As Thousands Cheer, Louisiana Purchase, This Is the Army, Annie Get Your Gun*, and *Call Me Madam*.

Berlioz (Louis) Hector: *b.* Côte St. André, December 11, 1803; *d.* Paris, March 8, 1869; Romantic composer and critic, outstanding master of orchestration.

As a youth, Berlioz was sent to Paris to study medicine but soon turned to music. Having had a smattering of experience in flute and guitar, he began to study with LE SUEUR and REICHA at the Paris Conservatoire. His strong individuality and distaste for mere routine often brought him into conflict with conservative authorities. He sought the Prix de Rome several times, winning it finally in 1830 with the CANTATA *Sardanapale*. Berlioz' vigor in championing progressive musical ideas was not limited to battles on his own behalf; as a critic and conductor he espoused the causes of many great musicians of his time. In later life he supplemented his earnings by acting as librarian at the Paris Conservatoire; this did not, however, preclude the continuation of his European tours.

Berlioz is best known for his contributions to program music, especially in the *Symphonie fantastique, Harold en Italie* (which contains an important solo viola part), and *Roméo et Juliette*, a "dramatic symphony" (i.e., one with choral and solo vocal parts). The actual extent to which he derived his musical ideas from extramusical sources is not too important because each of his finer works bears close musical scrutiny irrespective of its extramusical associations. Berlioz was one of the first of the ROMANTICS to believe in an extensive interpenetration of instrumental music and language, an example of fusion that is a characteristic trait of Romanticism. This interdependence is shown both by the descriptive nature of his instrumental music and by the presence of instrumental interludes in his OPERAS, such as *La Damnation de Faust* and *Les Troyens*. Somewhat paradoxically, it is these interludes, including the *Rákóczi March*, that are best known.

Another of the chief traits of Berlioz' music is the masterful handling of orchestral color. Berlioz revealed many possibilities of seldom used instruments and unusual instrumental combinations. In 1844 he issued his *Traité d'instrumentation et d'orchestration modernes*, the first work of its kind, and one of fundamental importance. In works such as the *Symphonie Funèbre et Triomphale* Berlioz delights in the massive sounds produced by large numbers of performers, an aspect that attracted many later Romantic composers.

Other important works include the ORATORIO *L'Enfance du Christ*, a REQUIEM, and the song cycle, *Nuits d'Été*.

Bernstein, Leonard: *b.* Lawrence, Mass., August 25, 1918. Bernstein completed his musical studies at Harvard, the Curtis Institute, and the Berkshire Music Center; PISTON, THOMPSON, and Koussevitsky were among his teachers. Following an auspicious debut with the New York Philharmonic in 1943, he rose steadily in the ranks of American conductors, becoming director of the Philharmonic in 1958. He has written scores for three musical comedies (including *West Side Story*), as well as two SYMPHONIES, two BALLETS (including *The Age of Anxiety*), an OPERA, songs, choral works, and miscellaneous instrumental compositions. His educational programs on television have reached a wide audience.

Bewegt (G): animated.

Biber, Heinrich Ignaz Franz von: *b.* Wartenberg, Bohemia, August 12, 1644; *d.* Salzburg, May 3, 1704. A violinist of importance, Biber served Emperor Leopold I and the Archbishop of Salzburg. His SONATAS and other works for violin—both solo and with keyboard ACCOMPANIMENT—are best known, but he also wrote sacred music and a few OPERAS.

Bibliography: Although musicology is one of the youngest of the humanistic disciplines, its literature is quite extensive. A useful survey of important monuments in this literature is furnished by Vincent Duckles' *Music Reference and Research Materials* (1954).

Most needs for further information may, however, be satisfied through the use of the larger music dictionaries and histories and through the bibliographical references provided there for individual persons and topics. The largest music encyclopedia in English is *Grove's Dictionary of Music and Musicians*, ed. Eric Blom (5th ed.; 9 vols., 1954, supplementary vol., 1961). The illustrations, music examples, and lists of primary and secondary source materials of a still larger, more authoritative German encyclopedia, *Die Musik in Geschichte und Gegenwart*, ed. Friedrich Blume (1949–?) may prove useful even to those with little or no reading knowledge of German. Less extensive and technical is the one-volume Thompson, *International Cyclopedia of Music and Musicians,* ed. Robert Sabin (9th ed., 1964).

Those wishing only biographical information will find *Baker's Biographical Dictionary of Musicians*, ed. Nicolas Slonimsky (5th ed., 1958) extremely useful. The topical counterpart to this work, though not equally comprehensive and even, is Willi Apel's *Harvard Dictionary of Music* (2nd ed., 1969).

Two of the better one-volume histories of music in English are Paul Henry Lang's *Music in Western Civilization* (1941) and Donald Grout's *A History of Western Music* (1960). Those desiring greater depth should know of an important series

published by W. W. Norton Co., New York, that presently included the following independent volumes: Curt Sachs, *The Rise of Music in the Ancient World, East and West* (1943); Gustave Reese, *Music in the Middle Ages* (1940), and *Music in the Renaissance* (rev. ed., 1959); Manfred Bukofzer, *Music in the Baroque Era* (1947); Alfred Einstein, *Music in the Romantic Era* (1947); and William Austin, *Music in the Twentieth Century* (1966). Another series, *The New Oxford History of Music* (New York: Oxford University Press) has thus far issued the first four of a projected set of eleven volumes (the last to include chronological tables and a general index).

A wide range of illustrative material may be found in Georg Kinsky's *A History of Music in Pictures* (reprint of English ed., 1951) and in Paul H. Lang and Otto Bettmann's *A Pictorial History of Music* (1960). A large German set, *Musikgeschichte in Bildern*, has been begun under the general editorship of Heinrich Besseler and Max Schneider.

There are a few widely-used general anthologies of music: Arnold Schering, *Geschichte der Musik in Beispielen* (1931; reprinted, 1950); Archibald Davison and

Willi Apel, *Historical Anthology of Music* (2 vols., 1946, 1950); William Starr and George DeVine, *Music Scores Omnibus* (1964); and Edward R. Lerner, *Study Scores of Musical Styles* (1968). A much greater range of material may be found in specialized collections; a valuable guide to these is provided by the article "Editions" in the *Harvard Dictionary of Music*. A more extensive survey is provided in the articles *"Denkmäler"* ("Monuments") and *"Gesamtausgaben"* ("Complete Editions") in *Die Musik in Geschichte und Gegenwart*. Collected editions are either available or in course of issue for most major composers.

Sibyl Marcuse's *Musical Instruments: A comprehensive Dictionary* (1964) offers information on both common and esoteric instruments. Other useful books within this area include Curt Sachs, *A History of Musical Instruments* (1940); and Anthony Baines, ed., *Musical Instruments* (1961).

Books on theoretical subjects reflect the wide variety of approaches possible within this area and their usefulness for a given reader may depend upon the reader's background and biases. Elementary material is covered by John Castellini in *The Rudiments of Music* (1962). Richard Franko Goldman's *Harmony in Western Music* (1965); Roger Sessions' *Harmonic Practice* (1951), and Kent Kennan's *Counterpoint Based on 18th Century Practice* (1959) are useful on a more advanced level.

Binary form: two-part form, a musical structure containing two main divisions. Often each of these is repeated. They may be equal or unequal in length; in the latter event the second section is normally the longer. Generally the first section leads from the TONIC key to a related one (most often the DOMINANT), while the second reverses this direction. Many dance movements of the 17th and early 18th centuries are written in binary form, as are most keyboard works by Domenico SCARLATTI and many short movements and works of the 18th and 19th centuries.

As a rule, the two sections of binary form have related or similar contents. When material used in the opening section returns at the end of the second section, the form is known as rounded binary. From this form evolved the SONATA FORM, which plays such a vital role in sonata, SYMPHONY, and CHAMBER MUSIC repertoires. Rounded binary form somewhat resembles TERNARY FORM. Both may be represented by the schema, *A B A*. However, the *B* section of a ternary form is contrasting rather than derivative and the return to the *A* section is handled differently in the two forms.

Binchois, Gilles: *b*. Mons, Belgium, *c*.1400; *d*. near Soignies, September 20, 1460. Soldier, priest, and musician to Philip the Good (duke of Burgundy), Binchois rivaled DUFAY as a composer of graceful three- and four-part CHANSONS. He wrote MOTETS, MAGNIFICATS, and MASS sections.

Bitonality: *see* POLYTONALITY.

Bizet, Georges (*bapt.* Alexandre César Léopold); *b*. Paris, October 25, 1838; *d*. zet's parents, who were professional musicians, entered their son at the Paris Conservatoire at the age of nine. Bougival, June 3, 1875. There he studied with Marmontel and HALÉVY. He won the Prix de Rome in 1857. Bizet was active chiefly as an OPERA composer, but neither *Carmen*, his masterpiece, nor his other two major operas— *The Pearl Fishers* and *La Jolie Fille de Perth*—won outstanding success during his lifetime. *Carmen*, now an operatic staple, was rejected by many critics because of supposedly Wagnerian traits and the coarseness of its subject.

Other important works by Bizet include the incidental music to DAUDET's *L'Arlésienne* (from which two SUITES were drawn), a SYMPHONY, the symphonic suite *Roma*, the OVERTURE *Patrie, Jeux d'Enfants*, and other keyboard pieces.

Blanche (F): half note.

Blasinstrumente (G): wind instruments.

Blechinstrumente (G): brass instruments.

Bliss, Arthur: *b*. London, August 2, 1891. Bliss, one of several English composers writing in a conservative RO-MANTIC idiom, was trained at Cambridge and at the Royal College of Music. He has written in a wide variety of traditional media, including SYMPHONY, CONCERTO, OPERA, BALLET, CHAMBER MU-SIC, and songs.

Blitztein, Marc: *b*. Philadelphia, March 2, 1905; *d*. Fort-de-France, Martinique, January 22, 1964. Active especially in the theater, Blitztein wrote a number of OPERAS, among them *Regina* and *The Cradle Will Rock*, a BALLET, and revised Kurt WEILL's *Three-Penny Opera* for U.S. production. His nonstage works cover a wide range.

Bloch, Ernest: *b*. Geneva, July 24, 1880; *d*. Portland, Oregon, July 15, 1959. Bloch studied under Émile Jacques-Dalcroze, Eugène Ysaÿe, and

Ludwig Thuille, a m o n g others. He taught briefly at the Geneva Conservatory and, in 1916, came to the United States as a conductor. He was director of the Cleveland Institute of Music (1920–25) and the San Francisco Conservatory (1925–30). Many prominent American composers, including SESSIONS and MOORE, are numbered among Bloch's pupils. His style is partly late ROMANTIC, partly NEOCLASSICAL. Although many of his forms are rhapsodic, others—such as the *Concerto grosso*—submit to strict discipline. Among his best-known works are several that develop Jewish themes: *Schelomo* (a cello CONCERTO), the *Israel Symphony, Baal Schem,* and the *Sacred Service.* His three STRING QUARTETS and piano quintet are prominent among 20th-century CHAMBER works. He composed numerous other works in a variety of traditional media.

Blockflöte (G): recorder.

Blow, John: *b.* Newark-on-Trent, February 1649; *d.* London, October 1, 1708. Trained at the Chapel Royal, Blow was organist at Westminster Abbey (1668–79, 1695–1708). He was named Master of the Children, organist, and composer to the Chapel Royal in 1674, 1676, and 1699, respectively, holding these titles until his death. PURCELL was the greatest of his pupils. A versatile and imaginative composer, he wrote ANTHEMS, odes, songs, keyboard and other instrumental music, and a MASQUE, *Venus and Adonis.*

Bocca chiusa (I): hum.

Boccherini, Luigi: *b.* Lucca, February 19, 1743; *d.* Madrid, May 28, 1805. After winning fame in Paris as a cellist, Boccherini went to Madrid as court composer to the Infante Luis. He became composer to Frederick William II of Prussia in 1787 and spent some time in Germany. His last years were spent in Madrid, where he died in poverty. Boccherini was especially prolific as a composer of CHAMBER MUSIC, writing 125 STRING QUINTETS. In addition, he wrote a number of SYMPHONIES, DIVERTIMENTI and orchestral dances, a few OPERAS and ORATORIOS, a CANTATA, and some CHURCH MUSIC. His harmonic and melodic style often closely resembles that of HAYDN although seldom displaying the degree of originality distinguishing the greater master.

Bogen (G): bow.

Böhm, Georg: *b.* Hohenkirchen, September 2, 1661; *d.* Lüneburg, May 18, 1733. An important composer for organ and harpsichord, Böhm was organist at St. John's in

Lüneburg from 1698 until his death. He also wrote some sacred vocal music.

Boieldieu, François Adrien: *b.* Rouen, December 16, 1775; *d.* Jarcy, October 8, 1834. From 1793 to 1825, Boieldieu composed some 40 OPERAS—the most enduring being *La Dame blanche* and *Le Calife de Bagdad*—and contributed to joint productions with other composers such as MÉHUL and CHERUBINI. One of the most successful French opera composers of his day, he was appointed conductor to the Imperial Russian Opera (1803–11) and professor of composition at the Paris Conservatoire (1817–26). He also wrote early keyboard works and songs.

Bois (F): wood, woodwind.

Boito, Arrigo: *b.* Padua, February 24, 1842; *d.* Milan, June 10, 1918. Although Boito's opera *Mefistofele* has held the stage in revised form for the past century, Boito is best remembered for his brilliant LIBRETTOS for VERDI's *Otello* and *Falstaff*, as well as for PONCHIELLI's *La Gioconda*.

Bolero: a Spanish dance in moderate triple METER for a soloist or couple. Characteristic repeated rhythmic patterns are marked out by CASTANETS. The most famous example of the music is the *Bolero* of RAVEL.

Bombard: the bass of the double-reed SHAWM family, used during the Middle Ages and RENAISSANCE.

Bombardon: a large, BRASS INSTRUMENT of circular shape.

Bononcini, Giovanni: *b.* Modena, July 18, 1670; *d.* Vienna, July 9, 1747. The most famous member of a family of musicians; he is best remembered as a rival of HANDEL in the composition of OPERAS for English audiences. He was active in Italy, Austria, Germany, England, and France as cellist and composer. Among his nonoperatic works are MASSES, ORATORIOS, CANTATAS, SINFONIAS, SONATAS, SUITES, and other instrumental works.

Borodin, Alexander Porfirievich: *b.* St. Petersburg, November 11, 1833; *d.* St. Petersburg, February 27, 1887; Russian nationalistic composer, one of the Mighty FIVE.

Borodin was a chemist by profession. He had an excellent education as a child and learned to play piano and flute. His music is lyrical, descriptive, and richly colorful. Under the influence of BALAKIREV and others, Borodin's style became suffused with Russian and Oriental folkloristic idioms. Borodin's major

works include three SYM-
PHONIES (the last incom-
plete), the symphonic sketch
*In the Steppes of Central
Asia,* two STRING QUARTETS,
and the OPERA *Prince Igor*
(completed by RIMSKY-KORSA-
KOV and GLAZUNOV). He
wrote also another opera,
operatic fragments, and miscellaneous piano, CHAMBER,
and vocal works.

**Bortniansky, Dmitri Stepa-
novich:** *b.* Glukhov, 1751; *d.*
St. Petersburg, October 7,
1825. Trained by GALUPPI
and other Italian composers,
Bortniansky became director
of the Russian court chapel
in 1796. He improved per-
formance standards greatly
and contributed extensively
to the repertoire of Russian
sacred music. He also wrote
OPERAS to French texts.

Bouché (F): a French horn
tone muted by hand, or, more
specifically, a soft tone so
muted. *See* CUIVRÉ.

Bouche fermée (F): hum.

Boulez, Pierre: *b.* Montbrison,
France, March 26, 1925.
Boulez studied with MESSAIEN
and René Leibowitz. As music director for a theater com-
pany, he toured widely. Active as a conductor, Boulez
organized the *Domaine Musicale,* a concert series of avant-
garde music. His earlier works
contributed to the further
evolution of serial techniques,
especially with regard to

rhythm. But after pursuing
a path leading to the prede-
termination of all musical
elements, he began to turn in
an opposite direction to explore elements of CHANCE. He
has been fascinated also by
the possibilities inherent in
electronic manipulations of
sound, including noise. His
works include three piano
SONATAS, a STRING QUARTET
and other CHAMBER MUSIC
for new combinations of instruments, a few orchestral
pieces, and works for mixed
vocal and instrumental groups,
of which *Le Marteau Sans
Maître* is the most famous.

Bourdon (F): (1) a drone
bass; (2) a soft-sounding OR-
GAN RANK employing stopped
pipes.

Bourgeois, Louis: *b.* Paris,
*c.*1510; *d.* Paris, *c.*1561; the
musician responsible for most
of the melodies of the Genevan Psalter. Many of these
were adapted from earlier—
often secular—models; some
were newly composed. Bourgeois issued two harmonized
sets of PSALMS in 1547. He
was an early advocate of
SOLFEGGIO.

Bourrée (F): (1) in the BA-
ROQUE, a French dance in
quick duple METER, with
phrases beginning on the
fourth quarter of the measure.
The *bourrée* was among the
optional movements of the

SUITE. (2) A folk dance of Auvergne in triple meter.

Bow: (1) an implement consisting of hair strung taut on a curved stick; its function is to set a string in vibration by means of friction. The violin, viola, cello, and bass are normally played with a bow (*see* VIOLIN FAMILY), as are the viols, now being used increasingly in the performance of early music. The modern bow stick is a round or octagonal rod of Pernambuco wood, with a slight curve that brings the center closer to the hair than either end. At the lower end of the bow, the hair is fastened to a movable section known as the nut or frog. A screw mechanism controls the precise position of the nut and therefore the degree of tension exerted on the hair. The basic design of the modern bow was established by François Tourte (1747–1833). Although most bows for the same instrument look alike, fine differences in balance and resilience may result in marked handling differences between outstanding and mediocre bows. The average violin bow is just over 29 inches in length. The viola, cello, and bass bows are progressively heavier, the latter two being also progressively shorter. *See also* BOWING.

(2) The musical bow is a stringed instrument of several preliterate peoples that is played by plucking or striking. Some musical bows have gourd or other resonators attached; others are played so that resonance is obtained from the mouth cavity of the player or from a covered pit dug into the ground.

Bow form: a musical structure in which the opening sections recur in reverse order at the conclusion. A pattern that may be represented by the letters *A B C B A,* would furnish one example of bow form. (A simple TERNARY FORM, *A B A,* may also be considered among box forms.)

Bowing: (1) the technique of bow handling in the playing of instruments of the VIOLIN (and related) FAMILIES; (2) the bow strokes required for the proper playing of a given passage. The movement of the elbow away from the body is known as down-bow, the opposite, as up-bow. *See also* DÉTACHÉ, LOURÉ, MARTELÉ, RICOCHET, SAUTILLÉ, and TREMOLO.

Boyce, William: *b*. London, 1710; *d*. Kensington, February 7, 1779. The most important of Boyce's several posts was that of organist and composer to the Chapel Royal. In 1769 he had to abandon music because of deafness. Boyce was a versatile composer, writing SYMPHONIES, OVERTURES, CHAMBER MUSIC, organ VOLUNTARIES, and both sacred and secular vocal music. He issued an important anthology, *Cathedral Music,* containing British works of the previous two centuries.

Brace: (1) a bracket placed at the left-hand edge of a group of STAVES, connecting these staves to indicate that they form one musical entity, whether in a keyboard, vocal, or instrumental score; (2) a set of staves so connected.

Brahms, Johannes: *b.* Hamburg, May 7, 1833; *d.* Vienna, April 3, 1897; the greatest ROMANTIC master of SYMPHONY and CHAMBER MUSIC.

The son of a double bass player at the Hamburg Opera, Brahms was trained first by his father and then by Otto Cossel and Eduard Marxsen. He became an excellent pianist and earned money as a youth by playing in taverns. A tour of north Germany in 1853 with the violinist Eduard Reményi began Brahms' rise to prominence. He deeply impressed the violinist Joseph Joachim, who became a close friend and who introduced him to LISZT and SCHUMANN. The latter arranged for the publication of Brahms' early music and, in a prophetic article, hailed the young composer as the coming genius of German music. Brahms joined Schumann, first in Düsseldorf and then in Bonn. From 1857 to 1859 he served as music director to the Prince of Lippe-Detmold. His later life was spent primarily in Vienna, although his residence there was interrupted on occasion by travel in Germany. In Vienna, Brahms conducted the concerts of the *Singakademie* (1863–64) and the *Gesellschaft d e r Musikfreunde* (1871–74). He received an honorary doctorate from the University of Breslau and, in 1886, was made a knight of the Prussian Order of Merit. In 1889, Hamburg presented him with the freedom of the city.

Brahms was a master of almost every contemporary medium except opera. His four symphonies, his *Variations on a Theme by Haydn,* two piano CONCERTOS, violin concerto, and concerto for violin and cello stand at the peak of Romantic achievements in these forms. The same may be said for his two dozen chamber works, scored for a wide variety of different instrumental combinations. Brahms' larger piano works include three SONATAS and five sets of variations, the last of which is a double set based on the PAGANINI *Caprice* treated also by Liszt and RACHMANINOFF. More familiar, however, are some 30 CHARACTER PIECES—intermezzos, ballades, rhapsodies, etc.—composed during the latter part of his life. As a composer of some 200 songs, Brahms is one of the great masters of the genre, together with SCHUBERT, Schumann, and WOLF. In general, the Romantics did not favor the choral medium, but Brahms created a wide variety of choral works, from deceptively simple arrangements of folk tunes to the magnificent *German Requiem, Alto Rhapsody, Song of Destiny,* and *Song of the Fates.*

Brahms' style combines a Romantic love of sonorous and chromatic harmonies and a rich orchestral palette with a CLASSICAL respect for form and craft. Although he admired WAGNER's music, he opposed the exalted position accorded program music by the followers of Liszt and Wagner. The sonata, theme and VARIATIONS, MOTET, and even the CHORALE PRELUDE were viable forms to Brahms, not outmoded genres. Because of his interest in ABSOLUTE MUSIC and in traditional forms, his opponents often considered Brahms a mere academician, although conceding his mastery of COUNTERPOINT, variation, and formal organization. His admirers, on the other hand, viewed Brahms as the inheritor of BEETHOVEN's mantle. Brahms himself was deeply conscious of his musical heritage. There is a wide emotional range to his music although it is rarely frolicsome. Most of the short piano pieces, for example, are highly condensed statements of deep emotions; a lighter vein appears in his waltzes. Though Brahms' settings of pastoral and amorous texts are remarkably fine, they are surpassed by his settings of more serious texts, such as the *Vier Ernste Gesänge.* Brahms' great interest in folksong is often reflected in his melodies; his harmonies are richly sonorous, his rhythms vigorous and often daring. One of the marks of his style is the simultaneous use of conflicting rhythmic patterns.

Branle (F), Brawl (E), Brando (I): a group of dances of the 16th and 17th centuries employing swaying movements; some were in duple METER, others in triple.

Brass instruments: wind instruments whose tones are initiated by the vibration of the player's lips, transmitted to the instrument via a cupped or funneled mouthpiece. Modern instruments are made of brass or some other metal, but their ancestors were made of various materials including horn, wood, shell, and glass. The orchestral brass include the trumpet, French horn, trombone, and tuba; other members of the family, used

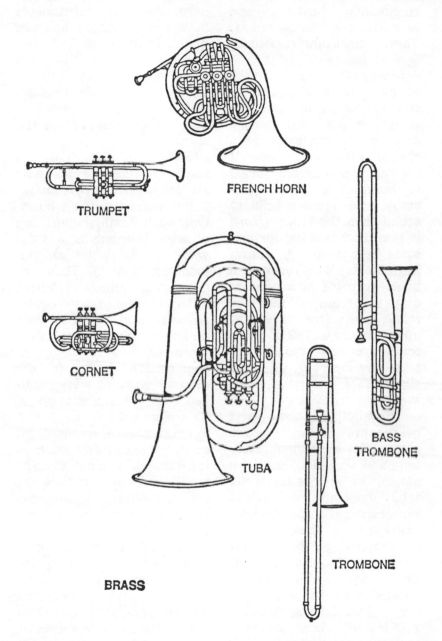

TRUMPET

FRENCH HORN

CORNET

TUBA

TROMBONE

BASS TROMBONE

BRASS

chiefly in bands, include the cornet, Flügelhorn, saxhorn, euphonium, baritone, and helicon (or sousaphone). These names are sometimes applied inconsistently.

Most modern brass consist of partly cylindrical, partly conical tubes, coiled into differing shapes. Instruments that are chiefly cylindrical are classed as trumpets; those that are chiefly conical are classed as horns. The former generally have a more brilliant sound than the latter. (*Horn* is also used as slang for any brass instrument.) A natural instrument is one—such as a bugle—capable of producing only the tones of the harmonic series (*see* ACOUSTICS, TONE COLOR). Intermediate tones are now usually obtained by means of valves or slides (*see section, Technique*).

The trumpet is the highest of the present brass instruments. It is comparatively long and slim, and has three valves; the last quarter of the tube flares gently into a bell of moderate size. The trumpet exists in many sizes, the most common being a B-flat instrument (*see* TRANSPOSING INSTRUMENTS), which, in orchestral parts, has a range of nearly three octaves, from the *e* below *middle c* to the *c* above the treble staff.

The trumpet has two counterparts in the horn family, the cornet and the Flügelhorn. All three instruments have similar ranges and are played in the same way. The cornet appears stubby and squat in comparison with the trumpet; the Flügelhorn is the widest of the three, with a bore larger than that of the cornet.

The term Flügelhorn is sometimes used to designate an entire family of instruments with expanding bores. One such family, consisting of seven instruments, was devised by Adolphe Sax and patented in 1845. These instruments, called saxhorns, differed little from others manufactured at that time under various names. Furthermore, the bores and other construction details of the original saxhorns were modified over the course of years. This situation has resulted in a confusion of terminology, compounded by differences in local usages. The baritone (or tenorhorn) and euphonium are medium-size instruments belonging to this general family. Most members have three piston valves and are held erect, with bells pointing upward or outward.

The French horn is the next highest of the orchestral brass. It is coiled to a circular shape and is held so that the bell is at the player's side, facing slightly backward. The right hand is inserted into the bell, adjusting both PITCH and tone color. The horn's timbre is normally mellow. The instrument has a wide range from the *b* below the bass staff to the *f* on the top line of the treble staff. A similarly shaped instrument, with a smaller range and with three upright piston valves, is the mellophone.

The trombone belongs to the class of trumpets; that is, its bore is cylindrical except for the lowest third, which widens into the bell. The trombone is the only one of the modern brass that normally uses a slide rather than valves. (Slide trumpets are known, but are rare.) Valve trombones are becoming increasingly popular, especially among JAZZ musicians, because they facilitate a rapid technique. Some feel, however, that their tone quality is inferior to that of the slide trombone. Trombones are made in several sizes, the most usual being the tenor trombone, which has an unbroken range from the *e* below the bass clef to the *d* nearly three octaves above. In addition, four pedal tones, *bb*, *a*, *ab*, and *g*, are obtainable below the continuous range. The bass trombone is a larger instrument, pitched a fourth lower. Because it is clumsy to

manipulate, it has been largely supplanted by the tenor-bass trombone. This instrument is similar to the tenor trombone in size, but has a larger bore and a valve, which, when used, lowers the pitch by a fourth. There is also a rarely used double-bass trombone, pitched an octave lower than the tenor.

Tuba is a generic term for the lower brass instruments, excluding the trombones. The euphonium is classed as a tenor tuba. There is also the bass tuba in *Eb* or *F* and the double-bass tuba in *Bb*. These instruments each have four or five valves, and have a three-octave range beginning respectively with the *bb* below the bass clef, with the *eb* or *f* below that, and with the *bb* an octave below the first. Tubas for marching bands are made in a wide circle so that the player may pass his head and shoulder through the circle and support the instrument on the other shoulder. Such instruments are known as helicons or bombardons. A variety with a bell designed by John Philip SOUSA is called the sousaphone. The so-called Wagner tubas—tenor and bass—have slightly smaller bores than other instruments of this group, and have funneled mouthpieces of the French horn type rather than cupped mouthpieces. They were designed for use in WAGNER's operas and have been used also by later composers. They are somewhat more agile than other tubas.

Experiments are still being carried out with brass instruments. Refinements are being devised for standard instruments. New instruments, varying somewhat from standard ones, continue to appear, but remain on the periphery of the musical scene.

Technique and History. A wind column vibrating at full length produces one note, but the column may be made to produce other notes by making it vibrate in halves, thirds, fourths, or still smaller fractions. This is done with brass instruments by increasing the tension of the lip muscles (which behave as a double reed) and by increasing the breath pressure. The notes thus produced will be those of the harmonic series (*see* ACOUSTICS). The player will obtain first the fundamental, then the octave above, the twelfth, the double octave, and so forth. (The lowest note obtainable on a narrow-bore instrument is the second harmonic.) The first several of these notes are widely separated, and the problem of producing a continuous scale is therefore basic to brass technique. Several solutions

are possible, and the evolution towards present methods was by no means a consistent and orderly one.

One can, for example, get an unbroken range by using only the higher harmonics, from the eighth upward. During the BAROQUE period, trumpet parts were differentiated according to range. The principal trumpeter played the lower register and was limited to sustained notes and fanfares. The clarin trumpeter was a skilled virtuoso in the upper register; he used a shallow mouthpiece with a broad rim and was capable of dazzling feats, such as are called for in certain Bach cantatas and in the *Brandenburg Concerto No. 2*. However, the continuous range of the clarin trumpet was relatively small. The system was abandoned in the late 18th century, when the power of the old trumpet guild was broken.

Other methods of obtaining a continuous range depend upon changing the length of the wind column itself. This may be done by boring holes into the side of the column. As the holes are covered consecutively from the top, the effective wind column becomes longer and the pitch lower; an individual harmonic series is available for each fingering. This principle was used in the construction of the cornett (= zink; not to be confused with the cornet) and serpent. The former was a treble instrument with a slightly conical bore, developed in the 15th century. It was either straight or slightly curved in shape and had six fingerholes. The cornett had a gentle sound and blended well with voices and strings. The serpent, a bass instrument, was of somewhat later origin. Because of its greater size, the column was designed in a serpentine shape so that the fingerholes remained within normal handspan. The cornett was discontinued after BACH's time, but the serpent remained in use until the mid-19th century, appearing in scores by MENDELSSOHN, Wagner, and VERDI. It submitted to different changes in shape; as a straight instrument, doubled back upon itself, it was called a Russian bassoon. An improved version of this instrument, known as a basshorn, appeared around 1800. During the CLASSICAL era, experiments were conducted with k e y e d trumpets; HAYDN's *Trumpet Concerto* was written for such an instrument. The experiments were discontinued when it was found that the drilling of holes into an instrument with a small, cylindrical bore lowers the tone quality. Keyed bugles

were more successful and were used during the early 19th century. A bass size, shaped like the Russian bassoon, is known as an ophicleide.

The length of a wind column may be altered also by means of a slide. That is, one section of tubing may fit within another for some distance. As the overlap is reduced, the wind column is lengthened and the tone lowered. Each of the lower tones serves as the basis for a different harmonic series. The modern trombone has seven different slide positions to fill the interval between the second and third harmonic. Slide instruments—both trumpets and trombones (sackbuts)—were used during the RENAISSANCE, although construction details were not the same as those of today. The slide trumpet (*tromba da tirarsi*) was still used by Bach; it was later supplanted almost entirely by the valve trumpet.

Most trumpets and horns of the Classical period were natural instruments. They were built in a specific key, and the players changed key (i.e., changed harmonic series) by adding on pieces of tubing, known as CROOKS. At first, the crooks were inserted between the mouthpiece and the body of the instrument. They were later made curved and inserted into the coils of the body itself. Valves, invented about 1815 by Stölzel and Blühmel, permit a series of crooks to remain in place. In the customary descending valve, the crook is not part of the wind column; when the valve is worked, the air is shunted through the additional tubing, lowering the pitch. The valve may be of the piston or the rotary variety. An ascending valve works by shutting off a section of tubing, raising the pitch. Most modern instruments have three valves or more. The three valves of a trumpet lower the pitch by a whole step, a half step, and a step-and-a-half, respectively. By combining these as necessary, a full chromatic compass may be obtained.

The problems of articulation on brass instruments are handled as on WOODWINDS (*see* description of "tonguing"). The TONE COLOR of trumpets, horns, and trombones may be altered through the use of mutes of various shapes and materials.

Music. The brass repertoire reflects the close association of these instruments with military ceremonies and other outdoor pomp. There is a large repertoire of marches for brass band, and many of the characteristic brass motives in orchestral music are of a fanfare nature. BAROQUE and Classical composers used the brass only sparingly in their orchestral music, but the ROMANTICS used them with gusto. The French horn was a particular favorite of 19th-century composers. The accompanied SOLO literature for these instruments is limited. Solo trumpets were featured in a few Baroque scores (e.g., by VIVALDI and Bach), while the Haydn *Trumpet Concerto* and the four Horn concertos by MOZART represent the best of the Classical repertoire. The French horn takes part in a modest amount of CHAMBER MUSIC since it is used in standard woodwind quintets and in other small ensembles. The chamber literature for trumpets and trombones is scantier, though these instruments are finding greater favor with modern composers than they enjoyed previously. They are both prominent in jazz bands.

Bratsche (G): viola.

Breve: a time-value equivalent to two whole notes. *See* also NOTATION (*History*).

Bridge: (1) a thin strip of wood or other material that serves to raise the strings of a string instrument from the sound-board, keep them in place, and define the beginning of the effective vibrating length. On bowed instruments (e.g., members of the viol and

VIOLIN FAMILIES) the upper edge of the bridge is arched, while on plucked and struck instruments it is usually straight. On most instruments —excluding stringed keyboard instruments and other zithers —the bridge rests on top of the belly, below the center, held in place by the tension of the strings. Some non-European instruments employ bridges that are to be moved about by the player. (2) A section of a composition that serves a connective rather than a thematic or developmental function. This connective function usually involves a change from one key to another.

Britten, Benjamin: *b.* Lowestoft, November 22, 1913. One of the major English composers of the mid-20th century, Britten studied with Frank Bridge and, at the Royal College of Music, with Ireland. Britten is essentially a lyrical composer and long melodic lines, clear textures, and generally NEOCLASSICAL orientation characterize his style. The most famous of his several OPERAS are *Peter Grimes* and *The Turn of the Screw*, while other important vocal works include the song cycle *Les Illuminations*, and *A Ceremony of Carols* (for chorus and harp). Britten's instrumental music includes *The Young Person's Guide to the Orchestra* (variations on a THEME by PURCELL) and two STRING QUARTETS. He also wrote music for well-known motion pictures.

Broken chord: the tones of a CHORD sounded successively rather than simultaneously. The PITCH outline thus formed may proceed in one direction (normally over a more limited range than in an arpeggio) or may alternate directions to produce patterns of different degrees of stability and complexity, as in an ALBERTI BASS.

Bruch, Max: *b.* Cologne, January 6, 1838; *d.* Friedenau (Berlin), October 2, 1920. As a conductor, Bruch was active in Germany, England, and the United States; from 1891 to 1910 he taught composition in Berlin. The most famous of his works are his first violin CONCERTO, the setting of *Kol Nidre* for cello and orchestra (commissioned by the Jews of Liverpool), and the *Scottish Fantasy* for violin and orchestra. He also wrote SYMPHONIES, OPERAS, CHORAL WORKS, and CHAMBER MUSIC.

Bruckner, (Josef) Anton: *b.* Ansfelden, September 4, 1824; *d.* Vienna, October 11, 1896; important ROMANTIC symphonist.

Bruckner learned the rudiments of music from a relative, J. B. Weiss, and as a choir boy at St. Florian. He became organist at Linz in 1856, studying theory and composition with Simon Sechter (1856–61). He wrote his first important work at the age of forty. In 1867 Bruckner succeeded Sechter as court organist in Vienna and, from 1868 to 1891 taught organ and harmony at the Vienna Conservatory. In 1875 he was appointed lecturer on music at the Vienna University.

Bruckner's simple and devout nature is exemplified by numerous sacred pieces—both liturgical and nonliturgical—for chorus and organ or orchestra. His major works in this area, the three numbered MASSES (Bruckner's early Masses are unnumbered, as are his first two symphonies), the *Te Deum*, and the setting of Psalm 150, are among the great CHORAL WORKS of the Romantic era. The nine numbered SYMPHONIES—the last incomplete at the time of Bruckner's death—are related to his choral music stylistically, and sometimes thematically also. Bruckner was an ardent admirer of WAGNER and adopted the latter's harmonic idiom and use of a large orchestra. As a symphonist, he was much influenced by BEETHOVEN and SCHUBERT. His THEMES are broad and lyrical. Some of the first and last movements are capped by hymn-like melodies stated by the brass. The SCHERZO movements are in the style of LÄNDLER. An expansive treatment of themes and the use of three thematic groups rather than two results in large structures. Size, coupled with a slow rate of harmonic change, gives the impression of placid movement even at brisk tempos. The monumental character of the symphonies has worked against their popular acceptance in non-Germanic nations; performances are sometimes based on cut versions prepared by his friends. Among Bruckner's chamber compositions, his string quintet is outstanding.

Brunette (F): a French song of the late 17th and early 18th centuries having a text dealing with love and nature.

Buffa, Buffo (I): comic; often designates a singer performing a comic part in OPERA, such as a buffo bass (e.g., Figaro).

Bugle: a BRASS INSTRUMENT with a conical tube used in the playing of military signals and fanfares.

Bull, John: b. 1563(?); d. Antwerp, March 12, 1628. Organist at Hereford Cathedral and later at the Chapel Royal, Bull was named the first professor of music at Gresham College in 1596. He went to Brussels in 1613 and in 1617 became organist at the Cathedral of Antwerp. Here he became acquainted with SWEELINCK. Best known for his virtuoso compositions for the VIRGINALS, Bull wrote also some sacred vocal music and some CHAMBER MUSIC.

Burla (I), Burlesca (I), Burleske (G), Burlesque (F): a movement or work in a playful style.

Busnois, Antoine: *d*. Bruges, November 6, 1492; a leading CHANSON composer of his generation. Priest and poet, Busnois spent several years in the chapel of Charles the Bold of Burgundy. Many of his more than 60 chansons display imaginative use of imitation. Although he wrote several fine MOTETS and MASSES, he did not equal OCKEGHEM (whose pupil he claimed to be) as a composer of sacred music.

Busoni, Ferruccio Benvenuto: *b*. Empoli, April 1, 1866; *d*. Berlin, July 27, 1924. Busoni's influence on early 20th-century music as virtuoso pianist, conductor, teacher, editor, theorist, and composer was far greater than is implied by the minor place of his music in the present concert repertoire. He was a child prodigy and was the youngest member to be admitted to the Accademia Filarmonica of Bologna since MOZART. Berlin was his chief residence, although he toured widely in both Europe and the United States. Busoni experimented with novel scales and with MICROTONES. He gave impetus to the NEOCLASSICAL movement through the emphasis on leaner, contrapuntal textures, formal clarity, and experiments with TONE COLORS. He also cultivated several 18th-century forms. Busoni wrote three OPERAS, two STRING QUARTETS, a quantity of piano music (including six SONATINAS and the *Fantasia contrappuntistica*), and a variety of vocal and orchestral music. He edited and transcribed much older music for piano.

Buxtehude, Dietrich: *b*. Oldesloe(?), 1637(?); *d*. Lübeck, May 9, 1707. The son of an organist, Buxtehude held posts at both Hälsingborg and Helsingör (across the straits), and from 1668 on, at St. Mary's Church at Lübeck. He wrote a wide variety of sacred vocal music, especially CANTATAS, as well as TOCCATAS, FANTASIAS, and CHORALE PRELUDES for organ, and music for harpsichord and instrumental ensembles. His reputation during his lifetime was vast and his influence, especially on BACH, significant.

Byrd, William: *b*. Lincoln, 1543; *d*. Stondon, July 4,

1623. The greatest of the Elizabethan composers and an influential teacher, Byrd served as organist at the Lincoln Cathedral (1563–72) and as gentleman of the Chapel Royal from 1570 (organist there, together with TALLIS, from 1572). In 1585 Byrd and Tallis were granted the exclusive right to publish music and music paper in England. Endowed with a masterful technique and a penetrating sense for textual values, Byrd excelled in nearly every genre known to his time. His *Gradualia* (settings of the Mass PROPER), polyphonic MASSES, and MOTETS made him famous all over Europe. He also wrote Protestant church music, including the *Great Service* and was equally preeminent in the field of MADRIGAL, VIRGINAL music and instrumental ENSEMBLE music.

C

Cabaletta (I): in OPERA, either a short song with simple and strong rhythm, or the final portion of an ARIA (or duet) in a fast, repeated rhythm.

Cabezón, Antonio de: *b.* Castrojeriz, *c.*1500; *d.* Madrid, March 26, 1566. Blind since childhood, Cabezón served as organist at the courts of Charles V and Philip II. His keyboard works include settings of PSALM tones and other liturgical melodies as well as variations and imitative works (TIENTOS). His influence on the development of the keyboard repertoire was considerable.

Caccia (I): a 14th-century Italian genre depicting outdoor scenes for two canonic voices and an accompanying one, the counterpart to the

French CHACE. *See also* PRO-
GRAM MUSIC.

Caccini, Giulio: *b.* Rome,
*c.*1550; *d.* Florence, December 10, 1618. An early composer of MONODIES (he
claimed to be the first), Caccini was singer and lutenist to
the grand duke of Tuscany.
He is remembered for his
monodic madrigal collection
Le Nuove Musiche, and for
his opera *Euridice* (1600).

Cachucha: a fast Andalusian
dance in triple METER, similar to the BOLERO.

Cadence: the conclusion of a
musical thought, normally a
variation of a standard formula. A cadence may arise in
a purely melodic context or
in contrapuntal or harmonic
contexts. Because Western
music of the past three centuries is preponderantly HAR-
MONIC, the term most fre-
quently implies a harmonic
function.

The governing of rhythmic
flow, the suggestion of having
reached a breathing point of
greater or lesser importance,
is basic to all cadences. The
only other element that may
be involved in melodic cadences is a sense of tonal order. A melodic cadence is
forceful if its last note is a
clearly established tone center; otherwise it may be am-
biguous. A sense of tonal
order may also serve to distinguish among contrapuntal and
harmonic cadences occurring
in traditional styles. A composer may employ cadences
that are equivalent in terms
of purely local functions and
yet the significance of these
cadences in terms of the larger
shape of the music may vary
considerably according to the
way in which each is related
to the composition's primary
tone center.

A strong contrapuntal ca-
dence ends with a perfect
octave or fifth, reached by
contrary motion. In some
styles an intermediate cadence
may end with a third. Among
numerous MEDIEVAL and
RENAISSANCE contrapuntal cadences are three designated
by special terms. The *Phrygian cadence* is characterized

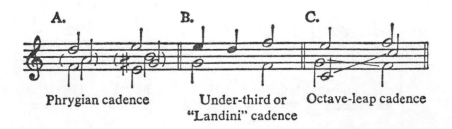

Phrygian cadence   Under-third or   Octave-leap cadence
                    "Landini" cadence

by a half-step descent to the tone center; the *under-third cadence* (or Landini cadence) avoids the direct upward progression of a half-step by a momentary downward movement. The *octave-leap cadence* conceals the presence of parallel, harmonic fifths through unusual voice leading.

In tonal harmony, there are four main cadential progressions. The most conclusive is a dominant-tonic progression, which is termed an *authentic cadence*. This cadence is perfect if the tonic chord presents the doubled root in the highest voice and imperfect if otherwise. A tonic-dominant cadence may be used to mark a mid-point within a larger thought and is thus designated as a *half cadence* or half close. British terminology for these two basic cadences varies from American usage: both forms of authen-

tic cadence are known as *perfect cadences,* while the half cadence is termed an *imperfect cadence.*

The subdominant-tonic close (familiar to most as the "Amen" conclusion appended to HYMNS) is called a *plagal cadence.* A cadence that leads the listener to expect the finality of a dominant-tonic progression, but which goes instead from the dominant to the submediant is known as a *deceptive cadence* (or interrupted or evaded cadence). Such a cadence usually leads into an extension involving a return to the tonic.

Cadences may also be classified according to their rhythmic structure. A cadence that ends with a stress is known as a *masculine cadence* (or masculine ending), while a cadence with an unstressed ending is known as a *feminine cadence* (feminine ending).

Cadenza: a SOLO section in

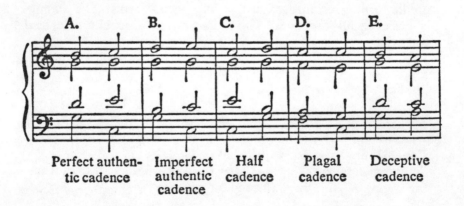

Perfect authentic cadence   Imperfect authentic cadence   Half cadence   Plagal cadence   Deceptive cadence

an improvisatory, virtuoso style occurring near the end of an ARIA or CONCERTO movement. This section is usually an interpolation inserted in the final cadence of the soloist. Allusion to previously stated themes is customary. In the 18th century cadenzas were improvised by the performers. However, MOZART wrote out cadenzas for a few of his piano concertos. BEETHOVEN composed a mandatory cadenza for his last piano concerto and this practice was followed by later composers, thus ensuring stylistic unity between the cadenza and the main body of the work. Sometimes the sense of the term is extended to include brief, virtuoso, interpolative passages occurring at any point in solo and ENSEMBLE works.

Cadman, Charles Wakefield: *b.* Johnstown, Pa., December 24, 1881; *d.* Los Angeles, December 30, 1946. Composer, organist, and critic, Cadman was especially interested in the music of the American Indians and used Indian themes in his works. His major opera is *Shanewis;* he wrote also orchestral and keyboard music and many songs, the most famous being *At Dawning.*

Cage, John: *b.* Los Angeles, September 5, 1912. One of the major figures among American avant-garde composers of the mid-20th century, Cage studied with SCHOENBERG, COWELL, and VARÈSE. He first attracted attention with his pieces for prepared piano (calling for the placement of various objects on and between the strings in order to produce new sound effects). He uses many sounds from extramusical sources and is one of the leading protagonists of CHANCE MUSIC.

Caisse (F): DRUM. *Caisse claire:* side drum; *caisse roulante, caisse sourde:* tenor drum; *grosse caisse:* bass drum.

Calando (I): getting softer and slower.

Cambiata, nota cambiata (I): (1) a melodic figure proceeding stepwise downward to a NONHARMONIC TONE, thence downward again by a leap of a third to a CONSONANCE, and moving upward stepwise; (2) an accented passing DISSONANCE (infrequent usage).

Cambini, Giovanni Giuseppe, *b.* Legborn, Feb. 13, 1746; *d.* Bicêtre, Dec. 29, 1825. Trained by Martini, Cambini was active chiefly in Paris as a composer and conductor. He wrote many symphonies, string quartets, and ballets, as well as some operas and oratorios; few, however, are performed today.

Camera (I): chamber. *Musica*

da camera is therefore music designed for the salon rather than the church or theater. For *Sonata da camera, see* SONATA; SUITE.

Camerata: a group of Florentines including Vincenzo Galilei, Giulio Caccini, Ottavia Rinuccini, and Count Bardi, whose discussions in the late 16th century led to the creation of MONODY, the stylistic basis for early OPERA.

Campana, Campanella (I): bell (the latter form, a diminutive).

Campion, Thomas: *b.* London, February 12, 1567; *d.* London, March 1, 1620. A poet and physician as well as a composer, Campion wrote several books of songs with lute accompaniment and music for court MASQUES. He wrote also a COUNTERPOINT treatise.

Campra, André: *b.* Aix-en-Provence, December 4, 1660; *d.* Versailles, June 29, 1744. After holding church posts at Toulon, Arles, Toulouse, and Paris, Campra became the most successful French OPERA composer between LULLY and RAMEAU. His varied output includes a MASS, MOTETS, PSALMS, CANTATAS, and songs, in addition to operas.

Canarie, Canary: a 17th-century French dance in 3/8 or 6/8, employing dotted rhythms.

Cancrizans (L): (1) retrograde motion (i.e., proceeding from the last note to the first; (2) a CANON in which one voice proceeds backward.

Cannabich, Christian: *b.* Mannheim, December 28, 1731; *d.* Frankfurt, January 20, 1798. A student of Johann STAMITZ and JOMMELLI, he was violinist in and later conductor of the Mannheim orchestra. As a composer he wrote many SYMPHONIES, CHAMBER WORKS, and BALLETS, a few CONCERTOS, and a SINGSPIEL.

Canon: (1) a contrapuntal work in which two or more VOICES present the same melody in overlapping succession. (2) in MEDIEVAL usage, the term referred to an inscription (usually a word puzzle) containing clues whereby a performer could derive unwritten notes from written ones. Some, but not all, of the resulting compositions fall within the present meaning of canon.

The imitative voices of a canon may be accompanied or unaccompanied. The former variety of cannon is called *mixed.* The first voice to enter is called the *dux* or antecedent, the later ones, *comes* or consequent(s). The imitation is most frequently at the octave or unison, but other intervals may also be employed, as in BACH's *Goldberg Variations.*

Canonic imitation may be carried out to the end of a piece or the last phrase may be freely composed so that a satisfactory end may be achieved more easily. Some canons are so fashioned that each voice may, upon reaching the end, begin immediately again, fitting smoothly into the polyphonic fabric furnished by the voice parts that have not yet concluded. Such works, known as circle canons or ROUNDS, include such folk favorites as *Three Blind Mice, Frère Jacques,* etc. *See also* CATCH.

INVERSION, RETROGRADE MOTION, AUGMENTATION, and DIMINUTION, and combinations of these techniques may be employed in canon. Canon by retrograde motion is known as *crab canon* or cancrizans. Methods of indicating time-values in the musical notation of the RENAISSANCE suggested canons in irregular augmentation, which proceed in different meters simultaneously and are known as *mensuration canons.*

The origins of canon are unknown. *Sumer Is Icumen in,* a four-part canon over a two-part repeated figure, is the earliest example yet discovered; its precise date is disputed, estimates ranging from *c.*1280–1310. In the 14th century, Italian *cacce* (singular, *caccia*) and French *chaces* vividly depicted in canon outdoor scenes, especially those of the hunt. Canon technique reached an early peak in the works of JOSQUIN DES PREZ and was later a favorite device of 17th- and early 18th-century composers. BACH was an outstanding master of canon. MOZART, BEETHOVEN, and some later composers often wrote canons for fun.

Cantabile (I): to be performed in a singing (i.e., flowing) manner.

Cantata: a term derived from *cantare,* to sing, designating a number of sectional, accompanied vocal forms, prominent chiefly during the BAROQUE. A solo cantata is a work written for a vocal soloist; a choral cantata is one that employs a CHORUS.

The cantata originated early in the 17th century as a work for vocal soloist and CONTINUO, set as a strophic variation, and often having a pastoral text. Each section employed the same bass line (or one with some variants) in combination with a new vocal melody. A contrast between sections in RECITATIVE, ARIOSO, and ARIA style evolved in the works of the following generation, including those by CARISSIMI, CESTI, and Luigi ROSSI. This contrast was the basis for later cantatas by both French and Italian mas-

ters, including works by STRA-
DELLA, Alessandro SCARLATTI,
CHARPENTIER, CAMPRA, and
RAMEAU. The standard Italian
cantata of the late 17th cen-
tury consisted of two or three
arias of contrasting nature,
each preceded by a recitative.
Gradually the ACCOMPANI-
MENT for the arias was en-
riched and scored for small
ORCHESTRA.

The cantata was taken up
by German composers, but
within a changed framework.
They used the musical form
for setting sacred texts and
the cantata was incorporated
into Protestant church services. It is this sort of cantata
that is best known, primarily
because of the magnificence
of J. S. BACH's sacred cantatas; the liturgical function of
these works requires that they
each be suited to a particular
Sunday of the church year.
These cantatas normally end
with a simple harmonization
of a chorale, the melody being sung by the congregation.
Often the chorale furnished
text, and sometimes melody,
for other movements of the
cantata; such works are
known as CHORALE CANTATAS.
Bach's *Christ Lag in Todesbanden* is among the most
notable of these.

In the mid- and late-Ba-
roque, the vocal forces employed in cantatas were
greatly expanded. Several vocal soloists were employed in
a single work, and stirring
movements for chorus were
created. From a purely musical point of view, the sacred
cantata was the equivalent of
contemporary MASSES, PAS-
SIONS, and ORATORIOS in most
matters except length.

Cantatas continued to' be
written after the Baroque, including examples by HAYDN,
MOZART, BEETHOVEN, SCHU-
BERT, SCHUMANN, MENDELS-
SOHN, LISZT, and BRAHMS, but
the genre was not particularly
important during the 19th
and 20th centuries. During
this time the term usually designated a sectional composition for mixed forces, similar
to a short oratorio.

Canticle: a scriptural text constructed in the fashion of a
PSALM, occurring within the
liturgy of the OFFICE. There
are three major canticles
(taken from the New Testament), the *Magnificat*, the
Nunc Dimittis, and the *Benedictus Dominus Deus Israel*,
and fourteen lesser canticles
(taken from the Old Testament).

Cantilena: (1) a lyrical melody; (2) a medieval designation for secular vocal compositions.

Cantillation: unaccompanied
liturgical chanting; the term
refers most often to music of
the Jewish service.

Canto (I): song, melody.

Canto fermo, see CANTUS FIRMUS.

Cantor: (1) the solo singer in Jewish and Roman Catholic services; (2) the music director of a German Lutheran church.

Cantus firmus (L), canto fermo (I): a preexisting melody used as the basis for a new composition or a COUNTERPOINT exercise. *Cantus firmi* provide the foundation for much MEDIEVAL and RENAISSANCE sacred music, as well as for some secular music of these periods. A *cantus firmus* is often stated in longer note values than are used for the other voices.

Canzona (I): song. More specifically: (1) in OPERA, a lyrical song, less elaborate than an ARIA; (2) in the 16th century, (a) the Italian designation for a French polyphonic CHANSON, (b) an instrumental transcription of such a work, (c) a newly composed instrumental piece in chanson style, or, (d) an Italian vocal work in a simpler style than the MADRIGAL; (3) in the 17th century, (a) an evolved form of *2c,* or, (b) a SOLO song accompanied by basso continuo (*see* FIGURED BASS). A large instrumental *canzona* is a lively work, normally featuring imitative openings in several contrasting sections. The *canzona* is among the precursors of both the SO-NATA and FUGUE, an enlargement of the individual sections leading toward the former, an increased emphasis on imitation, toward the latter.

Canzonet, Canzonetta (I): diminutive of *canzona,* a short piece of light character, scored either for two or more voices, for voice(s) and instruments, or — exceptionally — for keyboard.

Cappella: *see* A CAPPELLA; MAESTRO DI CAPPELLA.

Capriccio (I), **Caprice** (F): (1) a humorous or capricious piece; (2) a potpourri; (3) a technical study (rare); (4) in the BAROQUE, a work of fugal character with a lively theme.

Carissimi, Giacomo: *bapt.* Marino (Rome), April 17, 1605; *d.* Rome, January 12, 1674; outstanding early BAROQUE vocal composer. As choirmaster at St. Apollinare in Rome, Carissimi produced polyphonic MASSES and MOTETS. Most important, however, are his ORATORIOS (including *Jephte, Judicium Salomonis, Jonas,* and *Balthazar*) and his numerous secular CANTATAS in monodic style. He greatly influenced these forms by tightening the early recitativic style for narrative purposes, by allowing greater melodic freedom for lyrical purposes, and by providing more varied instrumental accompaniments.

Carol: (1) in the modern sense, a Christmas song; (2) in the MEDIEVAL sense, a polyphonic song constructed according to a certain refrain pattern. Medieval carols are often, but not necessarily, concerned with Christmas.

Carpenter, John Alden: *b.* Chicago, February 28, 1876; *d.* Chicago, April 26, 1951. Carpenter studied with PAINE at Harvard and entered his father's shipping supply business following graduation. Although he continued his musical studies with Edward ELGAR and then Bernard Ziehn, he did not devote full time to musical composition until his retirement in 1936. His style was influenced by French impressionism and by JAZZ. Among his better known orchestral works are *Krazy Kat, Skyscrapers,* and *Adventures in a Perambulator.* He wrote also CHAMBER and KEYBOARD MUSIC and songs.

Carter, Elliott Cook, Jr.: *b.* New York City, December 11, 1908. Carter studied with PISTON and Nadia Boulanger; he taught briefly at several American colleges and universities and has contributed meaningful criticism of modern music. He has composed a wide variety of CHAMBER WORKS (most importantly, two STRING QUARTETS), as well as a SYMPHONY, CON-CERTO, three BALLETS (among them *The Minotaur*), an OPERA (*Tom and Lily*), ORATORIOS, and other vocal works. Carter is keenly interested in COUNTERPOINT and in rhythmic constructions as one of the primary features of musical structure; he delights in the use of POLYRHYTHMS and carefully calculated changes in TEMPO.

Casella, Alfredo: *b.* Turin, July 25, 1883; *d.* Rome, March 5, 1947. Casella completed his studies under FAURÉ at the Paris Conservatoire and taught there and at the Conservatorio di Santa Cecilia in Rome. He was prominent as a pianist, conductor, and critic, as well as a composer, and did much to further the cause of modern music in Italy. His large output includes SYMPHONIES, CONCERTOS, OPERAS, BALLETS, CHAMBER MUSIC, piano music, and songs; his style is basically NEOCLASSICAL.

Cassa (I): drum. *Cassa rullante,* tenor drum; *gran cassa, cassa grande,* bass drum.

Cassation: a work in several movements, similar to a SERENADE or DIVERTIMENTO (i.e., suitable for outdoor performance by a small orchestra). The genre is proper to the 18th century.

Castanets: a percussion instrument popular especially in Spain, consisting of two shell-shaped, hardwood clappers, held loosely together at one end by a string. The traditional instrument is held within the palm, but modern orchestral castanets may have handles and springs.

Castelnuovo-Tedesco, Mario: *b*. Florence, April 3, 1895. A pupil of PIZZETTI, Castelnuovo-Tedesco has cultivated a facile, post-Romantic style that found favor in the period around World War II. His output includes OPERAS and other stage works, CONCERTOS, CHAMBER and KEYBOARD MUSIC, songs, and choruses. He has resided in the United States since 1939.

Catch: an English ROUND of the 17th or 18th century for male VOICES in three or more parts. The texts are normally humorous or earthy.

Cavalieri, Emilio de': *b*. Rome, *c*.1550; *d*. Rome, March 11, 1602. An amateur composer and member of the Florentine CAMERATA, Cavalieri helped create the monodic style of the early BAROQUE. Best known for his setting of the morality play, *La Rappresentazione di Anima e di Corpo* (1600)—often cited as the first ORATORIO—Cavalieri also composed *intermedii* (entertainments given between the acts of a play) and sacred works.

Cavalli, Pier Francesco: *b*. Crema, February 14, 1602; *d*.

Venice, January 14, 1676. Though his surname was Caletti-Bruni, Cavalli became known by the name of his Venetian protector, Federigo Cavalli. Much of Cavalli's life was spent at St. Mark's in Venice, where he sang in the choir under MONTEVERDI; he rose gradually in rank, becoming choirmaster in 1669. In addition to his more than 40 OPERAS in spectacular Venetian style—including *Il Giasone* (1649), *Il Serse* (1654), and *Ercole Amante* (1662), Cavalli wrote a variety of sacred music and some secular CANTATAS. He was an important force in the evolution of the early austere monodic style toward greater lyricism.

Cavatina (I): a song, in either an OPERA or ORATORIO, that is less elaborate in style and structure than an ARIA. By extension, the term may refer to an instrumental movement or work of similar style.

Cavazzoni, Marco Antonio: *b*. Bologna, *c*.1490; *d*. *c*.1570. Active in Urbino, Rome, Chioggia, and Venice (where he was a singer at St. Mark's under WILLAERT), Cavazzoni contributed to the development of the organ repertoire with his TOCCATA-like RICERCARS and transcriptions of MOTETS and CHANSONS. His son, Girolamo (*b*. Urbino, *c*.1520; *d*. Venice, 1560), followed in his footsteps, being among the first to write imitative ricercars and CANZONAS independent of vocal models.

Celesta: a keyboard instrument resembling a small upright piano, but whose hammers strike steel bars situated above wooden resonators. The instrument was invented by Auguste Mustel in 1886; its best-known use occurs in TCHAIKOVSKY's *Dance of the Sugar-Plum Fairy* (in the *Nutcracker Suite*).

Cello: a bass instrument of the VIOLIN FAMILY.

Cembalo (I), **Clavicembalo** (I): harpsichord.

Cent: a unit for measuring intervals, devised by Alexander Ellis. Each equal-tempered half step has a value of 100 Cents; an octave thus equals 1200 Cents. The system of Cents makes possible accurate comparisons between our equal-tempered intervals and others in different systems of tuning, both Oriental and Occidental.

Certon, Pierre: *b. c.*1510; *d.* Paris, February 23, 1572. A pupil of JOSQUIN and a member of the Sainte Chapelle, Certon wrote MASSES, MOTETS, PSALMS, and CHANSONS, his secular works being more successful than the sacred.

Cesti, Marc' Antonio (*bapt.* Pietro): *b.* Arezzo, August 5, 1623; *d.* Florence, October 14, 1669. Cesti contributed significantly to the development of the dramatic ARIA in both OPERA and secular CANTATA; his best-known work is the lavish opera *Il pomo d'oro*, staged in Vienna for the marriage of Emperor Leopold I.

Chabrier, (Alexis) Emmanuel: *b.* Ambert, January 18, 1841; *d.* Paris, September 13, 1894. Chabrier's place in the concert repertoire is maintained by his evocative orchestral RHAPSODY, *España*, and a few piano pieces such as the *Bourrée fantasque* and *Habanera*. His two OPERAS (influenced by his admiration for Wagner), operettas, and other miscellaneous works are largely forgotten.

Chace (F): a 14th-century French genre (the counterpart to the Italian *caccia*) depicting a hunt or other outdoor scene, set in CANON.

Chaconne (F), **Ciaccona** (I); **Passecaille** (F), **Passacaglia** (I): two terms for works of regular phrase structure, almost invariably in triple METER, and deriving ultimately from dances. (Normal usage favors the French form of the former term, the Italian of the latter.) A few of these works—mainly by French BAROQUE composers—are RONDOS, alternating a standard refrain with different couplets. Normally, however, the terms refer to works in

VARIATION form, based either on a repeated harmonic progression or on a recurrent bass melody, which may occasionally be transferred to an upper voice. No clear distinction between the two terms was maintained during the Baroque, the period in which most CHACONNES and PASSACAGLIAS were composed. The fact that a given work may be based on *chaconne-passacaglia* variation procedures is not always indicated in its title. (The *Crucifixus* movement of BACH's *B Minor Mass* is one of many such works.) To lessen terminological confusion, modern scholars have suggested that the term *chaconne* be employed for continuous variations founded on a harmonic progression, while the term *passacaglia* be reserved for similar works employing a recurrent bass line.

Chadwick, George Whitfield: *b.* Lowell, Mass., November 13, 1854; *d.* Boston, April 4, 1931. After study in Boston, Leipzig, and Munich, Chadwick became a composition instructor at the New England Conservatory in 1880 and was appointed director in 1897. One of the most prominent American composers of his day, he wrote in a richly romantic vein. He wrote in almost all genres then cultivated, but only a

few symphonic poems and OVERTURES are still known.

Chaikovskii: *see* TCHAIKOVSKY.

Chair organ: choir ORGAN.

Chalumeau (F): (1) the low register of the CLARINET; (2) in the early 18th century, the clarinet itself; (3) in the loosest sense, any primitive REED instrument.

Chamber music: In the broadest sense, music written for a small group of performers, each with an individual part. The term originated in the BAROQUE, mainly to designate a style proper for aristocratic homes (as opposed to church and operatic styles), but it may be applied to a large body of music—both vocal and instrumental—from the late Middle Ages to the present day. Normally, however, it is used to denote instrumental music alone, and often it is even limited to music of the CLASSICAL and later periods. It is customary to classify chamber music according to the number of parts: duets (duos), trios, quartets, quintets, sextets, septets, octets, nonets, and so forth.

While the outstanding genre of Baroque chamber music is the trio SONATA, there are also extensive literatures for various numbers of instruments, for viols, and for mixed ensembles. Indeed, many works were written so that they might be performed on a variety of instruments. After 1750 the outstanding medium is the STRING QUARTET, consisting of two violins, viola, and cello. There are, however, many other standard combinations, including the piano trio, comprised of piano, violin, and cello. Most Classical and Romantic works employ the forms of the sonata. Increasing interest in the modest repertoire of Baroque music for wind ensembles and in the smaller Classical and Romantic literature for such groups is now being shown, while modern composers are writing more frequently for heterogeneous groups and less often for standard ones. The nature of chamber music leads the composer to strive for ENSEMBLE balance and fine craftsmanship rather than for virtuosity and quick effect.

Chamber orchestra: a small orchestra.

Chambonnières, Jacques Champion de: *b. c.*1602; *d.* Paris(?), *c.*1672. As harpsichordist to Louis XIV, Chambonnières exerted great influence on the development of harpsichord music. Many important musicians, including D'ANGLEBERT and COUPERIN, numbered among his pupils. A collection of his KEYBOARD works was published in 1670.

Chance music, aleatoric music: music of the mid-20th century in which the composer assigns a major creative role to the performer. In such music the composer may provide a set of detailed materials or a vague outline of the entire piece, leaving the order of execution or the filling in of details to the performer. If the performer is to work out the actual pitches and rhythm, the composer will normally abandon traditional musical NOTATION and work out one that will convey his particular ideas. The shape of a musical gesture (phrase) may be suggested by a line, for example, or intensity or duration by the size of a figure. Different performances of the same work may vary greatly, and the receptivity and imagination of the performer becomes of far greater moment than in traditional music. Since neither composer nor performer is necessarily bound by the limitations of metrical rhythm, great rhythmic freedom may be achieved in chance music. In addition to traditional vocal and instrumental sounds, tonal resources comprise also vocal and instrumental sounds produced in abnormal fashion and sounds from extramusical sources (e.g., striking or dragging of chairs or stands). Intensive interest in chance music began in the 1950s with works of such diverse composers as STOCKHAUSEN and CAGE; Milhaud's *Cocktail* (1921) might be cited as an early example of the concept, as well as certain 18th-century works that assemble short bits of music in an order determined by the casting of dice.

Changing note: *see* CAMBIATA (sense 1).

Chanson: a SONG with French (or, rarely, Provençal) text.

Chant: (1) a generic term for various bodies of liturgical music, normally intended for unaccompanied unison singing; (2) in the Anglican church, the term refers specifically to the music for PSALMS and CANTICLES; (3) in French, a word meaning melody, song.

Character piece: a modern term for a work belonging to a 19th-century repertoire, mainly for piano, developing one or two moods within a small or moderate frame. Often a group of such pieces is designed to form one larger unit. Various BAGATELLES, BALLADES, MOMENTS MUSICAUX, PRELUDES, IMPROMPTUS, INTERMEZZI, and SONGS WITHOUT WORDS are among the works comprised within this term.

Charpentier, Gustave: *b.* Dieuze, June 25, 1860; *d.*

Paris, February 18, 1956. After study with MASSENET at the Paris Conservatoire, Charpentier won the Prix de Rome in 1887. His opera, *Louise*, written in a French kind of verismo style, achieved considerable success. In addition, he wrote some songs, orchestral works, and music for chorus and orchestra.

Charpentier, Marc-Antoine: *b.* Paris, 1634(?); *d.* Paris, February 24, 1704. As a youth Charpentier went to Rome to become a painter, but turned instead to music, studying with CARISSIMI. After his return to Paris he was music director to Mlle. de Guise, composer to the dauphin, and music director at the Church of Saint-Louis. In 1698 Charpentier became music director at the Sainte Chapelle. The greatest French composer of ORATORIOS, his large output of sacred music includes also MASSES, MAGNIFICATS, PSALMS, MOTETS, and LESSONS. Charpentier wrote music for a few stage works, collaborating briefly with Molière, but did not write OPERAS until late in life, owing to LULLY's monopoly on operatic productions. His work represents a blending of Italian and French traditions. Carissimi's influence is evident, but Charpentier employs greater contrasts of forces and textures and more varied harmonies than did his master. In the oratorios, instrumental interludes are prominent.

Chausson, Ernest: *b.* Paris, January 20, 1855; *d.* Limay, June 10, 1899. A pupil of MASSENET and FRANCK, Chausson developed a richly romantic style. His best-known works are his *Poème* for violin and orchestra and his *Symphony in Bb Major.* He wrote also some CHAMBER MUSIC, songs, works for voice and orchestra, and three OPERAS.

Chávez, Carlos: *b.* Mexico City, June 13, 1899. As conductor of the Orquesta Sinfónica and director of the National Conservatory and of the National Institute of Fine Arts, Chávez championed both the cause of modern Mexican music and the preservation of the ancient Mexican heritage. His own compositions employ national instruments; the strong rhythmic drive of his music derives from Mexican folk music, Indian as well as Spanish-Mexican. His works include five SYMPHONIES, five BALLETS, CONCERTOS, STRING QUARTETS and other CHAMBER MUSIC, choral works, songs, and piano music.

Cherubini, (Maria) Luigi Carlo Senobio Salvatore: *b.* Florence, September 14, 1760; *d.* Paris, March 15, 1842. The son of a musician, Cherubini completed his training under Guiseppe Sarti. After visiting London (1784–86) and being appointed composer to the king, Cherubini went to Paris, establishing a permanent home there in 1788. He was active first as an opera composer and producer; he became an inspector of the Conservatoire in 1795 and director of that school in 1821. Though Cherubini had a fine melodic gift, his dramatic sense was not equal to that of MOZART or GLUCK. The success of his *Les Deux Journées* (*The Water Carrier*) did much to further the vogue of OPERAS with plots turning on dramatic rescues. BEETHOVEN admired his music. After 1813 Cherubini turned more and more to the composition of church music, writing MASSES with orchestral accompaniment, MOTETS, etc. Other works include a SYMPHONY, a few CHAMBER WORKS, some piano SONATAS and other keyboard pieces, and orchestral marches and dances. His *Cours de contrepoint et de la fugue* was an influential text.

Chest: in the 17th century, a set—usually of four or more —of the principal sizes of an instrument family (e.g., a chest of viols). *See* CONSORT.

Chest voice: the lower register of the VOICE.

Chevalet (F): bridge; *see* PONTICELLO.

Chimes: (1) a set of about 18 metal tubes, tuned chromatically, suspended within a metal framework, and struck by a hammer. The instrument is known also as tubular bells. (2) A loose designation for the GLOCKENSPIEL.

Chinese block, Temple block: a hollowed-out wooden block, usually struck with a wooden drumstick.

Chitarra (I): guitar.

Chitarrone: a large LUTE, with bass strings lying outside the fingerboard. *See illustration, p. 167.*

Choir: (1) a homogeneous instrumental group (e.g., string, woodwind, or brass choir); (2) a particular ORGAN keyboard or division. *See also* CHORUS *or* CHOIR.

Chopin, Frederic François: *b.* Zelazowa Wola (Warsaw), March 1, 1810; *d.* Paris, October 17, 1849; great piano composer of the ROMANTIC school.

The son of a French schoolteacher and a Polish mother, Chopin began his musical studies under Adalbert Zwyny and continued with Joseph Elsner, the director of the Warsaw Conservatory. His great talent was soon apparent; he played in public before the age of eight and began to compose at the same time. His first tour as a mature performer took him to Vienna in 1829. Though he returned briefly to Warsaw, he set out again in November 1830, stopping at Breslau, Dresden, Prague, Vienna, and Munich, before reaching Paris late the following year. His enthusiastic reception in that city, coupled with adverse political conditions in Poland, caused Chopin to settle in Paris. He was much in demand as a piano teacher to the aristocracy and he appeared from time to time as a pianist at private salons and public concerts. In 1837 he began a liaison with George Sand (pen name of Mme. Dudevant) which lasted ten years and was finally broken under painful circumstances. In 1838 Chopin suffered a severe bronchial attack which left him in weakened health; he eventually succumbed to tuberculosis. His last spurt of energy was spent in a seven-month concert tour of Great Britain in 1848.

Both as a performer and composer, Chopin epitomized the Romantic concept of intimate art. Though a brilliant pianist, he shunned the showmanship of a LISZT. He exhibited a remarkable control over dynamic nuances. Although his music contains many heroic moments, the heroism is an inner personal quality and not a pose to obtain the adulation of the crowd. Within the personal realm Chopin was able to create an extremely varied world of piano color. In so doing he won the respect and friendship of many of his greatest peers, including BERLIOZ, MENDELSSOHN, BELLINI, Liszt, and MEYERBEER. Chopin was·one of the few masters of high eminence who wrote almost exclusively for the piano. His few songs and CHAMBER WORKS, though charming, are comparatively insignificant. The orchestral accompaniments to his two piano CONCERTOS and other similar works are lacking in depth.

It is possible to discern the influence of national folk elements in the 51 *Mazurkas* and 12 *Polonaises*, and that of HUMMEL and FIELD in the 19 *Nocturnes* and 17 *Waltzes*. The melodic style as a whole owes a debt to Italian OPERA. Chopin's great originality lies in the amalgam itself, in the instinct which permitted him to reach the peak of elegance without becoming precious or banal. His style is generally HOMOPHONIC; yet there are brilliant contrapuntal moments. Indeed, Chopin was much influenced by BACH; the arrangement of his *Preludes* according to key recalls similar practices of Bach. At times Chopin's harmonies are only pedestrian supports for delicate melody; yet he was capable of great harmonic daring. Though his 27 *Études*, as well as the 4 *Scherzos*, 3 *Sonatas*, 4 *Ballades*, 3 *Impromptus*, and the *Fantaisie-Impromptu*, present many technical difficulties, the technical element is always subservient to the needs of musical expression.

Choral: adjective form of CHORUS. The term may also occur as a variant spelling of CHORALE, but this usage is not correct.

Chorale: a German Lutheran HYMN. Some of the melodies are original compositions, but many of the famous ones were adapted from well-known secular songs of the 16th and early 17th centuries. The texts may be either free translations of Latin items of the Catholic liturgy, pre-Reformation German hymns, or original works created for Protestant use.

The earliest chorales were published shortly after the founding of the Protestant church in 1519. Luther, who was a competent musician, contributed actively to the early growth of the repertoire. Polyphonic settings of chorale tunes appeared as early as 1524. At first the tune was placed in the tenor and treated contrapuntally. In 1596, Lucas Osiander issued a collection in which the melody was given in the highest voice, accompanied by simple harmonies; this style then became prevalent. Chorale melodies originally had rhythmic individuality, but nearly all were leveled during the mid-17th century into simple, metrical p a t t e r n s. Even though BACH contributed a few chorale melodies, together with masterly harmonizations of traditional ones, the richest period of growth for the chorale took place before his birth. The main musical significance of the chorale lies in its use in CHORALE CANTATAS and CHORALE PRELUDES. Some chorale tunes are still popular as hymns in American Protestant churches.

Chorale cantata: a German sacred CANTATA employing the text and melody of a CHORALE (occasionally the text alone) in more than one movement. Many such works were composed during the BAROQUE p e r i o d, BACH's *Christ Lag in Todesbanden* and *Wachet auf* being among the most famous. In works similar to the latter, the first movement employs the chorale melody as a CANTUS FIRMUS, stated in long notes in the soprano. Each phrase of the chorale melody serves to cap a series of imitative entries, the individual phrases being separated from each other by orchestral material, often a statement of the RITORNELLO opening the movement. (*Christ lag* is exceptional in that all movements are based on material drawn from the chorale melody.) Most sacred cantatas, whether chorale cantatas or not, conclude with a simple harmonization of a chorale, sung by both the choir and congregation.

Chorale prelude: an ORGAN work designed to preface the congregational singing of the CHORALE on which it is based. A wide variety of treatments were developed by German BAROQUE organists. Modern terminology has been devised to differentiate among chorale preludes according to their most distinguishing trait. In a CANTUS-FIRMUS chorale prelude the melody is stated in long notes, usually in the lowest voice, with contrapuntal embroidery above. In the melody chorale prelude, on the other hand, the tune is in normal values in the highest voice; the contrapuntal parts below often develop characteristic melodic patterns. The ornamented chorale prelude also places the tune in the soprano; the individual notes are surrounded by expressive ornamentation, resulting in their partial concealment. A simple harmonization of the chorale may serve as the theme for a set of variations (chorale partita, chorale variations), or the melody may be treated in a free, improvisatory manner (chorale fantasy). In preludes termed chorale motets, each of the phrases of the tune is developed in imitation, while in chorale FUGUES or fughettas, only the first phrase is so treated. A chorale CANON combines a canonic treatment of the melody with additional free voices. Outstanding examples of each of these varieties were created by BACH, who represents the peak of a development which began a century earlier with the works of SCHEIDT. Though BRAHMS and REGER wrote chorale preludes, the form was seldom employed after the Baroque. **Chord:** a group of three or more notes forming a harmonic unit. The term usually implies a simultaneous sounding of the notes; if they are sounded successively, one may refer to a broken chord or ARPEGGIO. In composition, the tones of a chord may be combined with one or more

notes foreign to it. Generically the latter are termed NONHARMONIC TONES, and, in traditional practice, are expected to resolve to chord tones in specified ways.

Traditional theory dealing with chord structure ("harmony") is based on the triad, a three-note chord consisting of a root—the tone on which the chord is founded—combined with a third and a fifth (*see* INTERVAL). The triad may also be described as a chain of two thirds. The four varieties of triads are: major (with a major third and perfect fifth), minor (minor third and perfect fifth), augmented (major third and augmented fifth), and diminished (minor third and diminished fifth).

The octave positions of notes belonging to a chord may be changed freely without altering the identity of the chord. The lowest note may be either the root, third, or fifth; one would speak respectively of the root position, first inversion, and second inversion. Similarly, the highest note may be any of the three notes; one may refer to the position of the octave,

major   minor   augmented   diminished

position of the third, and position of the fifth.

In forming four-note chords, one of the notes of the triad may be doubled. Normally this is the root, occasionally the fifth, and rarely the third. In SEVENTH CHORDS, the chain of thirds is extended, while most SIXTH CHORDS (such as augmented sixths) have a more irregular construction. The former arose through the elaboration of a triad by a transitional dissonance; however, seventh chords soon gained independent status. The term close position indicates that the three upper notes of a chord are within the range of an octave; open position indicates that these notes exceed the range of an octave.

Modern chords are extremely varied. Some extend the chain of thirds still further, while others may be built of chains of fourths or display irregular structure. *See also* HARMONY.

Chordophone: *see* INSTRUMENTS.

Chorus: (1) music for a chorus or choir; (2) the refrain section of a SONG—often the main text is meant for a soloist, the recurrent text for a group; (3) term designating certain ORGAN reed stops; (4) medieval name for either the crwth (a bowed string instru-

ment) or the bagpipe. *See also* CHORUS or CHOIR.

Chorus or Choir: an ensemble of singers employing several performers for each voice-part. The two terms are often used interchangeably, although some hold that the former should denote only a group organized under secular auspices, the latter, a church group. A male chorus may be known as a glee club, and that name has also been adopted by some female choruses. A mixed chorus is comprised of both men and women. Usually such a chorus consists of four sections: soprano, alto, tenor, and bass (*see* VOICE). However, no fixed practice exists since choral music is written also for three, five, six, and more voice-parts. A semichorus is a smaller vocal ensemble used in conjunction with a full chorus. Some music, mostly written in the early BAROQUE, calls for two or more choruses, used together or antiphonally; hence the term double (or triple) chorus.

Choral singing—both monophonic and polyphonic—is undoubtedly of very ancient origin. Within the tradition of European art music, the history of the chorus begins with the performance of ecclesiastical CHANT (i.e., with monophonic music). Medieval POLYPHONY—organum, con-

ductus, motet, and chanson—
was performed by soloists.
The first unmistakable evidence of choral polyphony
dates from the early 15th century; from that time the chorus increased rapidly in importance. Until the mid-18th
century, the average church
or princely choir was comparatively small, usually numbering less than two dozen
singers. The performance of
BACH CANTATAS, PASSIONS,
and MASSES by groups of 60
to 100 is anachronistic, as is
choral performance of MAD-
RIGALS, CHANSONS, and other
MEDIEVAL and RENAISSANCE
works not envisaged for that
medium. Large choruses were
employed for festive performances of HANDEL's ORATORIOS
in the mid-18th century and
were adopted by the ROMAN-
TICS. During the mid-19th
century, the chorus declined
in overall importance as a
medium for new composition
despite fine works contributed by BERLIOZ, MENDELS-
SOHN, BRAHMS, BRUCKNER,
and others.

Works written for unac-
companied chorus are designated A CAPPELLA. The most
famous choral works, how-
ever, belong to genres employing mixed vocal and
instrumental forces, the cantatas, oratorios, Passions, and
Masses from 1650 to the present. Beginning with BEETHO-
VEN's *Ninth Symphony*, the
chorus was used also in works
normally written for orchestra alone. At first it was used
for its ability to convey verbal ideas; later it was used
chiefly for the sake of TONE
COLOR. Among the various
nations, England possesses an
outstanding choral tradition,
rivaled by those of Germany,
Austria, and the United States.
Chromatic: (1) a sequence of
three or more notes proceeding by half-steps. A chromatic
scale therefore includes each
of the twelve different pitches
of the octave, and a chromatic instrument is one capable of playing a chromatic
succession. (2) In tonal composition, a note or group of
notes foreign to the prevailing major or minor scale. A
chromatic chord has one or
more notes not in the key of
the work in which it is found,
and chromatic harmony uses
such chords in prominent
fashion. Very frequently
chromaticism is employed to
suggest heightened emotions.
(3) Any flat or sharp em-
ployed within a context in
which only naturals constitute
the norm (undesirable usage).
Church modes: ecclesiastical
modes, a system of eight
scales or MODES developed in
connection with GREGORIAN
CHANT, which provided the
basis for MEDIEVAL and RE-
NAISSANCE theory. The inter-

vallic structure of these modes is traditionally described by reference to scales using only the white keys of the piano. The eight modes are grouped in pairs (*maneriae*), each pair being comprised of an authentic and a plagal mode sharing the same final.

Originally the modes were known only by number. Later they acquired names previously used for classical Greek modes; however, no accepted connection between the two sets of modes has yet been discovered. A DOMINANT of a church mode is the main note for the intonation of the psalm-tone proper to that mode. It need not serve as the main center of contrast to the final as does a dominant in the major-minor system.

The Church modes were codified only after the earlier portion of the Gregorian repertoire had come into being. Although the system is a useful guide to most of the chant, individual pieces may have traits contrary to the specifications of the modes to which they are assigned. Furthermore, the scales themselves do not indicate the full range of possibilities open to the medieval musician. The composer could choose, for example, between *b* and *bb* (*see* HEXACHORD); the two notes could be used in the same chant, but not directly one after the other. Moreover, there are chants which end either on *a*, *b*, or *c'*. (These degrees are known as *affinales* or co-finals.) Many of these chants would require notation for either *eb* or *f♯* were they to preserve the same interval pattern and end with a

MODE	RANGE	FINAL	DOMINANT
1. Protus authenticus (Dorian)	d-d'	d	a
2. Protus plagius (Hypodorian)	A-a	d	f
3. Deuterus authenticus (Phrygian)	e-e'	e	c'
4. Deuterus plagius (Hypophrygian)	B-b	e	a
5. Tritus authenticus (Lydian)	f-f'	f	c'
6. Tritus plagius (Hypolydian)	c-c'	f	a
7. Tetrardus authenticus (Mixolydian)	g-g'	g	d'
8. Tetrardus plagius (Hypomixolydian)	d-d'	g	c'

normal final. It is thought that their NOTATION reflects a desire to avoid going beyond the bounds of the Gregorian system.

Still further exceptions were possible outside the realm of chant. As early as the 12th century, secular tunes employed modes equivalent to major and minor, as well as various sharps and flats ignored in the Gregorian system. ACCIDENTALS infiltrated both sacred and secular POLYPHONY in increasing numbers. The transposition of modes became more and more frequent. In the 16th century Glareanus sought to expand the modal system by admitting Aeolian and Hypoaeolian modes with finals on *a* (dominants on *e* and *c′*, resp.) and Ionian and Hypoionian modes with finals on *c* (dominants on *g* and *e*, resp.). Hyperaeolian (= Locrian) and Hyperphrygian (= Hypolocrian) modes, with finals on *b* were described, but rejected as impractical. During the BAROQUE, the system of Church modes was gradually superseded by the major-minor system.

Ciaccona: *see* CHACONNE.

Cimarosa, Domenico: *b.* Aversa, December 17, 1749; *d.* Venice, January 11, 1801. After completing his study at the Conservatorio di Santa Maria di Loreto, Cimarosa rapidly became one of the most successful OPERA composers of his generation. He worked chiefly in Naples and Rome, but also briefly in St. Petersburg and Vienna, in the service of Catherine II and Leopold II, respectively. In addition to his masterpiece, *The Secret Marriage*, he wrote some 75 other operas. Cimarosa's nonoperatic compositions include MASSES, ORATORIOS, CANTATAS, MOTETS, and a wide variety of other vocal works, a few SYMPHONIES, CONCERTOS, and a group of piano SONATAS.

Cimbalon: a Hungarian DULCIMER.

Cinquepace: a GALLIARD.

Circle of fifths: a schematic representation that is used to teach certain basic relationships among major and minor keys. The major keys that are most closely related to one another, that have the greatest number of tones in common, are located a perfect fifth apart. *C* major, which has neither sharps nor flats, is placed at the top of the circle, which then proceeds clockwise through the keys of *G, D, A, E, B, F♯,* and *C♯,* adding an additional sharp each time until the maximum of seven is reached. There is an overlap at the bottom of the circle, indicative of the

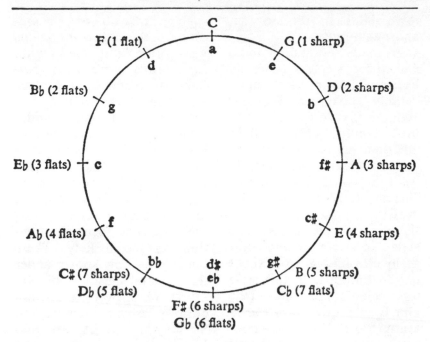

C
a
F (1 flat)   d   e   G (1 sharp)
B♭ (2 flats)   g   b   D (2 sharps)
E♭ (3 flats) c   f♯ A (3 sharps)
A♭ (4 flats)   f   c♯   E (4 sharps)
                  b♭   d♯   g♯
C♯ (7 sharps)   e♭   B (5 sharps)
D♭ (5 flats)   C♭ (7 flats)
F♯ (6 sharps)
G♭ (6 flats)

fact that it is possible to notate certain scales in two ways each, these forms of NOTATION being enharmonic equivalents. Minor keys are indicated at the interior of the arc occupied · by the major key with the same key signature.

Cithara: *see* KITHARA.

Cittern: an instrument of the LUTE family, with a flat rather than a rounded back.

Claquebois (F): XYLOPHONE.

Clarinet: a cylindrical WOODWIND instrument employing a single REED.

Clarino, Clarin trumpet: a BAROQUE trumpet used in the high register. *See* BRASS INSTRUMENTS.

Classical Era: music of *c*.1750 to *c*.1820. (In vulgar usage the term denotes all "art music," in contradistinction to popular and folk music.) During the late 18th century, interest in instrumental music began, for the first time, to outweigh interest in vocal music. The ORCHESTRA expanded, both in number and variety of instruments; the PIANO, invented during the first decade of the century, supplanted the HARPSICHORD and CLAVICHORD. The most characteristic forms of the period are the newly-developed SYMPHONY, piano SONATA, and STRING QUARTET. The era opened with such masters as C. P. E. BACH and GLUCK and culminated in the work of three giants: HAYDN, MOZART, and BEETHOVEN.

As the BAROQUE drew to an end, the old forms generally became longer and more densely textured. Whereas composers such as J. S. BACH probed more deeply into their inherited musical vocabulary, others felt that vocabulary to be too stilted and intense. The new trend was toward increasing lightness. In France, there developed the Rococo style, or *style galant*, normally classified as an offshoot of the Baroque. In this style the melodic lines are made airy by a profusion of ORNAMENTATION. The contemporary style in Germany is known as the *empfindsamer Stil*, or expressive style. Exemplified in the works of Bach's sons, this is usually considered as the beginning of the Classical Era, or a "pre-Classical period."

The Classical emphasis on melody and lightness of texture is reflected in the changed treatment of the lower parts. In the Baroque, the lowest line of the musical texture normally fulfilled two functions; it provided a solid harmonic foundation and served also as an interesting melody in its own right, a strong foil to the melody in the highest voice. At the close of the period, in the KEYBOARD works of composers such as D. SCARLATTI, the second of these two functions was often dispensed with. HARMONIES were then outlined by a few bold strokes, and the bass became less melodic, employing a wider range and more numerous leaps. In early Classical music, the harmonic structure was frequently expressed in conventional figurations of broken chords, encouraging the listener to focus all attention on the melody. These figurations, now known under the general heading of ALBERTI BASS, were used not only by lesser composers, but by Haydn and Mozart, and in early works by Beethoven as well. Since it requires more time to express a harmony one note at a time in repetitive patterns than with the various t o n e s distributed among different voice parts and sounded simultaneously, Classical harmonies tend to progress from one to the next át a somewhat slower pace than Baroque harmonies.

A second result of the trend towards lighter textures was the gradual abandonment of the BASSO CONTINUO. This had a vast effect, particularly on CHAMBER MUSIC. The trio and solo sonatas of the Baroque gave way to other media. On the one hand, the keyboard part was written out and strengthened, while the bass line was no longer doubled by cello or other bass instrument. This resulted in the creation of sonatas for piano and VIOLIN in which the piano part was the center of interest, the violin or other treble part serving as an artistic, but not necessarily essential, embellishment. Late in the Classical period, in the works of Mozart and Beethoven, the two instruments were accorded equal importance. Another offshoot of the trio sonata, involving the deletion of the keyboard part, was of even greater significance. The bass part was entrusted to the cello alone, and the resulting ensemble, a homogeneous group of bowed string instruments, was expanded into the STRING QUARTET. Some of the finest works of the Classical period were written for this medium, not only by Haydn, Mozart, and Beethoven, but also by lesser masters such as BOCCHERINI.

In the realm of orchestral music, use of the keyboard instrument was also gradually discontinued. Because the early Classical symphonies were often scored for comparatively few instruments and not all instruments were given independent parts, the realization of the *basso continuo* on the harpsichord helped provide sufficient body to the light texture. Haydn, for example, often directed the performance of his symphonies from the keyboard. Indeed, this practice continued from force of habit for some time after the number of independent orchestral parts was increased, eliminating the musical need for the keyboard filler and rendering keyboard participation superfluous since the light tone of the harpsichord would not carry over the more robust sound of the orchestral ensemble. The most vital change in the growth of the orchestra during the Classical period involved the expansion of the WOODWIND complement. By the end of the period, clarinets, as well as flutes, oboes, and bassoons, were demanded by most scores. BRASS INSTRUMENTS were used more frequently, but not in the profusion associated with ROMANTIC music. Much mid- and late-Baroque orchestral music may be described as monochromatic; it featured mainly string sound. Often the supporting parts for winds doubled extensively the string parts. On the other hand, an individual wind instrument could be used in primarily solo capacity as a significant color element over wide portions of the score. In Classical scores, the winds gained greater independence and were often used in short passages for color contrast. Orchestral playing gradually became more precise as exemplified by the orchestra at Mannheim, one of the celebrated ENSEMBLES of the early Classical period. Symphonic composers experimented with novel orchestral themes and with special dynamic effects, including both sudden changes of loudness and gradual CRESCENDOS.

The new style of the Classical period brought about new kinds of musical structures, emphasizing the sectional forms, such as SONATA FORM and RONDO, at the expense of continuous ones, such as FUGUE. Movements of mid- and late-Baroque w o r k s usually sought to present one central "affect," or emotion. THEMES were subjected to variation and numerous other manipulations, but only seldom dissected. In the Classical era, more and more attention was paid to motivic development, culminating in the tightly-knit works of Beethoven. At the same time, the individual themes of a movement became more sharply differentiated in character. Expanding the binary instrumental forms of the Baroque, the Classical period gradually evolved SONATA FORM, based on carefully chosen key contrasts. This form was employed in all instrumental repertoires. Since the development of sonata form was a gradual process, involving much experimentation, the details of the structure continued to change throughout its history.

Later periods have often exaggerated the Classical musician's preoccupation with matters of form. The area was, to be sure, of great concern; this was only natural in an age that esteemed reason and moderation. However, the Romantics often mistook concern for structural balance for a lack of emotional depth. Haydn was remembered affectionately as a genial patriarch; Mozart was pitied for his financial difficulties and untimely death. Their music, however, was not always considered meaningful and that of lesser masters was scorned. The basic artistic outlook of the Classical period was, of course, buoyant and extrovert rather than melancholy and introspective. But the music of the greater composers reveals considerable emotional depth, demonstrated chiefly through the sensitive use of unusual harmonies and dissonances. The main point is that these emotions are stated with great economy of means; they are not spotlighted as in Romantic music.

Classical composers kept

up the choral forms of the Baroque—the MASS, ORATORIO, and CANTATA — but these declined steadily in importance. They were permeated by new symphonic techniques and were more homophonic in texture than before. Some critics think the cheerful atmosphere exuded by many sacred works to be inappropriate to the gravity of their texts. However, massive pomp is not necessarily an accurate criterion of religiosity, and many Classical sacred scores abound in fine qualities.

Interest in OPERA continued unabated. The conventional sort of Neapolitan opera that provided the mainstream for the international operatic style prevalent in the early 18th century alternated narrative sections, set tersely in "dry" RECITATIVE, with more static expressions of emotion, expressed musically in florid ARIAS which constituted the chief attraction of the work. One of the most important Classical contributions was the movement towards the reassertion of principles of dramatic continuity, Gluck being among the outstanding composers working in this direction. The use of orchestrally accompanied recitative increased, and less dependence was placed on the DA CAPO form inasmuch as the use of the same music for both the beginning and end of an aria retards dramatic development. The simpler, bisectional CAVATINA was developed, more flexible SCENES were written, and vocal ensembles gradually became more important, reaching a height in Mozart's operas. The orchestra's potential for underscoring dramatic situations was increasingly exploited, and the OVERTURE was made an integral part of the work by drawing on themes used in the opera proper.

The small, secular forms for solo voice and keyboard or lute, comparatively neglected during the mid- and late-Baroque, began to come to the fore during the Classical era, especially in German-speaking countries, spurred by such great poets as Goethe and Schiller. Composers showed new sensitivity to poetic values and set texts dealing with a wide range of subjects. The songs themselves were often simple strophic settings of folklike character with economical, subordinate accompaniments.

The long-standing social and economic status of the composer, namely that of a servant in the employ of the church or nobility, began to change during the latter part of the Classical Era. The rise of the concert hall, together with the growing importance of the prosperous mercantile class and the contemporary political reforms and revolutions, led to greater freedom for the artist. Haydn was the last of the great masters to spend the major part of his life under the old system. Mozart quit the service of the petty archbishop of Salzburg, though he might have welcomed a more enlightened patron. Beethoven was the personification of independence. The composer was no longer bound to produce fresh cantatas, operas, or symphonies according to a prescribed schedule. He no longer had to cater to the tastes of a particular prince or write only for the instruments available at his place of employ. Often, however, he had to earn the major part of his livelihood as a concert artist, teacher, or critic. Composers gradually began, on the whole, to write at a somewhat slower pace and to spend more time in polishing individual works. The reuse of basically unchanged material, prevalent in earlier periods, began to disappear. In this way, emphasis on individuality, one of the hallmarks of Romanticism, began to grow.

Clausula: (1) a section of a piece of organum (*see* MEDIEVAL MUSIC), the forerunner of the medieval MOTET; (2) a cadential formula in RENAISSANCE music.

Clavecin (F), **Clavicembalo** (I): harpsichord.

Clavichord: a string KEYBOARD instrument that produces sound through the pressure of a brass blade (tangent) against a string. The instrument, which may have been known as early as the 12th century, is oblong in shape and the strings run nearly perpendicular to the keys. When a key is depressed, the vertical tangent presses against a string, dividing it into two sections; one is free to vibrate, while the other is damped. Since the PITCH is determined by the length of the string from the end that is free to vibrate to the blade of the tangent, it is possible to use one string for two pitches —or theoretically more—by placing tangents at different points along its length. This has the disadvantage that only one of these pitches is obtainable at a given time. Instruments constructed in this fashion are described as fretted. The clavichord produces a soft tone, eminently suited to small rooms, and is extremely responsive to variations in the player's touch. It was especially favored in Germany during the 17th and 18th centuries, particularly by C. P. E. BACH and others of his generation.

Clavier: a generic designation for KEYBOARD instruments. In the BAROQUE the term could designate the ORGAN, but now it is generally restricted to string keyboard instruments (harpsichord, clavichord, and piano). *See also* KLAVIER.

Clavioline: an electronic KEYBOARD instrument capable of producing different TONE COLORS.

Clef: a musical symbol which identifies the position on the staff of a single pitch. There are three families of clefs. The *c*-clef points out, by means of its center, the line on which middle *c* is located. The *g*-clef curls around the *g* above middle *c*, while the *f*-clef is center on the *f* below middle *c*. In past centuries, the *c*-clef might be employed on any line of the staff, the *g*-clef on any of the bottom three lines, the *f*-clef on any of the top three. Each position of each clef was designated by a different name. Now, the treble clef (= violin clef), a *g*-clef on the second line, and the bass clef, an *f*-clef on the fourth line, predominate. The alto clef (a *c*-clef on the third line) is used mainly in the notation of viola music, while the tenor clef (a *c*-clef on the fourth line) is used occasionally in the NOTATION of high phrases for cello, bassoon, or trombone. Some vocal music for tenors employs a treble clef with either an "8" added below or an added section on the third space, indicating that the music is to sound an octave lower than written.

Clemens non Papa, Jacobus (Jacob Clement): *b.* Walcheron, Netherlands, 1510(?); *d.* Dixmude, *c.*1557. A gifted and expressive composer, Clemens wrote a large number of polyphonic CHANSONS,

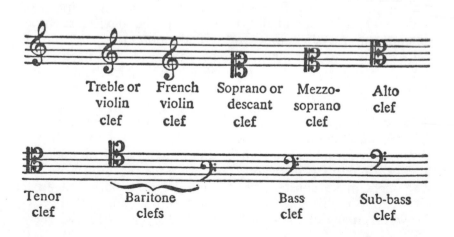

Treble or violin clef   French violin clef   Soprano or descant clef   Mezzo-soprano clef   Alto clef

Tenor clef   Baritone clefs   Bass clef   Sub-bass clef

MOTETS, PSALMS set to popular Dutch tunes, and MASSES. The words "non Papa" were perhaps adopted by Clemens to distinguish himself from a poet with the same given name.

Clementi, Muzio: *b*. Rome, January 23, 1752; *d*. Evesham, England, March 10, 1832. As a boy trained in Italy, Clementi's musical talents were so remarkable that he was invited to complete his studies in England under the patronage of Peter Beckford. After 1770 his chief residence was in London, although he spent several years on the Continent on tour as a pianist. After meeting MO-ZART, Clementi turned his attention from mere technical mastery to the development of a more lyrical and subtle touch and phrasing. He was an influential teacher—FIELD, KALKBRENNER, MEYERBEER, and Ignaz Moscheles being among his pupils—and also a successful publisher and PIANO manufacturer. As a composer he did much to help develop an idiomatic style of piano writing (as distinguished from that suitable for harpsichord). His collection of studies, *Gradus ad Parnassum*, is still a mainstay for advanced technical training of pianists, and beginners make constant use of a group of his SONATINAS. However, many of Clementi's

SYMPHONIES have been lost and his OVERTURES, CHAMBER MUSIC, and miscellaneous KEYBOARD pieces are rarely played.

Clérambault, Louis Nicolas: *b*. Paris, December 19, 1676, *d*. Paris, October 26, 1749. A student of André Raison, Clérambault served several Parisian churches as organist. A versatile composer, he wrote sacred and secular SONGS, CANTATAS, MOTETS, a MAGNIFICAT, an ORATORIO, trio SONATAS, and a variety of music for harpsichord and for organ.

Cluster, tone cluster, note-cluster: a group of adjacent notes, played simultaneously.

Coda: a concluding section designed to achieve a sense of finality, either by means of a last climax or by a gradual fading away. The former is the more frequent of the two methods. In a fugal coda, strict contrapuntal writing may be momentarily dropped, or a special device, such as a pedal point or a stretto may be employed. The need for a conclusive cadence in CANON may dictate the abandonment of strict imitation. The most frequent use of the term occurs in connection with SO-NATA FORM, in which the coda follows the recapitulation. Although rather brief at first, the section was greatly expanded by BEETHOVEN, serving as a second development and achieving a size comparable to that of the other major subdivisions of the movement.

Codetta: (1) a small CODA; in this sense, the term often refers to the conclusion of an exposition in SONATA FORM; (2) in a FUGUE exposition, a connective passage between the conclusion of one entry and the beginning of the next.

Colla parte (I): **Colla voce** (I): a direction for the accompanying player(s) to match the flexible rhythm of the soloist (the latter term specifies a vocal soloist).

Coll'arco (I): *see* ARCO.

Col legno (I): a direction ordering string players to use the stick of the bow against the string, rather than the hair.

Coloratura (I): (1) vocal passagework employing SCALES, ARPEGGIOS, TRILLS, or other ORNAMENTS in virtuoso fashion. Such flourishes are frequent in 18th- and 19th-century ARIAS. (2) A soprano whose VOICE is particularly suited to the performance of such florid passages.

Collegium musicum (L): a group of musicians, usually formed under the auspices of a college or university, normally meeting for the performance of early music.

Combination tones (Resultant tones): the auditory sensation of very faint tones occurring when two or more strong tones of different frequencies are sounded simultaneously. There are both difference (or differential) tones and summation tones. The most important difference tone may be calculated by subtracting the frequency of the lower of two strong tones from that of the upper. (This tone—known also as Tartini's tone—can be detected when two notes are played simultaneously on the violin and is used to check the accuracy of intonation.) Still fainter tones represent the difference in frequency between a twofold multiple of one of the primary tones and the other. If, for example, the frequencies of the two primary tones are 440 and 264, the difference tones will be equivalent to tones produced by the frequencies 176 (440 − 264), 88 (2 × 264 − 440), and 616 (2 × 440 − 264). Summation tones may be calculated by adding the frequencies of the strong tones. (Other possibilities may be obtained by using a twofold multiple of one of the frequencies.) Using the frequencies just mentioned, the summation tones will be equivalent to tones produced by the frequencies 704 (440 + 264), 968 (2 × 264 + 440), and 1144 (2 × 440 + 264).

Comes (L): the second of a pair of voices presenting the same melody in overlapping succession. *See also* DUX.

Comma: (1) a tiny difference between the PITCH of a tone calculated according to one system of TUNING and the pitch of the same tone calculated according to another system of tuning; (2) a tiny difference between the pitch of one tone and the pitch of its enharmonic equivalent within the same system of tuning. According to the harmonic series used in just intonation, the frequency of a note a major third above a given pitch is $5/4$ ($= 80/64$) of that of the chosen standard. According to the circle of fifths used in Pythagorean tuning, the frequency of a note a major third above a given pitch is $81/64$ of that of the chosen standard. The difference between these two pitches—represented by the ratio $81/80$ is known as the *Didymic* (or syntonic) *comma*. The Didymic comma also represents the difference between the two sizes of major seconds present in just intonation. In our present system of equal temperament any given note is exactly the same pitch as its enharmonic equivalent. There is, for example, no difference in pitch between $b\sharp$ and c; this identity is expressible by the arith-

metic ratio, $1/1$. In Pythagorean tuning, the pitches of $b\sharp$ and c are different; the ratio between their frequencies is $531441/524288$. This interval is clearly discernible, even though it is only about a fourth of a half step, the smallest interval normally used in Western music.

Common chord: (1) a major or minor triad in root position (obsolete); (2) in a modulatory passage, a pivot chord common to the preceding and following keys.

Common time: a synonym for $4/4$ time.

Compère, Loyset: *b.* northern France, *c.*1455; *d.* St. Quentin, August 16, 1518. After serving Galeazzo Maria Sforza and Charles VIII of France, Compère became canon and chancellor at St. Quentin. His MASSES, MOTETS, and CHANSONS were much esteemed by his contemporaries.

Compound meter (Compound time): meters whose main pulses are divided into three equal parts rather than two; these meters are represented by the time signatures, $6/8$, $9/8$, and $12/8$.

Computer music: a work or works created in whole or in part by means of a computer program. The physical characteristics of sounds—pitch, loudness, timber, duration, etc.—are capable of being described numerically, and it is thus possible to calculate as many of these characteristics as is desired by means of variously chosen mathematical procedures. The computer output may be transformed into a musical score to be performed by any of a wide number of combinations of traditional instruments, with or without vocal participation. Or the output may appear in graphic form and be converted for performance by a mechanical instrument such as a player piano. Lastly, it is possible to convert the digital expression of very closely spaced samplings of sound into an analog form which, when filtered, can be made to produce a magnetic tape that may be played on a tape recorder. It is possible to create computer music by analyzing probability tables for a given preexistent repertoire, but more frequently the composer will employ one or more random number generators and provide criteria whereby certain of these numbers will be accepted and others rejected. Interest in the possibilities of musical composition through computer programming began in the 1950s, and the *Iliac Suite* for String Quartet (1957) by Lejaren Hiller and Leonard Isaacson is one of the first significant works in this me-

dium. Other American composers who have created computer music include John CAGE, Herbert Brün, Salvatore Martirano, and James Tenney. European composers active in this medium include Yannis Xenakis and Pierre Barbaud.

Con brio (I): vigorously.

Concert: a public performance of music involving neither religious ritual nor theatrical or ceremonial production. Frequently the term recital is used to designate such performances given by only one or two musicians. The earliest known concerts for a paying audience took place in London in 1672.

Concertant (F), **Concertante** (I): a designation indicating the presence of two or more SOLO parts (or, rarely, one) within an ENSEMBLE framework. Usually the main ensemble is an ORCHESTRA, as in a *Symphonie concertante*.

Concertato (I): a term describing an early BAROQUE style in which VOICES and INSTRUMENTS of different rather than similar natures are combined and set off against one another.

Concertina: a hexagonal member of the ACCORDION family.

Concertino (I): (1) a short CONCERTO, usually light in style; (2) the SOLO group in a CONCERTO GROSSO.

Concertmaster: the first violinist of an ORCHESTRA. The concertmaster plays the occasional SOLO passages for violin in orchestral music and, unless overruled by the conductor, is responsible for the BOWINGS employed by the other violinists in his section. The equivalent British term is "leader."

Concerto (I), **Concert** (F), **Konzert** (G): (1) a work based on an interplay between one or more soloists and an ORCHESTRA. The SOLO parts, most frequently written for piano or violin, are designed to show the virtuosity of the performer.

This form originated during the late BAROQUE, but the most familiar works belong to the CLASSICAL and ROMANTIC periods. Works for two or three soloists are generally known as double or triple concertos, respectively. The Classical-Romantic form consists of three movements in a fast-slow-fast order. The first movement is usually cast in a modified SONATA FORM; the last is often a RONDO. Repeated statements of a theme —first by the orchestra and then by the soloist—and CADENZAS are the main modifications of standard symphonic forms. A small concerto, often in one movement with contrasting TEMPOS, is called either a *concertino* or a *Konzertstück*.

Although a large number of solo concertos were written during the late Baroque, the *concerto grosso*, written for a group of soloists, was both earlier and more widespread. The group of soloists, usually made up of two violins and CONTINUO, is called the *concertino* or *principale;* the full ENSEMBLE is known as the *(concerto) grosso, ripieno,* or *tutti.* The number of movements in early concertos varies; some works contain five or even more. The establishment of the modern, three-movement scheme was due in large part to VIVALDI. The BAROQUE concerto might be patterned after a *sonata da camera* or a *sonata da chiesa.* Or, individual movements might alternate a recurrent ritornello for the *tutti* with fresh material for the *concertino.* The *symphonie concertante* of the Classical period is similar in conception to the *concerto grosso,* although in the former the solo instruments may be each given greater individual attention.

(2) In both the Baroque and modern eras, the term concerto has designated orchestral works or movements (e.g., from CANTATAS) employing the principle of tonal contrast that characterizes

the *concerto grosso*, but without full-fledged solo parts. Bartók's *Concerto for Orchestra* is one such work. On the other hand, Bach used the term for a harpsichord work, the *Italian Concerto*, in which these contrasts are suggested by one instrument through the alternation of sections with different textures.

(3) The term was first used to designate compositions for one or more voices supported by continuo and sometimes by other instruments as well. That is, the term differentiated works for mixed forces from works for voices alone. This usage was prevalent in the first decades of the 17th century; the term was also employed in this sense by BACH, who so labeled several of his cantatas.

(4) The term was used occasionally during the late Baroque (e.g., by Vivaldi) to designate works for a small group of instruments without orchestral support. These follow concepts of form, rhythm, and tonal contrast similar to those of the *concerto grosso*.

Concert Overture: an OVERTURE not associated with music for an opera or play.

Concord: a CONSONANCE.

Concrete music: *see* ELECTRONIC MUSIC.

Conducting: the communication, by means of gesture, of an interpretation of a work to a group of musicians performing it. Usually a sizable group is involved: an ORCHESTRA, BAND, CHORUS, or mixed vocal and instrumental force; a CHAMBER GROUP of less than ten rarely requires a conductor. In the 17th and 18th century the direction of a musical performance was usually entrusted to the harpsichordist or the first violinist. Nowadays, a concerto soloist may still decide to act as conductor. However, the duties of a conductor are sufficiently numerous that they are normally handled by someone not engaged in singing or playing.

The conductor is responsible for setting and maintaining the basic rate of speed for each piece and for guiding any necessary deviations from it. He is responsible for regulating DYNAMICS, both in terms of large planes and delicate nuances. He must determine the balance between the various groups under his command, bringing out the significant parts of the music while keeping down the subsidiary parts. The conductor is also the final authority on details of phrasing. In addition, he is expected to cue important entrances, especially when those take place after long rests in the parts concerned. In order to obtain

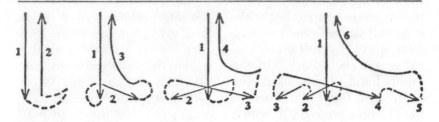

a fine performance, a conductor must convince his musicians, either by force of personality or by show of erudition, of the innate "rightness" of his interpretation; a docile obedience without this conviction will produce only lackluster results. Performances of the same work by different conductors might vary widely. At times conductors have indulged in highly subjective interpretations without concerning themselves with faithfulness to the composer's intent. However, increased stylistic awareness on the part of performing musicians and concert public alike has led most modern conductors to seek to work out their subjective interpretations within a stylistically appropriate framework.

A conductor must, of course, be able to read a full SCORE, which is apt to consist of more than a dozen STAVES with different CLEFS and TRANSPOSITIONS. He must be able to conceive sounds mentally. An excellent memory is necessary in order that he may free his eyes from the score and use them to command the attention of the performers. In addition, a conductor should have a sound knowledge of both instrumental and vocal techniques and of the history of musical style. Above all, he must be an effective leader.

The foundation for the conductor's gestures is a set of patterns, shown above, for beating time. The main pulse of each measure (i.e., the first) is indicated by a downward motion of the hand, with or without a BATON. The final pulse is indicated by an upward motion. A comparatively large gesture calls for a loud tone, a small one for a soft tone. However, conductors vary greatly in the size of their normal BEAT. The nature of the motion should suit the nature of the music. That is, a springy beat indicates energetic music, a flowing one, more lyrical music. The left hand is used primarily to indicate entries (by pointing) and shadings of loud and soft. If a conductor is leading an amateur group, he will usually find it necessary to adhere closely to the established beat patterns. However, conductors of professional ensembles often preserve only the most essential portions of these patterns, varying their motions freely in order to convey a more personal representation of musical rhythm. An ability to indicate rhythm clearly and yet freely is particularly important in directing both early and modern works not in standard meters. Orchestral conductors normally use a baton for the sake of greater clarity; many choral conductors, on the other hand, feel that they can achieve more flexible results without one.

Conductus (L): a MEDIEVAL setting of a metrical Latin text.

Consecutive intervals: *see* PARALLEL INTERVALS.

Console: the manuals, pedals, and stop controls of an ORGAN.

Consonance and dissonance: (1) a subjective judgment of INTERVALS in terms of sweetness and harshness, respectively; (2) a classification of intervals in theory.

It is often suggested that consonant intervals are those that have the simplest ratios between their vibration frequencies. However, this theory fails to recognize the complexity in the ratios of all tempered intervals now used in Western music. Other physical bases for consonance and DISSONANCE have been sought, but no satisfactory solution has been found. Subjective classification of intervals within these headings depends largely on the experience of the listener. As one becomes accustomed to a harsh-seeming interval, its harshness lessens or disappears.

In COUNTERPOINT and HARMONY, consonances are unisons, fifths, octaves, thirds, and sixths. A fourth above the lowest note is treated as a dissonance, but the same interval between upper voices is regarded as consonant. In traditional harmony and counterpoint, dissonances are required to resolve to consonances; consonances do not require resolution.

Con sordino (I): with a MUTE.

Consort: a 16th- and 17th-century term for an instrumental ENSEMBLE. A *whole consort* consisted of instruments of the same family. The most frequent of such consorts comprised six viols, two each of the three main sizes. A *broken consort* employed instruments of different families. By extension, the term was employed in the titles of music for instrumental ensembles.

Continuo, Basso continuo (I):

(1) a FIGURED BASS part; (2) the instruments responsible for the realization of that part.

Contrabass: (1) the bass viol, the lowest member of the VIOLIN FAMILY; (2) an adjective describing an instrument with a compass an octave lower than that of the normal bass of the pertinent family.

Contrabassoon, Double bassoon: a conical WOODWIND instrument of the double-REED family, having a very low range.

Contrafagotto (I): CONTRABASSOON.

Contralto: a female VOICE of low range, or a high male voice of similar range.

Contrapunctus (L): COUNTERPOINT.

Contratenor: the third VOICE of a 14th- or 15th-century work, with a range similar to that of the tenor. The contratenor often serves as a harmonic filler rather than as a structurally essential part.

Contrebasse (F): CONTRABASS.

Contrebasson (F): CONTRABASSOON.

Contredanse (F), **Contratanz** (G): a lively dance of the late 18th century, popular in France and Germany.

Converse, Frederick Shepherd: *b.* Newton, Mass., January 5, 1871; *d.* Westwood, Mass., June 8, 1940. Converse completed his studies with CHADWICK (in Boston)

and Joseph Rheinberger (in Munich). He taught at the New England Conservatory and Harvard University. He wrote *The Pipes of Desire,* the first American OPERA produced by the Metropolitan Opera Co. (New York) and *Job,* the first American ORATORIO performed in Germany, together with other operas, oratorios, CANTATAS, six SYMPHONIES and other orchestral music (including *Flivver Ten Million,* to celebrate the ten millionth Ford car), CHAMBER MUSIC, piano pieces and songs.

Coperto (I): covered; the term refers to a cloth covering used to mute drums.

Copland, Aaron: *b.* Brooklyn, N.Y., November 14, 1900. Copland studied under GOLDMARK and Boulanger (in Paris). Active as composer, pianist, conductor, lecturer, writer, and a participant in many organizations concerned with contemporary music, Copland has been a leading figure in American music. His best-known works are the SUITES drawn from the BALLETS *Appalachian Spring, Billy the Kid,* and *Rodeo,* and *El Salon México.* These show Copland's ability to capture the American and Mexican spirit, not merely through the use of folk tunes. JAZZ rhythms are incorporated into certain early works such as the *Piano Concerto*, while a modified serial technique is employed in the *Piano Quartet*. Other works include three SYMPHONIES, an OPERA *(The Tender Land)*, choruses and songs, CHAMBER MUSIC, piano music, and music for films.

Cor (F): horn. *Cor anglais*, English horn; *cor à pistons*, French horn; *cor de basset*, basset horn; *cor de chasse*, valveless French horn.

Corda (I), **Corde** (F): string.

Corelli, Arcangelo, *b*. Fusignano, February 17, 1653; *d*. Rome, January 8, 1713, one of the originators of the *concerto grosso*.

Corelli studied violin with Benvenuti and composition with Simonelli in Bologna. About 1671 Corelli went to Rome, his principal residence for the rest of his life. He was active as a violinist at the French Church (1675) and at the Teatro Capranica (1679). Later years were spent with Cardinals Benedetto Panfilio and Pietro Ottoboni. Among his pupils were GEMINIANI and LOCATELLI.

Corelli's works are comparatively few in number, but are of uniformly high quality. He issued six collections of a dozen works each, comprising either trio SONATAS, "solo" sonatas (for violin and CONTINUO), or *concerti grossi*. As a violinist, Corelli furthered the development of BOWING techniques and the use of DOUBLE STOPS; his compositions reveal a fine sense of the violin idiom.

Cornamusa (I), **Cornemuse** (F): bagpipe.

Cornelius, Peter: *b*. Mainz, December 24, 1824; *d*. Mainz, October 26, 1874. After brief experience as an actor, Cornelius studied with Dehn in Berlin. He became a friend of LISZT and WAGNER and wrote articles expounding the "New German" musical philosophy. He also wrote poetry. His most successful OPERA was *The Barber of Bagdad;* he also composed songs and choral works.

Cornet: (1) a BRASS INSTRUMENT similar to the trumpet; (2) an ORGAN stop (a mixture); (3) variant spelling of cornett.

Cornet à pistons (F), **Cornetta** (I): CORNET (1).

Cornett, Cornetto (I): a wooden wind instrument of the 15th to 18th centuries; *see* BRASS INSTRUMENTS.

Corno (I): horn. *Corno da caccia*, valveless French horn; *corno di bassetto*, basset horn; *corno inglese*, English horn.

Corrente: *see* COURANTE.

Counterpoint: (1) the art of combining melodic lines. To excel in this art, the composer must produce a convincing balance between the melodic and rhythmic independence of the several lines and their ability to combine and set each other off to form a greater whole. By independence is meant an avoidance of excessive parallel motion. Similarities or even identities of contour and RHYTHM occurring in succession between different VOICE-parts are characteristic of a large proportion of the finest contrapuntal music (e.g., FUGUE and CANON). A contrapuntal work may be created one complete voice-part at a time, or all voices may be worked out at the same time, each one helping shape the other as the polyphonic complex evolves, or an admixture of these techniques may be employed. The first method is by far the oldest within the history of Western art POLYPHONY. Often the first line, the structural foundation, consists of a preexistent MELODY (termed *cantus firmus* or *cantus prius factus*) to which the composer adds one or more new parts. Just as each tone of a melodic phrase carries with it certain implications or even requirements for the logical continuation of that phrase, so too do the intervals and chords formed by coincidence of two or more parts. These two sets of implications are not always in perfect agreement, and the balance between them in the shaping of the polyphonic complex has changed significantly over the centuries. Dur-

ing the High Middle Ages, greater attention was paid to the unfolding of the several melodies. Vertical ("harmonic") forces gradually became more important, achieving an equal balance with melodic forces in the style of PALESTRINA and acquiring a slight predominance in the contrapuntal style of BACH. In the past half-century the balance has again shifted in favor of linear considerations.

(2) a melody written to complement an existing one.

(3) A course of study leading to skill in the writing of complementary melodies. In traditional instruction, the student is given a melody in notes of equal value, and is required to construct a counter-melody to it. The latter is expected to be vocal in style. In other words, the total range must be within a normal vocal compass and skips considered difficult to sing are to be avoided. Five different rhythmic treatments (species) are introduced progressively. In first species, each note of the *cantus firmus* is set off by one note in the counterpoint. In second species, two equal notes in the counterpoint are set against one in the *cantus*, while in third species, the proportion becomes four to one. No dissonances are permitted within first species, but passing dissonances are permitted

on weak beats in second and third species. Fourth species is characterized rhythmically by SYNCOPATION, harmonically by SUSPENSIONS. Fifth species permits the combination of the rhythms and DISSONANCE treatment of the previous four. A codification of these practices that is of great historical importance is J. J. Fux, *Gradus ad Parnassum (Steps to Parnassus,* 1725).

Countersubject: a MELODY that accompanies a FUGUE subject with reasonable consistency throughout the course of the fugue.

Counter-tenor: (1) a male VOICE of light quality and particularly high range. *See* CONTRATENOR.

Country dance: a lively English dance of the 17th and 18th centuries.

Couperin, François: *b.* Paris, November 10, 1668; *d.* Paris, September 12, 1733; outstanding Rococo composer.

Nicknamed "le Grand," François Couperin was the greatest of a long line of able musicians. Trained by his father, Charles, and his uncle, also named François Couperin, he became organist of St. Gervais in 1685 and held that post until his death. From 1693 to 1717 he received a series of royal appointments; he taught several of the royal children. Couperin's early

works include two ORGAN MASSES, a MAGNIFICAT, and several MOTETS. A set of *Leçons de ténèbres* (publ. 1714) is among the greatest of his sacred works. From 1713 to 1730 he issued four volumes of harpsichord pieces containing 27 *Ordres* (SUITES). These comprise from a few to as many as a score of pieces in dance forms, most bearing fanciful programmatic titles. In melodic invention, delicate ornamentation, wit, and the coupling of extramusical connotations with carefully planned forms, these works epitomize the best of French style. Couperin's treatise on KEYBOARD playing— *L'Art de toucher le clavecin* (1716) — was an influential work. During his last eleven years Couperin composed trio SONATAS and other music for instrumental ENSEMBLE, including the *Concerts Royaux, Les Nations, Les Goûts Réunis, L'Apothéose de Corelli,* and *L'Apothéose de Lully.* Many of these demonstrate a new blending of the French and Italian traditions.

Coupler: a device that permits an organist or harpsichordist either to control the tonal resources of one KEYBOARD (manual or pedal) through the keys of another or to obtain octave doublings of each key that he plays.

Courante (F): a lively French

dance in triple METER, which originated during the late 16th century and became one of the standard movements of the BAROQUE suite. The Italian form, the *corrente* or *coranto*, is usually based on running figures. The French form proceeds at a more moderate TEMPO, in 6/4 or 3/2 rather than in 3/4 or 3/8. The measure may be subdivided into groups of either two or three quarters, and shifts from one subdivision to another are frequent.

Course: either a pair of strings lying closely parallel to each other and tuned to the same PITCH, or a single string.

Cowell, Henry: *b.* Menlo Park, Cal., March 11, 1897; *d.* Shady, N.Y., December 10, 1965. One of the most prolific among contemporary American composers, Cowell has been active also as a pianist, writer, and editor, and as one of the founders of the Pan-American Association of Composers. His experimental tendencies include the early use of percussive TONE CLUSTERS on the piano and the invention (with L. Theremin) of an instrument to produce different rhythms simultaneously. On the other hand, certain conservative, romantic traits appear in some of Cowell's SYMPHONIES using folk material. He wrote music for ORCHESTRA, band,

many different CHAMBER ensembles (including unusual combinations), and CHORUS.

Crab canon: a CANON employing RETROGRADE MOTION.

Cracovienne (F): *see* KRAKOWIAK.

Crecquillon, Thomas: *d.* Béthune(?), *c.*1557. A prolific composer of CHANSONS and MOTETS, Crecquillon also wrote some 16 MASSES. His style is primarily contrapuntal. For a time Crecquillon was in the service of Charles V of Spain.

Credo (L): the Catholic Creed, the third section of the MASS ORDINARY.

Crescendo (I): growing louder (no specific level of loudness is expected).

Crescendo pedal: a device that permits an organist to add or retire STOPS without removing his hands from the KEYBOARD.

Creston, Paul (bapt. Joseph Guttoveggio): *b.* New York City, October 10, 1906. Creston has written five SYMPHONIES, two CONCERTOS, and other orchestral music, CHAMBER, CHORAL, and piano music, and songs. His style intermingles many conservative post-romantic and impressionist elements with more modern idioms.

Croche (F), **Croma** (I): eighth note.

Cromorne (F), **Krummhorn** (G): a family of six double-

REED instruments with cylindrical, *j*-shaped outlines, employed *c*.1450–1620. Their reeds were enclosed in windcaps, through which the player blew; their tone was dark and subdued.

Crook: a narrow metal tube inserted either between the REED or mouthpiece of a wind instrument and the main body or within the main body of the instrument itself. *See also* BRASS INSTRUMENTS; WOODWINDS.

Cross-fingering: a method of fingering for WOODWINDS in which the player bypasses an open hole and closes one or more holes below it.

Cross relation: *see* FALSE RELATION.

Cross rhythm: the interplay resulting from the simultaneous use in different VOICES either of different equal divisions of a common timevalue (e.g., halves vs. thirds) or of different groupings of the same time-values (e.g., two groups of three vs. three groups of two).

Crotchet: a quarter-note (British usage).

Crwth, Crot, Cruit, Crowd: a bowed lyre, used much in the Middle Ages, and surviving in Wales until the early 19th century.

Csárdás: a Hungarian dance beginning with a melancholy section (*lassu,* or *lassan*) and

continuing with a gay one (*friss,* or *friska*).

Cui, César Antonovich: *b.* Vilna, January 18, 1835; *d.* Petrograd, March 24, 1918. A military engineer by profession and a composer and music critic by avocation, Cui was musically the least nationalistic and the least distinguished among the group known as the Mighty FIVE. His most successful works are among his songs and piano pieces rather than among his more extended CHAMBER WORKS and OPERAS.

Cuivré (F): a direction calling for a harsh, brassy tone on the horn.

Cuivres (F): BRASS INSTRUMENTS.

Cut time: *see* ALLA BREVE.

Cyclic, cyclical: (1) in the widest sense, any composition comprised of several MOVEMENTS that, while different in character and material, unmistakably form one musical unit. (2) More specifically, a work of several movements, two or more of which are thematically related. While several families of works possess such an attribute (including, e.g., certain BAROQUE SONATAS and SUITES), the term is used most often to refer to two of these. It designates especially certain ROMANTIC and late Romantic sonatas and SYM-

PHONIES. Further it distinguishes mid-15th-century and later settings of the MASS ORDINARY, each composed as a unit, from earlier settings that were composites of movements conceived independently or in pairs. The cyclic Mass could be unified either through the use of similar or identical openings to the movements (a motto or head motif) or through the use of the same CANTUS FIRMUS throughout.

Cymbals: a percussion instrument consisting of two round, slightly convex metal plates. These are normally clashed together with a sliding motion. A single cymbal may be held suspended and struck with one of several implements, most frequently a timpani or side drumstick or a wire brush. Both modes of playing produce an indefinite PITCH. *Cymbales antiques* or crotales, are small cymbals using thicker metal in order to produce a more definite pitch; these are made in different sizes. A definite pitch of unusual tone quality may be produced by drawing a cello or bass bow across the edge of a single cymbal. This method of playing is occasionally called for in modern SCORES.

Czardas: *see* CSÁRDÁS.

Czerny, Carl: *b.* Vienna, February 20, 1791; *d.* Vienna, July 15, 1857. A student of BEETHOVEN, Czerny became one of the important pianists and teachers of his day. LISZT and Sigismond Thalberg were among his pupils. He was a highly prolific composer, working in all genres then cultivated. His ETUDES and FINGER EXERCISES for piano, representing one of the first systematic approaches to technique, are still well-known.

D

Da capo (I): repeat from the beginning, either to the place marked *Fine* (end), or to an intermediate point marked by a special sign (*segno*). The term is often abbreviated D.C.

Dalayrac, Nicolas: *b*. Muret, June 8, 1753; *d*. Paris, November 27, 1809. After completing a set of six STRING QUARTETS in 1781, Dalayrac turned to the writing of OPERAS, producing 56 during his lifetime. These were successful almost throughout Europe, and were especially enjoyed by Napoleon.

Dallapiccola, Luigi: *b*. Pisino, February 3, 1904. Dallapiccola completed his training at the Cherubini Conservatory in Florence and was appointed to the faculty there in 1934. He has also taught in the United States, at the Berkshire Music Center and at Queens College. He is a leading Italian exponent of the TWELVE-TONE TECHNIQUE, which he handles with freedom. His melodies have a more even flow than those of SCHOENBERG and WEBERN

that are built on wide leaps. The OPERAS *Il Prigionero*, and *Volo Di Notte* are among his most famous works. Dallapiccola has written also a few sets of songs, as well as CHORAL, CHAMBER, orchestral, and KEYBOARD works.

Dal Segno (I): repeat from the place marked by the sign 𝄋.

Damper: a block of felt, glued to a wooden block, and made to rest on a PIANO or HARPSICHORD string in order to cut off the sound at the termination of a note or chord. A mechanism lifts the damper as the key is struck and returns it upon the release. The damper pedal is the right-hand pedal of the piano, which permits the simultaneous lifting of all dampers, resulting in a more sonorous tone. *See* MUTE.

Dämpfer (G): MUTE.

Daquin, Louis Claude: *b*. Paris, July 4, 1694; *d*. Paris, June 15, 1772. An eminent keyboard artist, Daquin served as organist at St. Paul from 1727 till his death; he was also organist at the

Chapel Royal from 1739. He composed many short pieces for harpsichord and organ.

Dargomyzhsky, Alexander Sergeivich: *b.* Tula, February 14, 1813; *d.* St. Petersburg, January 17, 1869. The realistic and nationalistic elements in Dargomyzhsky's major works—the OPERAS *Russalka* and *The Stone Guest* and three TONE POEMS—had considerable influence on BORODIN, MUSSORGSKY, and other nationalistic Russian composers, as well as on more cosmopolitan composers such as TCHAIKOVSKY. Dargomyzhsky wrote also many songs and piano pieces.

David, Félicien César: *b.* Cadenet, April 13, 1810; *d.* St. Germain-en-Laye, August 29, 1876. After having been active in Aix, David completed his training at the Paris Conservatoire. A stay in the Near East led David to exploit "Oriental" colors, much to the ROMANTIC audiences' liking for the exotic. His most successful works include the SYMPHONIC ODE *Le Désert,* and the OPERA *Lalla Roukh.* He wrote other operas, SYMPHONIES, CHAMBER MUSIC, piano pieces, and songs.

Debussy, Claude Achille: *b.* St. Germain-en-Laye, August 22, 1862; *d.* Paris, March 25, 1918; one of the greatest French composers, the creator of the IMPRESSIONISTIC STYLE in music.

After early piano study with a pupil of CHOPIN, Debussy entered the Paris Conservatory at the age of eleven. He studied there with Émile Durand, and, later, with Ernest Guiraud. From 1880 to 1882, he was engaged as pianist to Nadezhda von Meck (the patroness of TCHAIKOVSKY); in this capacity he traveled to Switzerland, Italy, and Russia. In 1884, Debussy won the Prix de Rome with his CANTATA *L'Enfant prodigue.* The symphonic SUITE *Printemps,* which he wrote in Rome was reproved by the jury at the Academy for an emphasis on color at the expense of form; the usual honorary performance was withheld. Although Debussy visited many important European musical centers—often to conduct his own works—he spent most of his life in and about Paris. He was active there as a critic and appeared also as a pianist. A contemplated tour of the United States in 1914 did not take place because of ill health; in the end Debussy succumbed to cancer.

The French tradition of SAINT-SAËNS, FRANCK, and MASSENET was imparted to Debussy at the Conservatory. Thanks to his trip to Russia, he became acquainted with the works of MUSSORGSKY, BORODIN, and BALAKIREV. As a young man, he was enthused with Wagnerian chromaticism, although later in his career—as his nationalistic feelings came to the fore—Debussy became anti-German. The performances of exotic music (Javanese and Spanish) at the Paris Exposition of 1889 aroused his interest. Furthermore, Debussy was much influenced by the ideas of the symbolist poets, Verlaine, Louÿs, and Mallarmé, and by the Impressionist painters, such as Monet, Pisarro, Degas, and Cézanne.

Many of the novel effects of Debussy's works aroused antagonism during his lifetime. His melodies are based not only on chromatically enriched major and minor modes, but on pentatonic, whole-tone, and irregular modal constructions as well. His harmonic palette is equally varied. There are numerous augmented chords, chords with sevenths and ninths, and chords of irregular construction. These chords are often employed for the sake of their color rather than for their traditional harmonic function. Often the same chord construction is repeated at different PITCH levels, a stringing together of so many daubs of sound. Characteris-

tic Debussy RHYTHMS, unlike those of many German Romantic works, may meander, eddy in gusts, or skip rapidly, and seem often unexpected. Debussy's ORCHESTRATION is rich and colorful, although it is seldom used to produce a weighty mass of sound. Instead, solo threads appear and disappear in great variety. Interest in thematic development is minimal, and form, on the whole, is treated freely.

Debussy made important contributions in almost all media. His two books of *Préludes*, his *Études* and SUITES are among the landmarks of the 20th-century piano repertoire. Among his CHAMBER WORKS are a fine STRING QUARTET (one of his first major compositions), a violin SONATA, a cello sonata, and a sonata for flute, viola, and harp. His most famous orchestral pieces include the *Prelude to the Afternoon of a Faun*, and three suites: *Nocturnes, La Mer,* and *Images.* Debussy's 60 songs stand in the forefront of the French segment of this literature. His works for mixed vocal and instrumental forces include *La Demoiselle élue, Le Martyre de Saint Sébastien,* and the operatic masterpiece *Pelléas et Mélisande.*

Decrescendo (I): growing

softer (no specific level of softness is implied).

Delibes, Clément Philibert Léo: *b.* St. Germain du Val, February 21, 1836; *d.* Paris, January 16, 1891. Organist, conductor, and teacher, Délibes is remembered for two of his OPERAS, *Lakmé* and *Le Roi l'a dit,* and two BALLETS, *Coppélia* and *Sylvia,* works of easy melodious charm. Other stage works and sketches, a CANTATA, choral works, and songs are now forgotten.

Delius, Frederick: *b.* Bradford, England, January 29, 1862; *d.* Grez-sur-Loing, France, June 10, 1934. Although regarded as the most prominent of late ROMANTIC English composers, Delius spent his adult life on the Continent (after a brief stay in the United States), studying at the Leipzig Conservatorium and settling in France in 1888. His early style was much influenced by GRIEG whom he met and admired. Although his melodies are DIATONIC, Delius's harmonies are richly chromatic and he employs a large orchestra to lush effect. His works include SYMPHONIC POEMS (e.g., *Brigg Fair*), CONCERTOS, two STRING QUARTETS and other CHAMBER MUSIC, compositions for vocal soloists, chorus, and orchestra (e.g., *A Mass of Life*) and for unaccompanied chorus, and six OPERAS (including *A Village Romeo and Juliet*).

Dello Joio, Norman: *b.* New York City, January 24, 1913. Dello Joio completed his studies under WAGENAAR and HINDEMITH. He taught subsequently at Sarah Lawrence College and other schools. He is prominent among American composers writing in a basically conservative idiom, drawing upon such diverse sources as GREGORIAN CHANT, Italian OPERA, and JAZZ. Dello Joio has written operas, BALLETS, and KEYBOARD, CHAMBER, CHORAL, and orchestral music.

Demi-semiquaver: a thirty-second note (British usage).

Deprès: *see* JOSQUIN.

Descant: (1) the highest part of a polyphonic work or the highest of a family of INSTRUMENTS; (2) a COUNTERPOINT —written or improvised—to an already existing MELODY, in particular to a HYMN or folksong; (3) English descant refers to a group of 3-voice English compositions of 1375–1450, employing successions of parallel HARMONIES built of thirds and sixths; (4) a variant spelling of DISCANT.

Des Prez, Des Prés: *see* JOSQUIN.

Destro (I), Destra (I): right hand.

Détache (F): (1) a style of BOWING employing a vigorous

stroke for each note. This style is used in passages of equal time-values and moderate speed. (2) In a wider sense, a style of playing midway between STACCATO, and LEGATO, each note detached from its neighbor.

Deutscher Tanz (G): a lively German dance in triple METER, in vogue during the late 18th and early 19th centuries.

Development: (1) the exploration of possibilities inherent in a THEME but not made apparent in its initial statement; (2) the middle section of a movement in SONATA FORM, based on techniques used in (1).

Most of the techniques employed in development are discussed under the heading VARIATION. There is normally, however, a difference in the connotation of the two terms. Development tends to imply a dramatic intensification, a heightened probing that is achieved less frequently in variation.

An important developmental technique in works cast in sonata form is thematic fragmentation. This involves the selection for intensive use of one or more motives from the principal theme. Because of the rapidity of reiteration in such development, intensity builds quickly. The simultaneous presentation of themes that had occurred originally in succession is another means of building a climax. MODULATION is an important harmonic characteristic of many developmental sections.

Diabelli, Anton: b. Mattsee (Salzburg), September 8, 1781; d. Vienna, April 7, 1858. A choirboy under Michael Haydn, Diabelli trained for the priesthood, but became in succession a music teacher and music publisher. (He published much of SCHUBERT's music.) As a composer he is best known for the waltz theme employed in BEETHOVEN's *Diabelli Variations*. (A composite set of variations by 50 other composers, including CZERNY, HUMMEL, LISZT, and Schubert was also issued by Diabelli.) Diabelli's SONATINAS for piano are still played by beginners; other works include a quantity of sacred vocal music, songs, OPERETTAS, dance music, and CHAMBER MUSIC.

Diamond, David: b. Rochester, July 9, 1915. Diamond completed his training under SESSIONS and Boulanger. His works include six SYMPHONIES, five CONCERTOS and other large-scale orchestral works, four STRING QUARTETS and other CHAMBER MUSIC, CHORAL MUSIC, and songs. His style, at first marked by atonal harmonic and melodic complexities, evolved toward a simpler neo-romantic expression.

Diapason: (1) a family of ORGAN STOPS; (2) obsolete term for OCTAVE; (3) a French term for TUNING FORK.

Diapente (Gr): obsolete term for the INTERVAL of a fifth.

Diaphony (Gr): early term for ORGANUM.

Diatesseron (Gr): obsolete term for the INTERVAL of a fourth.

Diatonic: (1) a style of writing in which the tonal resources are restricted either to the notes represented by the white keys of the piano or to the notes proper to the major or minor key of the piece. Notes other than these are described as *chromatic.* (2) A form of Greek tetrachord employing whole steps and half steps.

Dièse (F), **Diesis** (I): sharp.

Dieupart, Charles: *d.* London, *c.*1740. An excellent harpsichordist and violinist, Dieupart was active in London during HANDEL's time. His six SUITES were appreciated by BACH, who imitated their style in his *English Suites.*

Diferencia (S): 16th-century Spanish VARIATIONS.

Difference tones: *see* COMBINATION TONES.

Diminished: a quality of INTERVAL or CHORD.

Diminuendo (I): growing softer (no fixed level of softness is implied).

Diminution: (1) a restatement of a THEME in time-values smaller than those used originally; (2) during the late-16th century and 17th century, the practice—both written and improvised—of providing existing compositions with florid ornamentation.

Discant: (1) a MEDIEVAL polyphonic style in which all parts have metrically-organized rhythms; (2) a variant spelling of DESCANT.

Dissonance: a harsh-sounding interval; the opposite of CONSONANCE.

Dittersdorf, Karl: *b.* Vienna, November 2, 1739; *d.* Neuhaus, October 24, 1799. Dittersdorf's two most important posts were as music director to the bishop of Gross-Wardein (1764–69), in Hungary, and to the prince-bishop of Breslau (1769–95). He was famous in his time both as a violinist and composer and was awarded the Order of the Golden Spur by the pope and ennobled by the emperor. A prolific composer, he wrote OPERAS and SINGSPIELEN, ORATORIOS, MASSES, SYMPHONIES, CONCERTOS, CHAMBER MUSIC, and piano music. Although overshadowed by HAYDN and MOZART, his contribution to the development of the CLASSICAL symphony, SONATA, and OPERA should not be disregarded.

Divertimento: a late-18th-century, multimovement work for instrumental ENSEMBLE or chamber ORCHESTRA. The *divertimento* was light in style, employing elements of both the SUITE and early SYMPHONY.

Divertissement (F): (1) a FANTASY on familiar tunes, especially tunes drawn from an OPERA; (2) a series of dances, sometimes with songs, inserted in a stage work; (3) DIVERTIMENTO.

Divisi (I): an orchestral direction for string players, directing that the specified body of players be split into two or more groups, each group playing a different part. The term is often abbreviated *div.*

Divisions: a 17th- and 18th-century English term for: (1) the elaborate ornamentation of a MELODY by replacing individual written notes by various florid figures, or, (2) a VARIATION form based on the technique just described, usually employing a ground bass as a THEME.

Do (I, F): in SOLMIZATION either the first degree of the SCALE (movable *do*), or *c* (fixed *do*); the equivalent of *ut*.

Dodecaphonic: adjective describing a TWELVE-TONE work.

Dodecuple scale: a modern term for a chromatic scale furnishing the materials for a TWELVE-TONE composition rather than appearing as a momentary departure from the traditional major-minor system.

Dohnányi, Ernst von: *b.* Pressburg (Bratislava), July 27, 1877; *d.* New York City, February 9, 1960. After returning to Hungary in 1915 from Berlin, Dohnányi soon became the most prominent Hungarian musician. He was director of the Budapest Conservatory, the Hungarian Radio, and the Hungarian Academy, and conductor of the Budapest Philharmonic. He settled in the United States in 1949. He cultivated a readily acceptable post - Romantic style, modeled after BRAHMS, his best-known work being his *Variations on a Nursery Song* for piano and orchestra. His work includes a moderately large amount of KEYBOARD, CHAMBER, and orchestral music.

Dolce (I): sweet and soft.

Dolente (I), **Doloroso** (I): sorrowful.

Dominant: (1) the fifth degree of a major or minor scale, the main point of harmonic contrast with the TONIC key center; (2) the reciting tone (*repercussio, tuba,* tenor) of a CHURCH MODE.

Donizetti, Gaetano: *b.* Bergamo, Italy, November 29, 1797; *d.* Bergamo, April 8, 1848; prominent operatic composer.

A pupil of Mayr and Mattei, Donizetti was an amazingly prolific composer. Between 1818, the date of his first OPERA, and 1845, when he was paralyzed by a stroke that dimmed his mental powers, he produced some seventy operas, together with a quantity of church music, secular CANTATAS, songs, piano music, CHAMBER MUSIC, and SYMPHONIES. Donizetti was seldom painstaking. His HARMONIES and RHYTHMS are often dull; his MELODIES—though ingratiating—can be trivial. Nevertheless, *Don Pasquale* (1843), written in eight days, is a comic masterpiece, and *L'Elisir d'amore* and *The Daughter of the Regiment* offer many charming moments. *Lucia di Lammermoor* (1835) is by far Donizetti's finest serious opera; among his other works in this genre, it is approached only by *Lucrezia Borgia* and *Linda di Chamounix*.

Doppio movimento (I): twice as fast as the preceding TEMPO.

Dorian: (1) the first CHURCH MODE; (2) a Greek mode that may be represented by a scale descending through the white keys from *e'* to *e*.

Double (F): in the 18th century, a VARIATION, usually of a dance movement.

Double bar: two closely-spaced vertical lines used to mark the end of a composition or of a section thereof. In the former instance, the right-hand line is usually thick; in the latter, both lines may be thin.

Double bass: the deepest member of the VIOLIN FAMILY.

Double counterpoint (Invertible counterpoint): the technique of writing a pair of complementary melodies in such fashion that either may be placed higher than the other—usually through an octave TRANSPOSITION.

Double flat, Double sharp: symbols requiring the alteration of the pertinent note(s) by a whole step—downward and upward, respectively—from the natural form.

Double stop: the playing of two notes simultaneously on a bowed string instrument.

Double tonguing: *see* WOODWINDS (*Technique*).

Dowland, John: *b.* near Dublin, December 1562; *d.* London, January 21, 1626. Much of Dowland's maturity was spent on the Continent, but from 1612 to 1626 he was lutenist to Kings James I and Charles I. He is famed for his AYRES for voice and lute and for his instrumental ENSEMBLE music, including the *Lachrymae, or Seven Teares*. His works feature numerous passages of chromatic daring.

Down beat: the first or accented BEAT of a measure, indicated by a conductor through the downward motion of the hand.

Down-bow: the motion of *pulling* a bow across a string.

Drone: (1) a note, usually in the bass, sustained against a melody or a harmonic progression; (2) in a bagpipe, a large pipe that produces such a note.

Drum: an instrument normally consisting of one or two skins stretched over an enclosed space, and usually played by striking either with the hand or with one or two sticks. However, neither the presence of a skin nor the percussive mode of playing is obligatory. *Slit-drums* are made by hollowing out a tree trunk through a longitudinal slit and played by striking the thinned area flanking the slit. There are also the *steel drums* of the Caribbean, fashioned from metal barrels. Some drums may be played by friction. Drums may be made in the shape of a cylinder, barrel, cone, goblet, hemisphere, oval, or bowl, or they may employ a very shallow frame. The drums employed in modern orchestras and bands include the timpani (kettledrums), the snare, tenor, and bass drums, and the tambourine.

Timpani each employ a single head (i.e., skin), stretched over a metal hemisphere. Among the five drums listed immediately above, only the timpani produce sounds of definite PITCH. This pitch is determined by the size of the drum and the tautness of the head. The latter is controlled either by a set of hand-operated screws placed around the rim or by a pedal mechanism. Classical composers used timpani in pairs; usually one was tuned to the TONIC, the other to the DOMINANT. Late ROMANTIC and modern composers may use three or more timpani. TONE COLOR may be varied slightly by altering the material of the striking heads of the drumsticks. Normally felt is employed—either hard or soft—but leather, wood, or sponge may occasionally be used for special effects.

The *snare drum* (known also as the side or military drum) has a shallow cylindrical frame, with a head stretched over either end. A set of snares—cords of catgut or metal—is stretched over the lower head, emitting a rattling sound when the upper head is struck. A *tenor drum* is a larger double-headed cylindrical drum, deeper in proportion to its diameter than the snare drum. Both drums are played with slender wooden drumsticks. The *bass drum* is a still

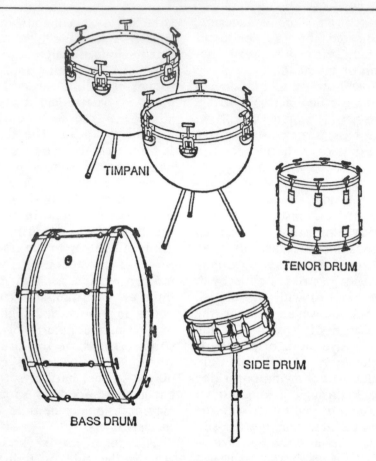

TIMPANI

TENOR DRUM

BASS DRUM

SIDE DRUM

DRUMS

larger double-headed cylindrical drum, set so that the heads are upright, and played with drumsticks having felt heads. The *tambourine* is an extremely shallow frame drum with a single head with pairs of circular metal jingles inserted into lateral slots cut out of the frame. The tambourine may be struck by hand, shaken, or rubbed.

Although a rich drum rep-ertoire exists outside of the European cultural tradition, the use of the various drums within that tradition is quite restricted. Before the 20th century, the drum was used only in large ENSEMBLES (except for certain military and ceremonial occasions), primarily for rhythmic accentuation or suggestive color (e.g., in evoking a military scene, a thunderstorm, etc.). Passages of thematic or developmental significance are comparatively rare. During the present century interest in percussion instruments has increased, and various members of the percussion family occur more frequently in mixed chamber ensembles. A few works have been written for percussion instruments alone; these may call for drums other than the traditional ones listed above.

Duet, Duetto (I): a work for two soloists, with or without ACCOMPANIMENT.

Dufay, Guillaume: b. Hainault(?), c.1400; d. Cambrai, November 27, 1474; the greatest composer of his generation. Trained at the Cambrai Cathedral, Dufay traveled widely during his prime. The most important of his posts was as singer in the Papal Choir (1428–33, 1435–37). After 1445 he spent much of his time at Cambrai, where he was canon at the Cathedral. Dufay's settings of the MASS ORDINARY occupy a central position in his output. Eight complete Masses survive, together with a few putative sets and a number of individual movements and pairs. Most of these use a preexistent melody as a structural framework, either in drawn out notes in the tenor or in decorated form in the highest voice. Dufay's role in the development of the cyclic Mass may be likened to that of HAYDN with regard to the SYMPHONY. A fairly large quantity of excellent MOTETS and secular works with vernacular texts (both French and Italian) also survive.

Dukas, Paul: b. Paris, October 1, 1865; d. Paris, May 17, 1935. After study at the Paris Conservatoire, Dukas became a critic and teacher (at the École Normale de Musique and at the Conservatoire). His most famous work by far is the orchestral SCHERZO *The Sorcerer's Apprentice*; other outstanding works are his OPERA *Ariane et Barbe-Bleue*, the BALLET *La Péri*, and a piano SONATA. He left a few other piano, CHAMBER, and orchestral works. His style shows the influence of IMPRESSIONISM.

Dulcimer: a string instrument, consisting of a shallow box (usually trapezoidal in shape), with a fairly large set of strings stretched parallel to it. The strings are normally struck by hammers held in the hands, but in colonial America, they were plucked. The *pantaleon*—popular during the 18th century—and the *cimbalom* are enlarged dulcimers.

Dulcitone: a small KEYBOARD instrument similar to the CELESTA, using tuning forks rather than steel bars as the sonorous material.

Dumka: a Slavonic BALLAD with a doleful or sentimental text, set in sections alternating sadness and exuberance. By extension, the term may be applied to instrumental MOVEMENTS of similar character.

Dump: a lament (vocal or instrumental), in vogue in England during the 16th century.

Dunstable, John: *b. c.*1380; *d.* December 24, 1453. Composer, mathematician, and astronomer, Dunstable, while in the service of the duke of Bedford, spent several years in Paris. The sonorous quality of his music, the prominence given to thirds and sixths, influenced Dufay and other Continental composers, and Dunstable's later works, in turn, reveal Continental influences. His surviving music consists largely of MASS sections and MOTETS, mainly in three parts.

Duo: a duet.

Duodecuple: same as DODE-CUPLE.

Duparc, (Marie-Eugène) Henri Fouques: *b.* Paris, January 21, 1848; *d.* Mont-de-Marsan, France, February 12, 1933. Duparc's career as a composer was terminated by a nervous disorder in 1885. His fame rests on a handful of fine songs that foreshadow elements of early IMPRESSION-ISTIC style. Two orchestral works and six piano pieces are also extant, while Duparc himself destroyed still other works.

Duplet: two equal notes (or a note and its equivalent rest) taking the time of a normal grouping of three equal values. A duplet is usually indicated by a *2* in italics.

Dur (G): major key.

Durante, Francesco: *b.* Frattamaggiore, March 31, 1684; *d.* Naples, August 13, 1755. Durante was an eminent teacher and one of the leading Italian composers of sacred music of his time. In addition to MASSES, MOTETS, PSALMS, etc., he wrote music for harpsichord and for string ENSEMBLE.

Dussek, Jan Ladislav: *b.* Cáslav, February 12, 1760; *d.* St.-Germain-en-Laye, March 20, 1812. As one of the leading pianists of his generation, Dussek traveled widely and enjoyed the assistance of many patrons. He was active in London for nearly 12 years in his father-in-law's music-publishing firm. His compositions include piano SONATAS and CONCERTOS, as well as works for piano for four hands and a large quantity of CHAMBER MUSIC. Many of Dussek's works are well wrought, and his use of chromatic HARMONY often foreshadows ROMANTIC developments in this sphere.

Dux (L): the first of a pair of VOICES that present the same melody in overlapping succession. (See also COMES.)

Dvořák, Antonin: *b.* Mühlhausen, September 8, 1841; *d.* Prague, May 1, 1904; the greatest of Czech composers.

Dvořák was the son of an innkeeper and butcher. He learned to play violin from the local schoolmaster and left home when sixteen in order to study at the Prague Organ School. He supported himself as a violinist in a small orchestra and then as a violist in the National Theatre Orchestra (1862–73). In 1873 he became organist at St. Adalbert's in Prague and won his first success as a composer with the patriotic CHORUS *Hymnus.* Thereafter, he won several Austrian state prizes and achieved steadily increasing fame, thanks in part to the interest of BRAHMS, HANSLICK, LISZT, and VON BÜLOW in the performance and publication of his music. Dvořák was appointed professor of composition at the Prague Conservatory in 1891, was director of the National Conservatory in New York (1892–95), and then returned to Prague, becoming director of the Conservatory in 1901.

A prolific composer with a great melodic gift, Dvořák was active in all traditional genres of composition. His *Slavonic Rhapsodies* and *Slavonic Dances* for orchestra, the *Dumky Trio,* and several of his piano works illustrate Dvořák's nationalistic affinities. His most famous SYMPHONY, *From the New World,* is generally taken to reflect the influence of American folk music (and of Negro spirituals, in particular), although Dvořák disclaimed any conscious intent in this direction. The *Symphonies Nos. 2* and *4* retain a place in the repertoire, as does the Violin Concerto, several CHAMBER works, and the *Stabat Mater.* Other music by Dvořák, including OPERAS, OVERTURES, SYMPHONIC POEMS, CONCERTOS, CHORAL MUSIC, songs, and piano music, is performed more frequently in Eastern Europe than elsewhere.

Dynamics: (1) shades of loudness and softness in performance; (2) the written indications for the particular shade desired by the composer or suggested by the editor. The more common dynamic indications are: *pianissimo (PP),* very soft; *piano (P),* soft; *mezzo piano (mP),* moderately soft; *mezzo forte (mF),* moderately loud; *forte (F),* loud; *fortissimo (FF),* very loud; *crescendo (cresc..* or ━━━━), growing louder:

decrescendo or *diminuendo* (*decresc.* or *dim.*, resp., or ═══════), growing softer; *forte-piano* (*FP*), loud attack followed by an immediate softening; *sforzando* and *sforzato* (*sFz, sF*), a marked accent. The symbol > stands for an accent. Dynamic indications begin to occur in the early 17th century, but were used very sparingly, if at all, before the late 18th century. During the course of the 19th century, composers gave more and more detailed instructions concerning the proper realization of dynamics in their individual works.

E

Ear training: instruction intended to develop the ability to recognize patterns of TONES, to retain them at least briefly in the memory, and to translate aural perception into proper NOTATION. The student is drilled in the recognition of basic INTERVALS and common rhythmic patterns and, in dictation, proceeds to increasingly complex problems. An adequately trained memory is of course necessary to the appreciation of the details of a musical masterpiece, while the ability to write that which one hears is a necessary prerequisite to most composition.

Ecclesiastical modes: *see* CHURCH MODES.

Échappée: a NONHARMONIC TONE that interrupts the main progression between two chord tones by movement in an opposite direction.

Eclogue: a poetic term used as a title for pastoral compositions.

Écossaise (F): a lively dance in duple METER, popular in

England and several Continental countries at the turn of the 19th century; the *Écossaise* did not originate in Scotland, despite the fact that its name means Scottish.

Egk, Werner: *b*. Auchsesheim, May 17, 1901. The tunefulness and neo-romantic spirit of such OPERAS as *Die Zaubergeige* and *Peer Gynt* have won moderate success for Egk's music. He has also written BALLETS, songs and CHORAL WORKS, orchestral SUITES, and a piano SONATA. Egk conducted the Berlin State Opera (1938–41), and was director of the Berlin Hochschule für Musik (1950–53).

Eighth note, eighth rest:

♪ ♪ , ♫ , 𝄾

Einem, Gottfried von: *b*. Bern, January 24, 1918. Von Einem was active on the staffs of the Berlin and Dresden state operas. As a composer, he is known particularly for his OPERAS — including *The Trial*—and BALLETS. He has written also several orchestral works that reflect a basically NEOCLASSICAL approach.

Electronic instruments: instruments whose TONE is either produced or amplified by electrical means. The former may be termed *radioelectric*, the latter, *electromechanical*. The THEREMIN (Thereminvox, Etherophone), Ondes musicales (Ondes Martenot), Solovox, Novachord, and Hammond Organ are among the better known radioelectric instruments. The Hammond Organ and others employing similar principles generate the desired frequencies directly and convert them into sound. Instruments such as the Theremin obtain the desired frequencies as the difference between two far higher frequencies. Many electromechanical instruments that amplify and modify the sound of the piano, reed organ, guitar, and other string instruments have been devised. Despite the modern composer's interest in electronically produced (or modified) sound, none of the above instruments has gained widespread acceptance outside of popular music.

Electronic music: music drawing on tonal resources made available through modern recording techniques and electronic generation of sound. Composers began to draw on these resources shortly before the mid-20th century, and have already evolved a variety of compositional procedures and styles. *Musique concrète* employs primarily material gathered from sources previously considered as nonmusical—that is, noises of all varieties. These are dissected, transposed, amplified, and otherwise manipulated electronically. The resultant sounds are recorded on tape and then assembled to form musical patterns. Pierre Schaeffer, Olivier Messiaen, and Pierre Boulez have worked in this medium. Sounds from conventional musical sources have been the primary materials utilized by composers of the New York "school," such as Otto Luening and Vladimir Ussachevsky in their music for tape recorders. Manipulations may involve change of tape direction or tape speed. Inasmuch as there is a perceptible difference in quality between the initiation (attack) of a normal instrumental or vocal tone, its continuation, and its end, sounds may be used fractionally, divested of their beginnings, ends, or both. Frequencies may be used to react against one another to produce combination tones. Tape assembly calls for complex splicing procedures. European composers of electronic music, including Karlheinz Stockhausen in Cologne and Luigi Nono in Milan, make extensive use of sounds produced by electronic means. Electronic generators, used in combination with filters, modulators, and similar devices may produce either nearly pure sounds or complex ones with any number of harmonics with any given order of emphasis. They may also produce irregular sounds or noises. Any of the resources listed above may be combined with traditional sources of musical sounds, such as voice or orchestra. The development of the RCA Electronic Synthesizer and its installation at a center directed by Columbia and Princeton Universities has stimulated much interest in this field, which allows the composer direct control over a vast range of tonal possibilities. The development of smaller systems, such as those of Buchla and Moog, has made the potential of electronic music available to a wide number of composers. Increasing interest has been shown in the creation of electronic music by means of COMPUTER programs, although such processes were still in their infancy in the 1960s.

Elegy: a poetic term employed as a title for mournful compositions.

Elgar, Sir Edward William: *b.* Broadheath, England, June 2, 1857; *d.* Worcester, February 23, 1934. Elgar is one of the few native-born English ROMANTIC composers to gain international recognition. He was trained chiefly by his father and was active as a conductor and organist early

in his career. His most enduring works are the *Enigma
Variations* for orchestra, the
Introduction and Allegro for
strings, and the ORATORIO *The
Dream of Gerontius*. Elgar
wrote a variety of orchestral
choral, and CHAMBER MUSIC,
as well as songs and organ
music. His music, full of romantic spirit, enjoyed wide
popularity during the early
20th century, especially one
of the four *Pomp and Cir-
cumstance* marches.

Embellishment: *see* ORNA-
MENTS.

Embouchure (F): (1) the lip
position assumed in playing
a wind instrument and the relationship between the lips
and the REED or mouthpiece;
an improper embouchure will
result in poor TONE, improper
PITCH, or both; (2) the mouthpiece of a wind instrument.

Enesco, Georges, *b*. Liveni,
Rumania, August 19, 1881;
d. Paris, May 4, 1955. The
most prominent among Ru-
manian musicians, Enesco
was active as violinist, conductor, and composer. He
wrote an OPERA, a few songs,
and a variety of orchestral,
CHAMBER, and piano music;
his two lilting *Rumanian
Rhapsodies* for orchestra still
occupy a peripheral place in
the repertoire.

English flute: an obsolete term
for the RECORDER.

English horn: an alto oboe
(*see* WOODWINDS).

Enharmonic: (1) the relationship between two notes of
different spellings that are
identical in sound on KEY-
BOARD instruments—e.g., *b*♯
and *c*. (A very slight difference in PITCH between such
notes may occur in vocal performance and on instruments
of the VIOLIN FAMILY.) A
direct change from one spelling of a pitch to another is
known as an *enharmonic
change;* such a change of
NOTATION often indicates a
changed harmonic or tonal
context for the note involved.
A harmonic progression that
changes key through the use
of an enharmonic change is
known as an *enharmonic
modulation*.

(2) In ancient Greek music,
a tetrachord that proceeded
downward by a major third
and then two quarter-tones.

Enigmatic canon: a CANON
notated as a single line without sufficient information regarding the point or points of
entry of the imitating voice(s)
or the interval of imitation.
Such canons are created as
musical puzzles, some of
which are capable of more
than one correct solution.

Ensemble: (1) a small or mod-
erate-size group of performers, generally with only one
or two musicians to a part;
(2) the quality of a concerted

performance. Good ensemble work goes beyond the requirements of keeping time and the observance of the grosser features of the SCORE. It demands familiarity with the music and with fellow performers such that the group achieves a flexibility and unity that would mark the artistry of a fine SOLO performance. (3) An operatic number scored for a group of solo singers, with or without CHORUS.

Entr'acte (F): music to be played between the acts of a stage work.

Entrée (F): (1) in French BAROQUE BALLET and OPERA, a self-contained dance number in which the characters are presented on stage; (2) in instrumental music, an opening piece of marchlike character.

Episode: (1) in a RONDO, a subsidiary section serving to provide contrast between entries of the main THEME; (2) in a FUGUE, a connective passage between entries of the theme.

Equal temperament: *see* TUNING (1).

Equale (I): a composition for a few INSTRUMENTS (or VOICES) of the same kind.

Escapement: the part of the piano action that permits the hammer to rebound after striking the strings.

Espressivo (I): expressive.

Essercizio (I): ETUDE, exercise.

Estampie (F): a French instrumental dance form of the Middle Ages, built of a series of repeated sections.

Étouffez (F): an indication to harpists and percussionists to damp (stop) the sound of their instrument immediately after plucking or striking.

Etude (F): study; a piece designed to help the performer develop his technical abilities, generally in one particular area. Many etudes are nearly devoid of musical interest and are used only for their mechanical value. However, the greatest examples of the genre—etudes of CHOPIN, LISZT, DEBUSSY, and a few others—arrive at musical distinction while ingeniously working out their individual technical demands.

Euphonium: a low-pitched BRASS INSTRUMENT.

Eurhythmics: the artistic expression of rhythm through simple body motions.

Exposition: the first full statement of the thematic materials of a FUGUE or SONATA FORM.

Expression: the nuances of TEMPO, PHRASING, and DYNAMICS necessary to all good musical performance. The composer can at best give the performer only an outline of his intentions. Music written before the mid-18th century is often without any explicit performance directions. Proper expression demands a thorough knowledge of the history of musical style, a keen awareness of both the large outlines and the significant details of musical architecture, and the ability to communicate both forms of knowledge in a convincing personal manner.

Expressionism: a term borrowed from painting for an early 20th-century style seeking to express man's harsher inner emotions. Wide melodic leaps, nonconsonant HARMONIES, and terse forms are often characteristic of this style. The term is sometimes employed to describe OPERAS by Richard STRAUSS, but more often denotes the music of SCHOENBERG, BERG, and WEBERN.

F

Fa: in SOLMIZATION, either the fourth degree of the scale, or the note *f*.

Faburden: a counter-melody sung above a well-known tune, often a HYMN. *See* FAUXBOURDON.

Fado, Fadinho: Portuguese popular music.

Fagott (G), Fagotto (I): BASSOON.

Fa-la: a late-16th- or 17th-century song using the syllables *fa-la* (*la*), as a refrain. Made popular through GASTOLDI's *balletti*, these songs spread over the Continent and especially to England.

Falla, Manuel de: *b.* Cadiz, November 23, 1876; *d.* Alta Gracia, November 14, 1946. One of the greatest Spanish composers, de Falla completed his studies under Felipe Pedrell. He was active in Europe as a composer, conductor, pianist, and teacher until 1939, when he moved to Argentina. His major works include the OPERAS *La Vida Breve* and *Master Peter's Puppet Show*; the BALLETS *El amor brujo* and *The Three-Cornered Hat*; and *Nights in the Gardens of Spain* (for piano and orchestra). His early works are colorfully nationalistic and impressionistic; in later works such as the *Harpsichord Concerto*, de Falla adopted a more restrained NEOCLASSICAL idiom.

False relation (Cross relation): the simultaneous or successive appearance of a note and one of its chromatic alterations (e.g., *d* and *d*♭) in different VOICE parts.

Falsetto: *see* VOICE.

Falso bordone (I): simple, four-part harmonizations of PSALM TONES, written in the 16th century. *See* FAUXBOURDON.

Familiar style: a term descriptive of a choral work or passage in which all parts employ identical or nearly identical RHYTHM and text (mainly one note to a syllable).

Fancy: a contrapuntal FANTASIA.

Fandango: a lively Spanish dance in triple METER. usually accompanied by guitars and castanets.

Fantasia (I), **Fantaisie** (F), **Fantasie** (G). **Phantasie** (G), **Fantasy, Fancy:** (1) a work of improvisatory style. for a KEYBOARD instrument or lute; (2) a keyboard work of the size of a SONATA, but employing forms not expected of a SONATA; (3) the development section (free fantasia) of a movement in SONATA FORM; (4) a CHARACTER PIECE suggesting a dreamlike mood; (5) a work in improvisatory style developing one or more preexistent THEMES, these often being drawn from an OPERA; (6) in 16th- and 17th-century usage, an instrumental work in imitative style, often in sections of different METERS and TEMPO; the English term *fancy* denotes this genre alone.

Farandole (F): a Provençal dance in which a chain of dancers follows a leader. The traditional music is in duple METER and is played on pipe and drum.

Fasch, Johann Friedrich: *b*. Buttelstadt (Weimar), April 15, 1688; *d*. Zerbst, December 5, 1758. A student of KUHNAU and Christopher Graupner, J. F. Fasch served as music director to the court at Zerbst. His music was admired by BACH. He wrote CANTATAS, MASSES, SUITES, CONCERTOS, and CHAMBER MUSIC.

Fasch, Karl Friedrich Christian: *b*. Zerbst, November 18, 1736; *d*. Berlin, August 3, 1800. Son of J. F. FASCH. Karl Friedrich served as accompanist to Frederick the Great (together with C. P. E. BACH) and as music director at the Berlin Opera. He founded an important Berlin choral society, the Singakademie, in 1791. He specialized in sacred vocal music.

Fasola: a system for simplifying sight-singing used in England and colonial America. The syllables, *fa, sol,* and *la,* were employed for the scale degrees 1-3 and 4-6, while *mi* indicated the seventh degree. In certain hymnbooks the letters *F, S, L,* and *M* were printed on the staff instead of notes. This system furnished the point of departure for shape notes, used after 1800. *See* SOLMIZATION.

Fauré, Gabriel Urbain: *b.* Pamiers, May 12, 1845; *d.* Paris, November 4, 1924. One of the most prominent late ROMANTIC French composers, Fauré was a student of SAINT-SAËNS. He was active as an organist (his last post being at the Madeleine) and was a highly influential teacher at the Paris Conservatoire. Among his students were RAVEL, ENESCO, and Boulanger. He became director of that school in 1905, retiring in 1920 because of deafness and ill health. Fauré excelled particularly in the smaller forms. Among the French, he is second only to DEBUSSY as a composer of songs, writing nearly 100, including the cycle *La Bonne Chanson.* His NOCTURNES, BARCAROLLES, IMPROMPTUS, PRELUDES, and other KEYBOARD works also rank highly. Fauré had a keen harmonic sense; he used the resources of late ROMANTIC HARMONY in fresh contexts and also anticipated some of the procedures of IMPRESSIONISM. Many of his melodies are cast in a modal idiom. His larger works include a REQUIEM, some CHAMBER MUSIC, the *Ballade* for piano and orchestra, and the incidental music to *Pelléas et Mélisande.* Fauré wrote also two OPERAS, sacred music, and miscellaneous orchestral and choral works.

Fauxbourdon (F): a 15th-century compositional TECHNIQUE employing two written parts—the lower either a sixth or octave beneath the upper—and one unwritten part which paralleled the uppermost part at the interval of a fourth below. *See* FABURDEN; FALSO BORDONE.

Feldpartie (G), **Feldpartita** (G): *a* DIVERTIMENTO for wind instruments or military band.

Fermata (I): see PAUSE.

Festa, Costanzo: *b.* Rome(?), *c.*1490; *d.* Rome, April 10, 1545. A prolific and important composer, Festa was a singer in the Papal Chapel from 1517. He was perhaps

the first native Italian MADRI-
GALIST and composed also
MOTETS, Vesper HYMNS, MAG-
NIFICATS, two MASSES, and
other sacred music, showing
a mastery of the Franco-
Flemish contrapuntal style.

Fiato (I): breath; *strumenti a
fiato,* wind instruments.

Fiddle: (1) loose term for various antecedents of the violin;
(2) slang for violin. *See* VIO-
LIN FAMILY.

Field, John: *b.* Dublin, July
26, 1782; *d.* Moscow, January 23, 1837. A descendant
of a family of musicians,
Field completed his studies
under CLEMENTI and was engaged by the latter to demonstrate pianos, first in London,
and then in France, Germany,
and Russia. Field remained in
Russia (1803–32). He wrote
chiefly for his instrument and
was the first to develop KEY-
BOARD.NOCTURNES. His singing melodic style influenced
that of CHOPIN.

Fife: a small flute, similar to
a piccolo but usually without
a key mechanism.

Fifth: an interval written by
skipping three alphabet letters
(e.g., *a♯-e, a-e, a-e♯*); unless
the augmented or diminished
form of the interval is specified, the perfect form is implied. Humming the first and
third notes of *Twinkle, Twinkle, Little Star* or *Dixie* will
produce the sound of a perfect fifth.

**Figured bass, Thorough bass,
Basso continuo** (I): an ACCOM-
PANIMENT consisting of a
BASS LINE and a set of Arabic
numerals indicating chords to
be added above it. (For technical details, *see* HARMONY.)
Such parts were written
largely during the BAROQUE
and are so characteristic of
the period that it has been
nicknamed "The Era of the
Thorough Bass." The part—
known also as a *basso continuo* or merely CONTINUO—
was performed on a keyboard
instrument (harpsichord or
organ) reinforced by one or
more bass instruments (cello,
double bass, bassoon, or even
lute). The term *continuo* may
refer to such an instrumental
combination as well as to the
part. A keyboard artist was
expected to supply the required chords when reading
at sight from a figured bass,
working the top notes of his
realization into a suitable melody. In modern editions, written realizations are often provided, though these incur a
loss of spontaneity and variety.

Filtz, Anton: *b. c.*1730; *d.*
Mannheim, March 1760. A
pupil of J. STAMITZ, Filtz became a cellist in the famed
Mannheim orchestra in 1754.
In his brief lifetime he contributed to the development
of the early CLASSICAL SYM-
PHONY, and he wrote more

than forty symphonies, as well as CONCERTOS and a quantity of CHAMBER MUSIC.

Final: the last note of a MELODY; the term is used especially with reference to melodies composed within the system of CHURCH MODES.

Finale (I): the concluding MOVEMENT of a multi-sectional work.

Finck, Heinrich: *b.* Bamberg(?), *c.*1445; *d.* Vienna, June 9, 1527. After spending his early maturity in Cracow, in the service of the Polish kings, Finck held posts in Stuttgart, Augsburg, Salzburg, and Vienna (music director to Ferdinand I). His polyphonic LIEDER, MASSES, and MOTETS show superior imagination and skill.

Fine (I): end. Many pieces end with the repetition of their initial sections. Since it is customary to indicate such repeats verbally rather than to write out the music in full, it is necessary to mark out the point of conclusion.

Fingerboard: a long strip of wood running beneath the strings of violins and related instruments; the fingers press the strings against the finger board to alter the vibrating length and thus obtain the desired PITCH.

Fingering: either the planned choice of finger and hand positions suitable to the playing of a given passage, or the written indications of this choice. The primary goals of proper fingering are: (1) the observance of correct PHRASING and tonal balance; (2) the minimization of mechanical problems through the avoidance of unnecessary displacements of the hand and needless use of weaker fingers. In KEYBOARD fingering, the thumb is numbered 1 and the other fingers, consecutively, 2-5. In fingerings for strings and WOODWINDS, the thumb is disregarded (or numbered 0) and the index finger is numbered 1.

Finney, Ross Lee: *b.* Wells, Minnesota, December 23, 1906. After completing his studies under Boulanger, BERG, and SESSIONS, Finney has been active on the faculties of Smith College and the University of Michigan. Elements of American folk songs appear in several of his works, including *Pilgrim Psalms* and *Barber Shop Ballad* (for ORCHESTRA). Finney has also employed SERIAL TECHNIQUES. His compositions include two CONCERTOS, STRING QUARTETS, piano sonatas and song cycles.

Fipple flute: a generic term for instruments similar to the RECORDER.

First-movement form: same as SONATA FORM.

Fischer, Johann Kaspar Ferdinand: *b. c.*1665; *d.* Rastatt,

March 27, 1746. Fischer, who served the margrave of Baden, was among influential German composers who assimilated French style. His collection of PRELUDES and FUGUES for organ, *Ariadne musica,* was a predecessor of Bach's *Well-Tempered Clavier.* He wrote also SUITES for KEYBOARD and for ORCHESTRA.

Five, The (The Mighty Five, The Mighty Handful): a nickname coined by the critic Stasov for BALAKIREV, BORODIN, CUI, MUSSORGSKY, and RIMSKY-KORSAKOV, who together championed the development of a national style in Russian music.

Flageolet: an instrument similar to a small RECORDER, but usually with a narrower bore. Double flageolets, with one mouthpiece and two tubes, are also known.

Flageolet tones: a seldom-used synonym for harmonics obtained on string instruments.

Flam: a pair of quick strokes on the snare drum.

Flamenco: the music and dances of Spanish gypsies.

Flat: (1) the sign, ♭, which calls for a PITCH a half step lower than that represented by an alphabet letter alone (e.g., *ab* is a half step lower than *a*); (2) the lowered pitch designated by means of the ♭; (3) an out-of-tune pitch an indeterminate distance lower than standard, brought about either by improper tuning or faulty performance.

Flautando (I), **Flautato** (I): a direction requiring either that string players bow near the bridge or that they play HARMONICS.

Flauto (I), **Flautone** (I): flute, bass flute, respectively. In BAROQUE SCORES, however, *flauto* indicates recorder, *flauto traverso* (or traversière), the flute. *Flauto piccolo* has changed similarly in meaning, formerly describing a small recorder, now, the piccolo.

Flicorno (I): BRASS INSTRUMENTS similar to the saxhorn and Flügelhorn.

Flöte (G): flute; Kleine Flöte, piccolo.

Flotow, Friedrich von: *b.* Teutendorf, Germany, April 26, 1812; *d.* Darmstadt, January 24, 1883. Although Flotow was a prominent OPERA composer of his day, his only lasting success was *Martha.* The son of a nobleman, Flotow studied in Paris with REICHA and was court director of music in Schwerin (1855–63).

Flue pipe: a class of ORGAN pipes with whistle-like construction.

Flügel (G): either a grand PIANO or a similarly shaped HARPSICHORD.

Flügelhorn (G): a family of BRASS INSTRUMENTS, or, more

specifically, the soprano member thereof.

Flute: a soprano WOODWIND instrument. The beaked or English flute is now referred to as a recorder.

Folia (S), **Follia** (I), **Folies d'Espagne** (F): a late RENAISSANCE or BAROQUE composition in variation form, based on a specific simple BASS LINE and written in triple METER.

Folk song: a vague term devolving upon two main concepts: (1) that the music so described gained such widespread popular acceptance that it became part of a people's oral tradition for a reasonable length of time; (2) that the authorship of this music is either unknown or disregarded. Often the application of the term is restricted —consciously or not—to music within or derived from the European cultural tradition. Since the folk performer is not concerned with adherence to a particular written form or with the inviolate preservation of the artistic creation of a particular individual, he is reasonably free to change many details of a given work; thus many folk songs survive in widely differing versions. The definition of the basic core of the folk song, that which should not be subject to change, is a personal one, varying from one singer to another. Most folk songs in current use are less than four centuries old, and many originated during the 19th century. There has been continuous interaction between folk and art music over the centuries, each contributing subtly to shape the other. Feelings of nationalism aroused during the 19th century led to an increased use of folk melodies in art music and to the imitation of folk styles in new compositions. Systematic efforts to collect folk melodies to prevent their future loss began in several countries near the turn of the 20th century. The musical materials of European folk song vary considerably. Extremely simple songs, including children's game songs, may be built on only three or four notes. Modes not customary in art music may be found in both the Balkans and Spain and microtones in the Balkans, but chromaticism is rare. STROPHIC construction predominates among European folk songs and there are frequently simple repetition patterns within the strophe. Metrical rhythms constitute the norm, although folk songs may contain several changes of METER. Rhythmic groupings of 5, 7, and larger prime numbers may be found in the Balkans, as well as irregular rhythms with beats of changing duration. Most songs are simple, relatively syllabic settings, but some Eastern European folk songs use small ORNAMENTS in profusion and a few folk songs, including some from Spain, are highly melismatic. While a few broad traits run through most European folk song, there are numerous differences of detail among various national styles.

Foot: a normal standard of length, used as an analogue for the designation of relative PITCHES. The analogue derives from practices observed in building ORGANS and is used most frequently in connection with that instrument. Notes sounding as written may be described as 8-foot tones; notes sounding an octave higher than written, two octaves higher, one octave lower, and two octaves lower would be described respectively as 4-, 2-, 16-, and 32-foot tones.

Foote, Arthur: *b.* Salem, Mass., March 5, 1853; *d.* Boston, April 8, 1937. A student of J. K. Paine, Foote received the first graduate degree (M.A.) in music granted in the United States. A skilled organist and pianist, Foote was among the more prominent American composers who worked in a lyrical ROMANTIC idiom. He wrote a variety of orchestral music, including a *Suite for Strings,* CHAMBER MUSIC, songs, vocal ENSEMBLE music, and church music.

Forlana (I): a lively, north Italian dance using dotted rhythms in 6/8 or 6/4 time, popular during the 18th century.

Form: (1) the organization of musical thought, obtained by the alternation of tension and repose; (2) a repetition pattern or a technical procedure in composition (e.g., CANON); (3) a loose synonym for medium or genre (e.g., OPERA).

Contrast between tension and repose may be obtained variously. In MELODY, notes of high register normally have greater tension than those of medium or low register. In RHYTHM, fast notes convey greater impulse than slow ones; unstressed notes suggest greater motion than stressed ones. In HARMONY or COUNTERPOINT, DISSONANCE implies tension, and CONSONANCE, repose. Passages that modulate from one key to another have greater impulse than those that remain within one key. In tonal music, the TONIC note and the tonic chord are the centers of response toward which all other notes and chords eventually flow. The degree to which music is impelled to move forward depends on the interaction of these various factors; particular combinations may result in the momentary negation of any one of these general principles.

The bulk of the music familiar to the average listener —the art music of 1700–1900, folk music, show music —exhibits a high degree of symmetry. Small units of regular size combine to form larger units; these are combined into still larger groups, and so forth. In a way, musical organization may be compared to the organization of a novel; there, related sentences form paragraphs; out of these arise chapters; and the chapters together form the book, which, if well written, displays a balance between unity and variety and a carefully proportioned set of climaxes.

The smallest complete unit of musical thought—akin to the sentence in literature—is known as a *phrase*. Like a sentence, the musical phrase may be built either as an indivisible whole or as a combination of two or more subdivisions. Subdivisions consisting of a few notes with a characteristic o u t l i n e are called *motives*. The most famous of these is the four-note cell that opens BEETHOVEN's *Fifth Symphony*. Below we show two motives from the opening of Beethoven's *Piano Sonata*, Op. 2, No. 2.

The most common organization of music proceeds according to powers of 2. That is, small groups containing two primary stresses combine into medium ones of four primary stresses; these in turn, combine into ever larger groups of eight, sixteen, and thirty-two stresses. In musical NOTATION, primary stresses are preceded by BAR-LINES, which recur regularly every few units of time. The above figures may therefore be stated in terms of MEASURES (= bars) instead of stresses. However, bar-lines do not necessarily mark the opening or conclusion of a musical thought. M a n y phrases begin and/or end in

the middle of a measure (i.e., the unstressed portion).

The average phrase consists of four or eight measures; a period consists of two phrases, a double period of four. Much dance music and music derived from dances is so constructed. On the other hand, there are instances in which the unit of construction is either three measures (the "broom theme" in DUKAS' *Sorcerer's Apprentice*) or five (the opening of the "St. Anthony Chorale" used in BRAHMS' *Variations*, Op. 56a). One way of avoiding monotony of phrase length is to use a deceptive CADENCE to prolong a phrase.

Contrapuntal compositions are usually much less regular in structure than homophonic ones. Analysis in terms of phrases, periods, and double periods has only limited application.

Most familiar music depends on repetition, literal or varied, for clarity and unity. Exceptions to this rule usually are either small works or small sections of larger works. Literal repetition involving melody, rhythm, and harmony is normally very obvious, but varied repetition or repetition involving only one of the three musical elements mentioned may be so subtle that a listener who has not studied the score may be unaware of its presence. Repetition may concern either the treatment of details or the overall "architectural structure." (*See also* DEVELOPMENT; VARIATION.)

One of the simplest repetitive schemes involves the use of two phrases of parallel construction. The first has an incomplete ending; the second begins in the same fashion as the first, but proceeds to a more positive termination. Paired phrases such as these are known as question and answer, antecedent and consequent, or *ouvert* (open) and *clos* (closed). Larger structures can be based on an expansion of this principle.

The number of repetitive patterns and technical procedures falling within the second meaning given for form is so large and varied that a fully satisfactory classification is difficult to achieve. One that has attained some currency distinguishes between simple (= single) and compound forms. The latter, including SONATA, SYMPHONY, CONCERTO, SUITE, MASS, CANTATA, and ORATORIO, consist of a number of semi-independent sections called MOVEMENTS. The simple (or single) forms consist of the individual movements themselves and of independent works that are not divided into self-sufficient sections.

This category may be further divided into *continuation forms* and *sectional forms*. The former either involve little or no large-scale repetition or else are based on the contrapuntal elaboration of one or more THEMES. The latter, as implied by the heading, are built from two or more small sections. One must bear in mind that the division lines in this system are by no means hard and fast. A FUGUE, for example, is normally classed as a continuation form; however, one may find reason to view it as a sectional form if one focuses attention on its contrasts between subject statements and episodes.

Sectional forms are of three main varieties: (1) VARIATION FORMS, (2) BINARY FORMS, and (3) TERNARY FORMS. In musical shorthand, the sections are represented by alphabet letters, a different letter being used for each section having individual content. Varied repetition of a section is indicated by a prime (′). The schema *A B A′* would denote a three-part work whose third section is a variation of the first and whose middle section forms a contrast to the outer two. The system is useful, but hardly precise. It does not indicate either comparative lengths or the degree of de-

tail represented. The schema *A A B* could be used either for a large work in three equal sections or for the setting of an eight-line poem in which the *A* sections consist of two lines each and the *B* section of four lines. The schema *A B A* might represent the details of a small three-part work, or it could represent the overall plan of works that might be described in greater detail as *AB CDC AB* or *ABA C ABA. See also* CHACONNE, PRELUDE, RONDO, TOCCATA.

Forte (I): loud (*F*); fortissimo (I), very loud (*FF*); fortississimo (I), extremely loud (*FFF*); forte-piano (I), a forceful attack, followed by an immediate drop in volume on the same tone (*FP*); mezzo forte (I), medium loud (*mF*).

Fortepiano: obsolete name for the piano.

Forzando (I): strongly accented (*fz*).

Foss, Lukas: *b.* Berlin, August 15, 1922. After coming to the United States when fifteen, Foss completed his training at the Curtis Institute. He has been active as pianist, conductor, teacher, and composer. His style is basically TONAL. His works include CONCERTOS, SYMPHONIES and other orchestral music, CHAMBER MUSIC, sacred and secular CANTATAS, a BALLET, and two OPERAS (one based on Mark Twain's story *The Jumping Frog*). Foss has also been actively interested in the development of group improvisations in modern idiom.

Foster, Stephen Collins: *b.* Lawrenceville (Pittsburgh), Pa., July 4, 1826; *d.* New York City, January 13, 1864. Foster worked for his brother as an accountant before devoting himself to music. His first success, *Oh, Susanna!*, was written in 1848. Other favorites include *Old Folks at Home (Swanee Ribber)*, *My Old Kentucky Home*, *Jeanie with the Light Brown Hair*, and *Beautiful Dreamer*. He usually wrote both lyrics and music for his songs, which number 189. He wrote also a dozen instrumental works in the salon style then popular.

Fourth: an interval notated by skipping two alphabet letters (e.g., *c♯-f, c-f, c-f♯*); unless the augmented or diminished form of the interval is specified, the perfect form is implied. Humming the first two notes of *Taps, Reveille,* or *Auld Lang Syne* will illustrate the sound of a perfect fourth. The augmented fourth is also known as a *tritone.*

Françaix, Jean: *b.* Le Mans, May 23, 1912. A pupil of Boulanger, Françaix ranks prominently among modern French NEOCLASSICAL composers. He displays the wit and clarity of traditional Gallic spirit, but not necessarily depth. His works include BALLETS and OPERAS, an ORATORIO, a SYMPHONY, a piano CONCERTO, and miscellaneous CHAMBER and CHORAL MUSIC.

Franck, César Auguste: *b.* Liège, December 10, 1822; *d.* Paris, November 8, 1890; influential Belgian-French composer, organist, and teacher.

Franck was trained at the Liège and Paris Conservatories. After 1843 he lived in Paris, where he was choirmaster (1853) and then organist (1858–90) at St. Clotilde. In 1872 he became professor of organ at the Paris Conservatory; in this capacity Franck influenced many French composers of the following generation, including D'INDY, CHAUSSON, and DUPARC.

Like BRUCKNER, Franck matured slowly as a composer; his finest works were written after he reached 50. His style combines a French respect for FORM and TECHNIQUE with a sonorous and rich harmonic idiom. Although he wrote four SYMPHONIC POEMS, *Les Éolides, Le Chasseur maudit, Les Djinns,* and *Psyché*, Franck avoided programmatic extremes. He is best known for his works in classical forms: his Symphony in D minor, the *Variations symphoniques* (for piano and orchestra), STRING QUARTET, piano quintet, and violin SONATA. In these he sought to strengthen unity through the use of related thematic material among the v a r i o u s movements. Among his major piano works are the *Prélude, choral, et fugue* and the *Prélude, aria, et final.* His organ works, including the *3 Chorales,* rank high in the ROMANTIC repertoire for that instrument. Franck composed also five ORATORIOS — including *Rédemption* and *Les Béatitudes*—miscellaneous church music, and two OPERAS, now forgotten.

French horn: a BRASS INSTRUMENT of circular shape.

Frescobaldi, Girolamo: *b.* Ferrara, September 1583; *d.* Rome, March 1, 1643; brilliant organist and KEYBOARD composer.

After studying with LUZ-ZASCHI in Ferrara, Frescobaldi visited Flanders briefly before becoming organist at St. Peter's in Rome. He occupied this post from 1608 to 1628, taking leave to become organist to the grand duke of Tuscany for six years. He returned to St. Peter's in 1634, remaining there until his death.

Best known for his organ and clavier works (TOCCATAS, RICERCARS, CANZONAS, CAPRICCIOS, etc.), Frescobaldi wrote also MADRIGALS, ARIAS, two MASSES and other sacred works, and instrumental ENSEMBLE music. He handled masterfully free imitative COUNTERPOINT as well as elaborations of Gregorian melodies; he had a fine feeling for chromaticism and for the virtuoso resources of the keyboard. Frescobaldi's prefaces to his works are rich sources of information about his performance style.

Fret: one of a series of narrow, transverse strips fixed to the fingerboards of certain string instruments. The frets mark the string lengths necessary for the various notes, thus making it simpler to obtain correct PITCH through accurate stopping. On fretted instruments there is no tonal difference between stopped notes and open ones. Frets are now made either of wood or metal (formerly they consisted of gut ties).

Friska (H), **Friss** (H): the fast section of a CSÁRDÁS.

Froberger, Johann: *b.* Stuttgart, May 18, 1616; *d.* Héricourt, France, May 7, 1667. A student of FRESCOBALDI, Froberger spent several periods as court organist in Vienna and then entered the service of the Duchess Sybille of Württemberg. One of the foremost KEYBOARD composers of his day, Froberger helped establish the standard form for the BAROQUE SUITE. He also wrote TOCCATAS, FANTASIAS, CANZONAS, and RICERCARS.

Frog: *see* NUT (1).

Frottola (I): (1) a generic term for a group of STROPHIC songs of light content popular in Italy around the turn of the 16th century. Most *frottole* are marked by simple HARMONIES and incisive RHYTHMS; they are generally in four voice-parts. Performance by vocal soloist accompanied by instruments and by vocal ENSEMBLE is possible; some *frottole* were written for VOICE and lute. The frottola was a forerunner of the 16th-century MADRIGAL. (2) One of the specific poetic forms comprehended under (1).

Fuga (L): (1) FUGUE; (2) in RENAISSANCE usage, CANON.

Fugato (I): a section of a non-fugal work in which a THEME is developed through a set of imitative entries.

Fughetta (I): a short FUGUE.

Fugue: a contrapuntal work for two or more voices that develops a main subject by means of several series of imitations. Fugal procedures are so variable, even within the works of individual masters, that one cannot speak of fugal FORM either in the sense of a fixed repetition pattern, a fixed sequence of events, or a fixed tonal scheme. Though certain norms may be outlined, there are exceptions to each, the nature of any given fugue being determined in large part by the nature of the subject.

The voices of a fugue enter normally one by one with statements of the subject, usually based alternately on the TONIC and DOMINANT degrees. The initial set of entries is known as an *exposition.* Sections of the fugue not presenting the subject in full are termed *episodes.* These may either be freely conceived or derived from thematic material; often they modulate from one key to another. The development of the fugue consists of an alternation between episodes and reappearances of the subject in one or more voices. Occasionally a fugue may be so tightly knit that episodes are dispensed with.

In the exposition, it is normal for each entry to await the completion of the subject in the previous voice. When the first voice has finished its presentation of the subject, it continues with a countermelody to the entry of the subject in the second voice. This process is repeated until all voices are employed simultaneously. After this, individual voices may rest from time to time during the remainder of the fugue. Thickness of texture need not remain constant. If the first countermelody to the subject recurs consistently in conjunction with later statements of the subject, it is known as a countersubject. Occasionally two statements of the subject will occur in a single voice during the course of an exposition. The second of these is known as a redundant entry.

The entries of the subject that are based on the dominant are known as answers. If the tonic statement of the subject features prominently both the tonic and dominant degrees, the INTERVAL pattern of the answer may vary slightly from that of the subject in order to reinforce a sense of tonality. That is, the answer may employ the dominant degree where the tonic occurs in the subject, and the tonic degree where the dominant occurs. Thus some patterns occupying a range of a fifth in the subject may be compressed to a fourth in the answer, while others having a range of a fourth may expand to a fifth. Such answers are known as *tonal* answers, exact ones as *real*.

In fugal development, the subject may occur in INVERSION, AUGMENTATION, or DIMINUTION. One entry may begin while the previous one is still in progress. Such a procedure is known as a *stretto* and is employed for heightened dramatic effect. In order to reach a final climax, the composer may briefly abandon normal part-writing and introduce a quasi-rhapsodic, virtuoso passage. Some fugues may develop two subjects (double fugues) and others even three (triple fugues).

The instrumental CANZONA and RICERCAR, which derived from imitative vocal forms of the 16th century, are the predecessors of the fugue. This form originated during the BAROQUE and reached its zenith in the works of J. S. BACH. Though many later masters wrote fugues—particularly HAYDN and BEETHOVEN—the form is not characteristic of either the CLASSICAL or ROMANTIC periods. (However, the use of fugue remained traditional for certain sections of the MASS.) Composers' interest in linear forces in the present century has kept alive some interest in further use of fugal procedures.

Fugues have been written for many media—CHORUS, ORCHESTRA, CHAMBER ENSEMBLES, etc. The largest single segment of the repertoire is intended for KEYBOARD performance: organ, harpsichord, or piano. Though best known as an independent piece or coupled with an introductory PRELUDE, the fugue may also constitute a movement in a SONATA, chamber work, SYMPHONY, Mass, cantata, oratorio, or even OPERA.

Fuguing tune: a colonial American or 18th-century English HYMN tune in a setting employing IMITATION.

Fundamental bass: the root of a CHORD, or a line formed by the roots of a series of chords. The latter may be a purely theoretical line inasmuch as any given chord may employ the root in a central or upper position rather than in the lowest.

Fuoco (I): fire.

Furiant: a lively Czech dance in triple METER, with shifting accent patterns.

Furniture: an ORGAN mixture.

Futurism: an Italian movement of the 1910s (initiated by F. T. Marinetti, Francesco Pratella, and Luigi Rossolo) advocating a heavy use of various noises in composition.

Fux, Johann Joseph: *b.* Hirtenfeld, Austria, 1660; *d.* Vienna, February 14, 1741. Active in Vienna from 1696, Fux was appointed to successively more important posts, becoming music director to the emperor in 1715. He was best known as the author of the treatise *Gradus ad Parnassum*, which furnished the cornerstone for the teaching of COUNTERPOINT for more than two centuries. A prolific and highly esteemed composer, Fux wrote many MASSES, as well as REQUIEMS, MOTETS, ORATORIOS, OPERAS (e.g., *Costanzo e fortezza*), ensemble SUITES and SONATAS, keyboard and orchestral works.

G

Gabrieli, Andrea: *b.* Venice, *c.*1520; *d.* Venice, 1586. Reputedly a pupil of WILLAERT, Andrea Gabrieli became second organist at St. Mark's, Venice, in 1564, and first organist in 1585. He was an eminent performer and an influential teacher. He was equally adept at writing sacred and secular music, vocal music such as MASSES, MOTETS, PSALMS, and MADRIGALS, and instrumental music such as RICERCARS, CANZONAS, and SONATAS. His mature madrigals usher in the final period in the Italian development of that form; they are more homophonic, dramatic, and declamatory than earlier examples. Several madrigal passages are set as dialogues, contrasting two groups of VOICES.

Gabrieli, Giovanni: *b.* Venice, 1557(?); *d.* Venice, August 12, 1612, nephew and pupil of ANDREA GABRIELI and teacher of SCHÜTZ and Michael PRAETORIUS. Although Giovanni Gabrieli was second organist at St. Mark's from 1585 to his death, he was not famed as a performer. He brought the development of the Venetian POLYCHORAL tradition of WILLAERT to great heights, often writing for mixed groups of VOICES and instruments. One of the early composers to specify instrumentation (but not consistently), he contributed to the developing sense of TONE COLOR. His MADRIGALS include examples of both the traditional polyphonic, vocal style and the new monodic style using BASSO CONTINUO. He wrote also MOTETS, MAGNIFICATS, SONATAS, TOCCATAS, RICERCARS, and FANTASIAS. His CANZONAS are quite popular among brass players.

Gade, Niels (Wilhelm): *b.* Copenhagen, February 22, 1817; *d.* Copenhagen, December 21, 1890. The leading Danish ROMANTIC composer, Gade was also a conductor and violinist. He was associated with MENDELSSOHN in Leipzig. His music shows the influence of Mendelssohn and SCHUMANN as well as that of Danish FOLK MUSIC. His compositions include 8 SYMPHO-

NIES, OVERTURES, miscellaneous CHAMBER MUSIC, short pieces and a SONATA for piano, songs, and CANTATAS.

Gagliarda (I), Gaillarde (F): GALLIARD.

Galant: *see* STYLE GALANT.

Galanterien (G): a generic term for the optional dance movements appearing in many BAROQUE SUITES. These include the minuet, bourrée, passepied, gavotte, and numerous others.

Galilei, Vincenzo: *b.* Florence, *c.*1520; *d.* Florence, June 1591. A lutenist, composer, and theorist, Galilei was active chiefly in Florence. As a member of the CAMERATA, he contributed—both in his treatises and his madrigals—to the development of accompanied SOLO song in declamatory style. He was the father of the famous scientist, Galileo Galilei.

Galliard: a lively dance in triple METER; it was frequently used in the 16th and early 17th century as a sequel to the slower PAVANE.

Galop (F): a lively dance in duple METER, popular in the 19th century.

Galuppi, Baldassare: *b.* Burano, October 18, 1706; *d.* Venice, January 3, 1785. A pupil of LOTTI, Galuppi was active in Venice, where he was director at the Ospizio dei Mendicanti and later music director at St. Mark's and at the Conservatorio dei Incurabili. As a successful OPERA composer, he traveled widely, spending periods at Turin, London, and at St. Petersburg, where he did much for Russian music. Especially noted as a composer of comic operas, Galuppi wrote also numerous MASSES, MOTETS, ORATORIOS and other sacred music, CANTATAS, SONATAS, SYMPHONIES, and a few CHAMBER works and CONCERTOS.

Gamba: short for viola da gamba.

Gamut: (1) the note, G (bottom line of the bass CLEF), the lowest note of the MEDIEVAL musical system; (2) the key of G (rare, obsolete); (3) the complete range of a voice or instrument.

Gapped scale: a scale employing INTERVALS of a minor third or larger.

Gastoldi, Giovanni Giacomo: *b.* Caravaggio, *c.*1550; *d.* unknown, 1622. Music director at the ducal chapel of Santa Barbara in Mantua (1582–1608), Gastoldi composed much sacred music, as well as a small quantity of instrumental music. He is best known, however, for his spirited BALLETTI and MADRIGALS.

Gavotte: a French dance of the 17th and 18th centuries in moderately quick duple METER, beginning usually on the second half of the measure. The gavotte is one of the more frequently employed optional movements of a SUITE.

Gebrauchsmusik (G): (1) 20th-century music intended for performers of average skill and for unsophisticated audiences. The term is often translated as "workaday music" or "utility music." The music itself avoids both extreme technical demands and the more advanced compositional procedures employed in some contemporaneous music. HINDEMITH has written a number of works falling under this heading, as have other composers, including KRENEK. (2) The term often refers to music for use in church, school, factory, etc., to "applied music" in general.

Gedämpft (G): muted.

Geige (G): violin, fiddle.

Geminiani, Francesco: *b.* Lucca, December 1687; *d.* Dublin, September 17, 1762. A student of CORELLI and A. SCARLATTI, Geminiani was active principally in London, Paris, and Dublin. He was one of the great violin virtuosos of his day, extending the technique of his instrument. He wrote the first known violin method and composed trio and solo SONATAS and CONCERTI GROSSI for strings.

Generalbass (G): thorough bass, FIGURED BASS.

Generalpause (G): one or more measures of RESTS for the entire ensemble (abbreviated G.P.).

German flute: the present transverse flute. *See also* ENGLISH FLUTE.

Gershwin, George: *b.* Brooklyn, N.Y., September 26, 1898; *d.* Beverly Hills, Calif., July 11, 1938. One of the most imaginative composers of popular music of the 1920s and '30s, Gershwin sought also to join elements of JAZZ with those of the European symphonic tradition. His major works in this direction include the *Rhapsody in Blue,* the *Piano Concerto in F, An American in Paris,* and the OPERA *Porgy and Bess.* These reveal a rich melodic and rhythmic sense that is unmistakably American in idiom.

Gestopft (G): 'stopped; a direction to French horn players to insert the hand into the bell in order to mute the tone.

Gesualdo, Don Carlo, Prince of Venosa: *b.* Naples, *c.*1560; *d.* Naples, September 8, 1613. A fine performer on the archlute and a friend of the poet Tasso, Gesualdo is known for the extraordinary chromatic progressions and emotionalism found in his MADRIGALS. His sacred music includes two volumes of MOTETS and one of RESPONSORIES.

Gibbons, Orlando: *b.* Oxford, December 1583; *d.* Canterbury, June 5, 1625. Trained at King's College, Cambridge, Gibbons was organist at the Chapel Royal from 1605, and at Westminster Abbey from 1623. He contributed significantly to the development of the verse ANTHEM; Gibbons was also an important composer of keyboard and instrumental ensemble music and wrote many fine MADRIGALS.

Gigue (F), **Giga** (I): jig, a lively dance in 6/8 time (or an equivalent), originating apparently in the British Isles in the late 16th century. By the 17th century, the *Gigue* became the last of the four standard dances found in most SUITES. Whereas the ALLEMANDE, COURANTE, and SARABANDE employed contrapuntal devices only rarely, the *Gigue* often made prominent use of imitation.

Ginastera, Alberto: *b.* Buenos Aires, April 11, 1916. The leading Argentinian composer of the 20th century, Ginastera has employed both traditional folk idioms and avant-garde procedures in his work. The colorful OPERA *Bomarzo* uses chance elements. Other works include a second opera, a CANTATA for soprano and 53 percussion instruments, a

SYMPHONY and a CONCERTO, CHAMBER and KEYBOARD MUSIC, and songs.

Giocoso (I): playful, joking.

Gioioso (I): joyous.

Giordano, Umberto: *b.* Foggia, August 27, 1867; *d.* Milan, November 12, 1948. Giordano's *Andrea Chenier* established his place as a prominent composer of veristic OPERA (*see* VERISMO). *Madame Sans-Gêne* is the best of his other nine operas, which are of uneven merit.

Giusto (I): a TEMPO designation meaning either meet and proper or strict (i.e., unfluctuating).

Glass harmonica: a series of concentric glass bowls of graded sizes, fixed to a common axle and turned by a treadle mechanism. The instrument was perfected by Benjamin Franklin. The friction of the moving bowl against the moistened fingers of the player produces sound. Works for this instrument were written by HASSE and MOZART.

Glazunov, Alexander Konstantinovich: *b.* St. Petersburg, August 10, 1865; *d.* Paris, March 21, 1936. A pupil of RIMSKY-KORSAKOV, Glazunov was appointed instructor at the St. Petersburg Conservatory in 1899 and director in 1905. From 1882– 1910 he wrote prolifically in all traditional genres except opera; his later works are few in number. His music displays nationalistic elements combined with others drawn from the music of LISZT and WAGNER. His violin CONCERTO, the SYMPHONIC POEMS *Stenka Rasin* and *The Kremlin,* and the BALLET *Raymonda,* are among his better known works.

Glee: a vocal work that is normally comparatively short, for men's VOICES alone, in HARMONIC STYLE, and with sectional contrasts. While the term occurs as early as 1652, the form flourished particularly in England from the mid-18th to the early 19th centuries. During that period several societies were formed for the composition and performance of glees, CATCHES, and other vocal part music. Glee clubs popular in U.S. colleges were concerned at first with various kinds of popular entertainments; after World War I, these organizations devoted themselves more and more to the performance of better CHORAL music.

Glière, Reinhold Moritsovich, *b.* Kiev, January 11, 1875; *d.* Moscow, June 23, 1956. A conservative and nationalistic composer, Glière was trained by Arensky, Taneyev, and Ippolitov-Ivanov. He was active on the faculties of the Kiev and Moscow Conservatories, PROKOFIEV being one of his pupils. He studied and collected melodies of the Asiatic regions of the USSR and used these in his music. The works by Glière that are best known in the West are the SYMPHONY *Ilya Murometz,* the BALLET *The Red Poppy,* and some songs and piano pieces.

Glinka, Mikhail Ivanovich: *b.* Novosspaskoye, June 1, 1804; *d.* Berlin, February 15, 1857. The son of a wealthy family, Glinka was given a fine education. As a young man, he continued his studies in Italy and Germany. His two completed OPERAS, *A Life for the Tsar* (now known as *Ivan Sussanin*), and *Russlan and Ludmilla,* were the first works written with the intent to create a nationalistic Russian idiom. The symphonic poem *Kamarinskaya* incorporates FOLK SONG elements. Other works by Glinka include sketches for unfinished operas, miscellaneous orchestral works (OVERTURES, dances, a SYMPHONY, etc.), CHAMBER and KEYBOARD MUSIC, songs, and CHORUSES.

Glissando (I): a scale or glide performed with great rapidity, often involving a special technique. On the piano, a glissando is executed by sweeping the nail of either the thumb or other fingers (normally the second and third) across the white keys with firm pressure. (The choice of fingering depends upon the direction of the glissando.) On rare occasions a black-key glissando or a glissando in parallel intervals may be employed. On the harp, the fingers are drawn rapidly across the strings. A violinist may obtain a glissando either through a series of rapid shifts or by smoothly drawing a finger up or down the string. Some writers prefer to exclude the latter effect, together with the trombone slide and the woodwind glissando (obtained by a combination of finger technique and varying lip pressure) from a more restrictive definition of glissando.

Glocken (G): bells.

Glockenspiel (G): a percussion instrument consisting of a set of thin steel bars of graded sizes arranged on a horizontal frame in a manner resembling a KEYBOARD. (The bars corresponding to the black keys are on the same level, but further back than the others.) The player normally uses sticks with globular wooden heads. The portable form of glockenspiel used by marching bands is known as a bell-lyre. In the 18th century, a form of glockenspiel similar to the CELESTA was employed—i.e., the instrument was equipped with a keyboard.

Gloria (L): (1) the second section of the MASS ORDINARY; (2) the doxology (*Gloria Patri*) sung following a psalm or canticle.

Gluck, Christoph Willibald: *b.* Erasbach, July 2, 1714; *d.* Vienna, November 15, 1787; outstanding composer of CLASSICAL OPERA. He received early musical training in local villages and probably continued his studies in Prague where he earned a living playing violin and cello. In the service of Prince Melzi he had the opportunity to go to Italy and to study under SAMMARTINI. From 1741 to 1745 he produced several OPERAS in various Italian cities. During the next four years he was active in London, Hamburg, Leipzig, Dresden, and Copenhagen. Gluck married in 1750 and made Vienna his principal residence thereafter, except for the years 1773–79, which were spent in Paris. He was associated with the musical establishment of the Prince of Sachsen-Hildburghausen and wrote operas for the Viennese court.

Gluck's talents matured slowly. *Orfeo ed Euridice* (1762), *Alceste* (1767), *Paride ed Elena* (1770), *Iphigénie en Aulide* (1774), *Armide* (1777), and *Iphigénie en Tauride* (1779) are the greatest of his more than

100 operas. In these late works to libretti by Calzabigi, Gluck turned from the traditional virtuoso quality of Italian opera, moving toward a simpler style with greater dramatic coherence. The influence of French tastes in Vienna led to the inclusion of CHORAL and BALLET sections in these works. Gluck's masterpieces influenced the works of later Classical and early ROMANTIC composers — including those of HAYDN, MOZART, and BEETHOVEN. In addition to operas, Gluck wrote BALLETS (the most successful being *Don Juan*), 11 SYMPHONIES, 7 TRIOS, a set of songs, *De profundis* (for chorus and orchestra), and other works.

Goldmark, Carl: *b.* Hesztheley, Hungary, May 18, 1830; *d.* Vienna, January 2, 1916. After completing his training at the Vienna Conservatory, Goldmark was active as a teacher and critic. He composed six OPERAS, the most successful being *The Queen of Sheba;* several OVERTURES (including *Sakuntala*); the SYMPHONY *The Rustic Wedding*, and other orchestral music; and an assortment of CHAMBER MUSIC, songs, and choral and keyboard compositions.

Gombert, Nicolas: *b.* southern Flanders, *c.*1490; *d.* Tournai(?), *c.*1560. A member of the imperial chapel of Charles V from 1526, Gombert possibly studied with JOSQUIN and continued the contrapuntal tradition of the latter at a time when Parisian and Italian composers were writing more and more in chordal texture. He is best known for his MOTETS, although he is equally gifted as a writer of MASSES, MAGNIFICATS, and CHANSONS.

Gong, tam-tam: a percussion instrument of indefinite PITCH, consisting of a large circular bronze plate with a turned rim a few inches deep. The gong is suspended in upright position and is struck with a felt or leather-covered beater. Gongs are made in several sizes.

Gopak: *see* HOPAK.

Gorgia (I): improvised vocal ornaments customary in performances around the turn of the 17th century.

Gossec, Francois Joseph: *b.* Vergnies, Belgium, January 17, 1734; *d.* Paris, February 16, 1829. During a long and successful career in Paris, Gossec served in the orchestra of La Pouplinière, was music director for the Prince of Condé, organized a concert society, was an associate director of the Paris Opéra, and taught at the Paris Conservatoire. He contributed significantly to the early development of the SYMPHONY and STRING QUARTET in France. From 1765 he devoted much of his energies to the composition of OPERAS. He wrote also a quantity of music celebrating the French Revolution. Gossec had a rich sense of color, and greatly expanded the normal French symphonic and choral forces, foreshadowing BERLIOZ's tastes in this direction.

Gottschalk, Louis Moreau: *b.* New Orleans, May 8, 1829; *d.* Rio de Janeiro, December 18, 1869. Trained in Paris, Gottschalk became a flamboyant piano virtuoso. Some of his several dozen piano pieces (e.g., *The Banjo Player*) have been revived since mid-century; his songs, SYMPHONIC POEMS, and two OPERAS contain Spanish idioms and helped establish a Latin American style.

Goudimel, Claude: *b.* Besançon, *c.*1514; *d.* Lyons, August 27, 1572. Known mainly for his settings of the Hugenot Psalter, Goudimel composed also MASSES, MAGNIFICATS, and MOTETS (before his conversion to Protestantism), together with excellent CHANSONS.

Gounod, Charles François: *b.* Paris, June 17, 1818; *d.* Paris, October 18, 1893. After study at the Paris Conservatoire, Gounod won the Prix de Rome in 1839. After his return he was active both as an organist and conductor. Gounod's fame rests on his masterpiece, the OPERA *Faust*. With the exception of *Roméo et Juliette* and *Mireille*, his other operas were unsuccessful. Gounod wrote a large quantity of sacred music in rich, ROMANTIC style. His *Ave Maria*, adapted from the first prelude of BACH's *Well-Tempered Clavier* has been exceptionally popular, together with the orchestral *Marche funèbre d'une Marionette*. Other works include two SYMPHONIES (and another for wind instruments), three STRING QUARTETS, piano pieces, and songs.

Grace: in 16th-century English usage, an ORNAMENT (e.g., trill, turn, mordent).

Grace note: an ornamental tone written as a small note; its time-value is dependent upon context, as is its position, either on or immediately preceding the BEAT.

Gradual: (1) a responsorial CHANT for soloist and choir constituting the second section of the PROPER of the MASS; (2) a book containing the GREGORIAN CHANTS for the Mass.

Grainger, Percy Aldridge: *b.* Melbourne, Australia, July 8, 1882; *d.* White Plains, N.Y., February 20, 1961. A concert pianist as well as composer, Grainger is known principally for his lively arrangements of

English FOLK TUNES. He has written for many different instrumental and vocal combinations.

Granados, Enrique: *b.* Lérida, July 1867; *d.* at sea, March 24, 1916. Trained at the Barcelona and Madrid Conservatories, Granados became a concert pianist and conductor and directed his own music school. One of the early nationalistic Spanish composers, Granados wrote his best works for the piano: *Goyescas* and the *Danzas españolas*. He also composed OPERAS, two SYMPHONIC POEMS and other orchestral works, CHAMBER MUSIC and songs.

Gran Cassa (I): bass drum.

Grand Choeur (F), **Grand Jeu** (F), **Grand Orgue** (F): full organ.

Grand Opéra (F): OPERA without spoken dialogue; in particular, 19th-century French operas with lavish settings.

Graun, Carl Heinrich: *b.* Wahrenbrück, May 7, 1704; *d.* Berlin, August 8, 1759. As music director to Frederick the Great, C. H. Graun was concerned primarily with the composition and production of Italian OPERA (both his own and by others); he was preeminent among his German contemporaries working in this area. Graun wrote also a large quantity of sacred music, including MASSES, a TE DEUM, a famous PASSION (*Der Tod Jesu*), MAGNIFICATS, etc., both sacred and secular CANTATAS, songs, and CONCERTOS and CHAMBER MUSIC.

Graun, Johann Gottlieb: *b.* Wahrenbrück, 1703(?); *d.* Berlin, October 27, 1771. Trained by Johann Georg Pisendel and TARTINI, J. G. Graun served as music director in Merseburg and then as concertmaster for the orchestra of Frederick the Great. He contributed to the development of the early Classical SYMPHONY and STRING QUARTET, writing other CHAMBER MUSIC, CONCERTOS, and some sacred music in addition.

Grave (I): slow and solemn.

Gravicembalo (I): HARPSICHORD.

Grazioso (I): gracefully.

Gregorian Chant (Plainsong, Plainchant): the unison melodies of the Catholic liturgy, some few thousand in number. According to its liturgical function, a CHANT may be sung by one or more soloists or by a CHOIR; responsorial chants alternate passages for soloist and for choir.

The liturgy, which comprises chiefly the MASS and the Daily Hours of Divine Service (the OFFICE), is the result of accumulated developments of many centuries. The earliest Christian services drew heavily upon Jewish tradition and liturgy; the

PSALMS are the largest single source of texts in Gregorian chant. Byzantine and other Near Eastern cultures also influenced the early development of chant.

During the period *c.*370 to *c.*600, several popes ordered codifications of the liturgy. The last of these was directed by Pope Gregory I (590–604), whose name is associated with the chant. According to tradition, the oldest of the chants in present use date back to Gregory's codification. The scarcity of musical documents from this era make it impossible to prove or disprove this tradition. Some scholars contend that the present form of the oldest chants arose over a century later. Most of the chants are anonymous; only a few written after 800, including HYMNS and ANTIPHONS, can be attributed to specific composers.

There is great stylistic variety to the chant. Its tonal realm—the eight CHURCH MODES—is capable of many more nuances than the major-minor system. Some chants are plain and severe, others jubilant bursts of energy. It is customary to distinguish between three kinds of settings: (1) *syllabic chants,* which have only one note per syllable; (2) *neumatic chants,* which use from one to four notes for each syllable; (3) *melismatic* chants, which employ groups of notes—from two to more than twenty—for each syllable, as in certain ALLELUIAS. In general, the chants for the Mass are more ornate than those for the Office, the responsorial chants being among the most ornate.

Another distinction between chants is based on the manner in which the MELODY was created. *Free melodies* are those newly composed for specific texts. *Type melodies,* on the other hand, are made to serve a group of texts by means of minor changes. *Centonized melodies* are constructed in mosaic fashion by assembling a number of standard formulas.

After the close of the Middle Ages, interest in the accurate preservation of the chant diminished sharply. The melodies became corrupt and the RHYTHM changed. The present form of the chant is the result of intensive efforts at restoration, carried out chiefly by the Solesmes monks. Present chant rhythm, which consists mainly of a succession of even values in very subtly articulated groups of twos and threes, represents their views on historically suitable performance. Although such performance does reflect late medieval practice—and produces results of great beauty—most scholars now agree that the earlier stages of chant employed two or three time-values in irregular alternation. *See also* MEDIEVAL MUSIC.

Gregorian Modes: *see* CHURCH MODES.

Grétry, André Ernest Modeste: *b.* Liège, February 11, 1741; *d.* Montmorency, September 24, 1813. After study in Rome (1759–66) Grétry went to Geneva and then, on the advice of Voltaire, to Paris (1768), where he quickly became the most successful composer of French OPERA of his generation. He was named to the Institut de France, was chosen Inspector of the Paris Conservatoire, and was named Chevalier of the Legion of Honor. He greatly influenced the further development of the *opéra comique*. Grétry wrote also some sacred music, CHAMBER MUSIC, a few piano SONATAS, and SYMPHONIES.

Grieg, Edvard Hagerup: *b.* Bergen, Norway, June 15, 1843; *d.* Bergen, September 4, 1907. Grieg's earliest musical training was provided by his mother; when fifteen, he entered the Leipzig Conservatory. In 1863 he went to Copenhagen for brief study with Niels Gade. There he met Rikard Nordraak, a young Norwegian composer who interested Grieg in the estab-lishment of a nationalistic style of composition. After Nordraak's early death, Grieg opened a Norwegian Academy of Music and gave concerts featuring Norwegian compositions. He also became conductor of the Christiana Harmonic Society. In 1867 Grieg married his cousin, Nina Hagerup, a fine singer. The success of his *Piano Concerto* and the incidental music to *Peer Gynt* led to the award of an annuity by the Norwegian government and to honors from England, France, and Sweden.

Grieg's numerous short piano pieces—e.g., the ten books of *Lyric Pieces*—and his songs represent him at his best. SCHUMANN, MENDELS-SOHN, and BRAHMS deeply influenced his style. In addition to the works cited above, Grieg wrote incidental music to *Sigurd Jorsalfar*, and a few CHAMBER and choral pieces.

Griffes, Charles Tomlinson: *b.* Elmira, N.Y., September 17, 1884; *d.* New York City, April 8, 1920. A student of HUMPERDINCK, Griffes was employed as a music teacher at the Hackley School for Boys in Tarrytown. His style was influenced particularly by DEBUSSY and RAVEL, and, to a lesser extent, by MUSSORG-SKY and SCRIABIN. His work may be loosely classed as IM-PRESSIONISTIC. Among his best known works are the SYMPHONIC POEM *The Pleasure Dome of Kubla Khan,* and the three *Roman Sketches* for piano, the first being *The White Peacock,* known also in an orchestral version. Griffes wrote also a number of songs and other piano pieces.

Grosse Caisse (F), **Grosse Trommel** (G): bass drum.

Ground (Ground bass, *Basso ostinato*): a BASS LINE, usually four or eight measures long, repeated constantly below one or more changing upper parts, these being either written or improvised. The resultant variation form might be termed a ground, division, *passacaglia,* *chaconne,* or *folía.* Ground basses were widely employed during the BAROQUE and may be found in ARIAS, choral movements, and instrumental works bearing titles that are not indicative of the formal technique involved.

Gruppo (I): an ORNAMENT, particularly a trill or turn (*grupetto*).

Guerrero, Francisco: *b.* Seville, 1528(?); *d.* Seville, November 8, 1599. Best known for his sacred works—MASSES, MOTETS, PSALMS, PASSIONS, MAGNIFICATS, etc.—Guerrero,

a pupil of MORALES, held posts in Jaén and Seville, but also traveled to Portugal, Italy, and Palestine.

Guidonian hand: a medieval teaching procedure in which each note but one of the then existing gamut was indicated by a special place on the instructor's hand and fingers. The device was named after Guido d'Arezzo.

Guitar: a plucked, fretted string instrument with a flat table, and back. The modern form employs six single strings, usually tuned *E, A, d, g, b, e'.* The RENAISSANCE guitar, somewhat smaller, narrower, and deeper, featured either four or five pairs of strings. Its forerunners were introduced to Spain by the Moors during the Middle Ages. The guitar is associated chiefly with FOLK and popular music, but there is a modest SOLO, CHAMBER, and orchestral repertoire for the instrument. BAROQUE literature for lute is often played on the guitar.

Gymel: a 15th-century term describing a still older English practice of two-part improvisational singing featuring extensive use of thirds and unisons.

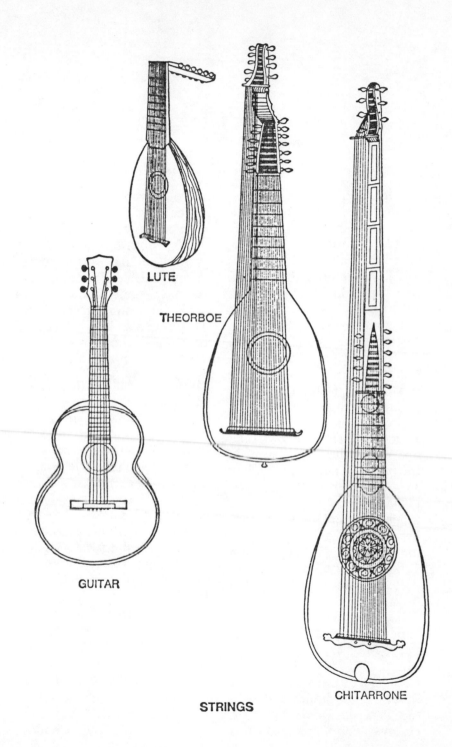

LUTE

THEORBOE

GUITAR

CHITARRONE

STRINGS

H

H: in German, the note B natural. (B, in German, indicates the note B flat.)

Hába, Alois: *b*. Vizovice, Czechoslovakia, June 21, 1893. An interest in Oriental music and in ideas put forth by BUSONI has led Hába to compose many works using quarter-tones and sixth-tones. Performances of Hába's MICROTONE music—including OPERAS, CHAMBER MUSIC, and KEYBOARD MUSIC—often make use of specially constructed instruments. Hába has also written much music in both a DIATONIC and a TWELVE-TONE style.

Habanera: a Cuban dance in moderate duple METER that became popular in Spain during the second half of the 19th century. It employs dotted and syncopated RHYTHMS.

Hackbrett (G): DULCIMER.

Halévy, Jacques François: *b*. Paris, May 27, 1799; *d*. Nice, March 17, 1862. Halévy was a student of CHERUBINI at the Paris Conservatoire and won the Prix de Rome in 1819. He was appointed professor of counterpoint and professor of composition at the Paris Conservatoire in 1833 and 1840. GOUNOD and BIZET were among his pupils. Among Halévy's numerous OPERAS, only *La Juive* achieved lasting recognition. He wrote also a few keyboard pieces and choral works.

Half close: *see* CADENCE.

Half note, half rest: ♩, ▬

Half step (Half tone, Semitone): the smallest INTERVAL commonly used in Western music. If written with consecutive alphabet letters, a half step is classed as a minor second. Its sound may be recalled by humming the first two notes of *White Christmas* or *The Londonderry Air*. Adjacent keys (black or white) of the piano form half steps.

Halling: an energetic Norwegian men's dance, usually in 2/4.

Hammerklavier (G): an obsolete German term for piano.

Handel, George Frideric (anglicized form of Georg Friedrich Händel): *b*. Halle, February 23, 1685; *d*. London,

April 14, 1759; great master of the late BAROQUE, famed for his ORATORIOS.

Handel's father, a barber-surgeon, intended a law career for his son; he provided the boy with musical training under Wilhelm Zachow only after much urging. After studying law briefly at the University of Halle, Handel became a violinist in Keiser's opera orchestra in Hamburg in 1703. In 1706 he left for Italy, where he became acquainted with the greatest Italian musicians of the day. In 1710 Handel was appointed music director to the elector of Hanover. Shortly thereafter, he received leave to produce an OPERA in London; he returned to Hanover, but requested another leave in 1712 for similar reasons. After the grant of an annuity by Queen Anne, Handel decided to remain in England. Royal favor was continued when his former master, the elector, became King George I of England. Handel served as music master to the daughters of the Prince of Wales and as music director to the duke of Chandos. However, from 1720 till his death, Handel was occupied chiefly with the production of his Italian operas and his oratorios. His fortunes alternately soared and plunged, owing to troubles with management, sing-ers, and rival companies, shifts in popular taste, and even side effects of political rivalries among the nobility.

STEFFANI, BUXTEHUDE, KEISER, and A. SCARLATTI, as well as Zachow, influenced Handel's early style. Handel turned early to the composition of opera, producing more than two score during the period, 1705–41. Of these, *Rinaldo, Il Pastor fido, Giulio Cesare, Sosarme,* and *Serse* are best known. Operatic style pervades the early Italian oratorios and the numerous Italian secular CANTATAS. While deftness in the treatment of the CHORUS appears at an early point in Handel's development, in the *St. John Passion* and settings of Latin sacred texts, Handel's greatest contributions in this medium date from his English period, including the Chandos AN-THEMS, the Coronation Anthems, two TE DEUMS, and especially the mature oratorios, beginning with *Saul* and *Israel in Egypt* (1738), and including Handel's best-known work, *Messiah* (1742), *Judas Maccabaeus,* and *Solomon.* While Handel's fame rests primarily on his vocal works, he produced much fine instrumental music, including three sets of harpsichord SUITES, solo and trio SONATAS, organ CONCERTOS, *concerti grossi,* and the well-known

Water Music, and *Fireworks Music.*

Handel was a fine keyboard artist and, like BACH, a master at IMPROVISATION. He was capable of composing with incredible speed. His music does not display the concentration and the occupation with thematic and technical development that characterizes Bach's music; it has instead a great flair for the dramatic. Handel used his German contrapuntal training to advantage in developing the English choral tradition in his oratorios. However, his style is based mainly on the Italian practices that gained international currency in his day. While often using either his own works or those of others as points of departure for new movements (and occasionally transferring entire movements almost intact), Handel was still a highly original composer. He surpassed his colleagues in melodic invention, in rhythmic and harmonic daring, and in a feeling for orchestral and vocal colors.

Hanson, Howard: *b.* Wahoo, Neb., October 28, 1896. After completing his studies at Northwestern University, Hanson taught at the College of the Pacific. In 1924 he became director of the Eastman School of Music in Rochester, holding that post until 1965. Hanson is a leading exponent of the ROMANTIC tradition, being much influenced by SIBELIUS. He has written five SYMPHONIES, SYMPHONIC POEMS and CONCERTOS, CHAMBER and KEYBOARD MUSIC, CHORUSES, songs, a BALLET, and an OPERA. He has been influential both as a teacher and conductor.

Hardanger fiddle: a Norwegian string instrument similar to the violin, but with four additional sympathetic strings.

Harfe (G): harp.

Harmonica: (1) the mouth organ or mouth harmonica is a wind instrument employing free, metal REEDS set into a very thin, small box. These are each set into a narrow channel and the player moves the instrument across his lips in order to direct the airflow into the desired channel, while masking out the others. Alternately blowing and sucking air into and from a single channel will produce tones a second apart. Harmonicas are made in different sizes and with different technical devices. They have achieved considerable vogue at times in the United States. The prototypes for present instruments were devised by Buschmann in 1821–22. (2) In French and German usage, a generic term for keyboard instruments, such as the ACCORDION and CELESTA, without either strings or pipes. *See also* GLASS HARMONICA.

Harmonics: (1) tones, at best

barely audible, representing the partial vibrations of a sounding medium (*see* ACOUSTICS; TONE COLOR); (2) light-bodied sounds obtainable on instruments of the VIOLIN FAMILY and the harp by touching a string at one of the simple fractional points (1/2, 1/3, 1/4, or 1/5) when playing. They may be played both on an open string (natural harmonics) and on a stopped string (artificial harmonics). The latter sort require that the touching finger be placed a fourth above the stopping one. In NOTATION, either a normal note may indicate the placement of the stopping finger, coupled with a diamond-shaped note immediately above to indicate the placement of the touching finger, or the desired PITCH may be indicated directly, together with a tiny circle placed above to indicate that it is to be played as a harmonic.

Harmonium: a small organ with free, metal REEDS and a bellows worked either by the feet of the player or electrically. (Also known as a *reed organ* or *house organ*.)

Harmony: (1) the theory of CHORD structures and functions; also, a course of instruction seeking to impart this theory; (2) the art of chord progression; (3) a generic designation for all music employing different sounds simultaneously; (4) in early medieval usage, a term synonymous with music; (5) a vague equivalent of CONSONANCE. Only the first two of these meanings will be discussed here.

Traditional harmonic theory is a legacy of the BAROQUE. It received its most important codification in the writings of RAMEAU, but continued to undergo modification until after the turn of the 20th century, at which time the gulf between the codified procedures and new techniques of composition deepened radically. The static unit of this theory is the chord, traditionally set for four VOICES: soprano, alto, tenor, and bass.

A chord may be founded on any degree of the SCALE and is identified either by the number of the degree or its name. The primary chords of each key are those on the first (*tonic*), fourth (*subdominant*), and fifth (*dominant*) degrees. These chords together contain all the notes of a key and often suffice for the harmonization of simple melodies. Secondary chords on the second (*supertonic*), third (*mediant*), and sixth (*submediant*) degrees share two of the three notes of the subdominant, dominant, and tonic chords, respectively, and are often considered as their subsidiaries. The *leading-tone* chord (seventh degree) often acts as a substitute for the dominant.

In harmonic analysis chords are normally identified by symbols. Capital roman numerals indicate the degree of the scale occupied by the root (not necessarily the lowest note) of the chord. In a further refinement, these numerals indicate only major chords; lower case roman numerals indicate minor ones. Arabic numerals designate intervals above the bass (lowest tone). These may indicate the presence of chord INVERSIONS or NONHARMONIC TONES. A bass part provided with such symbols is known as a FIGURED BASS or thorough bass. The numbers 6,3 or 6 indicate a first inversion; 6,4, a second inversion. If no numbers are given, root position is implied (5,3 structure). The number 7 may indicate a chord containing a seventh above the root: the inversions of such a chord are indicated by 6,5; 4,3 (or 6,4,3); and 4,2, respectively. If no chord is to be placed above the bass note, a 0 is used. A vertical or diagonal slash through a number indicates that the corresponding note is to be a half-step higher than normal. A sharp or flat appearing independently of a specific numeral normally alters the third of the chord.

In simple works in major keys, the I, IV, and V chords are major; the ii, iii, and vi chords, minor; and the vii° chord, diminished. In equally simple works in minor keys, the i and iv chords are minor; III, VI, and VII, major; and the ii° chord, diminished. The V chord, which would be minor according to the natural form of the minor scale, is normally changed to major. However, in works employing a more varied harmonic vocabulary, a composer may, within a predominantly major framework, occasionally use chords characteristic of the minor key with the same tone center, and vice versa. Chords characteristic of related keys may also appear, as well as certain o t h e r chromatic chords.

Harmonic style is not merely a matter of the richness or austerity of the vocabulary employed. Density and consistency of harmonic texture are also contributory elements. If the composer wishes a style stressing the close-knit melodic logic of each of several voice-parts, he is expected to follow rules of voice leading derived from counterpoint. These stress the desirability of oblique or contrary motion between the outer voices, the use of the smallest possible intervals for movement within a voice-part, and the avoidance of parallel (consecutive) fifths or octaves within any pair of voices. If, however, the melodic force is concentrated in a single line, these general considerations may be treated less strictly, and there is opportunity for greater freedom of motion, especially if there are changes in textural density.

Compositions employing similar harmonic vocabularies may also create contrasting impressions because of differences in the pace at which the harmonies change. In a fast harmonic rhythm, the notes of the individual chords will often be sounded simultaneously. By employing the notes of a chord successively as a melodic figuration, by repetition or by embellishment, a composer may create a slower harmonic rhythm. Progressions of two and three chords may have different degrees of force. Some produce a strong sense of directed movement by reaching a goal of greater or lesser importance. Others may represent means to a goal, rather than the attainment of the goal. Still others are primarily embellishments; these create a sense of variety and motion, departing from and returning to a given chord without producing a sense of essential harmonic change.

The nature of the harmonic idiom of the major-minor system is such that each of the chords within the idiom is associated with a few narrowly circumscribed functions, these being determined by the relationship of the chord to the prevailing key center. The ultimate purpose of these functions is to provide a harmonic drive that will achieve its goal through final repose on the tonic chord. The most basic progression is that leading from the dominant to the tonic. This kind of progression, namely of a root descending a fifth, may be extended to form a chain that will normally lead with increasing force back to the tonic. Progressions between chords with roots a third apart and a second apart may serve various purposes.

The breakdown of functional harmony began in the late 19th century. Composers sought out more and more alternatives to traditional modes of progression. Sometimes function was disregarded entirely and chords employed as elements of color. The 20th century has brought numerous changes in harmonic vocabulary and syntax. As yet, however, neither a universal vocabulary and syntax nor a widely accepted teaching method has been evolved for 20th-century harmony. *See also* CADENCE, MODULATION.

Harp: a family of plucked string instruments whose

strings are perpendicular to the sound board rather than parallel. The family is both ancient and widespread and its members exist in many different shapes and sizes. The modern orchestral instrument, known as the double action or double pedal harp, follows the basic construction of the harp brought out by Sébastien Erard in 1810. It is somewhat triangular in shape, with a vertical fore-pillar, a body (or sound-chest) which slants upward from the base of the pillar towards the player's body, and a curved neck, which holds the tuning pins. It has 45 or more strings tuned diatonically in the key of Cb major. Seven pedals, each controlling all strings producing pitches of the same letter (e.g., all C's), are located at the foot of the harp. Depressing a pedal one notch will raise the PITCH of all strings of that name by a half-step; they will sound as naturals rather than flats. Depressing that pedal still another notch will raise the respective pitches another half-step, producing sharps. A rapid, chromatic sequence is not obtainable on this sort of harp. This drawback has led to experimentation with harps having strings tuned in chromatic sequence. A chromatic harp with strings in two intersecting planes was introduced in 1897 by PLEYEL,

but the drawbacks of this instrument—poorer tone quality and more complex technique—have restricted its use; earlier chromatic harps suffered similar disadvantages. There are some harp CONCERTOS, including a Concerto for Flute and Harp by MOZART, and the harp is used as an orchestral instrument in a few BAROQUE and CLASSICAL scores, as well as in many more ROMANTIC and MODERN ones. (WAGNER employs six harps in *Rheingold*.) It appears in several fine CHAMBER works, including pieces by DEBUSSY and RAVEL, but the literature for harp alone is not particularly distinguished.

Harp-Guitar (Harp-Lute, Harp-Lute-Guitar, Harp-Lyre, etc.): hybrid instruments of the early 19th century, made by Edward Light. These instruments, which had only brief popularity and no significant repertoire, had the frets associated with lutes and guitars, and the yoke or curved neck and unstopped strings associated with lyres and harps.

Harpsichord: a stringed keyboard instrument using a set of jacks and plectra to pluck the strings. Instruments of this sort have existed since the 14th or 15th century, being known under the names harpsichord, spinet, virginal(s), cembalo, clavicembalo, gravicembalo, claveçin, etc.

The term harpsichord may be used as a generic designation for the entire family, although it more often denotes only the largest member, shaped like a grand piano. Smaller models, oblong or trapezoidal, are usually called SPINETS or VIRGINALS. All employ the same basic mechanism.

When a key is depressed, a long, upright jack placed on the inner end rises; a quill or leather tongue (plectrum) set in a sliver of wood balanced in the top center of the jack touches the string and forces its way past, making the string vibrate. When the key is released, the jack descends; the sliver of wood pivots slightly as the plectrum touches the string, allowing the plectrum to slide underneath without plucking the string anew. The tone is silenced by a small felt damper so placed in the upper corner of the jack that it touches the string when the key is at rest.

During the 16th century the harpsichord itself usually had a range of about four octaves; by the 18th century, its range was increased to five or even five and a half octaves. The harpsichordist cannot change loudness by altering the striking force as does the pianist; misplaced efforts in this direction result either in jangling tone or lack of rhythmic precision. It is, however, possible to alter the tone of the instrument by changing the material of the plectrum, by changing the place where the strings are plucked, and by using small leather or felt pads to damp the tone. The tonal resources of the instrument may be enlarged by adding 4-foot and 16-foot STOPS —the latter primarily a modern device—to the normal 8-foot stops, thus permitting a single key to sound the upper or lower octave as well as the regular pitch (*see* FOOT). To achieve this tonal variety, harpsichords often have two or even three keyboards and a single key may govern several strings. The jacks are held upright by wooden slides called registers and may be engaged or disengaged by moving the registers sideways. Changes of registration were effected in 18th century instruments by hand stops and were used sparingly. Modern instruments are equipped with pedals that allow the performer to make quick changes of registration not necessarily in accord with earlier performance practices. Virginals and spinets are limited to one keyboard and one jack per key. Among the famous harpsichord makers of the 17th and 18th centuries are the Ruckers family, the Silberman family, and Jacob Kirkman. The harpsichord has a sharp, clear sound, more pungent and percussive than that of the piano. Its fine qualities are becoming more widely appreciated once more.

The harpsichord was prominent both as a SOLO and ENSEMBLE instrument from the 16th to the 18th century. The peak of the repertoire comprises the masterpieces of BACH, HANDEL, SCARLATTI, COUPERIN, RAMEAU, and earlier composers, including PURCELL, FROBERGER, FRESCOBALDI, and the English virginalists (BYRD, MORLEY, BULL, and GIBBONS, among others). During the Baroque the harpsichord provided the essential realization of the FIGURED BASS for both CHAMBER and orchestral works. A few modern composers have also written for the instrument.

Harris, Roy: *b*. Lincoln Co., Okla., February 12, 1898. Harris, who completed his studies under Boulanger, has taught at many U.S. colleges and universities. He has composed prolifically in all traditional genres except opera, and has written several works for band. He employs modal and polytonal HARMONIES within a basically diatonic framework, and his music has a strong rhythmic drive. Several works make prominent use of American FOLK SONG. His best-known compositions include his Third Symphony

and the symphonic OVERTURE *When Johnny Comes Marching Home*.

Hasse, Johann Adolph: *b*. Bergedorf (Hamburg), March 25, 1699; *d*. Venice, December 16, 1783. Trained by PORPORA and A. SCARLATTI, Hasse was active in Naples, Venice, Dresden, Vienna, and again in Venice. He was one of the most popular composers of OPERA in the Neapolitan style, and wrote also a wide variety of sacred vocal music as well as CONCERTOS, and instrumental ENSEMBLE and SOLO music.

Hassler, Hans Leo: *b*. Nuremberg, October 25, 1564; *d*. Frankfurt, June 8, 1612. After studying with his father, Hassler went to Venice to complete his studies with Andrea GABRIELI. The most important of his posts were as organist to Count Octavian Fugger (1585–1600) in Augsburg and to the elector of Saxony (1608–12) in Dresden. Hassler was among the first to introduce Venetian polychoral and concertato TECHNIQUES to Germany. He wrote MADRIGALS, CANZONETS, LIEDER, and dances, in addition to a wide variety of sacred music (MASSES, MOTETS, settings of chorale tunes).

Hautbois (F): **Hautboy, hoboy:** oboe.

Hauptwerk (G): great organ.

Haut-dessus (F): soprano.

Haute-contre (F): alto.

Haydn, Franz Joseph: b. Rohrau, March 31, 1732; *d.* Vienna, May 31, 1809; the greatest of the CLASSICAL composers responsible for the early development of the SYMPHONY and STRING QUARTET.

The son of a wheelwright and amateur musician, Haydn received his first musical instruction from a paternal cousin, J. M. Franck. When eight, he joined the St. Stephen's choir in Vienna, where he remained until his voice broke. From 1748 to 1759 Haydn taught and eked out his precarious existence by doing odd jobs. As an assistant to Nicola Porpora, he gradually became acquainted with influential nobles and, in 1759, was engaged as music director by Count Morzin. Two years later Haydn entered the hire of Prince Paul Anton Esterházy. After the latter's death in 1762, he continued to serve Prince Nicholas (1762–90) and Prince Anton (from 1790 till Haydn's death). Most of his time was spent at the palatial estate, Esterháza, though Haydn often accompanied Prince Nicholas to Vienna. The temporary disbanding of the musical establishment in 1790 enabled Haydn to obtain leave for two triumphal trips to England—1791–92 and 1794–95. His last years were spent mainly in Vienna.

Haydn was responsible for the further musical training of his personnel, the supervision of their deportment, the maintenance of the music library and instruments, and for conducting the frequent OPERAS and symphonic and CHAMBER recitals. Moreover, he was to compose such music as the prince desired. These duties, though onerous by present standards, were customary in his day. Fortunately for Haydn, Prince Nicholas was passionately fond of music and wealthy enough to indulge this fondness on a grand scale. An orchestra of two dozen or so was recruited from the best talent; about a dozen singers were available.

Haydn's early style was shaped by the music of such Viennese composers as Monn, Wagenseil, and Reutter and by the works of C. P. E. BACH. Later, he formed a deep friendship with MOZART, each master learning from the other. Haydn was a patient and persevering worker. He matured slowly, attaining ever increasing originality in the process. His finest masterpieces were produced after sixty.

Although Haydn's contract forbade the gift or sale of his compositions, this provision was not enforced. By the 1780s, his fame had spread throughout Europe. As a result, publishers often attached his name to compositions by others, hoping to help sales. This fact, coupled with the loss or destruction of many of his earlier works, makes it impossible for scholars to determine the exact extent of his output. Among the major items are over 100 symphonies, 25 CONCERTOS, 84 string quartets, 52 piano SONATAS, about 24 operas, 12 MASSES, and 10 ORATORIOS and CANTATAS. Since Prince Nicholas liked to play the BARYTON, Haydn wrote 125 trios for this instrument, viola, and cello.

Though Haydn's operas contain much fine music and though he was proud of their success at Esterháza, he realized that he lacked the dramatic genius of Mozart. His most significant vocal music comprises the last six Masses (including the *Lord Nelson Mass*, the *Mass in Time of War*, the *Theresienmesse*, and the *Wind Band Mass*), written for Prince Anton, and the two oratorios, *The Creation* and *The Seasons*, which were inspired by a performance at Westminster of Handel's *Messiah*. Haydn's greatest contribution, however, lies in his symphonies and string quartets. Though not the first to write in these forms, he was the first to raise them to great heights; in so doing he played a vital role in the development of sonata form. His quick movements are characterized by great vitality and humor; the slow ones possess deep lyrical warmth.

Haydn, (Johann) Michael: *b.* Robrau, September 14, 1737; *d.* Salzburg, August 10, 1806. After following his older brother, Franz Joseph, in the choir of St. Stephen's in Vienna, Michael Haydn became music director at Grosswardein (1757) and then at Salzburg. He was an influential teacher, WEBER and REICHA being among his pupils. MASSES, REQUIEMS, ORATORIOS, and other sacred works comprise a substantial portion of his output; in addition, he wrote a few OPERAS, about threescore SYMPHONIES, CONCERTOS, miscellaneous orchestral works, and CHAMBER MUSIC.

Head voice: the upper portion of the vocal range.

Heckelclarina: a rarely-used single-reed WOODWIND with a conical bore and a range similar to that of the oboe and soprano saxophone.

Heckelphone: a rarely-used baritone oboe (designated as a bass oboe by DELIUS); i.e., a double-reed WOODWIND pitched an octave below the oboe.

Heinrich, Anthony Philip: *b.* Schönbüchl, Bohemia, March 11, 1781; *d.* New York, May

3, 1861. Heinrich was among the more influential musicians in the United States during the 1840s and 1850s. He was a prolific composer of SYMPHONIES, ORATORIOS, piano pieces and songs, and was one of the first to employ Indian themes and show other evidences of American nationalism.

Heldentenor (G): a brilliant male VOICE of high range and great power, such as is demanded by leading roles in Wagnerian OPERAS.

Helicon: a BRASS INSTRUMENT, a circular form of tuba.

Hemidemisemiquaver: a sixty-fourth note (British usage).

Hemiola, Hemiole, Hemiolia: (1) a RHYTHM which, in its simplest form, contrasts a group of two equal note values against a group of three equal values occupying the same total time. The contrast may be either simultaneous or successive. The individual values of the contrasting groups stand in the proportion of 3:2. In actual practice any specific value of either group may be replaced by two or more smaller values; or, two values of the group of three may be replaced by one larger value. The term is used especially with reference to music of the 14th to 16th centuries. In BAROQUE music, hemiola rhythms often occur in COU-RANTES. They are also to be found in works of such later composers as BEETHOVEN, BRAHMS, SCHUMANN, and CHOPIN. (2) In an earlier sense, now obsolete, the term denoted a pair of notes whose VIBRATION frequencies were related in the proportion of 3:2; such a ratio produces the INTERVAL of a perfect fifth.

Herbert, Victor: b. Dublin, February 1, 1859; d. New York, May 26, 1924. Trained in Germany, and active as a cellist in various European orchestras, Herbert came to the United States in 1886; here he was active both as cellist and conductor; he led his own light entertainment orchestra, a regimental band, and various symphony orchestras (including mammoth ensembles for charity benefits). From 1894 to 1924 he wrote 41 OPERETTAS, the basis for his fame. His two grand OPERAS, cello CONCERTOS, CHAMBER MUSIC, songs, and choral works are no longer performed. In 1914 Herbert helped found the American Society of Composers, Authors, and Publishers (AS-CAP).

Hérold, Louis Joseph Ferdinand: b. Paris, January 28, 1791; d. Thernes, January 19, 1833. Hérold was a student of MÉHUL at the Paris Conservatoire and won the Prix de Rome in 1812. He was active from 1815 till his death as a composer of OPERAS and BALLETS, his two best works being *Zampa* and *Le Pré aux clercs*. He wrote also a moderate quantity of piano music, now entirely ignored.

Heterophony: the simultaneous performance of variant forms of one basic MELODY; the variants may involve added or omitted notes and rhythmic changes. Heterophony is to be observed in some music of the Far East and may have been employed in ancient Greek and medieval Western music.

Hexachord: a SCALE of six notes following the pattern of the first six notes of a major scale. Hexachords formed part of the medieval theoretic system from the time of Guido d'Arezzo, a monk and influential teacher of the early 11th century. They were concerned primarily with sight-reading rather than composition. (*See* SOLMIZATION.)

In Guido's theory there are three varieties of hexachord. These are based on *C (c, d, e, f, g, a*: the natural hexachord), *F (f, g, a, b♭, c, d*: the soft hexachord), and *G (g, a, b, c, d, e*: the hard hexachord). These overlap and together contain all of the tones officially accepted in medieval theory. The hard hexachord, used in three octave positions, marked both

outer boundaries of the Guidonian system. The other hexachords were used in two positions each. In late RENAISSANCE practice it was possible to found hexachords on a wide variety of different notes. Hexachord patterns were employed as themes for MASSES and KEYBOARD variations in the late 16th century.

Hindemith, Paul: *b*. Hanau, November 16, 1895; *d*. Frankfurt, December 28, 1963. Composer, violinist, violist, conductor, theorist, and teacher, Hindemith was one of the most versatile musicians of this century. He was trained at the Frankfurt Conservatory and became successively violinist, concertmaster, and conductor of the Frankfurt Opera orchestra. He was also violist in the Amar-Hindemith quartet, which was famed for its performances of contemporary music in the 1920s. Hindemith taught at the Berlin Hochschule (1927–35). He left Germany after his music was banned by Nazi officials. He was asked by Turkey to reorganize that country's system of musical education. Hindemith first came to the United States in 1937; he joined the faculty of Yale University in 1940. In 1953 Hindemith went to Zurich as a faculty member of the university there.

Although Hindemith's music was considered very modernistic before World War II, his views on the function of music are essentially ROMANTIC. He does, however, draw on elements of form and texture that are characteristic of the BAROQUE and CLASSICAL periods, while employing melodic constructions and dissonant harmonic combinations according to an acoustically based method, described in his *Craft of Musical Composition*. Hindemith has contributed extensively to all traditional genres. Among his more important works are the OPERAS *Mathis der Maler* and *Die Harmonie der Welt;* the BALLET *Nobilissima Visione;* the *Symphonic Metamorphosis on Themes by Weber;* six STRING QUARTETS; the song cycle, *Das Marienleben;* and *Ludus Tonalis,* INTERLUDES and FUGUES for piano.

Hocket, Hoquetus (L): (1) a technique of the 13th and 14th centuries in which single notes or small groups alternate with short rests, thus breaking the melodic line into small fragments. Usually the technique was applied simultaneously to two parts, so that one was active while the other was silent. (2) A title for a work based on the technique just described.

Hoffmann, Ernst Theodor Amadeus: *b.* Königsberg, January 24, 1776; *d.* Berlin, June 25, 1822. Hoffmann spent most of his life as a civil serv-

ant, though he served as conductor during two brief periods. He composed 11 OPERAS, the best being *Undine*, a BALLET, a SYMPHONY, four piano SONATAS, and some sacred pieces. His greatest influence on music was as a writer of highly imaginative essays and tales, some of the latter being transformed into opera libretti. Some furnished ideas for SCHUMANN's *Kreisleriana.*

Hold: *see* PAUSE.

Holst, Gustav Theodore: *b.* Cheltenham, September 21, 1874; *d.* London, May 25, 1934. Holst completed his studies at the Royal College of Music under Stanford. From 1907 he was music director at Morley College in London and, from 1919 to 1924, composition professor at the Royal College of Music. His interests in Hindu culture and in English FOLK SONG are reflected respectively in his *Hymns from the Rig-Veda* and *Savitri* (a chamber opera), and in choral arrangements of folk tunes, a piano TOCCATA, and the *Somerset Rhapsody* (for orchestra). His best known work is the orchestral SUITE *The Planets.* Holst wrote a variety of orchestral, band, chamber, and choral works, as well as songs, piano pieces, and a handful of OPERAS.

Holzbauer, Ignaz: *b.* Vienna, September 17, 1711; *d.* Mannheim, April 7, 1783. The most important of Holzbauer's several posts was that of music director at Mannheim (1753 on). Although best known for his contribution to the development of the early CLASSICAL SYMPHONY, his sacred music was praised by MOZART. He was moderately successful as an OPERA composer, and also wrote DIVERTIMENTOS, CONCERTOS, and STRING QUARTETS.

Holzblasinstrumente (G): woodwinds.

Holzharmonika (G): xylophone.

Homophony: a TEXTURE in which a MELODY is supported by chordal accompaniment.

Honegger, Arthur: *b*. Le Havre, March 10, 1892; *d*. Paris, November 27, 1955. Trained at the Zürich and Paris Conservatories, Honegger was among the more prominent of the composers in post-World War I France who turned away from ROMANTIC and IMPRESSIONISTIC music. He was much interested in POLYPHONIC textures and made liberal use of polytonal and dissonant elements. Honegger wrote extensively for the stage: OPERAS, dramatic ORATORIOS, BALLETS, and incidental music for both plays and films. Among his most famous works are *King David* and *Jeanne d'Arc au bûcher*. His instrumental works include the SYMPHONIC POEMS *Pacific 231* and *Rugby*,

five SYMPHONIES, and CHAMBER and KEYBOARD MUSIC. He wrote also choral works and songs.

Hopkinson, Francis: *b*. Philadelphia, September 21, 1737; *d*. Philadelphia, May 9, 1791. A signer of the Declaration of Independence, and a lawyer by profession, Hopkinson was a poet and an ardent amateur musician and claimed to be the first native-born American composer. He wrote songs, and was probably the compiler of *A Collection of Psalm Tunes*.

Hopak, Gopak: a Russian dance in brisk duple METER.

Hoquetus: *see* HOCKET.

Horn: (1) normally, the French horn, a circular BRASS INSTRUMENT of conical bore; (2) the English horn is a conical, double-reed WOODWIND; (3) in slang, any brass instrument and occasionally other wind instruments as well. *See also* ALPHORN; BASSET HORN.

Hornpipe: (1) a single-reed WOODWIND, used in Celtic countries and known also as a pibgorn. Both ends of the instrument terminate in horns, one of which serves as a windcap, the other as a bell. (2) Different British dances of the 16th to 19th centuries. The 16th-century hornpipe was in triple METER; that of the late 18th and 19th centuries in duple.

Hovhaness, Alan: *b*. Somerville, Mass., March 8, 1911. Hovhaness is a pupil of CON-VERSE and MARTINU. A prolific composer, he is interested in the fusion of elements of Armenian and Indian music with traditional European techniques. His melodies often have the quality of cantillation and many of his works are built up by the frequent repetition of a small amount of thematic material. His orchestral music includes *Lousadzak (The Coming of Light), Arekaval (Season of the Sun)*, and two *Armenian Rhapsodies*. He has written for diverse CHAMBER groups, for piano, and for violin, and has composed both secular and sacred vocal music.

Hummel, Johann Nepomuk: *b.* Pressburg, November 14, 1778; *d.* Weimar, October 17, 1837. Hummel's earliest training was provided by his father; he later studied with MOZART and ALBRECHTS-BERGER and had the advice of HAYDN and SALIERI. He served as Haydn's deputy at Ester-háza (1804–11), was music director at Stuttgart (1816–19), and then at Weimar from 1819 on. One of the outstanding pianists of his day, he was regarded by some as the equal of BEETHOVEN. His main contribution lies in his solo piano works and piano CONCERTOS, which contributed to the development of piano technique. He wrote a wide variety of other music —OPERAS, BALLETS, CANTATAS, MASSES, and CHAMBER MUSIC, including a SEPTET that is still occasionally performed.

Humoresque (F), Humoreske (G): a title used by 19th-century composers for works of a playful or changeable character.

Humperdinck, Engelbert: *b.* Siegburg, September 1, 1854; *d.* Neustrelitz, September 27, 1921. Humperdinck was trained by Hiller and Rheinberger. He taught in Barcelona and Frankfurt, and was director of a Berlin school. An associate and admirer of WAGNER, he was able to combine FOLK SONG elements with Wagnerian color and texture in his one outstanding success, *Hänsel und Gretel*. His incidental music to *Königskinder* contains directions to the actors regulating speech rhythms and inflections (SPRECHSTIMME). Humperdinck wrote a handful of other OPERAS, together with incidental music for plays by Shakespeare, Maeterlinck, and Aristophanes; choral music, a SYMPHONY, SYMPHONIC POEM, and some songs.

Hurdy-gurdy: (1) a popular name for the barrel organ; (2) an obsolete string instrument, shaped like a large, deep, broad-necked violin, but producing sound through the friction of a rotating wheel, housed within the body and turned by a handle. The instrument is played resting on the lap. The strings are stopped by a simple, key-controlled mechanism. The instrument—in use from the 10th to the 18th centuries—has been designated variously as *organistrum, symphonia, chifonie, cinfonía, leier, vièlle à roue,* and *lyra* or *lira organizzata.* HAYDN wrote several works for the latter.

Hydraulis (Gr): an ORGAN of antiquity.

Hymn: in the widest sense, a song of praise or adoration, secular or sacred. Normally the term implies a sacred context. Although, during the first millennium A.D., the term could denote texts of disparate origin and structure (including PSALMS and CANTICLES, SEQUENCES and other TROPES, etc.), in modern usage, the term usually refers to poems with STROPHES of identical format, most often with the same or nearly the same number of syllables per line throughout the individual work. Most hymn MELODIES are comparatively simple; they are primarily syllabic, with occasional groups of two and three notes per syllable. However, there are some more ornate melodies also. Many texts have been set by more than one melody and several melodies have been adapted for use with more than one text.

Christian hymnody began in the Eastern Churches—Syrian, Byzantine, Armenian—and attained greater prominence there than in the West. In the Roman Catholic rite, a hymn is sung during each of the Hours of Divine Serve (OFFICE). St. Ephraim (*c.* 306–373) was the first important Eastern writer of Christian hymns, while St. Ambrose (*c.*340–397) was apparently the first to write Latin hymns. Several Eastern hymns of various periods are now sung in translation in the West. POLYPHONIC settings of hymn-texts, some based on plainsong melodies, some free, were composed frequently during the Middle Ages and RENAISSANCE. In 1524 the first collection of Lutheran CHORALES was issued. Throughout the BAROQUE the chorale was one of the main generative forces for German sacred music. English hymnody contemporary with the period of chorale writing was concerned with metrical translations of the psalms. Only later was the use of non-Scriptural texts admitted.

Hypoaeolian (Hypodorian, Hypoionian, Hypolocrian, Hypolydian, Hypomixolydian, Hypophrygian): *see* CHURCH MODES.

I

Ibert, Jacques: *b.* Paris, August 15, 1890. A pupil of FAURÉ and Paul Vidal, Ibert won the Prix de Rome in 1919. He was director of the French Academy in Rome from 1937 to 1955. His work displays a neoclassical style, technically polished, colorful, and often with pleasing wit. He has written several OPERAS, BALLETS, SYMPHONIC POEMS (such as *Escales, Divertissement*), CONCERTOS, CHAMBER and KEYBOARD MUSIC (including the popular *Little White Donkey*), songs and choral works.

Ictus (L): in poetry, a stress; in music, the term designates the subtle articulation of GREGORIAN CHANT following the theories of the Solesmes monks.

Idée fixe (F): BERLIOZ's term for a THEME which recurs in various guises, representing a specific idea or character in PROGRAM MUSIC (e.g., the artist's beloved in the *Symphonie fantastique*).

Idiophone: *see* INSTRUMENTS.

Imitation: the successive statement of identical or nearly identical material in two or more VOICES. If the identity of the several statements continues until the final phrase or throughout the piece, the work is termed a CANON. The term imitation, therefore, denotes the restatement of only a phrase or motive. Imitation may involve INVERSION, RETROGRADE MOTION, AUGMENTATION, or DIMINUTION. The consistent use of imitation to mark out the important formal divisions of a composition began during the late 15th century; all of the major forms of RENAISSANCE music made use of this principle at some time. The RICERCAR, instrumental CANZONA, INVENTION, and FUGUE are among the BAROQUE forms based on imitation. The emphasis on HARMONIC TEXTURES in the CLASSICAL and ROMANTIC periods lessened the importance of imitation during these eras.

Imperfect: a classification of CADENCE, INTERVAL, or note-value. In MEDIEVAL and RENAISSANCE NOTATION, a value containing two notes of the next smaller value was termed imperfect, a value containing three such notes being termed perfect.

Impressionism: a coloristic musical style, created by DEBUSSY, which flourished *c*.1890–1920. More often than not, impressionistic works have programmatic titles; however, they concern themselves with veiled suggestion rather than detailed realism. In this respect they are kin to the works of contemporary symbolist poets such as Verlaine and Mallarmé and to the works of impressionistic painters such as Monet and Seurat. The term itself was appropriated from the vocabulary of art history.

Some individual traits of Debussy's style appear in works by earlier composers, such as LISZT, LALO, CHABRIER, and FAURÉ. Although Debussy had no close followers in the manner of WAGNER, he strongly influenced many early-20th-century composers. Among them were RAVEL, ROUSSEL, DUKAS, DELIUS, BAX, ALBENIZ, RESPIGHI, LOEFFLER, and GRIFFES.

Impromptu: a title of some Romantic CHARACTER PIECES for piano, the most famous being by SCHUBERT and CHOPIN. The title suggests a casual extemporization; the works, however, have clear and sym-metrical forms rather than irregular, rhapsodic ones.

Improperia (L): in the Roman Catholic rite, certain CHANTS for Good Friday, or POLYPHONIC settings thereof.

Improvisation: the spontaneous composition or enrichment of either part or the entirety of a musical work during the course of performance. In spontaneous composition, the performer is often asked to work with specific materials. He may be given a well-known tune as a point of departure or a theme newly contrived to test his abilities. In CADENZAS, i.e., improvisations occurring as sections of written works, the performer is expected to expand on the materials provided in the main body of the work. The enrichment of a musical work by improvisation may entail the florid elaboration of a melody or theme notated in skeletal form, the addition of one or more voice-parts to an existing structure, or the development of a harmonic skeleton (as in the rhapsodic preludes for lute by Denis Gaultier and for harpsichord by Louis COUPERIN).

Because of its nature, an improvisation is not notated. (Some recent improvisations, however, have been recorded.) Thus our knowledge of various improvisational styles and techniques is dependent upon verbal descriptions, often vague, and examples written out primarily for teaching purposes. We are much better informed concerning improvisation within the framework of a written composition than free improvisation.

Improvisation has been employed during all periods of European musical history. During the Middle Ages, troubadour and trouvère performances were often accompanied instrumentally, but no written instrumental accompaniments survive; presumably these were improvised. Some forms of POLYPHONY based on plainsong were also improvised. During the RENAISSANCE, performers of *basses danses* customarily improvised simple counterpoints to preexistent tenor parts; later RENAISSANCE and BAROQUE instrumental practice often involved the improvisation of variations on simple bass parts. (*See* GROUND; DIVISIONS.) During the Baroque, slow melodies were usually notated in skeletal form. The performer was expected to add profuse ornamentation in accordance with the practices of the period. Examples of this practice were set down in various treatises. Quite possibly similar procedures were observed in earlier periods.

The outstanding use of improvisation during the Baroque concerned the elaboration of FIGURED BASSES in concerted music. Vocal and instrumental cadenzas furnished CLASSICAL performers with the opportunity to demonstrate their improvisatory powers. During the 19th century, solo recitals often included improvisations on tunes designated by the audience. CHANCE MUSIC of the mid-20th century employs improvisatory elements within a loose or strict outline determined by the composer. Group improvisation free of predetermined guides is also being explored. In "popular music," improvisation is an important technique in JAZZ. Before the 19th century almost all performers of consequence were adept at improvisation, but training in this skill has declined since. BACH, HANDEL, MOZART, BEETHOVEN, LISZT, FRANCK, and BRUCKNER were particularly famed for their improvisations.

Incidental music: music designed to enhance the production of a play or film. It may comprehend any or all of the following: PRELUDES, INTERLUDES, or POSTLUDES; music for songs, dances, or marches that are part of the dramatic action; and general background music. Some incidental music is performed independently of its dramatic function, often in the form of a SUITE. Beethoven's *Egmont*, Mendelssohn's *Midsummer Night's Dream*, and Grieg's *Peer Gynt* are among the best known examples from the 19th century; Prokofiev's *Alexander Nevsky* and Virgil Thomson's *Louisiana Story* were composed for motion pictures.

d'Indy, (Paul Marie Théodore) Vincent: *b.* Paris, March 27, 1851; *d.* Paris, December 2, 1931. One of the most versatile and influential musicians of his day, d'Indy was composer, organist, timpanist, choral director, conductor, teacher, one of the founders of the Schola Cantorum, secretary and then president of the Société Nationale de Musique, inspector of musical instruction in Paris, editor, scholar, critic, and writer. He completed his training under César FRANCK at the Paris Conservatoire, and his music shows the influence of Franck, together with that of LISZT and WAGNER, whom he met and admired. (D'Indy was also influenced by the music of BACH and by GREGORIAN CHANT.) The best known of his works are the *Symphony on a French mountain air* for orchestra and piano, and the *Istar Variations*. His works include OP-ERAS (the most important being *Fervaal*), TONE POEMS, SYMPHONIES, and other orchestral music, CHAMBER MUSIC, songs and choral works, and pieces for piano and organ.

In Nomine (L): a title used for numerous English instrumental compositions of the 16th and 17th centuries: the earliest of the group was transcribed from the section of the Benedictus of Taverner's MASS, *Gloria tibi Trinitas*, bearing the words "in nomine Domine" ("in the name of the Lord"). Later settings normally used the CANTUS FIRMUS employed by Taverner.

Instrumentation: *see* ORCHESTRATION.

Instruments: any of man's devices for producing music excepting the human voice. The study of instruments— their history and manufacture —is known as *organology*. Most musicians classify instruments according to the choirs of the orchestra: string, woodwind, brass, and percussion. To these four divisions a fifth may be added, keyboard instruments. This system is quite convenient for most discussions of European music and is employed in this dictionary for that reason. However, since the classification depends now on one criterion, now on another, there are many instruments known to man which cannot be classified accurately according to any of the above categories, as well as others, such as the piano and saxophone, that might well fit more than one.

Museum c u r a t o r s and others concerned with rare and exotic instruments often employ a more exact system of classification devised in the early 20th century by Curt Sachs and Erich von Hornbostel. This system divides all instruments into five groups according to their sound generators. It distinguishes between chordophones, aerophones, membranophones, idiophones, and electrophones.

A *chordophone* is any instrument on which sound is produced by means of a tightened string. There are four subdivisions to this group, each named after a representative instrument. A zither consists essentially of a body with one or more strings stretched parallel to it. This body may be either a stick (requiring a resonator, often a gourd), a tube, or a board (actually a box). The piano may thus be called a board zither. A lute consists essentially of a body plus a neck, with the strings stretched over both. All members of the violin family, the viols, guitars, etc., belong to this

subdivision. A lyre employs two projecting arms and a crossbar rather than a neck; the strings run across the body to the crossbar. A harp differs from the preceding instruments in that its strings are not parallel to the body, but rise vertically from it.

An *aerophone* is any instrument using air as a sound generator. A free aerophone produces sound independently of any enclosed column of air, although such a column may be used as a resonator. The accordion and mouth harmonica are among the members of this subdivision. The subdivision of wind instruments, on the other hand, is comprised of instruments whose pitch and tone color are shaped by an enclosed column of air. The subsection, pipes, comprises both the flutes and reed instruments and thus includes all of the orchestral woodwinds. In the flutes, the air column is set into vibration by splitting a windstream against a sharp edge; in the reeds, the windstream is interrupted by the extremely rapid opening and closure of a single or double reed. The other subsection of wind instruments, trumpets and horns, includes instruments which require the player's lips to act as reeds. In principle, the air columns of trumpets are primarily cylindrical, those of horns, primarily conical.

Membranophones are drums. These are classified mainly according to shape: cylindrical, barrel, conical, goblet, etc. *Idiophones* are instruments made of naturally sonorous materials; they include the xylophone, rattles, and gong. The group is subdivided according to the way in which the instruments are played; some are struck together, while others are stamped, shaken, scraped, plucked, rubbed, and so forth. *Electrophones* are instruments that generate their sounds by means of electricity. The various electronic organs are the most familiar members of this group. *See also* BRASS; DRUM; HARPSICHORD; ORGAN; PERCUSSION; PIANO; VIOL; VIOLIN FAMILY; WOODWINDS.

Interlude: a passage or MOVEMENT (frequently improvised) serving a linking function, e.g., between acts of an OPERA or play, between verses of a HYMN, between two movements of a larger composition.

Intermedio (I). Intermède (F): *see* INTERMEZZO (2).

Intermezzo: (1) the title of a Romantic CHARACTER PIECE; (2) in the 16th to 18th centuries, a musical entertainment performed between the acts of an elaborate play, OPERA, MASQUE, or BALLET.

The music might consist of various sorts of MADRIGALS, short ballets, operatic scenes, or, in the latter part of the period, short comic operas for two or three characters. Pergolesi's *La Serva padrona* was first performed in two sections, between the acts of *Il prigioniero superbo*, before achieving an independent life as an opera.

Interpretation: the performer's conclusions regarding the proper rendition of a given work. The term is closely connected with the term *expression*, but emphasizes judgment rather than communication. Interpretation is concerned chiefly with those elements not indicated precisely by the composer, either because of the inadequacies of NOTATION or because of the conventions of his time: the exact TEMPO, the degree of rhythmic freedom permissible, the principles by which individual dynamic nuances may be determined, and the resolution of musical shorthands (e.g., ORNAMENTS, FIGURED BASS, etc.). The goal of interpretation is the faithful recreation of the composer's intent. A thorough knowledge of music history and a certain amount of self-subordination are necessary to avoid distortion of that intent.

Interval: the distance in

PITCH between two tones. Intervals are measured according to the way they are written rather than according to their sound. Two tones of the same pitch are known as a unison or prime. Those written with successive alphabet letters (*a-b*, or *e-f*) are seconds, those that skip one alphabet letter (*a-c*, or *c-e*) are thirds, and so forth. An upward measurement of intervals is implied unless the writer specifies to the contrary.

Since the addition of flats or sharps to either or both notes of an interval leaves its numerical classification unchanged, it follows that there are several varieties or qualities of each interval. In principle, there are three varieties of unison, fourth, fifth, and octave, and four varieties second, third, sixth, and seventh. In practice, a few of these varieties are rare. The normal size of unison, fourth, fifth, or octave, is called *perfect*. An interval a half-step larger is called *augmented,* a half-step smaller, *diminished*. The second, third, sixth, and seventh are classed as *imperfect*. These intervals have two normal sizes, major and minor, major being a half-step larger than minor. In a major interval the upper note is present in the major scale based on the lower note. A size larger than major is augmented, a size smaller than minor, diminished.

In tonal music, harmonic intervals are also classified according to their relative stability. The perfect unison, fifth, and octave, together with major and minor thirds and major and minor sixths are termed consonances. These intervals are not equally stable, but they all possess sufficient stability not to demand further motion because of inherent quality. The remaining intervals lack stability in tonal context and require further motion in the form of resolution.

Examples of simple intervals, those not larger than an octave, are given on the following page. Terminology exists also for larger intervals; one may read of a ninth, tenth, twelfth, etc. These compound intervals are generally employed in the same fashion as their corresponding simple intervals, ignoring the difference of an octave.

There are several pairs of intervals, known as *enharmonic intervals,* that each employ different notation to express the same sounds. For example the augmented second, *c-d♯* has the same sound as the minor third, *c-e♭*. The two forms of notation imply different tonal contexts, however. Since an augmented

Prime	2nd	3rd	4th	5th	6th	7th	Octave

second is classified as a DISSO-NANCE, and a minor third as a CONSONANCE, the same sound in different notation is not only analyzed differently, but functions differently.

Two intervals combining to form an octave are known as *complementary intervals.* These occur when the lower note of an interval is shifted an octave higher and becomes the upper one; this process is known as INVERSION.

Intonation: (1) the observance of correct PITCH standards in performance; poor intonation means singing or playing "out of tune"; (2) in GREGORIAN CHANT, an opening phrase performed by a soloist before the entry of the CHOIR. *See* TUNING.

Intrada: in the 17th and 18th centuries, a march-like MOVE-MENT opening a SUITE or OPERA.

Introit: the opening item of the MASS, part of the PROPER.

Invention: the title of: (1) fifteen two-part keyboard pieces by BACH; (2) four violin partitas by BONPORTI.

Inversion: (1) the transfer of the lowest note of an INTER-VAL to an upper octave so

that it becomes the highest note; (2) the transfer of the root of a CHORD from the lowest position to a middle or upper position, either the third, fifth, or seventh then serving as the bass; (3) the transfer of the lower of two complementary melodies to an upper octave so that it becomes the highest; the technique of writing so that this procedure is feasible without breaking rules is known as *invertible counterpoint;* (4) the statement of a note sequence in contrary motion, so that upward-moving melodic intervals are replaced by similar downward-moving ones, and vice versa.

Invertible counterpoint: *see* DOUBLE COUNTERPOINT.

Ionian: *see* CHURCH MODES.

Ippolitov-Ivanov, **Mikhail Mikhailovich:** *b.* Gatchina, November 19, 1859; *d.* Moscow, January 28, 1935. A student of RIMSKY-KORSAKOV, Ippolitov-Ivanov was an instructor and director first at the Tiflis Conservatory and then at the one in Moscow. He was active also as a conductor. His only work widely known outside Russia is the *Caucasian Sketches.* Other works include a few OPERAS, SYMPHONIC POEMS, SUITES, CHAMBER MUSIC, and songs.

Isaac, Heinrich: *b.* Brabant, *c.*1450; *d.* Florence, 1517. Isaac entered the employ of Emperor Maximilian I in 1497, having previously served Lorenzo de' Medici. He remained with Maximilian until his retirement to Florence in 1515. Among his major contributions is the *Choralis Constantinus,* a collection of settings (MOTETS) for the MASS PROPER for the major festivals of the church year, together with settings of the ORDINARY. Isaac wrote other Masses and motets, as well as secular works in German, Italian, and French. His style embodies elements of Franco-Flemish polyphony together with techniques of the German LIED.

Isorhythm: in music *c.*1310–1440, the continual recurrence within one VOICE of a rhythmic pattern of at least moderate length, either in identical or proportional values. This rhythmic pattern is known as a *talea.* Isorhythm occurs primarily in MOTET tenors (i.e., the voice drawing on a GREGORIAN CHANT); occasionally it is to be found in more than one voice of a POLYPHONIC work. In some compositions repetition of a melodic pattern of a different length is also involved; the melodic pattern is termed *color.*

Istesso tempo, L' (I): a direction to maintain the same BEAT despite a change of METER.

Ives, Charles Edward: *b.* Danbury, Conn., October 20, 1874; *d.* New York City, May 19, 1954. Ives was the son of a bandmaster and completed his studies at Yale University under Parker. For practical reasons he turned to insurance as a profession, but composed extensively until his health failed in 1918. He wrote four SYMPHONIES and other orchestral works (including *Three Places in New England*), CHAMBER and piano music (including the *Concord Sonata*), songs, and choral works. Ives' music was rarely performed before 1939; but he is now recognized as one of the most original composers of his generation. Working apart from the mainstream of musical development, he evolved a style that fused elements drawn from the standard ROMANTIC vocabulary with elements of American FOLK MUSIC and with polyrhythmic and polytonal textures; he experimented with optional and interchangeable instrumentation and with quartertones.

J

Jack: an upright rod containing a mechanism to pluck the string of a HARPSICHORD.

Jacopo da Bologna: active in northern Italy during the second quarter of the 14th century. One of the first masters of the early 2- and 3-part Italian MADRIGAL, Jacopo also wrote CACCE, a LAUDA, and MOTETS (only one surviving complete).

Janáček, Leoš: *b*. Hukvaldy, Czechoslovakia, July 3, 1854; *d*. Moravian-Ostrau, August 12, 1928. Trained at the Prague, Vienna, and Leipzig Conservatories, Janáček was active in Brno (Brünn) and Prague as the director of an organ school, conductor of the Czech Philharmonic, and professor of composition at the Prague Conservatory. He wrote several OPERAS—including *Jenufa* and *From the House of the Dead*—SYMPHONIC POEMS, CHAMBER MUSIC, the *Glagolitic* (*Slavonic* or *Festival*) *Mass* and other choral works, and songs—including the cycle *Diary of One Who Vanished*. Janáček edited several collections of Moravian FOLK SONGS and wrote an essay on their structure. Much of his music has the kind of strength that is associated with folk art. (It is related stylistically to the music of MUSSORGSKY and DEBUSSY.)

Janequin, Clément: *b*. Châtellerault, *c*.1475; *d*. *c*.1560. Active in Bordeaux, Angers, and Paris, Janequin, though a cleric, wrote primarily lively CHANSONS. Most famous are his long, programmatic chansons, such as *Le Chant des Oiseaux* and *La Bataille*. The latter inspired several imitations.

Janissary (Janizary) Music: the music of the Turkish sultans' bodyguard, which made extensive use of percussion instruments: drums, cymbals, triangles, and crescent. (The latter is a pole, topped by a crescent and other symbols and fitted with bells and jingles.) Imitations of janissary music became popular in Europe during the 18th century, especially in Vienna, where MOZART, BEETHOVEN, and their contemporaries wrote movements and passages of "Turkish Music" (*alla Turca*).

Jazz: a generic designation for several 20th-century styles of popular music of the United States. Jazz developed during the mid-1910s from elements of ragtime and blues. (The latter, and occasionally the former as well, may be comprehended under the term jazz.) *Ragtime,* the favored style at the turn of the century, derived from marches and minstrel-show dances. Instrumentally orientated, it featured a strong rhythmic drive, comparatively rapid TEMPO, duple METER, regular phrase construction, and a prominent use of SYNCOPATION and CROSS RHYTHMS. *Blues,* which incorporates elements to be found in Negro spirituals and work songs, is of a mournful nature and uses a slower tempo. Its harmonies feature prominent use of seventh CHORDS, its melodies, the so-called "blue notes"— flatted thirds and sevenths. In its early stages jazz was normally improvised by small, irregularly constituted groups; the musicians would use a well-known tune as the basis for their IMPROVISATION. Brief SOLO passages ("breaks") were introduced in blues. Following the spread of jazz from New Orleans to other parts of the country, bands became larger, the style slicker and more pretentious (symphonic jazz). Carefully prepared arrangements became the rule, with improvisation being either more strictly controlled or only simulated. The older styles did not, however, die out, and fluctuations between different concepts may be found in the later development of jazz, together with the introduction of newer technical features (e.g., the ostinato basses of boogie-woogie, the flatted fifths of bebop, etc.). Jazz idioms have been used from time to time in works not intended for purely popular media. After mid-century, certain composers have sought to merge jazz traditions with those of "art music," the resultant works forming part of what has been termed a "third stream."

Jeté (F): *see* RICOCHET.

Jeu (F): organ stop: *jeux de fonds,* foundation stops; *jeux à bouche,* flue stops; *jeux d'anches,* reed stops.

Jeu de clochettes (F), **Jeux de timbres** (F); GLOCKENSPIEL.

Jew's harp, an instrument consisting of a frame, grasped by the jaws, and an elastic tongue, plucked either by a cord or by a finger. By varying the position of the tongue (as in the pronunciation of different vowels) different tones can be obtained. In

Southeast Asia, where the instrument apparently originated, bamboo is used; later copies are made of metal. In the earliest instruments, both frame and tongue are made of the same piece of bamboo.
Jig: *see* GIGUE.
Jommelli, Niccolò: *b*. Aversa, September 10, 1714; *d*. Naples, August 25, 1774. One of the foremost composers of Neapolitan OPERA, Jommelli was active in many Italian cities and also in Vienna, where he associated with METASTASIO. In 1753 he was appointed music director to the duke of Württemburg in Stuttgart; he returned to Italy in 1769. During his German stay, Jommelli modified the conventions of his Neapolitan style to allow for greater dramatic effect through a lessened dependence on the ARIA DA CAPO, a greater use of accompanied recitative, a richer harmonic foundation, and a fuller orchestral accompaniment. In addition to his operas, he wrote a number of sacred works, the most famous being a *Miserere* for two voices.
Jongleur (F): a medieval entertainer; some jongleurs may have performed songs by a troubadour or trouvère.
Josquin des Prez: *b*. Hainaut, Belgium. *c*.1450; *d*. Condé, August 27, 1521; the greatest composer of the early RENAIS-

SANCE. Josquin was trained at St. Quentin and spent most of his early manhood in Italy. He was in the employ of Galeazzo Maria Sforza (*c*. 1474), Cardinal Ascanio Sforza (*c*.1479), Popes Innocent VIII and Alexander VI (*c*.1486–94), and Hercules I of Ferrara (*c*.1499). Shortly after 1500, Josquin became music director to King Louis XII of France, remaining until the king died in 1515. The composer then became canon at St. Gudule in Brussels and provost of the Cathedral Chapter at Condé.

Josquin's work both summed up the evolution of 15th-century Franco-Flemish polyphony and foreshadowed much that was to follow. (In certain respects his historical position may be likened to that of BEETHOVEN.) Josquin's secular works range from jaunty, homophonic settings of Italian *frottole* to deeply moving contrapuntal works, such as his *Lament on the Death of Ockeghem*. A superlative composer of French CHANSONS, he set texts cast in traditional refrain forms (RONDEAUX and occasional VIRELAIS and BALLADES) and employing conservative rhetoric as well as newer texts of freer form and fresher content. His MASSES include outstanding examples of every structural procedure known to his age, and his MOTETS are of even greater importance. Josquin played a significant role in the development of IMITATION as a form-producing element. He had a keen sense for the textural contrasts obtainable by having a passage for one pair of VOICES imitated immediately by a different pair. Fond of CANON and a master of con-

trapuntal technique, Josquin did not permit artifice to overshadow musical expression. His music exerted a profound influence on many of his contemporaries and successors.

Jota: an Aragonese (Spanish) dance in fairly rapid triple METER.

Jubilus (L): a long series of notes sung to the final vowel of an ALLELUIA.

Just intonation: *see* TUNING.

K

Kabalevsky, Dmitri Borisovich: *b*. St. Petersburg, December 30, 1904. Kabalevsky was trained at the Moscow Conservatory under Nikolai Miaskovsky and was appointed to the faculty of that school in 1932. He is a conservative composer, stressing clear TONALITY and strongly marked RHYTHMS. His works include four SYMPHONIES,

several CONCERTOS, two OPERAS, CHAMBER MUSIC, and songs. He is best known for his piano SONATINAS and other pieces for beginners.

Kalkbrenner, Friedrich Wilhelm Michael: *b*. near Kassel, November 1785; *d*. Deuil, June 10, 1849. One of the outstanding virtuoso pianists of his day and an influential teacher, Kalkbrenner composed numerous works for the piano, including CONCERTOS and CHAMBER MUSIC.

Kammermusik (G): CHAMBER MUSIC.

Kapellmeister (G): *see* MAESTRO DI CAPPELLA.

Kazoo, Mirliton (F), Onion flute, Flûte-eunuque (F): a tube, with an opening (either at the side or end) covered by a membrane. The player hums into the tube, the vibration of the membrane making his voice sound raucous.

Keiser, Reinhard: *b.* Teuchern, January 9, 1674; *d.* Hamburg, September 12, 1739. Trained by his father and Schelle, Keiser began his career in Brunswick. He went to Hamburg in 1696 and became director of the Hamburg opera in 1703. He was named cantor to the Hamburg Cathedral in 1728. An outstanding OPERA composer, he was the first to write a comic opera in German. Of the nearly 120 operas he reportedly wrote, only 25 survive. These show a melodious style, a gift for the musical representations of the emotions, and skillful use of the orchestra. Keiser also wrote much sacred music—including PASSIONS, ORATORIOS, CANTATAS, and MOTETS—as well as secular songs and duets, and instrumental works. His music had considerable influence on HANDEL, MATTHESON, and other north German composers of the late BAROQUE.

Kerle, Jacobus de: *b.* Ypres, *c.*1531; *d.* Prague, January 5, 1591. Kerle traveled widely, his most important posts being those of organist at the cathedral of Augsburg and chaplain to Emperor Rudolph II in Prague. He wrote a collection of *Preces speciales* (Special Prayers) for the Council of Trent as well as much other POLYPHONIC sacred music, MASSES, MOTETS, MAGNIFICATS, and some MADRIGALS.

Kern, Jerome: *b.* New York City, January 27, 1885; *d.* New York City, November 11, 1945. Kern studied music both in New York and in Germany. He was a pianist and salesman for a publishing firm before achieving success as one of the best American composers of musical comedies. His best-known scores include *Showboat, Sally, Sunny, The Cat and the Fiddle, Roberta,* and *Very Warm for May.*

Kettledrum: *see* DRUM.

Key: (1) an indication of the primary TONE CENTER and SCALE formation underlying a tonal composition. The key of a work is sometimes given as an adjunct to its title, or it may be deduced by consulting the KEY SIGNATURE and final chord.

A key is perceived by the

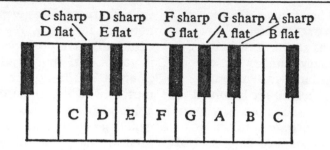

listener through the recurrence of certain HARMONIES at salient junctures. The tonic CHORD (the chord built on the keynote) is the most important of these. Notes foreign to the key of a work or movement may be employed in ornamental function, and, since extensive compositions seldom remain in one key, such notes may either lead into or function within a subordinate key. Even though all major keys are structurally alike (*see* SCALE), as are all minor keys of the same form, many composers have associated given keys with particular moods. Baroque composers were often concerned with elaborate doctrines covering relationships between keys and emotions.

(2) A key is one of a set of balanced levers that activate the tone-producing mechanism of a KEYBOARD instrument, e.g., piano, organ, or harpsichord.

(3) A key may also be a lever controlling the closure of a hole on a WIND INSTRUMENT, e.g., clarinet, saxophone, or key bugle. Such keys may be employed either for convenience or because the fingers cannot reach the holes themselves under normal playing conditions.

Keyboard: a set of keys (KEY, sense 2); except for pedal keyboards (used mainly in ORGANS), these are manipulated by the fingers. Modern compositions may, however, call for TONE CLUSTERS played with the fist or the entire forearm. The arrangement of keys on a modern instrument is as follows. The octave arrangement indicated above is repeated throughout the range of each instrument, the range of the modern piano being seven octaves and a minor third (a total of 88 keys). The lowest octave of 16th- and 17th-century instruments frequently presented another arrangement (*see* SHORT OCTAVE). The earliest keyboards were without black keys. HARPSICHORDS may have two keyboards, while organs may have as many as seven, four being the customary number for a moderately large instrument.

The techniques involved in playing the various keyboard instruments are similar. However, the keys of each sort of instrument respond differently to finger pressure, so that each instrument makes special demands on the player. A touch suitable for the piano, for example, will rarely produce equally satisfactory results on the organ, harpsichord, or clavichord.

Key Bugle: a BRASS INSTRUMENT with a chiefly conical bore and keys, which control the closure of holes pierced in the tube. The instrument was patented by Joseph Halliday in 1810.

Keynote: *see* TONIC.

Key signature: the constellation of sharps or flats (or the absence of both) occurring at the beginning of each staff, following the CLEF. Each such sharp or flat governs all notes of its name, regardless of their octave position. (This is not true of sharps and flats inserted in the course of the music.) The key signature enables the performer to tell which notes will normally be used in that piece and, hence, what the key is likely to be. The following signatures may be used: capital letters indicate major keys; lower-case letters, minor keys. The musician usually judges between the alternative key possibilities of a given signature by examining the opening CHORDS, although the final chord of a piece offers the simplest means of key identification. During the BAROQUE pieces in flat minor keys often displayed one less flat in their key signatures than they do now. A work in G minor, for example, would use a signature of one flat rather than two. Modern, atonal compositions dispense with key signatures.

C	G	D	A	E	B	F♯	C♯
a	e	b	f♯	c♯	g♯	d♯	a♯

F	B♭	E♭	A♭	D♭	G♭	C♭
d	g	e	f	.b♭	c♭	a♭

Khatchaturian, Aram: *b.* Tiflis, June 6, 1903. One of the best-known Soviet composers, Khatchaturian is a former student of Mikhail Gniessin and Miaskovsky. His BALLET, *Gayne,* and his violin and piano concertos have each won popularity in the West. Other works include two SYMPHONIES, CHAMBER and KEYBOARD MUSIC, and songs. Although basically a conservative composer, Khatchaturian was criticized by the Communist party for modernistic tendencies.

Kirchner, Leon: *b.* Brooklyn, N.Y., January 24, 1919. Among Kirchner's several teachers were SCHOENBERG, BLOCH, and SESSIONS. The composer has been on the faculties of various U.S. universities. Kirchner's dissonant, expressionistic style, possessed of a strong rhythmic drive, shows influences from the music of MAHLER and BARTÓK in addition to that of his teachers. His most important work is a piano CONCERTO; he has written also a TOCCATA for chamber orchestra, CHAMBER and KEYBOARD MUSIC, songs, and a SINFONIA.

Kit, Pochette (F), **Taschengeige** (G): a pocket-sized string instrument of the VIOLIN FAMILY used by dancing masters from the 16th to the 19th centuries.

Kithara: a large, heavy lyre of ancient Greece: a string instrument with a body, two upright arms and a crossbar, and four to twelve strings.

Klarinette (G): clarinet.

Klavier (G): (1) piano; (2) in an earlier sense, any KEYBOARD instrument.

Klavierauszug (G): a piano arrangement of a CHAMBER, choral, OPERA, or orchestral score.

Kleine Flöte (G): piccolo.

Kleine Trommel (G): snare drum.

Kodály, Zoltán: *b.* Kecskemet, Hungary, December 16, 1882; *d.* Budapest, March 6, 1967. Kodály was a classmate of BARTÓK and a close associate in collecting Hungarian FOLK SONGS. These influenced Kodály's style, although he did not exploit their asymmetrical rhythms as did Bartók; Kodály is a more traditional composer than his greater colleague. He has written OPERAS (including *Háry János*), choral works (including the *Psalmus Hungaricus* and much sacred music), orchestral works (e.g., *Dances of Galánta*), CHAMBER and KEYBOARD MUSIC, and songs.

Kontrabass (G): double bass.

Kontrafagott (G): double bassoon.

Konzert (G): (1) CONCERTO; (2) a CONCERT.

Konzertstück (G): a small CONCERTO.

Kornett (G): CORNET.

Krakowiak, Cracovienne: a Polish dance (named after the city, Cracow) in quick duple METER, often with syncopated RHYTHM.

Krenek, Ernst: *b.* Vienna, August 23, 1900. A student of Franz Schreker, Krenek was active in Cassel, Wiesbaden, and Vienna, before coming to the United States in 1938. He has taught at several American colleges and universities. Krenek has composed prolifically in a wide variety of genres and styles. His first works reflect a post-Romantic Viennese tradition, while those of the 1920s display several neoclassical elements. His most famous work, the OPERA, *Jonny Spielt Auf*, uses JAZZ. His later works employ an advanced TWELVE-TONE technique.

Kreutzer, Konradin: *b.* Messkirch, Germany, November 22, 1780; *d.* Riga, December 14, 1849. Active as a conductor in Stuttgart, Vienna, and Cologne, Kreutzer wrote some 30 OPERAS, including *Das Nachtlage von Granada* and *Jerry und Bätely*. He wrote also songs, choral music, CHAMBER MUSIC and piano pieces.

Kreutzer, Rodolphe: *b.* Versailles, November 16, 1766; *d.* Geneva, January 6, 1831. An outstanding violinist, Kreutzer is now remembered because of the dedication of BEETHOVEN's Sonata for violin and piano, Op. 47. His ETUDES are still used, and his OPERA, *Lodoiska*, is known. Other works—operas, CONCERTOS, STRING QUARTETS and other ENSEMBLE music—are nearly forgotten.

Kreuz (G): sharp.

Krieger, Johann: *b.* Nuremberg, December 28, 1651; *d.* Zittau, July 18, 1735. Organist at Zittau from 1681 till his death, Krieger wrote a wide variety of KEYBOARD music, together with MOTETS, MASSES, and secular POLYPHONIC music. His organ works were praised by HANDEL. He was a brother of J. P. KRIEGER.

Krieger, Johann Philipp: *b.* Nuremberg, February 25, 1649; *d.* Weissenfels, February 7, 1725. J. P. Krieger's most important post was as music director at Weissenfels and Halle. He wrote a variety of instrumental ENSEMBLE music together with OPERAS, church music, and organ works.

Kuhlau, Friedrich: *b.* Ülzen, Germany, September 11, 1786; *d.* Copenhagen, March 12, 1832. A court musician at Copenhagen from 1813, Kuhlau wrote a handful of OPERAS, ENSEMBLE music for flute and other instruments, two piano CONCERTOS, piano

SONATAS and SONATINAS (still used for teaching purposes), and songs.

Kuhnau, Johann: *b.* Geising, April 6, 1660; *d.* Leipzig, June 5, 1722. After studying law at the University of Leipzig, Kuhnau was appointed (1684) o r g a n i s t at St. Thomas's in that city, becoming cantor in 1701. (BACH succeeded to this post after Kuhnau's death.) Kuhnau was one of the leading CANTATA composers of his generation, judging from the surviving fraction of his works of this sort, and his music influenced that of Bach. He was the first German composer to write harpsichord works employing the structure of the Italian church SONATA (customarily written for two instruments and continuo). His *Biblical Sonatas* for harpsichord are among the most famous examples of BAROQUE PROGRAM MUSIC. He wrote theoretical works about music, as well as an amusing satirical novel, *The Musical Quack*.

Kutchka: *see* THE FIVE.

Kyrie (Gr): the first section of the MASS ORDINARY.

L

La: (1) the note *a*; (2) the sixth degree of the SCALE.

Lai (F), **Leich** (G), **Lay:** a variety of trouvère and, later, Minnesinger song, structurally similar to the SEQUENCE. In its strictest form, the lengthy text consists of a number of stanzas of varying structure, each stanza being divisible into two sections of equivalent form, set to the same or similar music. However, threefold and fourfold melodic repetition may occur within a stanza, while sometimes repetition is avoided. Almost all lais are written for unaccompanied voice.

Lalande, Michel Richard de: *b.* Paris, December 15, 1657; *d.* Versailles, June 18, 1726. The leading French composer of sacred music of his generation, Lalande became one of the superintendents of the chapel of Louis XIV in 1683. Later he became sole occupant of this post and held other royal titles as well. He wrote over 70 MOTETS for chorus and orchestra, together with other sacred music, BALLETS, and instrumental INTERLUDES.

Lalo, (Victor Antoine) Édouard: *b.* Lille, January 27, 1823; *d.* Paris, April 22, 1892. Lalo studied both at Lille and Paris, becoming a skilled violinist and violist. He achieved his first major success as a composer with his *Symphonie espagnole* for violin and orchestra. This work is still popular, and excerpts from his OPERA, *Le Roi d'Ys* and BALLET, *Namouna,* are still performed. Other works by Lalo include CONCERTOS, CHAMBER MUSIC, SYMPHONIES, and songs.

Lament: a generic designation for works commemorating a death or a departure. Laments played on bagpipes are part of traditional Scottish and Irish funeral rites. The earliest preserved laments, referring to the 7th-century Visigoths, King Chindasvinthus and Queen Reciberga, and to Charlemagne, are each entitled *planctus.* They are in staffless neumes and cannot be transcribed accurately. However, the pitches of the later *planh* by Gaucelm Faidit on the death of King Richard the Lion-Hearted may be read easily. Laments and elegies were frequently written in late-16th-century and 17th-century England, and several prominent examples are to be found in 17th-century OPERAS. The TOMBEAU is another 17th-century genre belonging to the category of laments; the title was used later by RAVEL.

Lamentations: the setting— in plainsong or polyphony— of a large portion of the Lamentations of Jeremiah, employed in the Roman Catholic rite at Matins on Thursday, Friday, and Saturday of Holy Week. The earliest setting, by OCKEGHEM, was followed by numerous others of the 16th to early 18th centuries. A 1588 setting by PALESTRINA is still performed at the Sistine Chapel. Other important composers of Lamentations include LA RUE, LE JEUNE, MORALES, LASSUS, BYRD, M. A. CHARPENTIER, and COUPERIN.

Landi, Stefano: *b.* Rome, *c.* 1590, *d.* Rome, *c.*1655. A student of G. M. and G. B. Nanino, Landi was a singer in the Papal Chapel from 1629. He was one of the earliest opera composers in Rome, his most important work being the sacred OPERA, *Sant' Alessio.* In addition, he wrote polyphonic MASSES and other sacred music, MADRIGALS, MONODIES, and instrumental CANZONAS.

Landini, Francesco: *b.* Fiesole, 1325; *d.* Florence, September 2, 1397; the most important Italian musician of his century. Blind since childhood, Landini was a gifted instrumentalist, particularly adept at the small portative organ. Over 150 of his two- and three-voice secular works survive, mainly *ballate,* together with a few MADRIGALS and CACCE.

Ländler (G): an Austrian dance, popular in the late 18th and early 19th centuries, similar in character to a slow waltz. MOZART, BEETHOVEN, and SCHUBERT all wrote Ländler.

Langsam (G): slow.

Larghetto (I): a slow TEMPO.

Largo (I): a TEMPO slower than LARGHETTO.

La Rue, Pierre de: *b.* Picardy, *c.*1460; *d.* Courtrai, November 20, 1518. After serving Archduke Maximilian, La Rue was employed successively by Duke Philippe le Beau, Margaret of Austria, and Charles V. He wrote more than three dozen MASSES, including one of the outstanding early polyphonic REQUIEMS. In addition, a substantial number of MOTETS and CHANSONS by La Rue are still extant.

Lassan, Lassu: the slow section of a CSÁRDÁS.

Lassus, Roland de (Orlando di Lasso): *b.* Mons, 1532; *d.* Munich, June 14, 1594. Famed as a child for the beauty of his voice, Lassus, when twelve, entered the service of Ferdinand Gonzaga, Viceroy of Sicily. In 1553 Lassus became choir director of St. John Lateran in Rome. After two years in Antwerp, Lassus was engaged by Duke Albert V of Bavaria in 1556 (in Munich). He was promoted to music director in 1560 and held this post until his death. Lassus was knighted by Emperor Maximilian II in 1570.

Lassus' works—over 2000 in number—encompass every major vocal genre of his time: CHANSONS, MADRIGALS, VILLANELLES, LIEDER, MOTETS, PSALMS, PASSIONS, MAGNIFICATS, MASSES, etc. His music, together with that of PALESTRINA and BYRD, represents the peak of late RENAISSANCE achievement. Lassus' style is more dramatic than that of Palestrina; it is terser and more harmonic. The melodies are more active and less sinuous. Exceptionally sensitive in the interpretation of the text, Lassus is equally adept in setting the light and humorous (e.g., *Audite Nova*) and the profound and moving (e.g., the *Penitential Psalms*).

Lauda (I): an Italian devotional song of the Middle Ages or RENAISSANCE. Two important repertoires survive. The first, belonging to the late 13th to early 14th centuries, comprises works for unaccompanied VOICE; many are comparatively simple and syllabic, some being elaborate and florid. The second, belonging primarily to the 16th century, comprises works that are normally set for four voices in a relatively simple, harmonic idiom.

Lauds: see OFFICE.

Laute (G): lute.

Lawes, Henry: *b.* Dinton, Wilts., January 5, 1596; *d.* London, October 21, 1662. A student of Giovanni Coperario, and a member of the Chapel Royal, Lawes wrote music for Milton's *Comus*, collaborated on Davenant's *Siege of Rhodes*, and wrote AIRS, PSALM tunes, and ANTHEMS.

Lawes, William: *b.* Salisbury, April 1602; *d.* Chester, 1645. Like his brother, HENRY LAWES, William Lawes was a student of Coperario. He served in the chapel of Charles I. He was an influential composer of instrumental ENSEMBLE music, as well as of ANTHEMS, songs, CATCHES, and MASQUES.

Leader: (1) concertmaster; (2) conductor; (3) the first violinist of a STRING QUARTET.

Leading tone (Leading note): the seventh degree of the major or harmonic minor SCALE. The leading tone is a half step below the TONIC, and its primary function is to lead to the tonic.

Lebhaft (G): lively.

Lechner, Leonhard: *b.* Etschtal, *c.*1553; *d.* Stuttgart, September 9, 1606. A choirboy under LASSUS, Lechner eventually became music director at Stuttgart (1587). One of the most important German composers of his generation, he wrote MOTETS, MASSES, MAGNIFICATS, penitential PSALMS, a PASSION, and sacred and secular German POLYPHONIC songs.

Leclair, Jean Marie: *b.* Lyons, May 10, 1697; *d.* Paris, October 22, 1764. As a young man Leclair forsook a career as dancer and ballet master for one as violinist and composer. He was active chiefly in Paris. A brilliant performer, Leclair was the greatest French composer of solo and trio SONATAS. He wrote also CONCERTOS, an OPERA, and an opera-BALLET. He required an advanced technique in the service of expressive music.

Ledger lines: short lines added above or below the STAFF to permit the precise NOTATION of PITCHES higher or lower than those within the staff.

Legato (L): a style of performance in which a group of notes is phrased as smoothly as possible, not permitting even tiny pauses between consecutive tones. *Legatissimo*, as smooth as possible.

Légèrement (F), **Leggiero** (I), **Con leggerezza** (I): lightly, gracefully.

Legno (I): wood. *Col legno* directs the string player to bounce the wood of the bow against the string(s). Older usages include *organo di legno*, a chamber organ with flue pipes; and *stromenti di legno*, woodwinds.

Legrenzi, Giovanni: *b.* Clusone, August 12, 1626; *d.* Venice, May 26, 1690. Active in several north Italian cities, Legrenzi settled in Venice, becoming head of the Conservatorio dei Mendicanti in 1672 and music director at Saint Mark's in 1685. LOTTI and CALDARA were among his pupils. Legrenzi helped further the development of individuality and independence among the movements of trio SONATAS. He was a key figure also in the development of Italian OPERA, furthering the evolution of the recitative and the development of more imaginative instrumental support for the ARIAS.

Lehár, Franz: *b.* Komáron, April 30, 1870; *d.* Bad Ischl, October 24, 1948. Following early instruction by his father, Lehár studied at the Prague Conservatory and worked privately with Fibich. The most successful composer of German OPERETTAS of his day, Lehár is remembered above all for *The Merry Widow, The Count of Luxemburg,* and *Gypsy Love.* In addition to his operettas, imbued with Viennese gaiety, in the spirit of J. STRAUSS, Jr., Lehár wrote many dances and marches, orchestral music, an OPERA, and a song cycle.

Leich (G): see LAI.

Leier (G): (1) hurdy-gurdy; (2) lyra.

Leitmotiv (G): a musical motive in an OPERA recurring in varied forms to symbolize a character, object, place, or idea. WAGNER's later operas —e.g., those of the *Ring of the Nibelung*—make extensive use of leitmotivs, as do several operas by Wagner's followers. The term was first used in a discussion of Wagnerian opera. Recurring themes may be found also in operas by MOZART, GRÉTRY, WEBER, and VERDI, as well as in 19th-century instrumental music and art songs.

Le Jeune, Claude: *b.* Valenciennes, 1528; *d.* Paris, September 25, 1600. Active chiefly in Paris, Le Jeune was a member of Antoine de Baïf's circle, the *Académie de poésie et musique.* He is best known for his CHANSONS and PSALMS set according to the principles of *vers mesurés,* long and short text syllables being each accompanied by equivalent note values. Le Jeune composed other secular and sacred music following more customary rhythmic organization and a few instrumental ENSEMBLE pieces.

Lento (I): a slow TEMPO.

Leo, Leonardo: *b.* San Vito degli Schiavi, August 5, 1694; *d.* Naples, October 31, 1744. Active in Naples as a composer, organist, and teacher, Leo held posts at the Conservatorio della Pietà, the Royal Chapel, and the Conservatorio di S. Onofrio. Among his pupils were JOMMELLI and PERGOLESI. His more than 50 OPERAS demonstrate the development of the large-scale coloratura ARIA DA CAPO. Leo wrote a wide variety of sacred vocal music, including MASSES, ORATORIOS, *misereres* and MOTETS. His instrumental music includes cello CONCERTOS, organ FUGUES, and TOCCATAS.

Leoncavallo, Ruggiero: *b.* Naples, March 8, 1858; *d.* Montecatini, August 9, 1919. After study at the Naples Conservatory Leoncavallo earned a living as a café pianist for many years, traveling widely in Europe and Egypt. His masterpiece, *I Pagliacci,* was patterned on MASCAGNI's *Cavalleria Rusticana,* and the two short OPERAS have been performed together ever since. Together they helped establish the trend towards realism in Italian opera around the turn of the century. Other operas, a BALLET, and a SYMPHONIC POEM met with minor success.

Leonin (Leoninus): mid-12th century composer, famed for the composition of a cycle of two-part organa (*see* MEDIEVAL MUSIC) for the major feasts of the church year, known as the *Magnus Liber Organi.* The first known master of the "Notre Dame School" (*see also* PEROTIN), Leonin was possibly active shortly prior to the founding of Notre Dame in 1163.

Lesson: a title for English compositions of the 17th and 18th centuries; frequently these were SUITES, but some examples were ETUDES or SONATAS. The title was customarily used for SOLO instrumental pieces, although ENSEMBLE works were occasionally so designated.

Le Sueur, Jean François: *b.* Drucat-Plessiel (Abbeville), February 15, 1760; *d.* Paris, October 6, 1837. After having served as music master at Dijon, Le Mans, and Tours, Le Sueur became music director at Notre Dame and served both Napoleon and Louis XVIII in the same capacity. He was also an inspector and professor at the Paris Con-

servatory, BERLIOZ and GOU-
NOD being among his pupils.
He composed MASSES, MO-
TETS, and other church music in a dramatic style, with
full orchestra, and was an influential composer of OPERAS,
these including *La Caverne*
and *Paul et Virginie.*

**Liadov, Anatol Konstantino-
vich:** *b.* St. Petersburg, May
10, 1855; *d.* Novgorod, August 28, 1914. After study at
the St. Petersburg Conservatory with RIMSKY-KORSAKOV,
Liadov was appointed theory
instructor at that school. PRO-
KOFIEV and Miaskovsky were
among his students. He composed SYMPHONIC POEMS and
other orchestral works—the
best known being *Baba Yaga,
Enchanted Lake,* and *Kiki-
mora*—and a wide variety
of piano music; he arranged
an extensive collection of
Russian FOLK SONGS for voice
and piano.

Liber Usualis (L.): a book containing the major portion of
the CHANTS and recited texts
of both the MASS and OFFICE
of the Roman Catholic rite.

Libretto: the text of an OP-
ERA, ORATORIO, MASQUE, or
other musico-dramatic work.
Normally the libretto is the
work of one man, the music,
that of another. However,
WAGNER wrote his own li-
brettos, as have other composers on occasion. A libretto
may be of scant literary merit
and yet be effective provided

that it satisfies the special
needs of the hybrid form for
which it is intended. Librettos
may be based on mythology,
the Bible, on actual incidents,
and on famous plays (e.g., by
Shakespeare), novels, and
stories. Almost invariably the
literary models are reworked.
Librettos for masques were
often written by famous poets
and dramatists, but only
rarely have opera and oratorio librettists achieved independent literary renown, as
did METASTASIO and SCRIBE.

Lied (G): SONG. In English
usage, the term denotes a
song with German text; very
frequently it denotes specifically a work of the ROMANTIC
period, e.g., by SCHUBERT,
SCHUMANN, BRAHMS, WOLF,
MAHLER, or Richard STRAUSS.

Liederkreis (G): song cycle.

Ligature: a compound symbol for a group of notes
(rather than for a single note)
used in MEDIEVAL and RENAIS-
SANCE NOTATIONS. Ligatures
were derived from the square
forms of NEUMES. Originally,
the various ligatures had no
fixed rhythmic values; specific ligatures were interpreted according to the context in which they appeared.
During the second half of
the 13th century a system was
evolved whereby one could
determine the time-value of
each note within a ligature according to the ligature's form.

Lira (I): the name for several

bowed string instruments of the VIOLIN FAMILY known in Europe from the 10th century (or earlier) to the 17th. These shared certain general characteristics: the use of drone strings, a heart-shaped pegbox, and rear (instead of side) pegs. The *lira da gamba* (*c.*1580–1650) was designed for the playing of chords rather than melodies. Concerning the *lira organizzata,* see HURDY-GURDY.

Liszt, Franz (Ferencz): *b.* Raiding, Hungary, October 22, 1811; *d.* Bayreuth, July 31, 1886; the greatest of the ROMANTIC piano virtuosos and the creator of the SYMPHONIC POEM.

Trained by his father, an official in the service of Prince Anton Esterházy, Liszt made his début when nine. Funds provided by a group of Hungarian noblemen enabled him to move to Vienna in 1821; there he met BEETHOVEN and SCHUBERT and studied with CZERNY and SALIERI. Two years later he went to Paris. Although CHERUBINI forbade his admittance to the Conservatory, Liszt remained in Paris, studying composition briefly with Ferdinando Paer and REICHA and continuing his career as a concert pianist. In 1835 Liszt began a liaison with the Countess d'Agoult; their daughter Cosima (one of three children) later married Richard WAGNER. Liszt's semiretirement ended in 1839, when he embarked on a series of tours throughout Europe, adding further laurels to an already prodigious reputation. From 1848 to 1861 he served as music director to the Weimar court; there he aided many musicians, especially Wagner. In these years Liszt turned his principal attention to orchestral composition. The period 1861–69 was spent primarily in Rome. Liszt took minor orders and was named abbé by Pope Pius IX in 1866. The master's last years were divided chiefly between Weimar, Budapest, and Rome.

As a virtuoso, Liszt was without a peer. As a teacher, he influenced many of the best pianists of the succeeding generation, including BUSONI, D'ALBERT, Alexander Siloti, and Moriz Rosenthal. He was among the foremost of those responsible for the concept of the musician as a creative genius, an artist rather than a craftsman. He believed ardently that music should be associated with poetic imagery and that abstract tone patterns were of small significance. He extended the path of BERLIOZ and, together with Wagner, was among the "New Germans," who opposed the classical orientation of BRAHMS and his followers.

Liszt created an orchestral style of piano writing that draws on the violin showmanship of PAGANINI and the expanded piano technique of CHOPIN, HUMMEL, Thalberg, and other virtuosi. His ability to transform works from the symphonic, operatic, organ, and song literatures into idiomatic piano pieces is evidenced in his numerous transcriptions. Although the technical demands of Liszt's piano works are subservient to musical expression, not even the most personal works achieve true intimacy; they all show an awareness of an audience. Because modern tastes have turned against the flamboyant rhetoric of Romanticism, Liszt no longer occupies the commanding position that he once did. However, his *Années de Pèlerinage* and *Harmonies poétiques et religieuses* contain many fine works and his various *Études* are still regarded as the ultimate test of piano technique. The rising tide of musical nationalism is exemplified in his 20 *Hungarian Rhapsodies*, which utilize gypsy airs. Liszt avoided the classical SONATA form; his *Piano Sonata in B minor* is written in one extended movement, based on the development of four themes. Similar techniques are employed in Liszt's 13 symphonic poems, which include *Les Préludes, Mazeppa, Orpheus,* and *Hamlet.* Liszt's *Faust* and *Dante* SYMPHONIES are equally descriptive. Some of his 60 SONGS possess great beauty, but they are seldom performed. Also neglected are his large religious works, including two ORATORIOS— *The Legend of St. Elizabeth* and *Christus*—a setting of Psalm XIII, and the *Grand Festival Mass* and *Hungarian Coronation Mass.*

On the whole, Liszt's output is of uneven quality. There are many moments that are banal posturing; yet there are others of great élan and of melodic and harmonic daring. Liszt deeply influenced the development of late Romantic harmony.

Litany: a long prayer, built of a series of supplications to God, the Virgin, and the Saints, alternating with congregational responses. In the Roman Catholic rite, litanies are chanted mainly on one tone with occasional inflections. POLYPHONIC settings have been composed by PALESTRINA, LASSUS, MOZART, and TALLIS (the latter furnishing two Anglican litanies).

Liturgical dramas: medieval plays, which developed from the expansion of dialogue TROPES, and which in turn gave rise to mystery plays. Some liturgical dramas—e.g., *The Play of Daniel, The Play of Herod* — survive with monophonic music.

Lituus: (1) an ancient Roman straight trumpet with an upturned, hooked bell; (2) a CROMORNE, in PRAETORIUS's usage (1619); (3) a BRASS INSTRUMENT of disputed identity in BACH's usage (Cantata 118), possibly either a trumpet or a horn.

Liuto (I): lute.

Locatelli, Pietro: *b.* Bergamo, September 3, 1695; *d.* Amsterdam, March 30, 1764. A student of CORELLI, Locatelli became one of the outstanding violin virtuosos of his day. He composed principally for his instrument, writing *concerti grossi*, violin CONCERTOS, trio and solo SONATAS, as well as sonatas for flute and *continuo.*

Locke, Matthew: *b.* Exeter, *c.*1630; *d.* London, August 1677. Locke served as composer to Charles II (1660) and as organist to Queen Catherine. He is best known for his stage music, including the MASQUES *Cupid and Death* and *The Siege of Rhodes;* he composed also SUITES for viols, songs, ANTHEMS, and other sacred music and wrote a treatise on FIGURED BASS.

Loco (I): a direction to play at the normal PITCH (following a direction to play an octave higher or lower), or—in string music—in normal position.

Locrian: an ancient Greek mode that may be represented by a scale descending through the white keys from *a'* to *a. See* CHURCH MODES.

Loeffler, Charles Martin: *b.* Mulhouse (Alsace), January 30, 1861; *d.* Medfield, Mass., May 19, 1935. Loeffler traveled widely in Europe as a child and youth, receiving his most important training in Berlin and Paris. He came to the United States in 1881, and played violin in New York and then in Boston until 1903. His compositions reveal both Russian and French IMPRESSIONISTIC influences. Among the best known of his orchestral works are *A Pagan Poem* (after Virgil), *Poem* (after Verlaine), *Memories of My Childhood,* and *La Mort de Tintagiles.* He also wrote CHAMBER MUSIC, choral music, songs, and two OPERAS that were never performed.

Loeillet, Jean-Baptiste: *b.* Ghent, November 18, 1680; *d.* London, July 19, 1750. After studying in Ghent and Paris, Loeillet went to London in 1705, where he became successful as a flutist, oboist, and harpsichordist. His main works include several SUITES for harpsichord, together with trio SONATAS and other CHAMBER works.

Loewe, (Johann) Carl Gott-

fried: *b*. Löbejün, November 30, 1796; *d*. Kiel, April 20, 1869. Loewe completed his studies under Türk at Halle. He was a teacher and organist in Stettin (1821–66), except for various periods spent in travel. Although Loewe was a versatile composer, he is known almost exclusively as a composer of German BALLADS, ranking among the masters of this genre. The dramatic elements of these strongly influenced BRAHMS, WAGNER, and especially WOLF. He also wrote many ORATORIOS, a CANTATA, five OPERAS, piano, CHAMBER and orchestral music.

Lombardic rhythm (Scotch snap): a rhythmic pattern consisting of a fast note on the BEAT followed by a dotted value three times its length, e.g.,

Long, Longa (L): in MEDIEVAL and RENAISSANCE NOTATION, a time-value represented by a square note with a descending tail at the right; the long is four to nine times as long as the semi-breve, the note equivalent to the modern whole note. (The various speeds of semibreves in medieval and Renaissance music were several times faster than those of modern whole notes.)

Lortzing, (Gustav) Albert: *b*. Berlin, October 23, 1801; *d*. Berlin, January 21, 1851. The son of wandering troupers, Lortzing led a varied career as singer, actor, composer, conductor, and impresario. He made a contribution to the development of German ROMANTIC OPERA, his most important work being *Czar und Zimmermann*. Lortzing wrote also two ORATORIOS, songs, and incidental music.

Lotti, Antonio: *b*. Venice, *c*.1667; *d*. Venice, January 5, 1740. A pupil of LEGRENZI, Lotti spent most of his life at St. Mark's, becoming first organist in 1704 and music director in 1736. He was an influential teacher. He was one of the more successful composers of OPERA, ORATORIOS, and CANTATAS of the late BAROQUE. While a progressive composer in these spheres, he was successful also in the conservative idiom that was expected of a church composer, writing MASSES, MOTETS, and other sacred music.

Loure (F): (1) Old French for bagpipe; (2) a dance of the 17th and 18th centuries, in 6/4 time and using dotted rhythms.

Louré (F): a style of BOWING, used in slow TEMPOS, which affords a slight emphasis and separation to each of a group of notes written within a slur.

Lübeck, Vincent: *b*. Padingbüttel, September 1654; *d*. Hamburg, February 9, 1740.

An organist at Stade and then at Hamburg, Lübeck was an important composer of CAN-TATAS, CHORALE PRELUDES, and other organ works.

Luening, Otto: *b.* Milwaukee, June 15, 1900. Luening completed his training at Munich and Zürich, also studying privately with BUSONI. He has been a member of several distinguished American faculties, including that of Columbia University. Although Luening has written numerous works for traditional media—often in a dissonant, polytonal style —he is now best known for his ELECTRONIC MUSIC, which uses conventional musical sounds transformed electronically and fixed by the use of tape recorder. He is one of the directors of the Electronic Music Center, operated by Columbia and Princeton Universities.

Lully, Jean-Baptiste: *b.* Florence, November 28, 1632; *d.* Paris, March 22, 1687; the composer chiefly responsible for the establishment of OP-ERA in French.

Lully went to Paris in 1646 as a page in the service of Mlle. d'Orléans and entered the service of King Louis XIV in 1652. He was shortly permitted to organize his own orchestra, "les petits violons," which he drilled into a famous ENSEMBLE. In 1661 he became court composer and, the next year, mu-

sic master to the royal family. In 1672 Lully obtained from Perrin the royal patent for the exclusive production of opera in France; he established the *Académie royale de musique* for the exercise of this privilege. While beating time with a heavy staff, Lully wounded his foot and died from the ensuing infection.

From 1664 to 1672, Lully collaborated with Molière in writing a series of *comédies-ballets;* in this genre he developed large CHORAL forms and more dramatic RECITA-TIVES. Thereafter Lully devoted himself chiefly to the composition of opera. He achieved the clarity demanded by the French by carefully molding the rhythm of his recitative after the speech rhythms of prominent actors. In his operatic style he avoids the florid melodies, the affective dissonances, and the set forms appearing in contemporary Italian opera. Both choral and BALLET sections are especially prominent in his works. Lully is responsible for the development of the French OVERTURE, a form that achieved widespread employment. In addition to his stage works, Lully wrote a few sacred pieces and some instrumental music.

Lur: an *S*-shaped Scandinavian horn of the Bronze Age. The planes of the two curves of the "S" are at right angles.

Lusingando (I): in a tender fashion.

Lute: a plucked string instrument with a body shaped like a halved pear and a longish neck; normally the fingerboard is fretted and the pegbox bent back. The term may refer to one variety of instrument, developed in early medieval Europe from Arabian ancestors, or it may denote a large family of instruments dating back to 2000 B.C. and distributed from the Far East to Western Europe. Only the former usage will be considered here. The medieval lute used four pairs of strings; each pair, tuned in octaves, is called a *course*. By 1500, the instrument assumed its final form, having added another double course as well as a single course (the highest in PITCH) for the MELODY. The courses were tuned a fourth apart except for a third between the middle courses. About 1640 Denis Gaultier proposed a tuning *A, d, f, a, d', f'*, and this *nouveau ton* was generally adopted by others. In the Middle Ages, the strings were plucked with a plectrum, but this device was discarded when a POLYPHONIC style of playing was developed during the RENAISSANCE. The increased use of the bass register led in the late 16th century to the development of a family of archlutes with additional bass strings. Because the widening of the fingerboard would have made the new instruments much more clumsy to play, the added strings were run outside the fingerboard. (Since these strings could not be stopped, their pitch could be altered only by retuning.) There are two main varieties of archlute, the chitarrone and the theorboe. The *chitarrone* had the body of a large lute and an extremely long neck, which extended the length of the instrument to upward of six feet. The stopped strings were run to a pegbox midway in the neck, while the bass strings were run to a second pegbox at the extreme end. In the *theorboe*, the additional pegbox for the bass strings was placed slightly higher and to the side of the first, the two being connected by a small, S-shaped neck. The lute was one of the most popular instruments of the 16th and 17th centuries, being used in ENSEMBLES, as ACCOMPANIMENT for a vocal soloist, and as a SOLO instrument in its own right. The solo literature includes arrangements of vocal polyphony, dance pieces, variations, preludes, and ricercars. The lute faded rapidly in importance during the 18th century, although both BACH and HAYDN used the instrument on occasion. Lute music is written in TABLATURE. *See illustration, p. 167.*

Lydian mode: (1) the fifth CHURCH MODE; (2) an ancient Greek mode that may be represented by a scale descending through the white keys from *c'* to *c.*

Lyra: (1) a member of the lyre family used in ancient Greece, lighter and of more recent origin than the KITHARA. Its body consisted of a tortoise shell or wooden bowl, covered by hide. Its arms were often made of horn. (2) A variety of medieval fiddle. (3) The *lyra organizzata* of the 18th century was a HURDY-GURDY. (4) Short for *lyra glockenspiel* or *bell lyre,* a portable instrument used in marching bands. A differentiation of meanings proper to the spellings *lira, lyra,* and *lyre* has been proposed, but has not achieved widespread acceptance.

Lyra viol: *see* VIOLA BASTARDA.

Lyre: (1) a generic name for a family of plucked string instruments having a body, two arms, and a yoke; (2) the specific name for the instrument indicated under LYRA (sense 1).

M

MacDowell, Edward Alexander: *b.* New York City, December 18, 1861; *d.* New York City, January 23, 1908. MacDowell received much of his training in Europe and began his teaching career at the Darmstadt Conservatory. He returned to the United States in 1888, living first in Boston and then in New York, where he was appointed head of the department of music at Columbia University in 1896. His mental health deteriorated rapidly after 1904. MacDowell enjoyed a greater international reputation than any other native American Romantic composer. His piano CONCERTOS and SONATAS are still played occasionally, together with some of his simpler piano pieces. He wrote also several SYMPHONIC POEMS, two SUITES, songs, and choral works.

Machaut, Guillaume de: *b.* Champagne, *c.*1300; *d.* Rheims, 1377; preeminent French poet and composer of the 14th century. A cleric, Machaut served first King John of Bohemia and then Charles V of France. In 1340 he became canon of Rheims. The major portion of his output is secular: BALLADES, RONDEAUX, and VIRELAIS. He wrote also nearly two dozen MOTETS and the first known setting of a complete MASS ORDINARY by one composer.

Madrigal: (1) a 14th-century Italian secular vocal form for two or three parts. The 14th-century madrigal texts consist of 1–4 stanzas of three lines, followed by a two-line RITORNELLO. The music is the same for each stanza, while new music is provided for the ritornello. The upper part is more ornate than the lower and florid passages often occur at the beginnings and ends of text lines. JACOPO DA BOLOGNA, Giovanni da Cascia,

Nicolo da Perugia, and LANDINI were among the masters of this form. (2) A secular vocal form of the 16th and early 17th centuries which originated in Italy. The texts of these works were based largely on pastoral subjects (although there are devotional madrigals by composers such as PALESTRINA) and did not follow any fixed poetic form. Early examples of this repertoire, written *c.*1530–50 by such composers as VERDELOT, FESTA, and ARCADELT, are for three or four parts, in a predominantly chordal style that derives from the FROTTOLA. With the works of WILLAERT, RORE, LASSUS, MONTE, and A. GABRIELI, the madrigal entered a "classic" period. IMITATION was used often, the number of voice-parts was usually five. A concern for the musical expression of the text was an important trait of the form: word painting and chromaticism (*see* PROGRAM MUSIC) were two of the chief means employed to underline key words. Daring chromaticism appears in late madrigals by composers such as MARENZIO and GESUALDO. After the turn of the 17th century, instrumentally accompanied madrigals for one and two voices, showing the influence of MONODY and OPERA, were written by composers such as MONTEVERDI. The Italian madrigal was well received in England in the 1580s and native English composers, such as BYRD, MORLEY, WEELKES, WILBYE, and GIBBONS, cultivated the form intensively c.1590–1630.

Maestoso (I): majestic, dignified.

Maestro di cappella (I), **Maestro de capilla** (S), **Maître de chapelle** (F), **Kapellmeister** (G): during the 17th to 19th centuries, the director in charge of the musical establishment of a ruler, nobleman, churchman, church, or township. In addition to rehearsing and leading all performances, the *maestro di cappella* was normally expected to compose a major share of the new music required for various occasions. In addition, he might be expected to supervise both the conduct and the further training of the musisians, take charge of the music library, and see that the musical instruments were properly maintained. Many such men, while adequate performers, were dull composers—hence, the derisive intent of the term, *Kapellmeistermusik*.

Maggiore (I): major.

Magnificat: the Canticle of the Virgin. In the Roman Catholic rite the Magnificat is sung at Vespers. The CHANT consists of a simple formula that is adapted to each of the ten verses and the two verses of the *Gloria Patri*. The Magnificat is both preceded and followed by an antiphon and the mode of this antiphon determines the choice of the formula for the Magnificat. In PLAINSONG performance, successive verses alternate between the two halves of the choir. POLYPHONIC settings of the Magnificat were composed frequently during the 15th to 18th centuries, either for voices or organ. In most RENAISSANCE settings only alternate verses (usually the even-numbered ones) were treated polyphonically, the remaining verses being performed in plainsong. In Magnificats of this period composers often maintained a free melodic relationship between the plainsong and the polyphony. In the BAROQUE the Magnificat was often treated as a multisectional work similar to the CANTATA and ORATORIO, employing soloists, chorus, and orchestra; the Magnificat by J. S. BACH is the most famous of such works.

Mahler, Gustav: *b*. Kalischt, July 7, 1860; *d*. Vienna, May 18, 1911; important late ROMANTIC symphonist and conductor.

Mahler began a career as an opera conductor in 1880, following study at the Vienna Conservatory and the University of Vienna. His great talent, high artistic standards, and executive ability brought him increasing success. From 1883 to 1897 he conducted OPERA in Kassel, Prague, Leipzig, and Budapest. As director of the Vienna Opera from 1897 to 1907, Mahler was responsible for a period of great brilliance. His inflexibility, however, created enemies who finally forced his resignation. From 1907 he was conductor of the New York Metropolitan Opera, and from 1909, director of the New York Philharmonic Orchestra.

The lyrical nature of Mahler's talent appears most clearly in his SONG CYCLES, including the *Lieder eines fahrenden Gesselen, Des Knaben Wunderhorn*, and the *Kindertotenlieder*. The first four of his ten SYMPHONIES— the tenth being incomplete when he died—use melodies from these songs. The Second, Third, Fourth, and Eighth symphonies use voices as well as instruments, an extension of a tradition that derives from BEETHOVEN's *Ninth Symphony. Das Lied von der Erde*, one of Mahler's best known works, is midway between a song cycle and a symphony. Mahler, like BERLIOZ and WAGNER, was a master orchestrator who contributed to the enlargement of the orchestra. Like BRUCKNER, he

expanded the symphony, lengthening the individual MOVEMENTS and increasing the number of movements. Unity is often achieved through thematic relationships between movements. Mahler's melodies have long lines and often use bold leaps for expressionistic purposes. His harmonies are richly chromatic. Critical evaluation of Mahler's work still varies widely. Some find it outstanding; others are unconvinced by its admixture of the simple and profound, the somber and playful.

Maître de chapelle: *see* MAESTRO DI CAPPELLA.

Major: a quality of INTERVAL, CHORD, mode, or SCALE.

Malagueña: an Andalusian dance in triple METER.

Malipiero, Gian Francesco: *b.* Venice, March 18, 1882. Both Malipiero's father and grandfather were musicians; Gian Francesco completed his training at the Bologna Conservatory and in Paris. He taught briefly at the University of Parma and was appointed director of the Liceo Musicale Benedetto Marcello in Venice in 1939. Malipiero's style, basically neoclassical, has been influenced by his interest in Italian BAROQUE music; he has edited the works of MONTEVERDI and has published works by numerous other Italian composers of the 17th and 18th centuries. A prolific composer, Malipiero has written numerous OPERAS, BALLETS, nine SYMPHONIES, several CONCERTOS and miscellaneous orchestral works, seven STRING QUARTETS and other CHAMBER MUSIC, choral and solo vocal works, and piano pieces.

Mandola (I): Mandora: a short-necked variety of LUTE used in 16th-century Spain.

Mandolin (Mandoline): a string instrument of the LUTE family strummed with a plectrum. Its body is in the shape of a halved pear; it has a short, fretted neck, and usually four pairs of strings. Although called for occasionally by HANDEL, MOZART, BEETHOVEN, MAHLER, SCHOENBERG, and lesser composers, it is chiefly a popular instrument.

Mannheim School: a loose designation for a number of mid-18th-century composers who wrote SYMPHONIES and CONCERTOS for the Mannheim orchestra. These men—including Johann, Karl, and Anton Stamitz, Cannabich, Toëschi, Filtz, Holzbauer, and Richter—made use of the famed skill and discipline of the ENSEMBLE and developed a homophonic orchestral style that featured rapidly ascending THEMES (often using scales or arpeggios), extended CRESCENDOS and DIMINUENDOS, and sudden dynamic contrasts.

Manual: a KEYBOARD (excepting one operated by the feet); the term ordinarily refers to an organ or harpsichord keyboard.

Maracas: a Cuban gourd rattle.

Marais, Marin: b. Paris, March 31, 1656; d. Paris, August 15, 1728. A student of Hottemann and LULLY, Marais was a famed virtuoso on the VIOLA DA GAMBA, serving Kings Louis XIV and XV in that capacity. He composed five books of pieces for his instrument and was among the earliest French composers to write trio SONATAS. He wrote also OPERAS and a TE DEUM.

Marcato (I): a direction indicating that the individual notes of a group are each to be played with greater than normal emphasis.

Marcello, Benedetto: b. Venice, July 24, 1686; d. Brescia, July 24, 1739. Trained as a lawyer and pursuing a career in politics, Marcello was a composer as well as a writer. His most famous work is the *Estro poetico-armonico,* comprising 50 settings of Giustiniani's PSALM paraphrases. Other compositions include MASSES, ORATORIOS, and other sacred music, CANTATAS, CANZONETTAS, music for the stage, CONCERTOS, and both chamber and keyboard SONATAS. A keen observer of the contemporary scene, he wrote a satirical description of operatic conventions, *Il teatro alla moda.*

March: music for parade or processional use, or of similar spirit. Marches may be written in 2/4, 4/4, or 6/8 time. The BEAT structure is meant to be clearly accented, and phrase construction is regular. Often a spirited main section frames one or two quieter sections, termed *trios.* Aside from military marches, there are marches in OPERAS, incidental music, SUITES, SONATAS, and SYMPHONIES. The greatest examples of the latter are those in BEETHOVEN's *Symphony No. 3 (Eroica),* his piano sonatas, Op. 26 and 101, and in CHOPIN's *Sonata in B♭ minor.*

Marcia (I): MARCH.

Marenzio, Luca: *b.* Coccaglio, 1553; *d.* Rome, August 22, 1599. One of the greatest of the Italian madrigalists, Marenzio served a number of Italian princes and churchmen (among them Cardinal Luigi d'Este) and King Sigismund III of Poland. His MADRIGALS summarize all the main techniques and styles of his period; Marenzio is particularly ingenious in the musical expression of poetic images. His sacred music includes several books of MOTETS.

Marimba: a member of the XYLOPHONE family of percussion instruments with tuned gourd. wooden box, or tubular metal resonators for each bar.

Marine trumpet: *see* TROMBA MARINA.

Marsch (G): MARCH.

Marschner, Heinrich August: *b.* Zittau, August 16, 1795; *d.* Hanover, December 14, 1861. After abandoning his study of law, Marschner became a pupil of Schicht. He was OPERA director at Dresden (1823) and Leipzig (1827), before becoming music director to the court at Hanover. As a leading opera composer, Marschner was an important l i n k between WEBER and WAGNER; his most successful works include *Hans Heiling, The Vampire,* and *Ivanhoe.* He wrote also songs, choruses, CHAMBER MUSIC, and works for piano.

Martelé (F), **Martellato** (I): a direction calling for a forceful, detached manner of playing a bowed string instrument or the piano.

Martin, Frank: *b.* Geneva, September 15, 1890. One of the foremost 20th-century Swiss composers, Martin studied under Lauber. He taught at several important European institutions. His early style, influenced by FRANCK and DEBUSSY, includes modal melodic elements and asymmetrical rhythms of FOLK MUSIC. Martin's later works employ TWELVE-TONE techniques, at first in a strict style, and then in a freer idiom. His output includes OPERAS, CANTATAS, SYMPHONIES, CONCERTOS, CHAMBER and CHORAL MUSIC.

Martini, Giovanni Battista: *b.* Bologna, April 24, 1706; *d.* Bologna, October 4, 1784. Ordained in 1722 (known therefore as Padre), Martini became music director for the church of San Francesco in Bologna in 1725. He was a versatile composer, producing vocal and instrumental music of every sort known to his day except for opera and ballet. Martini was also both historian and theorist, writing a three-volume history of music, and a two-volume COUNTERPOINT treatise, among other works. He was especially respected as the most learned musician of his day, and was sought as a teacher and adviser by many promising and prominent composers, among them GLUCK, MOZART, and GRÉTRY.

Martinu, Bohuslav, *b.* Polička, Bohemia, December 8, 1890; *d.* Liestal, Switzerland, August 28, 1959. Martinu studied with SUK and ROUSSEL. He was active in Prague, Paris, and New York, returning to teach composition at the Prague Conservatory after the Second World War. His work falls generally within the orbit of neoclassicism; his melodies and rhythms are of-ten influenced by elements of Czech FOLK MUSIC. Martinu wrote prolifically in a wide variety of media, being especially successful with smaller operatic forms.

Marziale (I): marchlike, martial.

Mascagni, Pietro: *b.* Leghorn, December 7, 1863; *d.* Rome, August 2, 1945. After study at the Milan Conservatory under PONCHIELLI, Mascagni became a conductor in the town of Cerignola. He achieved outstanding success in 1890 with the performance of his one-act OPERA, *Cavalleria Rusticana*. None of Mascagni's later operas approached the quality of this starkly realistic drama (*see* VERISMO), although *L'Amico Fritz* has retained a peripheral place in the Italian repertoire.

Mason, Daniel Gregory: *b.* Brookline, Mass., November 20, 1873; *d.* Greenwich, Conn., December 4, 1953. A member of a famous family of musicians, Daniel Mason studied at Harvard University and then with Percy Goetschius, CHADWICK, and D'INDY. He taught at Columbia University (1910–42). He wrote a wide variety of music in a lyric, conservative vein, including the OVERTURE *Chanticleer*, three SYMPHONIES and other orchestral music, choral and CHAMBER MUsic, songs, and piano music. He wrote many books and articles on music.

Mason, Lowell: *b.* Medfield, Mass., January 8, 1792; *d.* Orange, N.J., August 11, 1872. Self-taught, Lowell Mason became an influential teacher, organist, and conductor. He was president of the Handel and Haydn Society and one of the founders of the Boston Academy of Music. He was a prolific composer of HYMN tunes.

Masque, Mask: a lavish entertainment of the 16th–18th centuries, combining elements of ballet, drama, and song. Built about a set of masked stage dances and ballets performed by noblemen, the masque generally had a central THEME or device that was expressed also through recited poetry and song, the entertainment ending with a series of ballroom dances by the noble performers and the noble ladies of the audience. In the earlier masques, dialogue was spoken; the use of RECITATIVE was introduced perhaps in 1617. Owing to the genius of poets such as Jonson, Milton, Campion, Shirley, Beaumont, and Davenant and of designers such as Inigo Jones, the masque reached a peak in England during the first half of the 17th century. The English masque drew on earlier Italian masques and the French *ballet de cour* as well as on traditional English practices of mumming. Music was provided by such composers as the younger Alfonso Ferrabosco, William and Henry LAWES, Nicholas Lanier, and, later, LOCKE, BLOW, and ARNE. Often more than one composer contributed to a production. Music for 16th-century masques does not survive as such, although it is possible that some songs and dances still extant, e.g., by William Cornysh, were composed for masques. Although no complete scores survive for early 17th-century masques, much music has been preserved in outline form. The melody and bass are written down, but not the inner parts or the ORCHESTRATION.

Mass: the central rite of the Catholic Church, which, in its full form, consists of 18 items. Some of these are sung (*see* GREGORIAN CHANT); others are spoken or recited on a fixed PITCH. Some employ different texts according to the season or the festival of the day, while others have fixed texts, each with several musical settings. The former —including the Introit, Gradual, Alleluia, Tract, Offertory, and Communion—comprise the PROPER; the latter—including the Kyrie, Gloria, Credo, Sanctus (together with the Benedictus), and Agnus Dei—comprise the ORDINARY. In general, the chants of the Proper are older and more ornate than those of the Ordinary. The Proper was the first to be set polyphonically (*see* MEDIEVAL MUSIC for descriptions of organum), but composers' interest in this area declined sharply after the 13th century. Later collections of Proper settings— such as Isaac's *Choralis Constantinus* and Byrd's *Gradualia*—are infrequent. Thus a reference to a Mass by a particular composer implies a setting of the Ordinary.

Individual movements of the Ordinary, particularly the Kyrie, Sanctus, and Agnus, were set polyphonically during the 11–13th centuries. The first known setting of a complete Ordinary by one composer, that by MACHAUT, probably dates from the second quarter of the 14th century; however, the composition of single movements and of pairs remained the normal practice for this century. During the 15th century, the Mass attained a position in music comparable to that of the SYMPHONY during the CLASSICAL era. Most Masses of this time are based on pre-existent material and are classed according to the way in which this material is treated. A *Plainsong Mass* is one that uses in each movement a *cantus firmus* drawn from the corresponding part of Gregorian chant. Whether based on a chant, a voice-part of a CHANSON or MOTET, or a special melodic device, a *Cantus-firmus Mass* employs one *cantus firmus* throughout. This MELODY may be presented one or more times within a single division of the Mass, or it may be divided into sections that are each presented in successive divisions. Some portions of the Mass may dispense with the *cantus*. In the *Tenor Mass,* the *cantus* is treated in long notes in the tenor voice-part. This technique was one of the earliest to be explored and remained in use throughout the RENAISSANCE. As IMITATION became more and more important during the 15th century, fragments of the *cantus,* freely treated, began to appear in other VOICES as well. In another early form, the *Discant* or *Paraphrase Mass,* the *cantus*—often a liturgical melody—is freely elaborated in the highest voice. The *Parody Mass* of the mid-16th century draws upon the full fabric of a *polyphonic* composition, modified and interlarded with newly composed sections. In some instances the use of models of questionable propriety was too thinly disguised; this led the Council of Trent (1545–63) to ban the use of preexistent secular material.

During the RENAISSANCE and BAROQUE, Mass was sometimes celebrated in such fashion that individual phrases sung in plainsong alternated with polyphonic elaborations of the next section of plainsong performed on the organ; these polyphonic works are known as *Organ Masses.*

After 1600, some composers, such as ALLEGRI, Steffano Bernardi, and as late as LOTTI and FUX, wrote Masses in the *stile antico,* based on the style of PALESTRINA, but exhibiting also certain harmonic and rhythmic idioms that came into being with the development of MONODY. Others, especially BENEVOLI, expanded the Venetian polychoral style of Andrea and Giovanni GABRIELI to extraordinary lengths. Textures and forms associated with monody, OPERA, and chamber CANTATA in the 17th century were employed also in the writing of Masses. Orchestrally accompanied Masses employing both CHORUS and vocal soloists continued to increase in length during the 18th century, culminating in BACH's *B Minor Mass.* In works such as this, the texts for the five sections of the Ordinary were subdivided to provide the basis for several movements each. The ARIA DA CAPO with instrumental RITORNELLO was employed frequently for movements for soloists; the FUGUE occurred frequently in choral movements. The changes that are associated with the gradual development of the Classic style influenced the writing of Masses, and symphonic textures, idioms, and formal devices may be observed in the late Masses of HAYDN. (As a rule, the style of a Mass of any period differs little from other contemporary styles, and the comparative lack of a strictly liturgical style has clouded the appreciation of many fine works, especially of the Classical and ROMANTIC eras.) In addition to the *Missa Solemnis* and the *Mass in C* by BEETHOVEN, notable Masses of the 19th century include works by SCHUBERT, LISZT, FRANCK, and BRUCKNER. The Stravinsky Mass is among the best-known 20th-century contributions to this genre. Many Masses of the 18th and 19th centuries, including Bach's *Mass in B Minor* and Beethoven's *Missa Solemnis,* are more suited to concert than liturgical use, owing either to their length (excessive for normal liturgical occasions) and use of text repetition or to omissions or other departures from the liturgical texts.

Massenet, Jules Émile Frédéric: *b.* Montaud, May 12, 1842; *d.* Paris, August 13, 1912. Massenet was trained at the Paris Conservatoire under THOMAS and won the Prix de Rome in 1863. He was appointed professor of composition at the Conservatoire in 1878, remaining active until 1896. One of the most successful French OPERA composers of his day, Massenet is best remembered for *Manon, Werther, Thaïs,* and *Le Jongleur de Notre Dame.* He wrote also ORATORIOS, BALLETS, choral works, many songs, and a number of minor orchestral works.

Mastersinger: *see* MEISTERSINGER.

Matins: *see* OFFICE.

Mattheson, Johann: *b.* Hamburg, September 28, 1681; *d.* Hamburg, April 17, 1764. A lawyer and linguist who held important diplomatic posts, Mattheson was also a talented musician and writer on music. He worked intermittently at the Hamburg opera and in 1715 became music director at the Hamburg Cathedral. A competent composer, Mattheson wrote OPERAS, ORATORIOS, CANTATAS, a PASSION, a MASS, chamber SONATAS, and keyboard SUITES. He is best remembered, however, as a theorist and the writer of a biographical dictionary, *Grundlage einer Ehren-Pforte.*

Mazurka, Mazur: a Polish folk dance in triple METER, usually employing dotted rhythms and strong accents either on the second or third BEAT; the TEMPO is moderate to fast. The most celebrated works based on these rhythms are CHOPIN's Mazurkas.

Meantone tuning: *see* TUNING.

Measure: the segment of music contained between two BAR LINES.

Mechanical instruments: instruments that may be operated by someone without musical training. A few writers include the phonograph and tape recorder within this category, but electronic devices are usually excluded from the meaning. A rotating barrel with protruding pins at specially determined places is basic to many mechanical instruments. The rotation causes each pin either to strike directly the sounding material—e.g., a metal tooth in a music box—or to trip a lever or similar device that in turn permits wind to enter an organ pipe (as in the BARREL ORGAN), or activates a bell-clapper or other sound-producing device. The barrel itself may be turned manually, or it may be spring-driven, as in later examples. Mechanical carillons were known in the 14th century. Numerous mechanical instruments were created during the 18th and early 19th centuries, including musical clocks and music boxes. Among the most ambitious was Mälzel's mechanical orchestra, the Panharmonicon. BACH, HAYDN, MOZART, and BEETHOVEN each wrote works for a mechanical instrument. The mechanical piano, known as the *Player-Piano, Pianola, Phonola,* and under trade names, employs specially perforated paper rolls instead of a barrel-and-pin mechanism. The instrument is operated by air pressure; the perforations allow the air to pass into a cylinder with a slit leading to the mechanism that activates the key.

Medesimo tempo (I): the same TEMPO.

Mediant: the third degree of the major or minor SCALE.

Medieval music: European music of *c.*600 to *c.*1420. This period witnessed the richest development of liturgical CHANT and a subsequent flowering of secular SOLO song. POLYPHONY evolved from crude beginnings to highly artistic forms, some being more complex than any that followed during the next five centuries.

Information about the first four centuries of this period is scanty; much of it concerns liturgical chant. The most important of several codifications of the liturgy took place at the turn of the 7th century under Pope Gregory I (*see* GREGORIAN CHANT). Similar repertoires of chant developed in parallel fashion at various centers: Ambrosian chant in Milan, Gallican chant in France, and Mozarabic or Visigothic chant in southern Spain. In each, local elements were apparently combined with elements devised from Roman (i.e., Gregorian) usage and subjected to local modifications. The need for a common liturgy for all of Europe soon brought about conflict between the Roman rite and those of other centers. In France, Charlemagne outlawed the Gallican rite, which, however, survived for a while in areas not closely controlled by the court. Mozarabic rite continued unchecked until the 11th century, when the Roman rite was enforced in almost all except Moorish-held territories. (The rite still remains at the Cathedral of Toledo.) The Ambrosian rite was limited to the diocese of Milan and part of the diocese of Lugano.

During the early Middle Ages, new chants were created both for new feasts and for portions of the liturgy (e.g., the ALLELUIA) that did not have specific chants assigned to each of the various feasts. In the 8th or 9th century, composers began to expand certain chants by means of preludes, interludes, or postludes, some syllabic or neumatic, others melismatic. Certain of the new MELISMAS, as well as old ones belonging to the chant proper, proved difficult to memorize. New texts were therefore added to these melismatic sections, converting them into syllabic settings. The accretions to existing chants of new words, new music, or both are called TROPES. Some troped chants are nearly contemporaneous with the simpler versions, and it has been suggested that the definition of trope be expanded to provide for the possibility that in some instances the troped version represents the earliest form.

Among the most important tropes were the additions to the Alleluia chants, termed SEQUENCES. These long melodies were broken into segments of uneven length, which were often repeated in performance, normally using new text for the musical repetition. During the high Middle Ages, sequence texts, originally in prose, were more and more often metrical and rhymed; the repetition of segments, observed irregularly at first, became a rule for all except the first and last STROPHE. The peak of this development was reached in the late 12th century; the form itself influenced both Latin and vernacular poetry. All but four sequences were

banned by the Council of Trent (1545–63), though a fifth, the *Stabat Mater*, was later readmitted in 1727.

The liturgical drama developed from tropes for Easter and Christmas that were written in dialogue form. For example, the trope, *Quem quaeritis*, which prefaced the Introit for Easter MASS, contained dialogue between the three Marys and the Angel at the tomb of Jesus. At some late 10th-century centers, this trope was detached from the Introit itself and, expanded by the addition of other chants (an Alleluia, two antiphons, and the TE DEUM), was acted out at the end of Matins. The same subject was developed through other treatments, and the stories of Daniel, Herod, Rachel, The Foolish and Wise Virgins, etc., furnished materials for similar plays. In the later Middle Ages, the genre gave rise to miracle plays, which dealt with the miracles of various saints.

Polyphony as an art form (rather than a folk one) began as another means of embellishing liturgical chant. A 9th-century treatise shows that a solo section of a chant could be embellished by a second VOICE paralleling the chant at a fourth or fifth below. The resulting composition, called ORGANUM, is now termed parallel organum, so as to distinguish this type from others that developed later. Parallel organum in two voices is called simple organum; if one or both of the original parts is doubled at the octave, composite organum results.

From the first, a piece of organum could begin in unison, proceed in oblique motion until the two voices were at the interval of a fourth, remain in parallel motion for the central section, and close with oblique motion leading back to a unison. The added voice gradually acquired greater melodic independence, and by the 11th century organum used similar and contrary motion as well as oblique and parallel motion. The chant was then placed in the lower voice, but the two voices occupied similar ranges and crossed each other frequently.

In the 11th century, two notes were sometimes set against one in the chant, and in the 12th century, florid polyphony appears in which six or more notes in the upper voice may be set against one in the lower. Two surviving repertories of polyphony were apparently formed chiefly in the mid-12th century. One, preserved at Santiago de Compostela, comprises mainly settings of liturgical chants, responsories, Alleluias, Kyries, etc. The other, collected primarily in MSS that entered the library of St. Martial in Limoges before 1220, is concerned mainly with the setting of strophic, rhythmic poetry that may have served as an adjunct to the liturgy (used e.g., in procession). Considerable artistry is present in the melodic designs of both repertories. In both, the main structural INTERVALS are the unison, fifth, and octave. Because we have no external evidence to indicate whether the NOTATION possesses rhythmic significance, scholars disagree regarding the rhythmic style of these works.

A codification of rhythm, based on a small group of ternary quantitative meters known as RHYTHMIC MODES, was achieved in the first polyphonic repertory of wide international significance, that of the Notre Dame organa and *conducti*. The two great masters associated with this repertory are LEONIN (who may have been active even before the founding of Notre Dame in 1163) and PEROTIN, his successor a generation later. The Notre Dame organa display inner stylistic variety: that is, sections employing many notes to one in the chant contrasted with others in which rhythmic motion in all voices was similar. The latter style was employed especially for melismatic sections of the chant, the former for syllabic ones. Sections employing measured time-values in all voices were known as DISCANT. Perotin emphasized the discant style to a far greater extent than Leonin, often substituting discant sections, known as *clausulae,* for sections in organal style in works of the older master. Whereas almost all polyphonic works of previous centuries were in two parts, Perotin composed a few remarkable organa in three and four parts.

The Notre Dame *conducti* were usually created independently of preexistent liturgical chants. They are primarily in a syllabic, chordal style, though some have melismatic sections in discant style, primarily at the beginnings and endings of lines of verse. The term *conductus* has wide application. In the 12th century, it designated not only polyphonic works but also solo melodies with either sacred or secular metrical Latin texts.

The earliest sizable repertory of secular melodies, whether with Latin or vernacular texts, dates from the 12th century. Only a few melodies in staffless NEUMES survive from previous centuries; these include laments on the deaths of King Chindasvinthus (652) and Charle-

magne (814), and some settings of Horace, Juvenal, Virgil, and Boethius. These cannot be deciphered and are too few to even hint at the role of secular music in Europe after the fall of Rome. The *chansons de geste,* epic poems celebrating legendary heroes, were sung rather than recited. A simple MELODY served all lines of a section except the last, which was set by a different tune. Except for two late excerpts, no remnant of this music survives.

Nearly 300 troubadour melodies and more than 1500 trouvère melodies are preserved. The troubadour movement began among courtly circles in southern France at the end of the 11th century; its influence spread first to the trouvères of northern France and then to the MINNESINGERS of Germany. By the mid-12th century, the ranks of these poet-musicians included commoners as well as nobles. The main subject of the poems is unrequited love; however, there are also groups dealing with religious and political subjects. The melodies are usually rather simple; many possess great charm. Those of the troubadours are more ornate than average, while those of the minnesingers are apt to be stolid. Many of the French and Provençal works of the 13th century were governed by the rhythmic modes, but the rhythm of most pieces is not indicated by the notation and is much debated. Some melodies are through-composed; that is, each text phrase is set by new music. A form in which the first two phrases are immediately repeated is frequent among all of these repertoires. During the mid-13th century there evolved three refrain forms—the RONDEAU, BALLADE, and VIRELAI—which served as the basis for two centuries of further development. Although the earliest examples of polyphonic song —including works by Adam DE LA HALLE—are attractive, they do not equal the artistry of the contemporaneous late-13th-century MOTET.

There are no records of Spanish, Italian, or English secular repertoires comparable to those of the troubadours and trouvères. However, both Spain and Italy left a rich heritage of devotional song. The former was collected for King Alfonso the Wise (1252–84). The music, the *Cantigas de Santa María*, is similar to much late trouvère and troubadour music; refrain forms are prominent. The Italian melodies, known as *laude*, began as simple tunes, but a few of the later examples are quite ornate.

The mainstream of 13th-century music concerns the development of the motet. This form originated around the turn of the century through the addition of a Latin text to the upper voice of a Notre Dame *clausula*. Originally this text was sacred and had some bearing on the text of the liturgical chant from which the tenor of the *clausula* was abstracted. Soon, however, motets were composed without concern for the liturgical origin of the form and some of these used secular French texts. Three- and four-voice motets would employ a different text for each upper voice. By the late 13th century, trouvère melodies and dance tunes, as well as chants of types not employed in Notre Dame organa, were employed as motet tenors. It was customary for the tenor to employ a short rhythmic pattern that was repeated over and over until the end; the preexistent melody forming the basis of the tenor was also normally presented more than once. Important changes in the rhythmic style of the upper voices occurred after mid-century when notational developments permitted greater precision in the recording of rhythm. Shorter time-values were used increasingly. In the late 13th-century motets of Petrus de Cruce, the three voice-parts of the motet each have their individual character, the uppermost having a profusion of fast notes, the lowest using longer notes. Ternary rhythms dominated polyphonic music throughout the 13th century.

The acceptance of duple rhythm (*see* METER) was heralded in the 14th century by Philippe de VITRY. The title of his treatise, *Ars Nova,* has been used by modern scholars as a designation for the music of this century (or at least for the French music of the first half), while the motet repertoire of the 13th century is designated as the *Ars antiqua.* The repetitive rhythmic patterns of the 13th-century motet tenors were enlarged, developing into the isorhythmic patterns of Vitry, MACHAUT, and their successors. Settings of individual movements of the Mass ORDINARY became more frequent and a complete setting of the Ordinary by a single composer was provided by Machaut. In this composer's works, polyphonic settings of secular refrain forms achieve high artistic stature for the first time. The main form is that of the ballade. The uppermost part is a gracefully decorated vocal line; the angularity of the lower part(s) suggests instrumental performance.

During the second quarter of the century Italian composers, such as JACOPO DA BOLOGNA, and, a generation later, Francesco LANDINI, become prominent. The main forms are those of the ballata, MADRIGAL (not related to the more familiar RENAISSANCE madrigal); and CACCIA. The latter comprises vivid descriptions of outdoor scenes, set in CANON. In general, the ·Italian music of the 14th century is more mellifluous than the French. During the latter part of the century both French and Italian composers indulged in extravagant rhythmic arabesques of great complexity. Different metric divisions were often employed simultaneously, and unusual syncopations were frequent.

These qualities were the excesses of a waning period. A significant impetus toward the new style of the Renaissance came from England. Through the works of such composers as Lionel Power and DUNSTABLE, English music entered the main stream of continental art. A greater exploitation of thirds and sixths was one of the important characteristics of this new art.

Medley: a work made by stringing together a group of

well-known tunes (e.g., patriotic songs, FOLK SONGS, operatic AIRS), either used in their entirety or in part. An equivalent French term used frequently is *pot-pourri*.

Méhul, Étienne-Nicolas: *b.* Givet, June 22, 1763; *d.* Paris, October 18, 1817. One of the most prominent French composers at the time of the Revolution, Méhul is known primarily for his OPERAS. He wrote more than two dozen, some in collaboration with CHERUBINI, BOIELDIEU, and other composers. The best of Méhul's operas are *Uthal* and *Joseph;* his other works, rarely played, include BALLETS, patriotic songs, a few SYMPHONIES, OVERTURES, piano SONATAS, and a handful of sacred works.

Meistersinger (G): a member belonging to the highest rank of a German guild of amateur poet-musicians of the 15th and 16th centuries. These artisans and merchants were the successors to the aristocratic MINNESINGERS; they were active in southwest Germany, particularly in Mainz and Nuremberg. The various steps leading to the rank of master involved, in order, the learning of the rules, the ability to sing certain of the standard melodies, the writing of a new poem to fit a preexistent standard MELODY, and, finally, the composition of a new song whose melody became one of the accepted standards. Characteristic STROPHES are in BAR form: they open with two sections (*Stollen*) having the same poetic structure and the same melody, followed by a free section (the *Abgesang*) that employed no fixed repetitive scheme. Some of the guild practices are depicted in WAGNER's opera *Die Meistersinger.*

Melisma: a group of notes (usually a large group) set to a single syllable. The term is used especially with reference to GREGORIAN CHANT and other MEDIEVAL MUSIC.

Mellophone: a BRASS INSTRUMENT similar to the French horn.

Mélodie (F): (1) in a loose sense, MELODY; (2) in more technical usage, a song with piano ACCOMPANIMENT.

Melodrama: a stage work or a section thereof employing both spoken text and music; the two elements may be used alternately or simultaneously. Melodramatic scenes appear in OPERAS by MOZART, BEETHOVEN, CHERUBINI, and WEBER.

Melody: a logical succession of tones, as opposed to a random one. From an analytical standpoint, melody is compounded of: (1) MOTION or contour, (2) RHYTHM, (3) MODE, (4) FORM, (5) emotional connotation. However, from an aesthetic standpoint, melody, like protoplasm, cannot be split into component parts without losing its identity. A melody may itself comprise the full musical fabric, or it may be complemented by a chordal accompaniment or combined with one or more other melodies.

Normally a melody has an expressive quality that distinguishes it from mere figuration. However, the range of melodic styles known to man is so vast that attempts to render the term more precise and to arrive at evaluative criteria involve the elimination of one or more meaningful styles. Often, for example, the term is used to denote lyrical, vocal phrases of recurrent rhythmic patterns and balanced form. Consistent application of such limitations would force one to brand much medieval and modern music, music of strictly instrumental style, and much non-European music as "unmelodic." Although this position has been taken at times by some, it is now recognized as untenable.

Within the idiom proper to most familiar music, numerous melodic conventions operate to shape and direct the composer's melodic imagination. Melody is normally expected to move by steps and small skips rather than by large skips. A certain balance is expected of PITCH contour; motion in one direction for too long a period may be awkward. And, melody is expected to unfold against a HARMONIC background, whether real or supplied by the imagination. The greater the number of SKIPS, the larger the range of melodic motion, or the faster the rhythmic pace, the greater are the demands for simplicity and strength of harmonic logic. The most basic forms of melodic impulse are derived from SCALE segments and broken CHORDS, either unadorned or concealed by ORNAMENTATION. Under normal circumstances the harmonic logic is such that major harmonic changes occur between one measure and the next rather than within the measure. Both the harmonic and rhythmic substructure of melody are normally such that the listener is able to perceive at least subconsciously a distinction between those melody notes that are vital to the structure and those that are ornamental in function.

In a more modern idiom, melody is often either partly or entirely freed of a preconceived harmonic background. In such an idiom melody is often more active—i.e., it has more skips. It is more difficult for the inexperienced listener to perceive the melodic logic of such music.

Mendelssohn-Bartholdy, (Jacob Ludwig) Felix: *b.* Hamburg, February 3, 1809; *d.* Leipzig, November 4, 1847; a major ROMANTIC symphonist and an influential conductor and educator.

Descended of a cultured and wealthy Jewish family, Mendelssohn enjoyed all of the educational advantages his father could provide. (He had excellent linguistic ability and talent in painting and poetry.) His musical training was begun by his mother and continued under a variety of teachers, the most prominent being Carl Zelter. He made his début as a pianist at the age of nine and began to compose a year or so later. His subsequent progress was rapid: the maturity of his *String Octet* (1825) and his *Overture to A Midsummer Night's Dream* (1826) is remarkable.

As a symphonist and CHAMBER MUSIC composer, Mendelssohn accepted the forms of the CLASSICAL period, but his THEMES are generally lyrical rather than concise, his developments discursive rather than dramatic. His most famous SYMPHONIES, the *Scotch* (No. 3) and the *Italian* (No. 4) derive mildly programmatic elements from BEETHOVEN's *Pastoral Symphony*. More deeply imbued

by Romantic tone-painting are his several fine OVERTURES, including *The Hebrides,* also known as *Fingal's Cave.* Mendelssohn's music ranges from gay to melancholy. He normally avoids the portrayal of the more violent emotions.

Partly because of the sentimental nature of some pieces, Mendelssohn's piano music is no longer as popular as it had once been. However, the eight books of *Songs without Words* contain many fine examples of the Romantic CHARACTER PIECE, while the *Variations sérieuses* is a large work deserving of greater attention.

As a pianist and conductor, Mendelssohn toured widely, visiting England several times. He gave the first performance of Beethoven's *Emperor Concerto* there, and in turn was inspired by the English choral tradition to write his ORATORIOS, *St. Paul* and *Elijah.* In 1829, he directed BACH's *St. Matthew Passion* in Leipzig; this, the first performance since Bach's death, provided strong impetus to the Romantic revival of the BAROQUE master's works. Mendelssohn himself was influenced by Bach, as shown in his PRELUDES and FUGUES both for piano and organ.

In 1833 Mendelssohn was appointed music director for the town of Düsseldorf and two years later became conductor of the Leipzig Gewandhaus Orchestra. He succeeded in raising the standards of this well-known EN-SEMBLE, welding it into one of the finest in Europe. In 1841 he was invited by King Friedrich Wilhelm IV of Prussia to take charge of court · musical activities in Berlin. Mendelssohn was impeded in his duties by minor officials and wished to resign the following year. However, he accepted the title of Royal General Music Director, which did not require continuous residence in Berlin, and eventually directed the reorganization of the cathedral music and the cathedral CHOIR. In the winter of 1842–43, Mendelssohn, together with several colleagues, founded the Leipzig Conservatorium and arranged for its financial support through the King of Saxony. SCHUMANN and Mendelssohn were among the first of the eminent faculty. These numerous activities cut heavily into the time available for composition, but Mendelssohn's last years were productive of two of his best-loved works, the *Violin Concerto in E major* and the incidental music to *A Midsummer Night's Dream*.

Mennin, Peter: *b*. Erie, Pa., May 17, 1923. Mennin was trained at the Oberlin Conservatory and at the Eastman School of Music, under HAN-SON and Bernard Rogers. He has been director of the Peabody Conservatory and of the Juilliard School of Music. Mennin's music is largely in a neoclassical vein, with a strong feeling for TONE CEN-TERS and DIATONIC writing. His works include seven SYM-PHONIES, CONCERTOS and other orchestral music, CHAM-BER, KEYBOARD, and choral music, and songs.

Meno (I): less; *meno mosso*, less quickly.

Menotti, Gian Carlo: *b*. Cadegliano, July 7, 1911. Trained at the Milan Conservatory and at the Curtis Institute of Music, Menotti has won fame as a composer of short OPERAS, most of them his own libretti. His works include *Amahl and the Night Visitors, The Medium, The Telephone, The Consul,* and *The Saint of Bleecker Street*. He has written also BALLETS, two CONCERTOS, orchestral and piano pieces, and some CHAMBER MUSIC.

Mensural notation: a generic designation for the NOTA-TIONS of *c*.1260–1600.

Menuet (F), **Menuett** (G), **Menuetto** (G): MINUET.

Messa di voce (I): a vocal TECHNIQUE involving an increase and then a decrease of loudness while sustaining a single tone; the technique was especially important during the 18th century.

Messe (F, G): MASS. *Messa per i Defunti* (I), *Messe des Morts* (F), Requiem Mass; *Messe solennelle* (F), *Missa solemnis* (L), Solemn Mass.

Messiaen, Olivier: *b.* Avignon, December 10, 1908. Messiaen studied under DUKAS at the Paris Conservatoire. He has been organist at the Church of the Trinity since 1931 and professor of harmony at the Conservatoire since the end of World War II. Messiaen is among the more romantic and expansive of 20th-century French composers. His interest in the modes and rhythms of Hindu music, in GREGORIAN CHANT, and in IMPRESSIONISTIC music is reflected in his style. Many of his works —both vocal and instrumental—mirror a religious outlook. He has written for a wide variety of media, especially those that use new and different sound effects (e.g., electronic ones).

Meter: the organization of musical time into regularly recurring patterns of pulses. This organization is essentially a standard of measurement against which a composer may project a RHYTHM, rather than the time-values of that rhythm or the sense of flow produced. While most familiar music is metric, there is also a large body of music that is not so organized.

Qualitative meters, which govern the majority of Western music, comprise patterns of stressed and unstressed pulses of equal duration. These are subjected to a twofold classification: according to the number of time units contained in the pattern and according to the subdivision of these time units. *Duple meters* contain patterns of two time units; *triple meters,* patterns of three; and *quadruple meters,* patterns of four. Many writers refer to *quintuple meter,* which may be explained as a compound of duple and triple meters, but many others prefer not to use the term meter in connection with patterns of more than four units or with patterns having asymmetrical groupings. *Simple meters* are those in which the time unit is divisible into two parts, while *compound meters* comprise those in which the time unit is divisible into three. In a simple triple meter, for example, the pattern consists of one primary time unit, followed by two secondary time units, each being divisible into two parts; in a compound triple meter, the pattern contains the same number of time-units, but these are each divisible into three parts. In standard NOTATION, qualitative meters are indicated by TIME SIGNATURES. The sensation of stress that coincides with the first pulse of each group may be produced by actual dynamic stress, by regulating the rhythmic flow so that the longer values coincide with the stressed pulses, by regulating the PITCH contour so that the most essential notes fall on the stressed pulses, by regulating the HARMONIC rhythm so that important harmonic changes take place on the stressed pulses, or by any combination of these means.

Quantitative meters, which underlie some music from Greece and India, as well as certain European music of the Middle Ages and RENAISSANCE, comprise patterns formed by different time lengths. Most frequently these patterns combine longs and shorts related to each other in the proportion 2:1, but there are also meters that display the proportions 3:1 and 3:2. It is possible for a value in a quantitative meter to be represented by two or more notes in music provided that such subdivision does not destroy the feeling of unit necessary for that value.

Metronome: an apparatus to indicate TEMPO by maintaining a steady beat at speeds from 40 to 208 beats per minute. The rate of speed desired by a composer or suggested by an editor is often indicated at the beginning of a work: M.M. ♩ = 60 (M.M. stands for Mälzel's

Metronome), means that 60 quarter notes are to occupy one minute. The traditional metronome consists of a spring-driven pendulum with an adjustable weight on the upper end. As the weight is pushed lower, the metronome beats faster. An audible click is produced when the pendulum passes close to each end of its swing. The principle behind this metronome was apparently discovered by Winkel in 1812, but the device is normally associated with Johann Nepomuk Mälzel (an acquaintance of BEETHOVEN), who established the first metronome factory in 1816. Modern metronomes may be governed by electrical rather than mechanical means and may employ light flashes in addition to clicks.

Meyerbeer, Giacomo (original name: Jakob Liebmann Beer): *b.* Berlin, September 5, 1791; *d.* Paris, May 2, 1864. Following study with CLEMENTI and VOGLER, Meyerbeer began a twin career as concert pianist and OPERA composer; he soon abandoned the former calling. In 1815 he went to Venice, where he adopted the dominant Italian style, that of ROSSINI. After seven poor operas, Meyerbeer achieved success with *Il Crociato in Egitto* (1824); in 1826 he went to Paris to supervise a

French production of this work. From 1830 on Meyerbeer was the dominant composer of French opera (his libretti were provided by Scribe), setting the style for the elaborate spectacle of grand opera. His major works of this period are *Robert le Diable, Les Huguenots, Le Prophète,* and *L'Africaine.* He wrote miscellaneous nonoperatic works including songs, sacred and secular choruses, and compositions for orchestra.

Mezza (I), **Mezzo** (I): half, moderate. *Mezzo forte,* moderately loud; *mezzo piano,* moderately soft; *mezza voce,* moderated vocal tone (i.e., not full strength). Mezzosoprano, *see* VOICE.

Mi: in SOLMIZATION, either the third note of a diatonic SCALE, or the note *e.*

Microtone: any INTERVAL smaller than a half-step. Such intervals (and others of sizes judged irregular according to the tempered Western scale) exist in music of nonliterate and Oriental cultures. They formed part of classical Greek theory and have been used by Western composers in sporadic experiments (e.g., in the 16th and 20th centuries). Irregular intervals may be measured in terms of CENTS.

Milhaud, Darius: *b.* Aix-en-Provence, September 4, 1892. Milhaud completed his studies at the Paris Conservatoire under D'INDY and DUKAS, among others. He assimilated musical ideas from many sources, and his friend Cocteau imparted Satie's esthetics to him. A stay in Brazil as Claudel's secretary and later tours in the United States brought Milhaud in touch with South American rhythms and the JAZZ idiom. Although Milhaud sometimes writes in a complex, polytonal style, he normally stresses readily comprehensible melody. Gallic wit is characteristic of many of his better known scores. Milhaud has written prolifically in all traditional genres: OPERA, BALLET, SYMPHONY, CONCERTO, SUITE, STRING QUARTET, song, etc.

Minim: a half-note (British usage). *See also* NOTATION.

Minnesinger: a medieval German poet-musician, the counterpart of the Provençal troubadour and the French trouvère. The Minnesingers were active *c.*1150–1460. Among the most famous were Walter von der Vogelweide, Neidhart von Reuenthal, Tannhäuser, Heinrich von Meissen (Frauenlob), and Oswald von Wolkenstein.

Minor: a quality of INTERVAL, CHORD, MODE, or SCALE.

Minore (I): MINOR.

Minuet: a courtly French dance in moderate triple METER. It was frequently employed in stylized form in both BALLETS and instrumental SUITES from the mid-17th century on. Normally these minuets were cast in rounded BINARY FORM. Occasionally two minuets would follow one another in a suite; a repeat of the first minuet might sometimes follow the completion of the second, thus creating a composite TERNARY FORM. It is this composite form that is employed in classical SONATAS, CHAMBER works, and symphonies, most often as the third MOVEMENT (occasionally as the second). The central section is known as a *trio*. In orchestral works the trio is usually scored for fewer instruments than the minuet proper; it often features prominent solo wind passages. In the late CLASSICAL period, the minuet became quicker and acquired greater rhythmic energy. This transformation led, in the works of BEETHOVEN, to the creation of the SCHERZO.

Mirliton (F): *see* KAZOO.

Missa (L): MASS. *Missa pro defunctis*, Requiem Mass; *Missa solemnis*, High Mass (a composition bearing that title is normally an elaborate one).

Mixolydian: (1) the seventh CHURCH MODE; (2) a Greek mode that may be represented by a SCALE descending the white keys from *b'* to *b*.

Mixture: an ORGAN stop that employs pipes of different PITCHES coupled to the same key.

Mock trumpet: an English name for the *chalumeau* (predecessor to the clarinet).

Mode: the basic group of tones that underlies a piece of music. The characteristics that usually define a given mode include the number of tones used in an octave, the INTERVAL relationships between neighboring tones, and the functions of salient notes. Very frequently mode implies a selection of PITCHES made from the total number available within a particular musical culture. This selection is rarely made afresh by a composer; rather he casts his ideas in one of a group of established patterns. Indeed, modes may sometimes be characterized by the presence of certain melodic stereotypes peculiar to each. In Western music and other music employing the octave as a basic melodic and harmonic CONSONANCE, repetition of tones at the octave (or over several octaves) is taken for granted and does not enter into considerations of modal structure. But there is also music that does not employ perfect octaves, and a discussion of mode under such circumstances must include a description of pitch relationships over the total range. For analytical purposes the tones comprising a mode are normally arranged in consecutive order from the lowest to the highest, or vice versa (*see* SCALE).

Modes are classified in various manners according to their structures. *Authentic modes* are those in which the final note of a MELODY is the lowest or next lowest of its tones and serves as the first note of the scale. *Plagal modes* are those in which the final note is in the center of the range and the scale begins a fourth below the final. The modern major and minor modes always have authentic scale forms, but it is possible to distinguish between melodies with an authentic range (e.g., *Three Blind Mice*) and others with a plagal range (e.g., *La Marseillaise*). Such distinctions become blurred in melodies of very large or very small range.

Modes may also be classified according to the number of tones per octave. *Pentatonic modes* contain five pitches per octave; *hexatonic*, six; *heptatonic* or *diatonic*, seven; and *chromatic*, twelve. Pitches extraneous to a given mode may be drawn upon for compositional purposes provided their use is clearly subsidiary. Mode transformations have resulted in both ancient and modern times, in both Orient and Occident, from the evolution of these auxiliary pitches toward equal and independent status. It has been conjectured that the heptatonic modes of classical Greece arose as expansions of earlier pentatonic forms. Within the past century, the diatonic system of major and minor—a system of seven main and five auxiliary pitches —has given way in some music to a chromatic system in which each of the twelve pitches of the octave has equal importance.

Pentatonic modes are ancient and widespread, particularly in the Orient. The most familiar forms are those which employ whole steps and minor thirds; the black keys of the piano represent such patterns. Numerous American cowboy songs and Scottish FOLK SONGS employ pentatonic modes (e.g., *Bury Me Not on the Lone Prairie* and *The Campbells Are Coming*). Pentatonic modes with major thirds and half steps were known in ancient Greece and are still common in Japan.

Hexatonic modes are infrequent. They apparently were used in ancient India. They appear in occasional modern compositions based on the whole-tone scale, such as DEBUSSY's *Voiles*.

Heptatonic (or diatonic) modes are frequent in the Orient and provide the basis for most European music from the time of our earliest records. The CHURCH MODES formed the keystone for much MEDIEVAL and RENAISSANCE composition and for the theoretical discussions of these periods. The present major and minor scales were given theoretical recognition during the 16th century, but the conventions governing familiar usage were not codified for another century.

Mode, Rhythmic: *see* RHYTHMIC MODES.

Moderato (I): a moderate TEMPO.

Modern music: Western art music of *c.*1910 to the present; more specifically, that music which departs in some significant measure from the practices of late ROMANTICISM. The term suffers from the fact that it has been used by several successive generations, each time with new meaning. Furthermore, it fails to distinguish between new in date and new in style. Unfortunately, the term contemporary music is similarly vague.

The 20th century has been a period of rapidly widening creative horizons. The breakdown of the major-minor system of tonality has brought in its wake a search for new methods of melodic, rhythmic, and harmonic organization. Previously established limitations of sound material have been broken as composers have sought to use different kinds of sounds not previously considered "musical." Traditional forms, such as the SYMPHONY and SONATA, have been replaced by more flexible forms; some of these still depend upon traditional concepts of thematic development, while others consciously avoid both repetition and development. The trend toward massiveness in late Romantic music has been reversed. Works characteristic of the second quarter of the 20th century are terser than those of the late 19th century. The orchestra no longer occupies the dominating position it held previously as composers are turning more and more to a wide variety of differently constituted CHAMBER ENSEMBLES. IMPROVISATION, which played a minimal role in Romantic music, began to be combined with a number of different compositional procedures in music of the second half of the 20th century. The major figures of the era include SCHOENBERG, STRAVINSKY, BARTÓK, BERG, and WEBERN.

European HARMONIC thinking from the late 17th century to the turn of the 20th is founded upon three basic premises: (1) the harmonic unit is the triad, formed of a chain of two thirds; (2) in each work there is one triad that represents the primary harmonic goal of that work; all other triads function to channel the harmonic drive toward that goal; (3) a clear distinction between CONSONANCE and DISSONANCE, between harmonic and NONHARMONIC TONES, is possible, and all dissonances must resolve to consonances. All three of these premises have been challenged and overthrown in a major segment of 20th-century music. The changes in harmonic thinking represent the extension of trends apparent in late Romantic music. There the use of chromatic harmonies to produce rapid shifts from one TONE CENTER to another resulted in the weakening of the sense of primacy formerly accorded to the main tone center. The number of functions possible to a given CHORD in a given context increased. The concept of function itself was challenged in IMPRESSIONISTIC harmony. Debussy showed that any given harmonic constellation could be employed for the sake of its own particular quality of sound, rather than for its capacity to drive the harmony in a specific direction. Methods of chord building changed gradually. The chain of two or three thirds traditionally employed was expanded in the 20th century to chains of as many as six thirds. Furthermore, chords were built in chains of fourths and also had irregular structures. Schoenberg demonstrated, as did several others, that traditional distinctions between consonance and dissonance were useful only in particular context, but not immutable artistic law. Composers began to use harmonic constructions previously considered dissonant in an ever wider variety of situations.

A still more fundamental difference between newer and traditional styles concerns TEXTURE. Although the late Romantic composer was trained in COUNTERPOINT, his interest in the unfolding of a number of lines was normally secondary to his interest in the harmonic development accompanying one main line. Counterpoint was a matter of detail technique rather than a generative principle. In a significant segment of more recent music, the opposite is true: the unfolding of a group of melodic lines generates the harmonic development.

On the whole, the conservative composers of this century have retained a large number of elements associated with traditional techniques. They do admit triadic constructions, although treating them merely as one of several possibilities. They seek the establishment of primary tone centers, although these are handled with greater freedom than previously; the concept of function remains, although the details of function are changed. There is a general distinction between consonance and dissonance although dissonance is employed more frequently than previously. Harmonic textures continue to be prominent. In the musical vocabulary of more progressive composers of mid-century, triadic constructions, primary tone centers, functional progressions, and distinctive treatment of consonance versus dissonance are, if present, incidental rather than essential elements.

These profound changes in harmonic thinking are mirrored by equally basic changes in melodic thinking. Actually, European melodic thinking from the late 17th century to the turn of the 20th rests upon and is inextricably interwoven with the traditional harmonic premises described above. This accounts for the prominence of triadic melodic constructions, the importance of tonal centers, and the concept of melodic functions in traditional music, as well as the very strong subconscious tendency to interpret solo melody against a presumed harmonic background. The breakdown of the major-minor system was accompanied by melodic experimentation in several different directions. Several composers investigated the possibility of creating new music in the CHURCH MODES and in Oriental modes. Passages based on the whole-tone SCALE were written by Debussy, REBIKOV, and BUSONI. Composers extending the nationalistic paths of the 19th century employed modal constructions belonging to FOLK music; their number includes men of such diverse talents as Bartók and Vaughan Williams. In the TWELVE-TONE technique of Schoenberg and his followers, melodies are constructed on the basis of an afunctional chromatic MODE. (In theory this would mean an equality among the twelve tones of the octave; in actual practice, the composer may emphasize, without regard to key function, any chosen tone.) Experiments with INTERVALS smaller than those previously used in Western music (carried out by HÁBA, Busoni, and others) are presently outside the mainstream of 20th-century music, but are symptomatic of the inquisitiveness of the period. The fact that the composer is not necessarily concerned with the creation of MELODY against a harmonic background—real or imagined—

has led to far greater freedom in melodic movement. Intervallic successions—particularly wide SKIPS that have no harmonic anchor—previously avoided are now part of the newer idioms.

Changes in rhythmic style involve the exploration of alternatives to metrical rhythm, with its fixed stress patterns and the same number of beats in each measure. Even in the 19th century composers such as BRAHMS began to challenge the restrictions of such patterns; but these challenges were worked out within an overall metrical framework, whereas the 20th-century composer often steps boldly beyond such bounds. Composers such as Bartók and Stravinsky may employ rhythm as a powerful driving force of unbridled, primitive energy. Others, including those who employ serial techniques in the realm of RHYTHM, may create rhythms in which the elements of symmetry are too complex to permit ready aural recognition.

The rhythmic freedom of modern music is in turn reflected in greater freedom of form. Individual phrases are more frequently of irregular construction and length. Balance is less dependent upon the construction of phrases of equal lengths and upon such devices as literal REPETITION and antecedent and consequent phrases. Repetition is used with greater restraint (if not avoided), and far less space is given to passages which are purely transitory in function (the episodes and bridges of traditional forms). The composer may build on certain characteristic intervals or rhythmic cells but may use these in such varied contexts that they do not appear as readily recognizable motives to the untrained listener.

The dissolution of familiar guideposts has precipitated a continuing outcry by those seeking to judge modern music by former standards. The gap between the composer and his audience has widened considerably during this era. The audience itself is larger than ever before and many new members are not adequately prepared to deal with the challenges of modern music. Many composers, on the other hand, are more intransigent than their predecessors, more intent on filling personal artistic needs than in catering to the tastes of the general community. Some men, including HINDEMITH, have become alarmed at the lack of true communication between the composer and the average audience, and have advocated a more moderate course (*see* GEBRAUCHSMU-SIK). Others, especially after the Second World War, have felt free to explore still further afield and to address only a select audience. Often, greater importance is attached to newness and vitality than to the merely attractive. It remains for later generations to winnow out that which is both new and vital from that which is presently only new.

For more detailed descriptions of 20th-century trends and techniques, see IMPRESSIONISM, EXPRESSIONISM, NEOCLASSICISM, TWELVE-TONE MUSIC, ELECTRONIC MUSIC, CHANCE MUSIC, and COMPUTER MUSIC.

Modulation: a transition from one key to another. One of the chief functions of modulation is to mark divisions of FORM. Episodes and bridge passages of FUGUES, RONDOS, and SONATA forms are frequently modulatory, and modulation is usually employed extensively in development sections. A modulatory passage may also be written or improvised to connect two MOVEMENTS or pieces in different keys.

The simplest modulations employ CHORDS that are common to both the former and the future key. Such a "pivot chord" is often used to lead to a cadence in the new key. In modulating to or from a major key, one may draw on chords of its TONIC minor, and vice versa. That is, one may draw on chords of C minor when leading to or from C major. Modulations are also effected by chords that progress chromatically. Diminished seventh chords and augmented triads are particularly useful in this respect. If any of the four notes of a diminished seventh chord is lowered a half step, a new dominant seventh chord is formed. If any of the three notes of an augmented chord is either raised or lowered by a half step, a new triad is formed.

In BAROQUE and CLASSICAL music most keys reached by modulation are clearly established. Otherwise one speaks of a false or passing modulation. A *false modulation* is one that returns to the initial key, as in the bridge section of a sonata recapitulation. A *passing modulation* progresses to a third key. During the course of the ROMANTIC period, modulations were used with ever increasing rapidity until the feeling of a primary TONE CENTER was seriously weakened and eventually lost.

Moll (G): minor.

Molto (I): very.

Monn (Mann), Matthias Georg: b. Vienna, April 9, 1717; d. there, Oct. 3, 1750. Active at the Karlskirche in Vienna, Monn composed some sacred music as well as a few symphonies, concertos, string quartets, trio sonatas, and keyboard works. His symphonies influenced the Austrian development of that genre in the early Classical period.

Monochord: an instrument employing a single string stretched over a long, thin, wooden resonator. By means of a movable bridge, the monochord may be used to demonstrate the relationship between string-length ratios and musical INTERVALS. It was used extensively by medieval pedagogues.

Monodrama: a dramatic work for only one character (e.g., SCHOENBERG's *Erwartung*).

Monody: (1) an Italian style of vocal composition of the very late 16th and early 17th centuries, in which one or more soloists were accompanied by BASSO CONTINUO. A highly expressive style, monody was employed both in song and in OPERA. (*See also* BAROQUE music.) (2) A synonym for MONOPHONY, used often by earlier writers, but now discouraged. (3) Certain extended art songs with lyric texts and nonstrophic settings (i.e., the music is not identical for successive STROPHES) composed by SCHUBERT and his contemporaries.

Monophony: a musical TEXTURE consisting of unaccompanied MELODY. GREGORIAN CHANT constitutes the most important European repertory of monophony in terms of both artistry and size. Secular monophony was cultivated during the Middle Ages by the troubadours, trouvères, and MINNESINGERS, and much later European FOLK SONG is monophonic. Medieval examples of sacred monophony include the Spanish CANTIGAS, the Italian LAUDE, and the musical sections of religious dramas. Most music outside the European cultural tradition is monophonic.

Monothematic: an adjective describing a work or MOVEMENT developing one main THEME; the corresponding adjective for works developing two or more themes is polythematic. While SONATA form, for example, is normally polythematic, certain examples by HAYDN are essentially monothematic. The FUGUE, on the other hand, is normally monothematic, although double and triple fugues are polythematic.

Monotone: (1) a recitation on one PITCH, with possible slight inflections at phrase beginnings and endings; (2) a person with a small vocal range who is unable to reproduce desired pitch patterns.

Monsigny, Pierre Alexandre: *b.* Fauquembergues, October 17, 1729; *d.* Paris, January

14, 1817. Although his training was scanty, Monsigny's melodic gifts enabled him to become a highly successful composer of comedies with music, 1759–77. His *Rose et Colas* and *Le Déserteur* are among the important precursors of French comic OPERA.

Monte, Philippe de: *b.* Malines, 1521; *d.* Prague, July 4, 1603. Widely traveled, Monte's main post was as music director to Emperors Maximilian II and Rudolf II, from 1568 on. One of the leading composers of his generation, Monte produced numerous MADRIGALS, CHANSONS, MASSES, and MOTETS in a cosmopolitan style.

Montemezzi, Italo: *b.* Vigasio, August 4, 1875; *d.* Vigasio, May 15, 1952. Montemezzi's only work to achieve recognition is *L'Amore dei tre re.* He was trained at the Milan Conservatory and was active in the United States, 1939–49. He wrote also a few SYMPHONIC POEMS and other instrumental music.

Monteverdi, Claudio: *bapt.* Cremona, May 15, 1567; *d.* Venice, November 29, 1643; one of the greatest of the composers bridging the RENAISSANCE and the BAROQUE eras.

Monteverdi was trained by Marc'Antonio Ingegneri, music director at the Cathedral of Cremona. He entered the service of the duke of Mantua in 1590 as singer and violist and became the duke's music director in 1602. From 1613 until his death, Monteverdi was music director at Saint Mark's in Venice. He became a priest in 1632.

Monteverdi wrote both sacred and secular vocal music —including MASSES, MAGNIFICATS, MOTETS, MADRIGALS, CANZONETTE, OPERAS, and dramatic scenes—but no independent instrumental music. Like other late madrigalists, Monteverdi was deeply interested in the expression of the more extreme emotions, often by means of chromaticism and daring DISSONANCE. In his use of the latter, he departed from older Renaissance practices. His melodies became more frequently declamatory in style and his basses more strongly harmonic. Accepting the monodic theories of CACCINI and others of the Florentine CAMERATA, Monteverdi went on to surpass these men by virtue of his superior technical mastery and imagination. He created the first operatic masterpieces: *Orfeo* (1607), *Il ritorno d'Ulisse* (1641), and *L'incoronazione di Poppea* (1642). Nine other operas are largely or entirely lost. While the few previous operas comprised sparse RECITATIVES and CHORUSES, Mon-

teverdi employed in addition
varied instrumental sections,
repetitive vocal forms, duets
and more imaginative cho-
ruses, and dances. The monodic style is present also in
his later madrigals, which use
a FIGURED BASS.

Moore, Douglas Stuart: *b.*
Cutchogue, N.Y., August 10,
1893. After graduating Yale
University, Moore studied
further with D'INDY, Bou-
langer, and BLOCH. He was
on the faculty of Columbia
University, 1926–63. Moore's
works, of conservative and
nationalistic character, include OPERAS on American
themes, SYMPHONIES and programmatic orchestral music,
and a few CHAMBER works.

Morales, Cristóbal de: *b.* Seville, *c.*1500; *d.* Málaga, 1553.
A member of the Papal
chapel (1535–45), Morales
became music director at the
Cathedral of Toledo in 1545
and at Málaga in 1551. His
MASSES, MOTETS, LAMENTA-
TIONS, and MAGNIFICATS mark
him as the outstanding Spanish composer of his generation. He wrote also a handful
of secular works.

Mordent, inverted mordent:
ornaments in which the
written note alternates rapidly
once or twice with its neighbor. According to proper
usage, the mordent (or *pincé*)
involves the written note and
the note below. The inverted
mordent (*Schneller* or *Prall-
triller*) involves the note
above. The symbol for the
inverted mordent, as shown
below, is identical with the
symbol for the *trillo*.

Within the past century the
meanings of these two terms
have unfortunately been interchanged by some writers
and it is sometimes necessary
to deduce their meaning from
context. To lessen confusion,
some have proposed the terms
upper mordent and *lower
mordent.*

Morendo (I): fading away.

Moresca (Moresque, Morisca,
Morisque, Morris dance):
terms, some synonymous, for
a group of related dances
known in Europe at least as
far back as the 15th century.
While the entire group contains examples of solo and
pair dances, as well as dances
for large numbers, the most
familiar of these dances employ from six to ten men.

Mordent

Usually costume and pantomime are involved—often a mock fight between Christians and Mohammedans. The dances appear to trace back to primitive fertility rites. They have been employed in FOLK festivals, in semireligious celebrations, and, in stylized form, in BALLET and OPERA.

Morley, Thomas: *b.* 1557; *d.* 1602. A pupil of BYRD, Morley became organist at St. Paul's Cathedral in 1591 and a Gentleman of the Chapel Royal in 1592. He is best known for his MADRIGALS and their lighter counterparts, BALLETTS and CANZONETS, which he introduced to England from Italy. He wrote also some sacred music, a set of works for instrumental ensemble, and a few keyboard pieces. Morley's *Plaine and Easie Introduction to Practicall Musicke* (1597) was the first theory textbook printed in England.

Morris dance: *see* MORESCA.

Mosso (I): lively, animated. *Più mosso,* faster; *meno mosso,* slower.

Motet: a term applying to various groups of vocal and mixed vocal and instrumental pieces in different styles and forms from the 13th century to the present. (Concerning the origin and early stylistic history of the motet, *see* MEDIEVAL MUSIC.) The most frequent references are to the RENAISSANCE motet of *c.*1450–1600 and the BAROQUE motet.

The motet of the very early 13th century may be described as a polytextual, sacred form, based on a PLAINSONG *cantus firmus* stated in the lowest part (the tenor). Allowance must be made for the possible instrumental performance of the tenor; in that event polytextuality in two-part works would be implied rather than actual. During the latter part of the century a large group of secular motets were written. Polytextuality remained the rule, and many works were also polylingual (French and Latin). The tenor was sometimes derived from trouvère melodies and dance tunes as well as from plainsong.

During the 14th and early 15th centuries both sacred and secular motets flourished. Many of the latter have texts of political nature or texts celebrating festive occasions. Polytextuality is customary, but no longer universal. The customary motet of this period is for two texted parts plus a tenor, but there are also several examples that employ an additional part without text, the CONTRATENOR. The upper parts were performed vocally, sometimes with instrumental doubling; the tenor, which often displayed a rhythmic organiza-

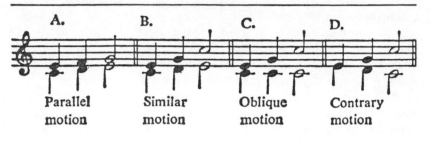

A. Parallel motion   B. Similar motion   C. Oblique motion   D. Contrary motion

tion known as ISORHYTHM, was frequently performed instrumentally, as was the contratenor.

The Renaissance motet of *c.*1450–1600 was normally a sacred form with one Latin text for all parts. The use of *cantus firmi* declined sharply during this period. Characteristic motets, for 4–6 VOICE parts, generally employ different musical ideas for the various text phrases, developing most or all of these by means of IMITATION. (Motets for larger numbers of performers are known, as well as motets employing predominantly chordal textures.) Choral performance was customary, although the voices might be assisted or replaced by instruments. In certain low MASSES it was permissible to substitute motets for various sections of the ORDINARY.

The BAROQUE motet is a sacred form, most frequently intended for mixed forces. Many works share the stylistic features of the sacred CAN-TATA. Solo voices and/or CHORUS may be employed to-gether with instruments. However, there are also many examples for unaccompanied chorus or double chorus. Both Latin and vernacular texts are employed.

After the Baroque the motet lost considerably in importance. It remained a sacred genre, but one with considerable stylistic variety. The most important post-Baroque motets are for unaccompanied chorus.

Motion: (1) the PITCH contour of a MELODY, as distinguished from its durational organization (RHYTHM). One may speak of *ascending* or *descending motion. Conjunct motion* proceeds stepwise, *disjunct motion* in skips. (2) The relationship between the contours of two parts written to be performed simultaneously. If these parts progress in the same direction, either similar or parallel motion results. In *similar motion,* the INTERVAL distance between voices changes, while in *parallel motion* it remains constant. *Oblique motion* results when one part remains stationary and the other moves. *Contrary motion* arises when the two voices move in opposite directions. (3) A steady rhythmic movement, often a pulsating AC-COMPANIMENT supporting a melody in long values.

Motive (Motif): a melodic cell whose characteristic PITCH outline or rhythm serves as the basis for musical development. An intensive treatment of one or more motives extracted from the principal themes is characteristic of the development sections of many works in SONATA FORM. FUGUE episodes may also be based on the expansion (often sequential) of a motive taken from the subject. *See also* FORM, LEITMOTIV.

Moto (I): Motion. *Moto perpetuo, see* PERPETUUM MOBILE.

Moussorgsky: *see* MUSSORG-SKY.

Mouthharmonica: Mouth organ, *see* HARMONICA.

Mouthpiece: the small, separate section of a wind IN-STRUMENT that is held to the player's lips or between them. Mouthpieces of brass instruments differ significantly both in size and in the shape of the bore. Larger (lower) instruments naturally employ larger mouthpieces. The initial section of a trumpet mouthpiece is cup-shaped, that of a French horn mouthpiece is shaped like a funnel. The proportions of the cup (shallow or deep) and the width of the rim of the mouthpiece has a definite effect on lip technique.

Mouton, Jean: *b.* Haut-Wignes, *c.*1470; *d.* St. Quentin, October 30, 1522, one of the leading composers of MASSES and MOTETS of the JOSQUIN generation, and teacher of WILLAERT. From 1513 on Mouton served in the chapels of Kings Louis XII and Francis I.

Mouvement (F), **Movimento** (I): (1) TEMPO; (2) movement.

Movement: a semiindependent section of a larger work, such as a SONATA, CHAMBER WORK, SYMPHONY, CONCERTO, SUITE, CANTATA, MASS, or ORATORIO. A movement is distinguishable from its fellows by virtue of its individual character; TEMPO, METER, key, melodic and rhythmic motion, orchestration, etc. Most movements come to a halt at their conclusion and are separated from the succeeding movement by a brief pause. A composer may choose, however, to run two or more movements together. He may choose also to interrelate two or more movements by means of common thematic material.

Mozart, (Johann Georg) Leopold: *b.* Augsburg, November 14, 1719; *d.* Salzburg,

May 28, 1787. Although overshadowed by his son, Wolfgang, Leopold Mozart was an important violinist, composer, and pedagogue in his own right. He served the count of Thurn and Taxis and then the archbishop of Salzburg, becoming assistant music director to the latter in 1762. His treatise on violin playing is one of the important documents of his time. He wrote a variety of sacred music, including ORATORIOS, as well as SYMPHONIES and other orchestral music, CHAMBER MUSIC, and KEYBOARD music. The famous *Toy Symphony*, often attributed to J. HAYDN, may be by L. Mozart.

Mozart, Wolfgang Amadeus (*bapt.* Johannes Chrysostomus Wolfgangus Theophilus): *b.* Salzburg, January 27, 1756; *d.* Vienna, December 5, 1791; perhaps the most universal musical genius of all time.

When four, Wolfgang began to study harpsichord with his father, Leopold. His amazing talent was such that by the age of six he began to concertize, first in Vienna and Munich, and later throughout the major European musical centers. Acclaimed for his virtuosity on the harpsichord and piano, he also mastered both violin and organ by the age of seven. Mozart began to compose when only five; his first SYMPHONY was written when nine, his first opera when twelve. As was customary for his time, his CONCERTS featured prominently his own works and IMPROVISATIONS. These childhood journeys enabled Mozart to meet many of the prominent musicians of his day and to become acquainted with a vast amount of music then in vogue. The styles of men such as J. SCHOBERT, J. C. BACH, and Padre G. MARTINI were assimilated quickly and young Mozart soon surpassed his older colleagues. The journeys also accustomed him to a restless mode of living and sharpened his eyes to the provincial narrowness of Salzburg, where he served as concertmaster in the archbishop's orchestra when not on tour. Mozart's relations with the lenient Archbishop Sigismund von Schrattenbach were friendly enough, but those with the more authoritarian Hieronymus Colloredo, who succeeded Sigismund in 1771, became increasingly strained. Mozart sought situations at various courts, but was not as adept at political maneuvering as his less-gifted colleagues, a failing that frequently hampered the production of his OPERAS. In 1781 he left Salzburg for Vienna, where he spent much of the last decade of his life. Though he worked with great energy, he did not spend his money wisely and was often in need. In 1787 Mozart was given the minor post of chamber composer to the Austrian emperor. In 1791, while composing a REQUIEM commissioned by an unknown nobleman, he fell prey to typhus; the work was completed by his pupil, Süssmayr.

Mozart excelled in a greater number of music forms than any other composer. His 49 surviving symphonies, 26 STRING QUARTETS, and 20 piano SONATAS and FANTASIAS are on a par with the masterworks of HAYDN, but he far surpasses his close friend in other CHAMBER WORKS and in his CONCERTOS (including 21 for piano and 5 for violin). His operas—including *The Abduction from the Seraglio* (actually a *Singspiel*), *The Marriage of Figaro, Don Giovanni, Così fan tutte*, and *The Magic Flute*—are among the outstanding works of his time. Mozart was gifted with a keen dramatic instinct and a sense for musical characterization. From the different operatic stereotypes of his day, he evolved individual, sparkling, and intensely human masterpieces. In the realm of opera he surpasses both Haydn and BEETHOVEN. The greatest of his contributions to sacred music include such works as the *Coronation Mass*, the *Mass in C Minor* (K. 427) and the REQUIEM. Possessed with tremendous inventive facility—rivaled perhaps only by that of SCHUBERT—Mozart created well over 600 works during his brief lifetime. (A "work" may range in size from a dance of a few measures to a full-length opera.) These were catalogued by Ludwig Köchel, whose researches have been kept up to date by more recent scholars, especially Alfred Einstein. It is customary to refer to a Mozart work according to its "K. number." Mozart's style represents a fusion of the national styles of his period, of Italian facility and German craft. It does not reveal the earthy roots of a Haydn or the seething intensity of a Beethoven. Mozart's music, whether vivacious or reflective, light or passionate, is the epitome of CLASSICAL aristocracy.

Muffat, Georg: *b.* Megève, May, 1653; *d.* Passau, February 23, 1704. As an organist Muffat held posts in Molsheim (Alsace), Salzburg, and Passau. A student of CORELLI and PASQUINI in Rome, Muffat became thoroughly acquainted with LULLY's music during six years of study in Paris, and, together with Johann Sigismund Cousser and FISCHER, helped introduce French and Italian elements into German BAROQUE composition. His major works include orchestral SUITES, chamber SONATAS, organ works, and *concerti grossi*. The prefaces to his publications furnish valuable information about the contemporaneous musical scene.

Musette: (1) a French BAG-PIPE; (2) an instrumental piece imitating the sound of a bagpipe, often featuring a drone.

Musica da camera (I): CHAMBER MUSIC.

Musica falsa (L): *see* MUSICA FICTA (sense 2).

Musica ficta (L): (1) the editorial addition of ACCIDENTALS to transcriptions of MEDIEVAL and RENAISSANCE works in accordance with the performance principles presumably observed by the musicians of those periods. Such accidentals are normally placed above the staff rather than on it. (2) In medieval usage, synonymous with *musica falsa* and indicative of any note or notes not included within Guido d'Arezzo's system of hexachords.

Musical Glasses: *see* GLASS HARMONICA.

Musica mensurata (L): mensural music, a MEDIEVAL designation for polyphonic music (with "measured" note-values (i.e., ORGANUM, CONDUCTUS, MOTET).

Musica plana (L): plainsong (i.e., GREGORIAN CHANT).

Musica reservata (L): a 16th-century term of disputed meaning. It is now held to be music to be performed in intimate surroundings, seeking the expression of a moving text, and often employing chromaticism to a significantly greater extent than was to be observed in more popular media. The music was "reserved" in the sense that its full values were appreciable only by the connoisseur.

Music box: a MECHANICAL musical instrument.

Music Drama: a term for Wagnerian OPERA, emphasizing the importance of dramatic continuity in his later works.

Music printing: a handful of chant books and theoretical treatises with musical examples were printed before 1501, when Ottaviano de' Petrucci brought out the first printed collection of polyphonic music, the *Harmonice Musices Odhecaton A*. In the earliest examples, either the staves were printed without notes or the notes without staves, the remaining component being handwritten. By 1476, Missals were issued in which the staves were printed first and the notes afterwards. This process, known as double impression, was employed by Petrucci, who issued about

60 collections (including re-editions) between 1501 and 1520. To avoid the difficult alignment of the paper for a second impression, a series of type pieces, each containing a note or rest on a small fragment of staff was devised. The printing of any voice-part merely required the assemblage of a long series of these pieces. This method of printing was adopted by Pierre Attaingnant in 1528 and by his competitors and successors. Music engraving began in Italy during the latter part of the 16th century. The clarity of engraved music of this period depended upon the handwriting of the engraver. In the early 18th century the engraving process was standardized by John Walsh's invention of a series of metal punches, each with a note or rest on one end. Lithography was adapted to music printing about 1800, the composer WEBER being among the first to use this technique. Modern music printing employs the photo-offset process. Handwritten or typewritten rather than engraved originals are often used for reasons of lower cost.

Musicology: the study of music from the scholarly and aesthetic rather than the purely aesthetic or purely practical standpoint. Although

Guido Adler and Hugo Riemann, among the first great musicologists, felt that musicology embraced theory, aesthetics, pedagogy, and musical ethnography, as well as history, present tendencies are to restrict the coverage of the term primarily to the last-named discipline. The penultimate of these disciplines, formerly called comparative musicology, is now designated as *ethnomusicology*. (The other musical disciplines mentioned may be subsumed within historical musicology, depending upon the manner in which they are approached.)

Musique concrète: *see* ELECTRONIC MUSIC.

Musique mesurée à l'antique: a 16th-century vocal repertoire in which the RHYTHM of the music is derived from the METER of the text. Important text syllables generally receive twice the time value of unimportant syllables; the texture is predominantly chordal. The repertoire came into being under the impulse provided by the poet Baïf and his associates, including Ronsard. Among the composers working in this style were LE JEUNE and Mauduit.

Mussorgsky, Modest Petrovich: *b.* Karevo, March 21, 1839; *d.* St. Petersburg, March 28, 1881; the greatest of Russian nationalistic composers, one of the Mighty FIVE.

A musician of outstanding gifts, Mussorgsky earned a living as a government clerk. His training was limited to childhood piano lessons and advice from BALAKIREV and RIMSKY-KORSAKOV. The roots of his highly original art lie in Russian folksong, with its modal melodies, irregular rhythms, and asymmetrical forms. However, Mussorgsky seldom quoted actual FOLK SONGS. Among his best and most famous works are the SYMPHONIC POEM *A Night on Bald Mountain*, the piano SUITE *Pictures at an Exhibition*, some songs (including the cycles *The Nursery*, *Sunless*, and *Songs and Dances of Death*), and the OPERAS *Boris Godunov* and *Khovanshtchina*. His songs are the finest Russian contribution to the repertoire, while *Boris Godunov* ranks high among the operatic masterpieces of all nations. Mussorgsky pays careful heed to PROSODY in his terse vocal lines. His music possesses tremendous color and evocative power. His colleagues—particularly Rimsky-Korsakov—and successors completed, revised, and reorchestrated several of his works: their polishings of crudities were often a debatable service.

Muta (I, plural: *mutano*): change. A direction to a wind player to change from one instrument to a related one (e.g., from flute to piccolo, or from oboe to English horn), or for a timpani player to change the tuning of one or more of his drums.

Mutation: (1) the change of VOICE experienced by adolescent boys; (2) in MEDIEVAL and RENAISSANCE SOLMIZATION, the change from syllables of one hexachord to those of another.

Mutation stop: an ORGAN stop producing a tone a twelfth or seventeenth (or any other interval not an octave or a multiple thereof) above the proper PITCH for the key that is depressed.

Mute: a device to soften the tone of a musical instrument; the mute also produces a change in TONE COLOR. The instruments of the VIOLIN FAMILY employ a pronged mute attached to or slid against the bridge. BRASS INSTRUMENTS employ mutes of various shapes; most are essentially conical, the small end of the cone being inserted in the bell of the instrument. These mutes may be made of wood, metal, or covered cardboard. The French horn may also be muted with the hand. DRUMS are muted either by covering the head with a cloth or by using sponge-headed drumsticks.

Mystic chord: a CHORD devised by SCRIABIN, consisting of a chain of fourths. These are, in order, augmented, diminished, augmented, perfect, and perfect. The notes *c-f♯-bb-e′-a′-d″* for example, would form such a chord.

N

Nachschlag (G): (1) the two-note turn at the end of a TRILL; (2) a BAROQUE ornament consisting of a quick note (sometimes more than one) whose value is subtracted from that of the main note it follows. The ornamental note is customarily a step above or below the main note and frequently serves as a passing note filling in a third.

Nachtanz (G): in the 16th and 17th centuries, any lively dance in triple METER designed to follow a more stately one in duple meter (e.g., the GAILLIARD that follows a PAVANE). Other terms for this second dance were *Proportz* and *Tripla*.

Nachtmusik (G): a seldom used synonym for SERENADE.

Nachtstück (G): a term equivalent to NOCTURNE.

Nail violin (Nail harmonica): an instrument of the mid-18th century, consisting of a wooden resonator shaped as a shallow, halved cylinder with *U*-shaped nails of graded lengths driven into the convex side. Sound is produced by the friction of one or two violin bows against the nails. The exposed length of the individual nail determines the PITCH.

Naker: a small, medieval kettledrum.

Nardini, Pietro: *b.* Leghorn, April 12, 1722; *d.* Florence, May 7, 1793. A pupil of TARTINI, and solo violinist for the duke of Württemburg at Stuttgart (1753–67), Nardini succeeded his teacher as music director at the Florentine court in 1771. A prominent virtuoso, he also wrote CONCERTOS and CHAMBER MUSIC for violin, keyboard SONATAS, and chamber music for flute.

Natural: (1) a NOTE neither flat nor sharp; (2) an accidental canceling a previous flat or sharp, ♮; (3) a form of minor SCALE.

Natural horn (Natural trumpet): *see* BRASS INSTRUMENTS.

Neapolitan sixth: the first inversion of a major triad whose root is a minor second above the TONIC.

Neck: the stick projecting from the body of violins, guitars, and similar instruments. In instruments such as the violin, the fingerboard, which extends over the body, is superimposed over the neck.

Neefe, Christian Gottlob: *b.* Chemnitz, February 5, 1748; *d.* Dessau, January 26, 1798. Neefe was a student of Hiller. After serving as conductor at Leipzig and Dresden and with two opera troupes, he became deputy organist and then electoral music director at Bonn. There BEETHOVEN was his pupil. He wrote eight SINGSPIELE, choral music, songs, and piano music.

Neighbor (Neighboring tone): *see* AUXILIARY TONE.

Neoclassicism: a 20th-century style that represents a reaction against the programmatic emotionalism of the ROMANTICS. In this style there is a return to objective, ABSOLUTE MUSIC, to leaner (and often contrapuntal) TEXTURES, simple and often stark TONE COLORATION, and clear FORMS. Many neoclassical composers chose BAROQUE models, which they adapted to modern idioms. JAZZ also exerted some influence on neoclassicism. Among the various composers working partly or entirely in the neoclassical style are BUSONI, STRAVINSKY, HINDEMITH, CASELLA, MALIPIERO, HONEGGER, MILHAUD, and PISTON. The term is sometimes applied to the music of certain late Romantic composers (such as BRUCKNER, FRANCK, and REGER), who also drew inspiration from earlier masters; however, this usage is discouraged.

Neoromanticism: (1) in recent usage, a designation for the general style employed by certain mid-20th-century composers who write in a lyrical fashion and employ many musical traits associated with romanticism, although with greater freedom in CHORD construction, more liberal use of DISSONANCE, and more varied rhythms. (2) The style of the last portion of the ROMANTIC period, also designated as postromanticism and late romanticism. Works by Richard STRAUSS, MAHLER, and SCRIABIN, among others, are representative of this style.

Netherlands Schools: different generations of RENAISSANCE composers who were born in northern France, Belgium, and Holland during the 15th and early 16th centuries. Agreement among scholars in the numbering of these generations is lacking; for this reason, and because of misleading implications of the term regarding cultural history, the term has largely been abandoned.

Neume: a symbol for a single note or a group of notes, either according to the notational system developed for GREGORIAN CHANT or according to that developed for Byzantine chant. The neumes of Gregorian chant were used also in the notation of non-liturgical melodies. *See* NOTATION *(History).*

Nicolai, Otto: *b.* Königsberg, June 9, 1810; *d.* Berlin, May 11, 1849. Nicolai received his final training from Zelter and Klein in Berlin. He was music director to the Court in Vienna (1841–47) and director of the opera and the cathedral choir in Berlin (1847–49).

He founded the Vienna Philharmonic Concerts in 1842. Nicolai enjoyed several temporary successes with his Italian OPERAS; only the German opera *The Merry Wives of Windsor*—produced shortly before his death—remained in the repertory. He wrote also a number of songs, choral works, and miscellaneous instrumental music.

Nielsen, Carl August: *b.* Nörre-Lyndelse, June 9, 1865; *d.* Copenhagen, October 2, 1931. An outstanding Danish composer, Nielsen studied at the Copenhagen Conservatory. He was active chiefly in Copenhagen as a violinist, conductor, and teacher. He is best known as a programmatic symphonist. In addition to six SYMPHONIES, he wrote three CONCERTOS, four STRING QUARTETS and other CHAMBER MUSIC, two OPERAS, ten CANTATAS, songs, and KEYBOARD music.

Ninth: a compound INTERVAL comprising an octave and a second.

Nocturne: a title (equivalent to *Night Piece* or *Nachtstück*) coined by John FIELD and adopted by CHOPIN for CHARACTER PIECES of lyrical and melancholy mood. Chopin's nocturnes are usually in TERNARY FORM, with a more dramatic middle section. Elaborate melodic ORNAMENTATION is frequent.

Noël (F): a Christmas carol.

Nonet: an ENSEMBLE work for nine parts, instrumental or vocal.

Nonharmonic tones: a generic term for tones whose melodic function is ornamental and which are not part of the basic harmonic structure. They are usually dissonant, but even if not, are treated as if they were. The term may occur not only in the analysis of works with a traditional harmonic orientation, but also in the analysis of contrapuntal works antedating the formulation of the harmonic theory underlying the major-minor system. The main sorts of nonharmonic tones are the ANTICIPATION, APPOGGIATURA, AUXILIARY (or neighboring) TONE, CAMBIATA, ÉCHAPPÉE, PASSING TONE, and SUSPENSION. Except for the appoggiatura and suspension, non-harmonic tones are in weak (unaccented) rhythmic position.

Notation: the written representation of musical sound or motion. The traditional Western notation in present use has evolved gradually over a period of more than a thousand years. Its primary purpose is to fix the PITCH and relative duration of individual notes. Sometimes, however, special conventions dictate the use of symbols that are not meant to be interpreted strictly, either from the rhythmic standpoint or from both the melodic and rhythmic standpoints. The indication of TEMPO, PHRASING, and of large outlines of shadings of loud and soft has become a secondary goal of notation, particularly since the turn of the 18th century; however, nuances of tempo, phrasing,

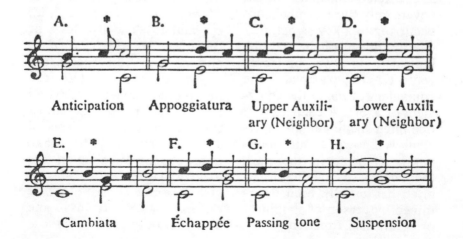

A.   B.   C.   D.

Anticipation   Appoggiatura   Upper Auxiliary (Neighbor)   Lower Auxiliary (Neighbor)

E.   F.   G.   H.

Cambiata   Échappée   Passing tone   Suspension

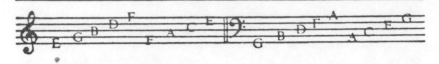

and shading depend largely upon an oral tradition for their transmission.

There are twelve pitches to the octave in Western music. These are identified by means of seven alphabet letters, from *a* to *g*, either with or without modifying symbols. A *sharp* (♯) indicates a pitch a half step above the pitch designated by the letter, while a *flat* (♭) indicates a pitch a half step below the lettered pitch. *Double sharps* (✕) and *double flats* (♭♭) indicate respectively pitches a whole step above and a whole step below normal. These four signs, together with the *natural* (♮), which acts as a cancellation, are known as ACCIDENTALS. (This term also has a restricted meaning which covers only those symbols not occurring in a key signature.)

Any given pitch may be indicated in two or three ways. C♯, for example, is the equivalent of *d*♭, *f*♭ the equivalent of *e*, etc. A change from one pitch spelling to an equivalent is known as an *enharmonic change*. In the past, the choice of spelling for a pitch has usually been determined by reason of simplicity or of musical function.

Pitches may be represented either by staff notation or by TABLATURE. A staff now consists of a set of five lines and four spaces, each of which provides place for an alphabet letter. The staff itself does not fix the identity of a note; this function is performed by a CLEF, a sign which identifies the position of a single pitch on the staff. The identities of other notes are deduced by determining how much higher or lower they are than the note identified by the clef. In modern practice, two clefs are predominant: the *treble clef*, which identifies *g'* on the second lowest line, and the *bass clef*, which identifies *f* on the second highest line. Thus the five lines of the treble clef are *e'*, *g'*, *b'*, *d''*, and *f''*, while the spaces are *f'*, *a'*, *c''*, and *e''*. The five lines of the bass clef are *G*, *B*, *d*, *f*, and *a*, while the spaces are *A*, *c*, *e*, and *g*. (Various mnemonics have been devised to aid the memorization of this information; for special devices employed to make note-recognition simpler, *see* FASOLA; SHAPE NOTES.)

Notes may consist of either outlines or solid forms; some have stems, others none; those with stems often have beams or flags attached. All of these notational variations serve to distinguish between different durational values. Each basic rhythmic symbol indicates a duration twice as long as the next smaller value and half as long as the next larger value. No symbol has an absolute time value that holds true for all works. In fact, the actual time accorded any given symbol may vary radically according to the rate of speed indicated or implied for the individual piece. For each symbol of sound duration there is an equivalent symbol for silence, known as a *rest*.

A dot appearing after a note, rest, or another dot lengthens that symbol by half its value. Two and even three dots may be used in succession. Because each dot receives progressively less time, it is never possible to double the value of the original symbol merely by means of dots. The normal meaning of the dot is not always observed exactly in BAROQUE notation and in the notation of modern popular music.

Two adjacent notes of the same pitch may be connected by a horizontal curved line known as a *tie*. The tie directs that the second of these notes is not to be articulated but is to serve merely to lengthen the first. Very long tones may be notated by a series of notes, each connected to the note following by a tie. Ties serve also to notate values intermediate between those that

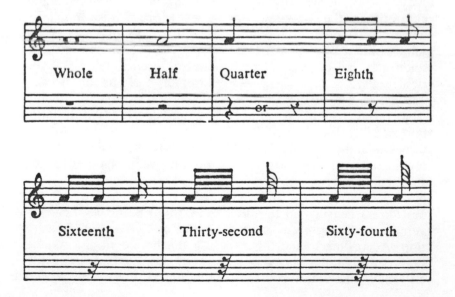

can be expressed by single notes, with or without dots. (For other methods of notating intermediate values, *see* DUPLET, TRIPLET.)

In most familiar music there is a regular pattern of stressed and unstressed units of time (*see* METER). These patterns are reflected in notation by grouping individual symbols into measures (= bars). Each measure has an opening stress and the measures are set apart from each other by a thin vertical line, the *bar-line*. A TIME-SIGNATURE is placed at the beginning of each piece in order to indicate the organization of time within the measure. While bar-lines may lend a closed and self-contained appearance to the music contained within each measure, they do not necessarily indicate either the opening or closing of a musical thought (*see* FORM); the measure is seldom a self-contained musical entity.

History. The roots of European musical notation cannot be traced with certainty. The Greeks and possibly other civilizations of antiquity developed musical notations, but these seem not to have had direct bearing on the development of present notation. According to the theory that has obtained the widest currency, the oldest roots of

our notation lie in adaptations of speech accent signs. Presumably an acute accent indicated a rising vocal inflection, a grave accent, a falling inflection. The circumflex represented a combination of the two, and so forth. By the 8th century, a set of musical symbols known as NEUMES had evolved in connection with the PLAINSONG of the Western church.

The neumes—written in various styles in different localities—indicated the number of notes in a MELODY and melodic direction, but neither exact pitches nor specific time-values. They could therefore be used only as memory guides for performers already familiar with the liturgical CHANTS. As the chant repertoire increased in size, so did the burdens on singers' memories. More precise indication of pitch became necessary. Theorists combined neumes with different sets of alphabet letters as early as the 9th century. Various experimental systems of INTERVAL notation were devised in the 9th century, but these did not provide the main channel for further developments.

In the 10th century Italian and English scribes began to indicate relative pitch by varying the height of the neumes in relation to an imaginary horizontal line. The use of

Late Medieval Neumes

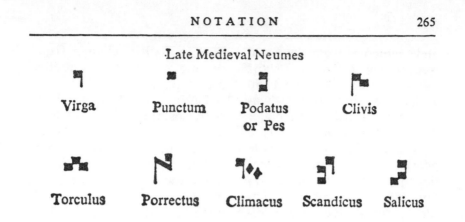

"heighted neumes" spread rapidly; by the end of the century the line itself was indicated, first by being scratched on the parchment with a dry point, later by being written in colored ink. A second line was added subsequently, and, in the Antiphoner of Guido d'Arezzo (*c*.1025), a four-line staff was employed. Such a staff is still used in the notation of liturgical chants. (The staff did not, however, win immediate, universal adoption.) The present five-line staff was known as early as A.D. 1200 and gradually became standard for all non-liturgical music. (In the 16th century, staves of six to eight lines were sometimes employed for KEYBOARD music.)

Diastematic (or staff) *notation* satisfied the needs for precise indication of pitch. It would seem that early neumes conveyed some rhythmic indications to contemporary singers, but this matter is disputed. At any rate, such

rhythmic tradition as did exist was lost during the 11th century, and a consistent search for a precise rhythmic notation awaited the development of complex POLYPHONY during the late 12th century. The first such repertoire had two important characteristics that influenced notation: (1) the upper voices contained many notes sung to a single syllable; (2) the rhythms of these voices were derived from one of a few simple patterns (*see* RHYTHMIC). Symbols—known as *ligatures*—indicating two or more pitches were used whenever possible, and each rhythmic mode was represented by a specific succession of ligatures. This system is known as *modal notation*. When musical styles changed during the first half of the 13th century, and syllabic or nearly syllabic settings predominated, methods of indicating time-values of individual notes had to be found. The square forms of the *virga* and *punctus* were equated respectively to long and short (*breve*) values. Around 1250 a diamond-shaped note was used for a third, still smaller value, called a *semibreve* (the equivalent of a modern whole note). This system of notation is known as *mensural notation*. In succeeding centuries, time-values were divided further and further, and ligatures were used less and less. There is a practical limit to the creation of shorter time-values even if no theoretical limits exist. Each time that theory overruled practical considerations, the result was that all of the older time-values became somewhat longer in order to accommodate the presence of the newly created shortest value. Over a period of centuries the breve, the short value of the early 13th century, became so long that it was discarded for all practical purposes during the 17th century. During the middle of the 15th century, the older black note-forms were changed to white, this change being roughly contempo-

raneous with a change from the use of parchment to the use of paper.

During the 14th to 16th centuries, the long might contain either two or three breves, the breve either two or three semibreves, and the semibreve either two or three *minims*. (If a value contained three of the next smaller value, it was termed *perfect;* if it contained two, it was termed *imperfect.*) The customary relationships prevailing within a given piece between the long and breve, the breve and semibreve, and the semibreve and minim were classified respectively under the headings *modus, tempus,* and *prolatio.* There are four possible combinations of *tempus* and *prolatio,* corresponding to the four combinations of simple and compound, duple and triple meters. These were indicated by the signs ⊙, O, ℂ, and C — these being the forerunners of present time-signatures. A vertical slash through a mensuration sign indicated a doubling of TEMPO. By plac-

Mensurel note-forms in black and in white notation

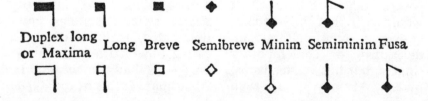

Duplex long or Maxima   Long   Breve   Semibreve   Minim   Semiminim   Fusa

ing a pair of numbers after the mensuration sign (or sometimes only one), other departures from the tempo norm could be indicated as in a ratio. The musical style of the late RENAISSANCE was dominated by simple duple meter, and notation in which values were related by multiples of two became standard. This relationship has been retained to the present day, notwithstanding numerous changes in rhythmic styles.

The music written during the 17th to 19th centuries required very few basic changes in the notational practice that had been standard since the late 16th century. (Changes in note shapes, for example, or adaptations to accommodate quarter tones are not basic changes.) For the written transmission of music created before the mid-20th century, the present system of notation will undoubtedly persist in all essentials for a long time to come. Indeed, this system is still adaptable to the widest segment of music now being written. However, the use of freer rhythms and of controlled IMPROVISATION in mid-20th-century music has involved experimentation with a large number of different notational systems, while ELECTRONIC MUSIC and music composed through the use of COMPUTER programs each pose special problems with regard to written forms. The notations developed for modern performers may employ various graphic concepts (lines, dots, differently shaped areas, etc.) in order to suggest to the performer musical gestures that may not be translatable in any fixed manner. Some of these may be brought into existence to express the ideas of only one work. Some may employ traditional elements of notation in new contexts, while others may be entirely independent of traditional concepts. Often the composer provides a verbal explanation of his intentions. The interpretations of these notations demands an awareness of current styles and a receptivity to the composer's ideas rather than a mechanical memory. In electronic and computer music, musical notation may be supplanted by technological descriptions.

Notes égales (F), Notes inégales (F): terms referring to a rhythmic convention of French BAROQUE NOTATION. Passages in stepwise motion written in equal values of moderate speed (usually halves of the main time-unit) were to be performed as an alternation of long and short values (*notes inégales*). If, however, a dot was placed either above or below each note, the performer was warned to disregard the convention and play the notes equally, as written (*notes égales*).

Notturno (I): (1) NOCTURNE; (2) an 18th-century work in several movements, similar to a SERENADE, often scored for a CHAMBER ENSEMBLE.

Novellete (G): a title given to some Romantic CHARACTER PIECES for piano. Those constituting SCHUMANN's Opus 21 are built of a number of contrasting sections, almost as a series of narrative episodes.

Nuove Musiche, Le (I): the title of a book of MONODIES by Caccini, published in 1602; the title is sometimes used as a designation for the modern style of the early 1600s.

Nut: (1) the device at the lower end of a BOW that maintains the tension on the bow hairs; (2) the strip of wood at the upper end of the fingerboard of a string instrument that raises the strings slightly so that they do not touch the fingerboard itself.

O

Obbligato (I): (1) an instrumental part, often a SOLO part, that is essential to the fabric of an ENSEMBLE or orchestral work. (In some scores c.1650–1750, there are nonessential parts that may be omitted without serious detriment.) Solo obbligato parts often occur in ARIAS in BAROQUE CANTATAS and ORATORIOS. (2) In 19th-century usage, still prevalent, an optional instrumental part.

Oberwerk (G): swell ORGAN.

Oblique motion: *see* MOTION.

Oboe: a conical WOODWIND instrument employing a double REED.

Oboe da Caccia (I): an alto

oboe of the BAROQUE with a range equivalent to that of the English horn.

Oboe d'amore (I): *see* WOODWINDS.

Obrecht, Jacob: *b.* Bergen-op-Zoom, November 22, 1452; *d.* Ferrara, 1505. In the North, Obrecht held posts in Bergen - op - Zoom, Utrecht, Antwerp, Bruges, and Cambrai, and, in Italy, at Ferrara. The majority of Obrecht's secular works have texts or titles in Dutch. However, the bulk of his output is sacred: MASSES and MOTETS. Obrecht's use of SEQUENCES, passages in parallel tenths, and clear-cut CADENCES contrasts with the more involved contrapuntal style of OCKEGHEM.

Ocarina (I): Sweet potato, a simple (keyless) globular flute, shaped like a bird or a sweet potato.

Ockeghem, Johannes: *b.* Flanders(?), *c.*1425; *d.* Tours, *c.*1495; the leading composer between DUFAY and JOSQUIN. A chorister at the Antwerp Cathedral and then in the Chapel of Duke Charles of Bourbon, Ockeghem was in the service of King Charles VII of France by 1453 and remained in royal service for the rest of his life. He became chaplain, then composer and music director; in 1459 he was appointed treasurer of St. Martin's Abbey in Tours.

Although several of Ockeghem's CHANSONS achieved widespread fame, he made his greatest contribution as a composer of MASSES and MOTETS. His style is characterized by a smooth flow, obtained by overlapping phrases in different voice parts and the avoidance of numerous strong cadences.

Octave: an interval formed by combining a note with the next higher or lower one of the same name. Octaves result when men and women sing the same MELODY; the sound of octaves may be recalled by humming the first two notes of *Over the Rainbow.*

Octet: an ENSEMBLE work for eight parts, instrumental or vocal.

Offenbach, Jacques: *b.* Cologne, June 20, 1819; *d.* Paris, October 5, 1880. Trained at the Paris Conservatoire, Offenbach was a cellist, conductor, theater manager, and, from 1853 on, the outstanding French composer of OPERETTAS. Among his most popular works are *Orpheus in Hades, La Belle Hélène, La Vie parisienne, La Grande Duchesse de Gérolstein,* and *La Périchole.* His finest work is the grand OPERA *Tales of Hoffmann.* He wrote a book regarding his musical experiences on a United States tour.

Offertory: (1) in the Roman

Catholic rite, the fourth item in the PROPER of the MASS. It is sung while the priest prepares and places the bread and wine upon the altar. Several 17th- and 18th-century composers wrote instrumental works to be performed at this point in the rite. (2) In the Protestant service, a work performed while offerings are collected.

Office (Daily Hours of Divine Service, Canonical hours): in the Roman Catholic ritual, a set of eight prayer hours that run from before sunrise to nightfall. These include Matins, Lauds, Prime, Terce, Sext, None, Vespers and Compline. The chanting of PSALMS, each preceded and followed by an ANTIPHON, comprises a major portion of the musical content of each of the Hours. Matins, now celebrated regularly only in monastic churches, includes in addition elaborate CHANTS known as Great Responsories. Vespers, of particular musical interest since it admits polyphonic music, contains the MAGNIFICAT, set frequently by composers of the 15th to 18th centuries. Other POLYPHONIC music intended for Vespers includes several 12th-century organa by LEONIN (*see* MEDIEVAL MUSIC). The four Marian antiphons, *Alma Redemptoris Mater, Ave Regina caelorum, Regina caeli,* and *Salve Regina,* are sung during Compline, one for each season of the Church year; these were frequently set as MOTETS during the 15th and 16th centuries.

Ondes musicales (F), **Ondes Martenot** (F): an ELECTRONIC INSTRUMENT devised by M. Martentot in 1928. The instrument produces only one tone at a time. The player may obtain either infinitely subtle gradations of PITCH or normal INTERVALS without an intermediate glide.

Open notes: (1) notes produced by strings vibrating at full length (i.e., on unstopped strings); (2) notes produced by instruments of the BRASS family without use of valves or keys.

Opera: a stage work that is sung throughout or in greater part, normally to an orchestral accompaniment. Opera, COMIC OPERA, OPERETTA, and musical comedy differ from each other with regard to the balance between the use of song and speech—the lighter the form, the more extensive the use of spoken dialogue. In serious opera, it is rarely used at all.

Opera originated during the last years of the 16th century. The genre was influenced at first by the BALLET DE COUR, by 16th-century dramatic entertainments that employed MADRIGALS and sometimes instrumental music at appropriate places in the loose-knit action, and possibly also by the heritage of medieval liturgical drama. The stylistic basis of early opera arose from the musical philosophies of the Florentine CAMERATA, led by Count Bardi, although the first productions were organized by other noblemen, including Count Corsi. Even though the Camerata had no precise idea of Greek music, they sought a return to the principles they thought governed ancient Greek drama. They held that music should follow the PITCH inflections of fine orators in order to present with utmost effectiveness the emotions suggested by the text. This resulted in a style known as MONODY, in which a SOLO vocal melody was supported by an instrumental BASS LINE and a harmonic filler. In opera, monody employed limited melodic range, numerous pitch repetitions, occasional affective melodic leaps, and a highly fluid (rather than symmetrical) RHYTHM. Because monody was avowedly patterned after speech, the music was known as RECITATIVE.

The music for the first opera, Peri's *Dafne* (1597), is lost. This work was followed in 1600 by two settings of *Euridice,* one mainly by PERI, the other by CACCINI. These consist chiefly of monodies, together with occasional CHORUSES. In MONTEVERDI's *Orfeo* (1607), the role of the chorus and ORCHESTRA is enlarged, and greater stylistic variety is achieved. His harmonies are more imaginative, his melodies more lyrical than those of his predecessors. In succeeding decades a distinction between narrative and lyrical melodic styles gradually sharpened, the former remaining irregular, the latter making greater use of symmetrical melodic and rhythmic constructions and of REPETITION. The term recitative was retained for the narrative style; sections of greater melodic interest were known as ARIAS.

From Florence, opera spread to Rome and then to Venice, where the first public opera house opened in 1637. Previously, opera had been a private spectacle commissioned by a nobleman for a particular celebration; an opera was performed once or twice and then discarded. With the opening of the theater to the public—nobility and rich merchants—magnificent sets and extravagant stage machinery were designed and more attention was paid to vocal display. Whereas during the first half of the 17th century there was often a fluid succession of recitative, aria, and ARIOSO styles (the last combining features of the first two), during the last half, these styles were more sharply separated into distinct sections. Arias became longer and demanded greater technical virtuosity; the ABA structure of the *aria da capo* became predominant. By the end of the century, a classic style had developed under Neapolitan leadership, with such masters as PROVENZALE and Alessandro SCARLATTI. This style emphasized the aria and aimed at producing a balance between the numbers and kinds of different arias. In the hands of lesser librettists and composers, the style could lapse into artificial conventionalism.

Italian opera began in France in 1645, but met with mixed reception and was modified to suit French taste. The strength of spoken drama and BALLET in France was such that: (1) clarity of text in opera was insisted upon, thus curtailing excessive vocal flourishes; (2) ballet was incorporated into French opera whenever possible. The first master of French opera was the Italian-born LULLY; in the 18th century, there followed RAMEAU and the Viennese GLUCK. The latter is especially known for his renewed emphasis on dramatic values.

Both Rameau and Gluck added immeasurably to the importance of the orchestra in opera.

Opera in England also competed with traditions of spoken drama and ballet (i.e., the MASQUE). Few operatic masterpieces of native English inspiration were produced, the last being by the late 17th-century master, PURCELL. However, a local offshoot of some importance was the ballad opera, a light work originally employing popular tunes and spoken dialogue. The first example was GAY's *Beggar's Opera* (1728). Otherwise, Italian opera was dominant. It was in England that HANDEL produced his finest Italian operas. Opera in the German principalities and in Austria during the 17th and 18th centuries was dominated by Italians and by Germans and Austrians writing in Italian style. Both HAYDN and MOZART wrote chiefly Italian opera.

The subject matter of most opera in the 17th century was mythological or historical. In order to counterbalance the stylized, heroic characters, comic episodes were introduced in the mid-17th century, either as subplots within the score or as separate entertainments (*intermezzi*) between the acts. In the 18th century, the heroic and natural (or comic) elements were separated, the former constituting *opera seria*, the latter, *opera buffa*. PERGOLESI's *La serva padrona* (1733), the first masterpiece of the latter genre, originated as an intermezzo and then was presented independently. The scope of this lively medium broadened, giving rise to such masterpieces as Mozart's *Marriage of Figaro, Don Giovanni,* and *Così fan tutte. Opera seria* was transformed into the grand opera of the 19th century.

During the 19th century, most important operas were written by masters who concentrated their creative efforts largely in this realm. Men such as ROSSINI, DONIZETTI, BELLINI, VERDI, and WAGNER wrote comparatively little besides opera, while symphonic masters such as MENDELSSOHN, SCHUMANN, and BRAHMS either never composed opera or were unsuccessful in the medium. During this century the awareness of national styles sharpened. German opera developed to great heights in the hands of WEBER and WAGNER; Russian opera was created by GLINKA, BORODIN, RIMSKY-KORSAKOV, and MUSSORGSKY, the latter's *Boris Godunov* being outstanding; the Czechs

contributed a comic gem in SMETANA's *Bartered Bride.*

On the whole, the Italian composers emphasized beautiful and effective vocal MELODY that often rested on simple HARMONIES. The individual arias were usually self-contained entities loosely connected by terse recitatives; the genre is known as *number opera.* Even Verdi's early masterpieces—*Rigoletto, Il Trovatore,* and *La Traviata*—follow these conventions. Late in his career, Verdi turned to a more continuous flow of music, with richer harmony and orchestration, reaching a peak in *Otello* and *Falstaff.*

The strongest reaction against number opera came from Wagner, who conceived of Music Drama as a *Gesamtkunstwerk*, a union of all arts, each sacrificing part of its identity as a contribution to the greater whole. His theories are exemplified in the four operas of the Ring (*Das Rheingold, Die Walküre, Siegfried,* and *Götterdämmerung*), *Tristan und Isolde,* and *Parsifal.* Wagner dispenses with the contrast between recitative and aria; his vocal style is homogeneous, instrumentally derived, and uses rhythms that reflect proper text declamation. Literal, large-scale repetition is avoided, though the heavily symbolic music employs recurrent motives (LEITMOTIVS) representing important persons, things, or ideas. Closed forms and conclusive cadences are also avoided; tonal centers shift continually. The orchestra becomes a commentator on the drama and equals, if not surpasses, the voice in importance.

In retort to Wagner's turgid symbolism, Italian composers of the late 19th century turned to more realistic treatments of the passions of everyday persons in a concise style known as VERISMO. PUCCINI is the most important representative of this school. DEBUSSY, the leading French composer, turned to a more ethereal form of mysticism in his impressionistic masterpiece, *Pelléas et Mélisande*. In BERG's expressionistic *Wozzeck* (composed 1918–21), the composer adapts various traditional instrumental forms in order to create a sense of structural unity. It is difficult to discern a central stream in modern opera, as various composers employ different techniques in seeking balance between music and drama and between personal expression and mass communication.

Opera buffa (I): opera with characters that are prey to normal human weaknesses—rather than idealized stereotypes—and with comic elements in the plot (though not necessarily a farce). MOZART's *Marriage of Figaro* and *Così fan tutte,* ROSSINI's *Barber of Seville,* and DONIZETTI's *Don Pasquale* are well-known examples of *opera buffa.*

Opéra comique (F): opera with spoken dialogue; the plot may be comic or, as in BIZET's *Carmen,* tragic.

Opera seria (I): late BAROQUE and CLASSICAL opera with characters of heroic stature; the plot is usually tragic. Most HANDEL opera belongs on the whole to this genre; MOZART's *La Clemenza di Tito* (1791) is its last significant example.

Operetta: a play with an amusing plot, numerous songs, and an orchestral accompaniment. Ensemble, choral, and dancing scenes are frequent. The dialogue is spoken. The heyday of operetta was the mid-19th and early 20th centuries. The most celebrated composers were OFFENBACH, Johann STRAUSS, Jr., LEHÁR, SULLIVAN, and, in the United States, HERBERT. The 20th-century equivalent of operetta is musical comedy; GERSHWIN, KERN, BERLIN, PORTER, and RODGERS composed the music for many of the best known of these shows.

Ophicleide: a keyed BRASS INSTRUMENT of low range.

Opus (plural: *opera* [L]): Work: a single piece or a set of pieces. The term, abbreviated op., is followed by a number which, more often than not, indicates the relative chronological position of the work in the composer's output. If the opus comprises a set of pieces, these too are distinguished by number— e.g., Op. 10, No. 1; Op. 10, No. 2, Op. 10, No. 3. In the 17th and 18th centuries, opus numbers were used only sporadically, and even in the early 19th century opus numbers were assigned erratically, especially by SCHUBERT and occasionally by BEETHOVEN. **Oratorio:** a sectional form for VOICES and instruments. Most oratorios are lengthy settings for vocal soloists, CHORUS, and orchestra of sacred, epic, or contemplative narratives. Often, the lack of costumes, scenery, and acting in oratorio is seized upon as a means of comparison with OPERA, but costumes and scenery were employed for many early oratorios and for STRAVINSKY's *Oedipus Rex*. The extensive role of the chorus, the frequent presence of a narrator, and the absence of brief exchanges of dialogue are traits often found in oratorio that distinguish it stylistically from opera.

The oratorio developed from a popular, late-16th-century practice, fostered by St. Philip Neri, of singing LAUDE; these were then folk-like polyphonic pieces with sacred text, sometimes in dialogue form. CAVALIERI's *Rappresentazione di anima e di corpo* (1600), which employs numerous choral numbers punctuated by dry RECITATIVES, is often named as the first work within the category proper. However, this work found comparatively few immediate successors. Toward the middle of the century, CARISSIMI produced several fine oratorios, using Latin texts. The popular function of the form is revealed by the simplicity of the harmonies of early examples; in these works, musical interest resides in their rhythmic and dramatic drive. However, the influence of contemporary opera led to the composition in oratorios of increasing numbers of brilliant ARIAS for virtuoso singers, and the momentary lessening of the importance of the chorus. Among Carissimi's greater contemporaries and successors active in oratorio composition are STRADELLA, Alessandro SCARLATTI, and CHARPENTIER (Carissimi's pupil). Most BAROQUE oratorio composers, with the exception of Charpentier, SCHÜTZ, and BACH, were also prolific operatic composers.

The oratorio is best known through a few of HANDEL's masterpieces in this form, including *Messiah, Israel in Egypt*, and *Judas Maccabeus*. However, the fact that many of Handel's other contributions in this field are seldom performed or recorded, tends to create an unbalanced conception of his oratorio style.

Although no later period displayed the intensity of interest in the oratorio shown by the Baroque, masterpieces of the genre continued to be produced. These include two by C. P. E. BACH, two by HAYDN (*The Creation* and *The Seasons*), two by MENDELSSOHN (*St. Paul* and *Elijah*), BERLIOZ' *L'Enfance du Christ*, FRANCK's *Les Béatitudes*, WALTON's *Belshazzar's Feast*, and HONEGGER's *King David*.

Orchestra: a group of instrumentalists employing more than one player for each of several parts. Numerous changes in constitution occurred during the evolution of the orchestra from its beginnings in the early 17th century to the present, but at all times string instruments have occupied a central place. (In vulgar usage, orchestra is a high-flown synonym for dance band; in that event string instruments may not be present.)

The modern professional symphony orchestra usually consists of approximately 100 instrumentalists. Its makeup is roughly as follows:

Strings	
Violin I	16–18
Violin II	16
Viola	12
Cello	10–12
Double Bass	8
Harp	2
Woodwind	
Flute	4
Oboe	4
Clarinet	4
Bassoon	4
Brass	
Horn	6–8
Trumpet	4–5
Trombone	4
Tuba	1–2
Percussion	6

The chief percussionist is the timpanist; the others perform the parts for the other drums, cymbals, triangle, xylophone, glockenspiel, chimes, etc., as called for. The larger orchestras contract also for the services of a pianist and employ additional instrumentalists—e.g., saxophonist, further percussionists, etc.—as needed. Instruments related to each of the four main woodwinds are usually entrusted to the fourth player of each group. The fourth flutist, for example, may be called upon to play piccolo or alto flute; the fourth oboist performs the English horn parts; and so forth. Ensembles of approximately 20–40 members are usually termed *chamber orchestras*. The musical direction of an orchestra is en-

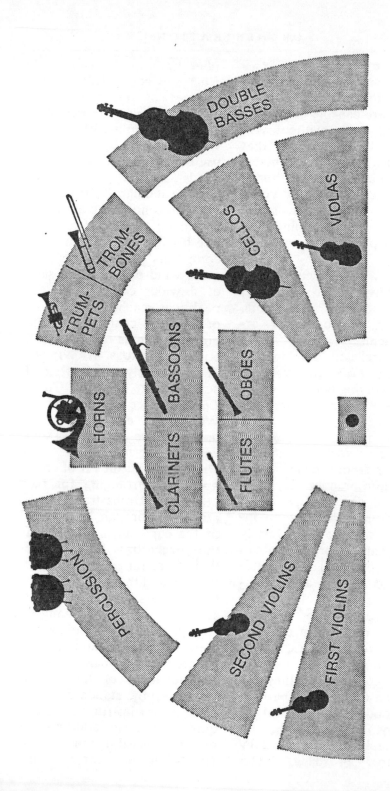

A COMMON ORCHESTRAL SEATING PLAN

trusted to a conductor (*see* CONDUCTING); experiments indicate that well-trained musicians are capable of playing standard works without visible outside direction, but that the musical results are below par. Subject to the authority of the conductor, BOWINGS and FINGERINGS for string passages are determined by the first player of each string group.

One widely used seating plan is given in the illustration section. Many conductors, however, employ other arrangements.

The orchestra developed in the early 17th century as an accompanying body for opera and only later acquired an independent existence. The instrumentation of the earliest orchestras would be judged irregular from the standpoint of modern practices. By mid-17th century, orchestras based largely or exclusively on instruments of the violin family (plus harpsichord or organ for the continuo) were standard, and there is a large BAROQUE repertoire for string orchestra. Oboes and bassoons were the most frequently employed winds. Flutes, horns, and trumpets were used in many scores; often they are intended to suggest a particular mood—e.g., pastoral or military. Although the famous orchestra of Louis XIV numbered 24 string players (*Les Vingt-quatre violons du Roi*) and could draw on the services of additional wind players, many orchestras through the mid-18th century were smaller. By 1800, the use of two each of the woodwinds, trumpets, and horns became standard. Throughout the 19th century the orchestra continued to grow steadily in size because of the ROMANTIC composers' use of more and more wind parts for the sake of a wider color palette. A peak was reached at the turn of the 20th century with the gigantic scores of MAHLER, Richard STRAUSS, STRAVINSKY (i.e., the early BALLETS), and SCHOENBERG (i.e., the *Gurre Lieder*). Since the First World War, more and more composers have been working with smaller ensembles.

Orchestration: the art of composing or arranging for ORCHESTRA. Orchestration requires a thorough knowledge of the capabilities of each of the orchestral instruments: their total ranges, their TONE COLORS and the ways in which these colors vary in different sections of their ranges, strong and weak points in their TECHNIQUE, and special effects that they can produce. A knowledge of the colors produced by standard combinations of instruments is required, and, in addition, a master orchestrator must possess an instinct for the unusual and effective. While a composition may be created without specific instruments in mind or for piano and later scored for orchestra, most composers think in orchestral terms from the first, their ideas being shaped by their knowledge of instrumental tone colors and capabilities. Occasionally a famous composition by one composer may be orchestrated or re-orchestrated by another. The RAVEL orchestration of MUSSORGSKY's *Pictures at an Exhibition* is the most famous example of this practice. While many 18th-century composers (e.g., HANDEL and RAMEAU) exhibited masterly instinct for orchestral color, it was BERLIOZ who made musicians acutely aware of techniques of orchestration through the writing of his pioneering treatise.

Ordinary: the sections of the MASS (and sometimes, by extension, also those of the OFFICE) that do not change text according to the particular feast being celebrated. The sections of the Mass Ordinary that are of importance for the musician are the *Kyrie, Gloria, Credo, Sanctus* (including the *Benedictus*), and *Agnus Dei.*

Ordre (F): title employed by François COUPERIN for several groups of KEYBOARD pieces, roughly equivalent to SUITES.

Orff, Carl: *b.* Munich, July 10, 1895. Orff completed his training at the Munich Academy of Music. He has been active as a conductor and teacher, particularly in Munich. He has written chiefly for the stage: OPERAS (e.g., *Die Kluge*), scenic CANTATAS (e.g., *Carmina Burana, Catulli Carmina,* and *Trionfo di Afrodite*), and plays with music (e.g., *Antigonae*). Orff's style is both reactionary and simple for its day: rhythmic and melodic cells are repeated rather than developed. The use of DISSONANCE does not obscure a clear sense of tonality. The suggestion of folk strength has, however, made for effective theater.

Organ: an instrument having one or more sets of pipes and an artificial wind supply, both governed by one or more KEYBOARDS and a connecting action. (*See also* ORGAN, ELECTRONIC.) Organ design has varied greatly from place to place and from one period to another. A tiny medieval instrument might have only one keyboard and a few dozen pipes, while a huge modern one might have as many as eight keyboards (including a pedal keyboard) and nearly 33,000 pipes. By varying the construction of the pipes, organ builders are able to vary the timber, allowing the organist to select at will from numerous TONE

COLORS. These may be blended, or distinctive colors may be employed simultaneously by using different keyboards. It might seem that the largest organs would be best because they offer the widest assortment of tone colors. However, these instruments are usually based on tonal concepts incompatible with those of the finest segment of the repertoire. Current design favors instruments of moderate size, having perhaps three manual keyboards and one pedal keyboard, each controlling 8–20 different sets of pipes.

An organ pipe may be made of wood or metal; its cross-section may be round or square; the body may be shaped as a cylinder, cone, or inverted cone; the upper end may be open, completely stopped, or partially stopped; the ratio of length to diameter (termed *scale* or *scaling*) may vary. The most fundamental difference between pipes, however, involves the nature of the aperture. A flue pipe is one constructed like a whistle or recorder; the air is forced past the sharp edge of a plane slanted into a hole cut in the side. A REED pipe is one that employs a single, beating reed. (The reed not only initiates the sound, but determines the PITCH, the pipe itself acting primarily as a resonator.) A set of pipes —one for each pitch—of the same characteristics of construction is known as a *rank, register, stop,* or *set.* The three main classes of flue pipes are called *diapason* or principal, *flute,* and *string.* The first produces a tone with a moderate number of harmonics (*see* ACOUSTICS), the second a gentler tone with fewer harmonics, and the last a penetrating tone, high in harmonics. The three classes of reed pipes are *solo, semichorus,* and *chorus,* in order of increasing stridency. Names of individual stops are sometimes used inconsistently and are often drawn from names of other instruments, both modern and medieval. Sometimes the tonal resemblance between the organ stop and its namesake is strong, sometimes not.

A second method of classification correlates factors of size, pitch, and NOTATION. In the average flue rank, the pipe for the C below the bass staff is 8 feet long. In such a rank, the notes will sound as written, and the entire rank is known as an 8' stop. In a 16' stop, the sounds produced will be an octave lower than written, while in a 4' stop, they will be an octave higher. Several still smaller ranks are also employed.

The basic ranks of the organ are known as *foundation stops.* Among the subsidiary ranks are *mixture* and *mutation stops*. The former are compound stops which permit each key to sound simultaneously from two to seven pipes; the tones produced are related to each other in terms of the harmonic series (*see* ACOUSTICS). A mutation stop is a rank of soft pipes representing an upper harmonic of a much louder foundation stop with which it is combined. It is not heard as a separate sound but as an alteration of the tone quality of the foundation stop. A *harmonic stop* utilizes a small hole in the side of each pipe; the sound produced is an octave higher than normal for the pipe's size. Placing a stopper in the end of a pipe not only lowers its pitch an octave but results also in a distinct tonal change. A vibrato or CELESTE effect may be suggested by coupling two pipes barely out of tune with each other, thus producing beats (*see* ACOUSTICS). A tremolo is produced by mechanically introducing small variations in the wind pressure at regular intervals.

Several ranks of pipes are grouped together into units known as *divisions* or *organs*. Each keyboard may govern either one or more divisions or organs. The three chief manual keyboards are called the *Great, Choir,* and *Swell.* Each possesses individual tonal capabilities, the Great being the most powerful, the Swell, the least. Most organs possess couplers which enable the organist to employ the stops of one division through the keyboard of another or to play at either the octave above or the octave below on the same or different keyboards.

Technique. Before an organist can begin to play a wind supply must be brought into action. In previous centuries, a group of men were required to work several sets of bellows; now machines perform this task, usually rotary electric fan blowers. Next, the tone quality must be selected. This is done by pushing down tilt-tablets or by pulling out knobs governing the individual stops. When the organist strikes a key, a connecting action—either mechanical, electropneumatic, or electric—permits the wind to enter the corresponding pipes of the selected ranks. When he removes his finger and the key returns to its normal position, the sound stops immediately. Great attention must therefore be paid to FINGERING in order to ensure the exact length of tone necessary to artistic interpretation. Because the wind supply of each rank is constant, there is no response to striking force on an organ key as on the piano. The organist must change dynamics by other means. Certain divisions—chiefly the Swell and the Choir—are enclosed in shuttered chambers. When the shutters are closed, the tone is soft; it becomes louder as the shutters are progressively opened by a tilting pedal near the bottom of the console. The chamber itself is known as a *Swell Box* or *Expression Chamber*. A second method of varying dynamics is either to add or retire stops. On some organs this can be done mechanically by means of a crescendo pedal. The pedal keyboard is played either by alternating the feet on different pedals, or by going from one pedal to another with a heel-and-toe action. In order to facilitate complex changes of registration while playing, it is possible to preset desired combinations of stops, using push-buttons (known as *combination stops*) located immediately below the keyboards to bring these registrations into action.

History. The earliest organ, operated by water pressure and known as a *hydraulis*, was presumably made in Alexandria *c*.250 B.C. by Ktesibios. Its Hebrew counterpart was known as a *magrepha*. Because of its loudness, the hydraulis was used chiefly for outdoor functions, including the Roman circuses. Pneumatic organs were apparently in use before A.D. 393. Early organs had no keyboards. They were worked directly by sliders, which when pulled out, permitted the wind to enter the pipes; several pipes were coupled together, as in a mixture. In the 13th century, this clumsy arrangement was gradually supplanted by a lever system, first operated in the manner of a typewriter keyboard, and later in a variant of the present keyboard. MEDIEVAL instruments were made in a wide variety of sizes. The *portative* was a small organ, held on the lap; one hand worked the bellows attached to the back, while the other played the keyboard. The *positive* was a larger instrument, suitable for home use and capable of being transported in large carts for use in processions. Some had two or three stops; they required one person to operate the bellows while another played. During the RENAISSANCE, the stylistic differences in organ design arose among the various leading musical nations; in general, the Dutch and Germans were the most progressive builders from the 16th to the 18th centuries, pioneering especially in the development of solo stops. The peak of the BAROQUE organ is represented by instruments of Gottfried and Andreas Silbermann. The Swell Box was invented in 1712 by Abraham Jordan. The improvements achieved during the 19th century involve chiefly mechanical details, particularly those dealing with the action. Wind pressures were gradually boosted and tonal concepts revised. The clear, contrasting tone colors of Baroque organs were replaced by rounder, fuller ones. These trends eventually resulted in the huge organs and theater organs of the early 20th century; however, the present tendency is to join the better features of the Baroque organ with those of the ROMANTIC organ.

Literature. Little is known of the earliest literature for organ. Possibly the organ assisted in the performance of GREGORIAN CHANT and perhaps played the long notes of early organa (*see* MEDIEVAL MUSIC). The earliest surviving music specifically for organ is in the Robertsbridge Codex of c.1325; the next sources are about 100 years later. Much early organ music consists of transcriptions of vocal pieces—CHANSONS and MOTETS. Gradually, however, composers began to create an independent repertoire for the instrument, based either on imitative COUNTERPOINT—

the CANZONA, RICERCAR, etc. —or on the flexible technical resources of the instrument— the TOCCATA, and VARIATION forms, etc. There were organ composers of merit in most major European countries at the beginning of the 17th century; however, after FRESCOBALDI, interest declined in the southernmost countries. French organ music continued to develop, culminating in the works of François COUPERIN, Louis Marchand, Jean François Dandrieu, and DAQUIN. However, the greatest contribution to the literature came from Germany, the home of innumerable organ masters, crowned by BACH. Romantic composers had less interest in the organ, although some fine works were written by MENDELSSOHN, LISZT, BRAHMS, FRANCK, WIDOR, and REGER.

Organ, Electronic: a KEYBOARD instrument — such as the Hammond, Novachord, Solovox, or Compton Electrone—which produces and amplifies the sound through the use of electricity. The Hammond Organ employs a series of motor-driven generators to produce alternating current with frequencies equivalent to those of the tempered scale. The Novachord and similar instruments produce such currents by means of vacuum tube oscillators. Both types employ amplifiers and loudspeakers. Both make available a variety of TONE COLORS by controlling the relative strengths of the partial vibrations that are the "hidden" constituents of the individual tones. These and similar instruments are used in popular music and in churches and other places of assembly instead of more expensive pipe organs.

Organetto (I): portative ORGAN.

Organistrum (L): HURDY-GURDY.

Organ Mass: organ settings of the MASS ORDINARY, written during the RENAISSANCE and BAROQUE. In this practice, the CHOIR first sang a section of PLAINSONG, the organ following with a polyphonic setting.

Organ Point: pedal point.

Organum: MEDIEVAL polyphonic setting of PLAINSONG.

Orgel (G), **Orgue** (F): ORGAN.

Ornaments, Graces, Agréments (F), **Manieren** (G), **Abellimenti** (I): conventional decorative figures. Among the most common are the APPOGGIATURA, MORDENT, NACHSCHLAG, TRILL, TURN, and certain forms of ARPEGGIO. Whereas more elaborate ornaments are either written out by the composer or improvised by the performer, the above are often indicated by standard signs. BAROQUE performers made particularly

extensive use of ornaments; their conventions were so widespread that composers frequently omitted to specify the placement of desired ornaments, leaving this matter to the discretion of the performer.

Ossia (I): or else; the word is used to indicate an alternative version of a particular passage, usually one that is simpler to perform.

Ostinato: a figure or phrase that is repeated persistently. With but few exceptions the repetition occurs at the same pitch and usually in the same voice. Many BAROQUE compositions are based on the use of an ostinato in the lowest voice (BASSO OSTINATO). *See also* CHACONNE and PASSACAGLIA; GROUND.

Ottava (I): OCTAVE. The abbreviations *8va* and *8*, and, rarely, the fully written-out directions *all'ottava, ottava alta,* and *ottava sopra* may be placed above a series of notes to indicate that these are to be played an octave higher than written. A dotted line often indicates how long the direction remains valid. The purpose is generally to avoid an excessive number of ledger lines in the NOTATION, making reading simpler. The same abbreviations and the directions *ottava bassa (8va bassa)* and *ottava sotto* may be placed below a series of notes to indicate performance at the octave below. *Coll' ottava* and *con ottava* require the doubling of the highest (or lowest) line at the octave.

Ottavino (I): piccolo.

Ottone (I), **Ottoni** (I), **Strumenti d'Ottone** (I): BRASS INSTRUMENTS.

Overtones: partial vibrations of the harmonic series (*see* ACOUSTICS).

Ouverture (F): OVERTURE.

Overblowing: a technique employed by wind players. Through subtle alterations of breath pressure and of the position of the lip muscles, the player is able to obtain different notes with the same FINGERING. Notes obtainable with a single fingering are related as members of the same harmonic series (*see* ACOUSTICS).

Overture: (1) an instrumental movement serving as an introduction to an OPERA, ORATORIO, stage play, SUITE, etc., or an independent work of similar style. A late BAROQUE Italian overture was usually entitled a *sinfonia* (*sinfonia avanti l'opera*), while the late Wagnerian overture is entitled *Vorspiel* (i.e., prelude). The earliest operas either had no overture or at most a brief one. The custom of providing a substantial opening MOVEMENT began, however, in the 1630s. The overtures to Venetian operas of the mid-17th century often featured slow introductory sections in duple RHYTHM, followed by fast movements in triple METER. The French overture, developed by LULLY, probably derives from such works. This overture begins in slow, majestic fashion, characteristically developed by dotted rhythms. There then follows a lively movement in pseudo-fugal style. A return at the end to the style of the opening is frequent, but optional. The instrumental works entitled French Overture are suites which employ the above form as an introductory movement. A second type, the Italian overture, became popular through the works of A. SCARLATTI toward the end of the 17th century. These *sinfonias* were in three sections, following a fast-slow-fast TEMPO pattern. These works constituted an important source for the development of the classical SYMPHONY. During the CLASSICAL period, SONATA FORM was used in the writing of overtures. From the time of GLUCK and MOZART it became customary to anticipate some of the important themes used in the opera itself. In the hands of lesser 19th-century composers, this practice degenerated into the construction of overtures as mere

MEDLEYS. The independent concert overture of the 19th century was generally of programmatic content and, as such, a forerunner of the SYMPHONIC POEM. Some were composed for special occasions. (2) In 18th-century English usage, a synonym for symphony.

P

Pachelbel, Johann: *b.* Nuremburg, August 1653; *d.* Nuremburg, March 6, 1706. An organist, Pachelbel held posts in Vienna (1674), Eisenach (1677), Erfurt (1678), Stuttgart (1690), Gotha (1692), and Nuremburg (1695). Although he wrote a few CAN-TATAS and MASSES, several MOTETS, MAGNIFICATS, and ARIAS, and a small body of CHAMBER MUSIC, Pachelbel's chief contribution is his organ music. He was one of the most important writers of chorale variations and CHO-RALE fughettas of the generation preceding BACH; he was also important as a composer of SUITES.

Paderewski, Ignace Jan: *b.* Kurylówka, November 18, 1860; *d.* New York City, June 29, 1941. Paderewski completed his piano studies under Theodore Leschetizky in Vienna. He soon became the most celebrated pianist of his day, exerting a hold over his audiences greater than can be accounted for by mere technical achievement. He composed a variety of works, chiefly for piano, but including also songs, an OPERA, CHAMBER MUSIC, and orchestral compositions. With the exception of a *Menuet in G*, none of his works achieved widespread acceptance. An ardent patriot, he was the first premier of the Polish republic (1919–20).

Padovana (I), Paduana (I): a name given to some 16th-century Italian dances of various rhythms. Padovanas are stylistically similar to PAVANES.

Paganini, Niccolò: *b*. Genoa, October 27, 1782; *d*. Nice, May 27, 1840. The most dazzling violin virtuoso the world has known, Paganini received his earliest musical instruction from his father, on the mandolin. He gave a public concert on violin when eleven and began touring Italy when thirteen. The European tour through Vienna, Berlin, Paris, and London that established his supremacy above all others began in 1828. Paganini's most important works include a set of 24 *Caprices*, two violin CONCERTOS, and several sets of VARIATIONS. The technical demands of these works influenced not only the development of violin playing, but also—through transcriptions by LISZT and SCHUMANN—the development of ROMANTIC piano style. Other works include a set of SONATAS for violin and guitar and a set of STRING QUARTETS for violin, viola, guitar, and cello.

Paine, John Knowles: *b*. Portland, Me., January 9, 1839; *d*. Cambridge, Mass., April 25, 1906. The son of a music dealer, Paine completed his musical studies in Berlin. He served as organist in Boston and taught at Harvard University, holding the first American professorship in music. Among his pupils were CARPENTER, CONVERSE, FOOTE, and D. G. MASON. He wrote a variety of works for chorus and orchestra, SYMPHONIES and SYMPHONIC POEMS, CHAMBER MUSIC, piano pieces and songs, organ works, and an OPERA.

Paisiello, Giovanni: *b*. Taranto, May 9, 1740; *d*. Naples, June 5, 1816. A student of DURANTE, Paisiello began as a composer of sacred music, but turned to the writing of comic OPERAS in 1763. He quickly became a leading master of the genre. Among his better-known operas are *The Barber of Seville* and *Nina*. Paisiello served Catherine II in St. Petersburg (1776–84), Ferdinand IV in Naples (1784–99), and Napoleon Bonaparte in Paris (1802–3) before returning to Naples. In addition to his vocal works, Paisiello wrote also SYMPHONIES, piano CONCERTOS, CHAMBER MUSIC, and piano SONATAS.

Palestrina, Giovanni Pierluigi da: *b*. Palestrina, *c*.1525; *d*. Rome, February 2, 1594; outstanding composer of sacred music of the late RENAISSANCE. Palestrina received his training at the Cathedral of Palestrina and at Santa Maria Maggiore in Rome. After a few years' service in his native town, Palestrina was appointed music director of the Julian Chapel in Rome in 1551. Pope Julius III made him a member of the Papal Chapel in 1555, but Palestrina was dismissed late that year by Pope Paul IV. He then succeeded LASSUS at St. John Lateran, and, during later years, was music director at Santa Maria Maggiore, at the Roman Seminary, and at the residence of Cardinal Ippolito d'Este. In 1571, Palestrina was reappointed director of the Julian Chapel, remaining there until his death.

Palestrina wrote over 100 MASSES. His fame is based on these and other liturgical works—MOTETS, HYMNS, LAMENTATIONS, MAGNIFICATS, etc. His secular and sacred MADRIGALS are of lesser importance. He cultivated a diatonic style of admirable restraint and balance. His melodies flow smoothly, ascending curves characteristically being followed by descending passages of similar length. Though a conservative composer in many respects, Palestrina contributed significantly to the evolution of a carefully controlled DISSONANCE treatment. Active during the period when the Council of Trent was consid-

ering the reform of liturgical music, Palestrina, together with a few other composers, produced POLYPHONIC Masses judged acceptable from the devotional standpoint. The story that the outstanding effect produced by his *Mass for Pope Marcellus* was the main reason why the Council did not ban polyphonic settings of the Mass is unfounded.

Pandiatonicism: a 20th-century style of composition based on the resources of the diatonic SCALE, but freed of some of the conventions associated with the major and minor modes. In this style all diatonic INTERVALS (i.e., including seconds and sevenths) may be treated as consonant and harmonic progressions may proceed without reference to traditional concepts of function. This style is present in certain works of SATIE, STRAVINSKY, POULENC, and COPLAND, among others.

Pandora: a plucked string instrument of the late 16th and 17th century, distinguished by a body with deeply scalloped sides.

Panpipes: a set of whistle flutes of graded sizes, bound together, usually as a raft, but sometimes as a bundle. The pipes may be made of bamboo, cane, or clay.

Pantaleon: a large DULCIMER, devised by Pantaleon Hebenstreit c.1690. Played with felt hammers, it is often considered a forerunner of the piano.

Parallel motion: *see* MOTION.

Parallel (or Consecutive) **intervals:** a succession in the same two voice parts of the same INTERVAL, based on different PITCHES. In the teaching of traditional COUNTERPOINT and HARMONY, parallel fifths and octaves are forbidden. Parallel thirds and sixths occur frequently, but their overuse produces a weak, overly sweet musical fabric.

Paraphrase: a free arrangement of the musical material in a previously existing work. There are paraphrases by LISZT, for example, that transform works from the operatic, song, and violin literatures into idiomatic piano works. Often a paraphrase may be an extensive improvisation on a short MELODY.

Parlando (I), **Parlante** (I): (1) in vocal music, a direction to simulate speech in the matter of TONE COLOR; (2) in instrumental music, a direction calling for expressive performance, approaching impassioned speech or song in its intensity.

Parody: (1) a work in which preexistent music is accompanied by a newly written text; this practice undoubtedly existed at all stages of music history, but it was particularly important during the Middle Ages, when sacred and secular texts were often interchanged. (2) A work that draws simultaneously on the several voice parts of a preexistent model, interspersing newly composed sections among derivative ones, and presenting derivative sections in new contrapuntal guises. Parody technique was especially important in the MASS compositions of the late 16th century. (3) In the nontechnical sense, a musical passage that refers satirically to a previously known work.

Part: (1) any one of the two or more melodic lines comprising a contrapuntal fabric; (2) in ENSEMBLE works, the music for any one instrument or voice; (3) a subdivision of a musical form.

Part-book: a print or MS of the 16th or 17th century containing the music for an individual voice or instrument for a group of works.

Partials: the set of vibrations constituting a given sound. Most sound-producing media vibrate simultaneously both in full and in various segments (*see* ACOUSTICS).

Partita (I): a BAROQUE term for: (1) a set of VARIATIONS; (2) a SUITE.

Partition (F), **Partitur** (G), **Partitura** (I): SCORE.

Part-song: a short choral work in a harmonic rather than contrapuntal TEXTURE. Most part-songs are secular works written for unaccompanied CHORUS. The term usually refers to a 19th- and early 20th-century repertoire. (2) In American library usage, a work for chorus or vocal ensemble that may be either polyphonic or homophonic.

Paso doble (S): a 20th-century Spanish dance in lively duple METER.

Passacaglia: *see* joint entry under CHACONNE.

Passamezzo (I): a moderately quick dance in duple METER of the late 16th and early 17th centuries; the music was customarily composed as a continuous VARIATION above one of two traditional OSTINATO patterns (*passamezzo antico, passamezzo moderno*). The *passamezzo* was usually followed by a SALTARELLO.

Passecaille: *see* joint entry under CHACONNE.

Passepied (F): a French dance in lively 3/8 or 6/8 time. It was introduced into French BALLETS of the mid-17th century and later became one of the optional movements of the SUITE.

Passing note (Passing tone): a NONHARMONIC TONE appearing in scalewise progression between two harmonically consonant tones.

Passion: a liturgical narration of the Crucifixion according to one of the four Evangelists (St. Matthew, St. Mark, St. Luke, or St. John), part of the rite during the week beginning with Palm Sunday. PLAINSONG settings, based chiefly on intonations relieved by simple inflections, were designed for performance by three singers as early as the 13th century. The parts of Christ, the *Chronista* (Narrator, Evangelist), and the *Synagoga* representing the remaining participants, including the *turba*, "crowd," were differentiated according to PITCH (from low to high in the order mentioned) and TEMPO (from slow to fast).

In the late 15th century, the part of the *Synagoga* was set polyphonically, while the parts of Christ and the *Chronista* remained in plainsong. In the 16th century there appeared settings of the entire text; these were usually in MOTET style, the music often drawing on the plainsong formulas. Victoria's two Passions are among the finest of RENAISSANCE settings.

In the BAROQUE, newly created poetry was interpolated into the Passion text, greatly expanding it. The dramatic resources of the ORATORIO—CHORUSES, RECITATIVES, and ARIAS, all with instrumental ACCOMPANIMENT—together with CHORALES were employed by Lutheran composers. BACH's two Passions, according to St. Matthew and St. John, stand at the peak of the genre. Bach apparently wrote three other works in this form; one survives in part in other contexts; two are entirely lost. The St. Luke Passion once ascribed to Bach is not his.

Pasticcio (I): a composition put together from works by several composers. The term often refers to light, 18th-century French and English *operas* thus constructed; many of these were little more than MEDLEYS of tunes then in vogue.   •

Pastorale (F); music suggestive of an idyllic scene. Conventions established for such works during the BAROQUE included the use of a moderate TEMPO, 6/8 or 12/8 METER, and long bass notes suggestive of bagpipe drones. (The *Siciliano* is closely similar in style.) The term may refer to a song or an instrumental piece, or, in 16th and 17th century usage, to an OPERA, MASQUE, BALLET, or CANTATA.

Pauken (G): TIMPANI.

Pause, Hold, Fermata (I): the sign ⌒ directing that the note or rest immediately above or below be prolonged beyond its normal duration. The length of the additional duration is not measured but is left to the discretion of the performer. (In French and German, *Pause* indicates a REST.)

Pavane: a dance in slow duple METER employed in the 16th and early 17th centuries; in the latter part of this period it was usually followed by a GALLIARD.

Pavillon en air (F): a direction to horn and trumpet players to point the bell of the instrument upward.

Pedal: (1) that part of an instrumental mechanism which is operated by the feet. A pedal may be part of a KEYBOARD controlling the production of sound (on the organ), or may adjust PITCH (on the harp); it may prolong or soften the sound (on the piano), or it may control OCTAVE register or TONE COLOR (on the harpsichord). (2) short for PEDAL POINT; (3) short for PEDAL TONE, pedal note.

Pedal harpsichord (Pedal piano): a harpsichord or piano with a pedal KEYBOARD. The former were used occasionally during the early 18th century (e.g., by BACH), the latter during the 19th century (e.g., by SCHUMANN and GOUNOD).

Pedal point: a note sustained against a changing series of HARMONIES. Normally this note is the lowest of the several parts; should it occur in a middle or upper part, it is customary to speak of an *internal* or *inverted pedal point*, respectively. Most pedal points are founded either on the first or fifth degree of the SCALE.

Pedal tone (Pedal note): a low tone producible on certain BRASS INSTRUMENTS, but lying outside the normal, continuous range of the instrument. The tone is produced by the vibration of the air column as a unit rather than in segments.

Pentatonic: a term descriptive of a MODE, SCALE, or MELODY that utilizes five tones to the OCTAVE.

Pepusch, Johann Christoph: *b.* Berlin, 1667; *d.* London, July 20, 1752. After serving at the Prussian court and a short stay in Holland, Pepusch settled in London. He was active with various theaters and was Handel's predecessor as organist and composer to the duke of Chandos. He is most famous for the arrangements provided for the *Beggar's Opera,* and wrote besides MASQUES, CANTATAS, ODES, CONCERTOS, and SONATAS. He also published a HARMONY treatise.

Percussion instruments: generally speaking, instruments played by striking or shaking. (When dealing with non-orchestral instruments, the term is imprecise in that not all instruments capable of being played in these manners are actually classified as percussion instruments; the dulcimer, for example, is considered a string instrument.) The group is subdivided into instruments of definite PITCH and instruments of indefinite pitch. To the former category belong (among others) the timpani or kettledrums, xylophone, marimba, vibraphone, glockenspiel, celesta, and chimes. To the latter category belong (among others) the snare, tenor, and bass drums, the tambourine, triangle, cymbals, gong, Chinese block, rattles, and scrapers. In traditional scores percussion instruments are most frequently employed to reinforce rhythmic definition. In modern scores they are employed more often for the sake of their special TONE COLORS. *See also* articles on individual percussion instruments.

Perfect: a classification of either INTERVAL, CADENCE, or note value (*see* IMPERFECT).

Pergolesi, Giovanni Battista: *b.* Jesi (near Ancona), January 4, 1710; *d.* Pozzuoli, March 16, 1736. Pergolesi's fame rests chiefly on his *Stabat Mater* and his comic OPERA, *La Serva Padrona.* The latter originated as an INTERMEZZO to the serious opera *Il Prigioniero superbo* (1733). When performed independently in Paris, in 1752, it helped spark a spirited controversy regarding the merits of French versus Italian music. Pergolesi wrote a large number and variety of works during his brief lifetime, CHAMBER MUSIC, CANTATAS, etc., but *Il Maestro di musica* and several concertinos are

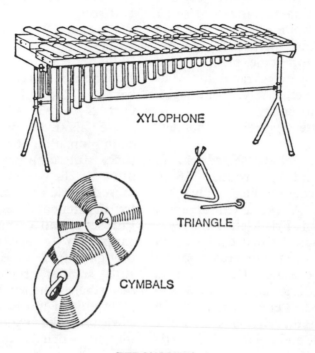

XYLOPHONE

TRIANGLE

CYMBALS

PERCUSSION

of questionable authenticity if not spurious.

Peri, Jacopo: *b.* Rome(?), August 20, 1561; *d.* Florence, August 12, 1633. The composer of *Dafne*, the first OPERA (1597), Peri was an accomplished singer and organist, who served both the Medici and Gonzaga families. Peri's *Euridice* (1600), which includes songs by CACCINI, is the first opera fully preserved.

Peri wrote, singly and jointly, other operas as well as MADRIGALS, monodic songs, and music for intermedii.

Period: in music of simple, symmetrical FORM, a section comprised of two "thoughts" (phrases).

Perotin (Perotinus): late 12th-century composer active in Paris—possibly at Notre Dame. Perotin wrote three- and four-part ORGANA, CON-

DUCTI, and provided numerous alternative sections (CLAUSULAE) to LEONIN's cycle of two-part organa. (*See also* MEDIEVAL MUSIC.)

Perpetuum mobile (L): a title meaning perpetual motion, used for some pieces which employ even, rapid notes almost exclusively, from beginning to end.

Pesante (I): weighty, ponderous.

Peter, Johann Friedrich: *b.* Heerendijk, May 19, 1746; *d.* Bethlehem, Pa., July 13, 1813. A Moravian organist, Johann Friedrich Peter was perhaps the first composer to write CHAMBER MUSIC in the United States. He wrote also many fine accompanied ANTHEMS. Peter was active in Nazareth, Bethlehem, Lititz (Pa.), and Salem (N.C.). His older brother, Simon Peter, was a minister who composed a few anthems.

Petite flûte (F): piccolo.

Pezzo (I): piece.

Pfitzner, Hans (Erich): *b.* Moscow, May 5, 1869; *d.* Salzburg, May 22, 1949. Trained at the Hoch Conservatory in Frankfort, Pfitzner was active as a conductor and teacher in numerous German cities. His work, in a late ROMANTIC style akin to that of Richard STRAUSS, was much admired in Germany and Austria. His best-known work is the OPERA *Palestrina*;

he wrote other operas, two SYMPHONIES and four CONCERTOS, a few choral pieces, CHAMBER MUSIC, and over 100 songs.

Phantasie (G): fantasy (FANTASIA).

Philidor, François André Danican: *b.* Dreux, September 7, 1726; *d.* London, August 24, 1795. After having made his mark as a chess champion, Philidor became a successful composer of comic OPERAS. He wrote also some sacred music and some works for instrumental ENSEMBLES.

Phrase: a unit of musical organization (*see* FORM), which, though often divisible into still smaller segments, is nevertheless the smallest complete unit of musical thought.

Phrasing: the exposition of the fine details of musical architecture by means of nuances of ARTICULATION, RHYTHM, and DYNAMICS in performance. The importance of a given note may be made clear not only by dynamic stress, but also by slight prolongation or distinctive attack (or by a combination of these methods). The segregation of a given note group is often accomplished by a slight shortening of the late note of the group, thus introducing a tiny breath of silence before the first note of the following group. The distinction thus achieved is frequently reinforced by a slight softening of the last note of a group. Actual techniques involved in phrasing depend both upon the nature of the instrument or voice being used and upon musical context. See Articulation.

Phrygian: (1) the third CHURCH MODE; (2) a Greek MODE that may be represented by a SCALE descending the white keys from *d'* to d.

Pianissimo (I): very soft (*PP*); piano (I), soft (*P*).

Piano (full name *pianoforte*): a stringed KEYBOARD instrument with a mechanism that employs felt hammers to strike the strings. Modern instruments may vary both in shape and range. Grand pianos, whose strings run horizontally, may vary in length from a little over five feet (a baby grand) to nearly nine (a concert grand). Upright pianos, whose strings run vertically, may vary in height, the true upright being the tallest, the console and spinet being much shorter. Most American pianos have a compass of seven octaves and a minor third (88 notes). Approximately the upper five octaves use three strings for each note, the octave-and-a-half below using two strings for each note, and the lowest notes using only one. The upper strings are made of steel; the lower ones have a steel core which is wound with copper wire. Resting on the strings are a set of wooden blocks with thick felt pads; these are known as *dampers*. The striking of a key causes the corresponding damper to rise and causes the hammer to pivot, strike the string(s), and rebound halfway. When the key is released, the damper descends and cuts off the sound and the hammer returns to its position of rest. It is possible to raise the entire bank of dampers by means of the damper PEDAL (known also as the sustaining or loud pedal, the right pedal). This leads to greater resonance and to the blurring of tones if several are struck. The soft (or left) pedal functions differently on grand pianos and uprights. On grand pianos it shifts the entire keyboard and action a tiny distance to the side so that the hammers are no longer centrally placed under the strings. On upright pianos the bank of hammers is shifted forward so that the individual hammer traverses a smaller distance before striking the string(s). In either event, the effect is one of softer sound and a slight change in tone color. (The change of color was more distinct in late 18th century pianos.) American grand pianos are also equipped with a middle pedal, known as a *sostenuto pedal*, which keeps raised the dampers of the keys that are down when the pedal is depressed. This pedal is used only rarely.

History. Bartolommeo Cristofori (1655–1731), who produced his first *gravicembalo col pian e forte* about 1709, is generally credited with the invention of the piano, although an earlier, imperfect instrument of the same type is known. The pianoforte was so named because the performer could play softly or loudly according to the striking force used, obtaining a direct control over dynamic range not possible on the harpsichord. The earliest action (single action) was quite primitive: a nearly vertical jack, placed on the portion of the key inside the instrument, would strike the hammer just below its hinge, causing it to fly upward and hit the string. By 1726 Cristofori perfected a much more refined action (double action), which transmitted the pressure of the key to the hammer through an intermediate lever; the main line of future developments stemmed from this sort of action. It was an action designed by the Viennese Johann Andreas Stein (1728–92) that was prominent when the piano first began to become popular during the last third of the 18th century. MOZART enjoyed the Stein piano; it had a light, sensitive action and a well-balanced tone. BEETHOVEN, however, demanded a heavier action capable of producing a louder tone; he preferred the instruments of the Englishman John Broadwood (1732–1812), which had a heavier structure, permitting higher string tension; they also had the two main pedals of the modern piano. Broadwood's patent for these dates from 1783. (Still other pedals, some providing special tonal effects, were available on some pianos built around the turn of the 19th century.)

During the 19th century, the range of the piano was increased. The action was refined on numerous occasions, the most important contribution being the invention of the double escapement by Sébastien Érard of Paris in 1821. This is a device permitting the hammer to rebound halfway, allowing a more rapid repetition of individual notes. Increased demands for dynamic power and increased string tensions went hand in hand. To compensate for the resultant stresses, Alpheus Babcock of Boston devised a full cast-iron frame by 1825. He also began to alter the angles of the strings, which had heretofore run in roughly parallel courses, crossing the lower strings over the middle ones.

This principle, known as *cross-stringing*, was perfected by Steinway and Sons about the middle of the 19th century. It makes possible a reduction in the total length of the instrument and increases its resonance.

Technique. Most keyboard techniques are based on similar principles. The fingers are kept curved so that, with the exception of the thumb, they strike with the tips. Normally they pivot from the knuckle. Connected lateral movement over extended range is provided chiefly through the use of the thumb. Since piano tone is determined by the nature of the striking force, the pianist must be able to exercise great control over his touch. He must be able to range from the softest, clear murmuring tone, to a "singing" tone that will project an important lyrical line over its subordinate background played simultaneously in more subdued colors, to tremendous bursts of octave and chordal power with maximum loudness without harshness. This demands a fine sense of balance and weight, not restricted to the fingers alone, but including the hands, wrists, arms, and body as well.

Music. The piano literature is undoubtedly the richest of those devoted to any one instrument. The current repertoire begins essentially with the works of HAYDN, Mozart, and Beethoven, although fine works by other masters active in the last half of the 18th century (including C. P. E. BACH) are gradually winning a wider place. The main stream continues with the numerous compositions—large and small—by SCHUBERT, CHOPIN, SCHUMANN, MENDELSSOHN, BRAHMS, LISZT, and DEBUSSY, and is enriched by the works of WEBER, GRIEG, FAURÉ, MACDOWELL, MUSSORGSKY, ALBENIZ, DE FALLA, RAVEL, REGER, and SCRIABIN, among others. Among the most important 20th-century composers for piano are BARTÓK, SCHÖNBERG, and PROKOFIEV. The pianist is able also to draw on the rich literature created originally for harpsichord and clavichord, including masterpieces by BACH, HANDEL, and SCARLATTI. Transcriptions of varying quality have made many examples from other repertoires accessible as well. The piano occupies first rank as a solo instrument in combination with orchestra and is of great importance as the ACCOMPANIMENT to ROMANTIC and modern LIEDER. It has a considerable CHAMBER repertoire, comprising duo SONATAS with violin, other string or wind instruments, as well as trios with violin and cello, quartets, and quintets. Included are master-pieces by Haydn, Mozart, Beethoven, Schubert, Brahms, Debussy, and others.

Pianola: a MECHANICAL keyboard INSTRUMENT.

Piatti (I): CYMBALS.

Picardy third, Tierce de Picardie (F): a major third appearing in the final chord of a section in a minor key.

Piccini, Niccolò: b. Bari, January 16, 1728; d. Paris, May 7, 1800. A student of LEO and DURANTE, Piccini became a successful and prolific composer of OPERAS, first in Rome and Naples, and later—in competition with GLUCK—in Paris.

Piccolo: a small flute, the highest-pitched of the WOODWIND family.

Pieno (I): full: *organo pieno*, full organ; *a voce piena*, with full voice.

Piston: (1) a valve of a BRASS INSTRUMENT of the plunger rather than the rotary type; (2) in French, a shortened name for the *cornet à pistons* (CORNET); (3) on the organ, a button or stud that places into operation a preset group of STOPS.

Piston, Walter: b. Rockland, Me. January 20. 1894. After graduating from Harvard University, Piston completed his musical training in Paris under Boulanger. From 1926 until his retirement in 1960, Piston was a member of the Harvard faculty. He wrote four books dealing with various aspects of music theory. Piston is among the outstanding American NEOCLASSICAL composers; his concern for craftsmanship is balanced by an elegance of idea. His works include seven SYMPHONIES, SUITES, CONCERTOS, and other orchestral music; a BALLET, and CHAMBER MUSIC.

Pitch: the vibration frequency of a sound, perceived in terms of a spectrum from low (few vibrations per second) to high (many vibrations per second). The *a* above middle *c* is presently assigned a standard of 440 vibrations per second, pitches of other notes being calculated in relationship to this standard. *See also* ACOUSTICS; TUNING.

Pitch-pipe: a simple wind instrument, employing either free REEDS (as a mouth harmonica) or a whistle mouthpiece with a tube having a graduated stopper, used for giving an opening pitch to an unaccompanied CHORUS.

Più (I): literally, "more": *più mosso*, faster (more movement); *più forte*, louder (more loudly).

Pizzetti, Ildebrando: b. Parma, September 20, 1880; d. Rome. February 13, 1968. A graduate of the Parma Conservatory. Pizzetti taught there, and in Florence, Milan, and Rome. He was also a prominent critic, writer, and editor. Pizzetti was particularly active as an operatic composer, writing in a lyric, post-ROMANTIC vein. Other music includes a SYMPHONY, CONCERTOS, CHAMBER and piano music, and songs.

Pizzicato (I) (abbr. *pizz*.): a direction in music for instruments of the VIOLIN FAMILY ordering that the strings be plucked rather than bowed. Normally the player plucks the strings with the right hand (i.e., the BOWING hand), but certain virtuoso passages may require left-hand pizzicatos either in rapid sequence with bowed notes or even simultaneous with them.

Plagal: a variety of CADENCE or MODE.

Plainsong: a term normally synonymous with GREGORIAN CHANT, but occasionally used also to refer to other bodies of liturgical CHANT.

Plectrum: a small, thin piece of ivory, horn, quill, wood, metal, or plastic used to pluck the strings of instruments such as the mandolin, banjo, and zither, and also as part of the harpsichord mechanism.

Plein Jeu (F): full ORGAN.

Pleyel, Ignaz Joseph: *b*. Ruppertsthal, June 1, 1757; *d*. near Paris, November 14, 1831. A student of Johann Baptist Wanhal and J. HAYDN, Pleyel was active in Rome, Vienna, Strasbourg, and London, before settling in Paris in 1795. There he founded a music store and the piano factory that still bears his name. He wrote a large quantity of CHAMBER MUSIC, together with SYMPHONIES, CONCERTOS, piano SONATAS, and songs. His style shows the marked influence of Haydn.

Plica (L): in medieval NOTATION, a tail added to a NEUME, long, breve, or ligature, indicating that the main tone was to be followed by an ornamental tone, either higher or lower according to the direction of the tail. The vagueness of the symbol sometimes causes doubt concerning the actual PITCH of the ornamental tone; it is usually thought to be a second from the main tone.

Pochette: *see* KIT.

Poco (I): little; *poco a poco*, gradually (little by little).

Poi (I): then, afterward.

Polacca (I): POLONAISE.

Polka: a dance in fairly rapid duple METER which apparently originated in Bohemia about 1830. The polka quickly became very popular and spread to other European countries and to America.

Polo: an Andalusian dance in moderate triple METER, popular especially during the 19th century. Syncopations and florid vocal passages are characteristic of the music.

Polonaise (F): a stately Polish court dance in triple METER. Purely instrumental versions appear in SUITES and CON-

CERTOS by BACH and HANDEL and in works by MOZART, BEETHOVEN, WEBER, and SCHUBERT. The most familiar polonaises, however, are those by CHOPIN, which are extended, independent works for piano.

Polychoral: a term descriptive of works for two or more CHORUSES, with or without instrumental ACCOMPANIMENT. In polychoral composition, the composer usually seeks to exploit the tonal contrasts obtainable by alternating passages among the various groups and by alternating passages for one group with others for the full ENSEMBLE. In performance the several groups are usually some distance apart so that a sense of spatial as well as tonal contrast results. For the sake of clarity, polychoral style is normally harmonic rather than contrapuntal, and the HARMONIES do not change as rapidly as in music for smaller groups. Polychoral works were cultivated especially in Venice during the late 16th and early 17th centuries (e.g., by Andrea and Giovanni GABRIELI, among others). A peak of massiveness was reached slightly later with works by the Roman BENEVOLI, who wrote music in as many as 53 parts. The medium was employed also by German, French, and English composers of the mid- and late BAROQUE.

Polymeter: see POLYRHYTHM.

Polyphony: a TEXTURE arising from the simultaneous combination of two or more melodic lines. (The term may also refer to early medieval ORGANUM, which employs essentially a single melodic line, duplicated strictly or freely at the fourth or fifth and sometimes reinforced at the OCTAVE; however successions consisting solely of octaves do not constitute polyphony, the notes of this INTERVAL being regarded as equivalent rather than as different.

Polyrhythm: the simultaneous occurrence of conflicting rhythms in different VOICES. Normally polymeter—the simultaneous use of different METERS—is involved. For example, recurrent patterns three eighth notes in length may contrast with others of four eighth notes, the time-value for the individual eighth note or for each group being the same in both cases. The simplest examples of polyrhythm are usually described as CROSS RHYTHMS, the former term being frequently reserved to denote bolder contrasts.

Polytonality: the simultaneous combination of different melodic or harmonic patterns, each being characteristic of a different key. Polytonal passages were used on rare occasions in earlier centuries, either as curiosities or for humorous effect. They occur more frequently in 20th-century music, and are often a means to powerful expression. In most instances, bitonality—the use of two different keys—is involved. Some writers prefer to reserve the term polytonality for those few instances in which more than two keys are combined simultaneously.

Pommer, Pomhart (G): a SHAWM.

Pomposo (I): pompously.

Ponchielli, Amilcare: b. Paderno Fasolaro, August 31, 1834; d. Milan, January 16, 1886. Ponchielli completed his musical training at the Milan Conservatory. He was active as an organist, bandmaster, music director, and composition teacher. The OPERA *La Gioconda* is the only one of several composed by Ponchielli to achieve lasting recognition. He wrote also sacred music.

Ponticello (I): the bridge of a string instrument. *Sul ponticello,* a direction to bow very close to the bridge.

Porpora, Nicola Antonio: b. Naples, August 17, 1686; d. Naples, March 3, 1768. Porpora was trained at the Conservatorio dei Poveri in Naples, and became a prominent teacher and conductor

as well as a prolific composer of OPERAS. He was a rival of HANDEL and of HASSE. In addition to his operas, Porpora wrote ORATORIOS, MASSES, MOTETS and other church music, SINFONIAS, violin SONATAS, and harpsichord music.

Portamento (I): (1) a vocal TECHNIQUE whereby a singer proceeds from one written tone to the next by means of a glide of subtle PITCH gradation. A similar effect, possible on instruments of the VIOLIN FAMILY and on the trombone, is normally termed a GLISSANDO. (2) A frequent, but improper, synonym for PORTATO.

Portative: a small, medieval ORGAN, placed on the lap (or on a table), and played by the right hand, while the left worked a bellows.

Portato: (I): a manner of playing in which the continuity between successive tones is broken by tiny gaps; yet the tones are not sharply detached from one another, as in STACCATO playing.

Port de voix (F): (1) PORTAMENTO; (2) a BAROQUE term for APPOGGIATURA.

Porter, Quincy: b. New Haven, February 7, 1897. Trained by Horatio Parker (at Yale University), D'INDY, and BLOCH, Porter has been on the faculties of several major American schools, including Yale (from 1946 on). His music features a NEO-CLASSICAL concern for craft and contrapuntal textures. Nine STRING QUARTETS and other CHAMBER works occupy a central place in his output, which includes also orchestral works, piano and organ music, and some songs.

Posaune (G): trombone.

Positif (F): the choir division of a large organ.

Position: (1) the spacing or harmonic order of the notes of a CHORD. (2) The placement of the FINGERING hand on the neck of a bowed string instrument; in first position, the hand is at the highest point of the neck (closest to the scroll); in each of the next positions the hand is shifted closer to the bridge of the instrument. (3) The placement of the slide of a trombone; the slide is fully retracted in first position and at its maximum practical extension in seventh.

Positive: a small ORGAN of the Middle Ages and RENAISSANCE, of a size that could be transported on a cart.

Postlude: (1) an organ work intended for the conclusion of a church service; (2) a synonym for CODA (infrequent).

Potpourri (F): a MEDLEY; a group of well-known tunes assembled loosely into a piece of popular nature.

Poulenc, Francis: *b.* Paris, January 7, 1899. Poulenc studied piano with Ricardo Viñes and composition with Charles Koechlin. The influences of SATIE and RAVEL on his early style are noticeable. Poulenc has written four CONCERTOS and a few other orchestral works, CHAMBER and KEYBOARD MUSIC, songs, choral works, a CANTATA, OPERAS, and BALLETS. He is best known for those works displaying a light Gallic wit and elegance, but has written also a religious opera, *Les Dialogues des Carmélites,* and liturgical music.

Praetorius, Michael: *b.* Kreuzburg (Thuringia), February 15, 1571; *d.* Wolfenbüttel, February 15, 1621. Praetorius was music director to the duke of Brunswick for much of his life. A prolific composer and an important theorist, he wrote many CHORALE settings of widely different degrees of complexity, MAGNIFICATS, MOTETS, HYMNS and other sacred music, MADRIGALS, instrumental dances, and organ music. His 3-volume *Syntagma Musicum* (1615–20) includes much valuable information concerning instruments and performance practices of his time.

Prelude, Praeludium (L), **Préambule** (F), **Preludio** (I), **Vorspiel** (G): a short instrumental work, often functioning as an introduction. While there are some orchestral preludes—chiefly operatic—the genre is primarily a SOLO form. Preludes for KEYBOARD instruments are most numerous, followed by those for lute or guitar.

The prelude is one of the earliest specifically instrumental genres. It is not dependent either upon transcriptions of vocal models or upon procedures customarily associated with vocal composition. Most RENAISSANCE preludes are free in form; many are improvisatory and moderately brilliant in nature. During ing the BAROQUE, preludes frequently headed groups of dance movements (SUITES) or preceded FUGUES (e.g., as in the 48 sets of preludes and fugues comprising BACH's *Well Tempered Clavier*). A wide variety of styles is to be found among these works. No important preludes were written during the CLASSICAL era, but CHOPIN revived the title in connection with a set of 24 short keyboard compositions. These ROMANTIC works, together with IMPRESSIONISTIC, post-Romantic, and later works by DEBUSSY, SCRIABIN, RACHMANINOFF, and SHOSTAKOVICH fall essentially under the heading of CHARACTER PIECES.

The operatic prelude is normally shorter and freer in form than the operatic OVERTURE; the music usually foreshadows selected themes ap-pearing in the main body of the work. WAGNER, in particular, preferred the title prelude. *See also* CHORALE PRELUDE.

Preparation: in traditional HARMONY, a note that is a member of the CHORD in which it is used initially, but which becomes a nonchordal DISSONANCE when repeated immediately in the same voice in conjunction with the following change of chord.

Prepared piano: a piano made capable of producing special tone colors and noise effects. The composer may direct that certain objects be placed across the strings or that the unison tuning of a pair or trio of strings struck by one hammer be altered, or that objects be placed in the body of the piano. Works for prepared piano have been written by John CAGE and Lou Harrison, among other modern composers.

Près de la table (F): a direction to the harpist to pluck the strings close to the soundboard in order to obtain a more metallic tone.

Presto (I): a very fast TEMPO; *prestissimo*, the fastest tempo possible to the performer.

Prick-song: a 16th-century English term designating POLYPHONIC music in contradistinction to PLAINSONG. At first the term denoted only handwritten music, but its meaning was later extended to include printed polyphonic music.

Prima donna (I): the singer of the leading female role in an OPERA. The term is capable also of a derogatory sense, indicating a vain, willful, and capricious person.

Prima vista, a (I): at first sight; performance without previous visual acquaintance with the music. *See* SIGHT READING.

Prima volta, Seconda volta (I): first time, second time. Repeated passages often employ different endings for the first presentation and the repeat. To conserve effort and space, the material common to the first and second times is written out only once, followed by the ending proper to the first time and then the ending proper to the second. These endings are usually indicated by the signs, ⌐1. and ⌐2. . (The first ending terminates, of course, with a repeat sign.)

Prime: (1) a UNISON; (2) the normal form of a TWELVE-TONE row; (3) in the Roman Catholic rite, the third of the Hours of Divine Service (OFFICE).

Primo (I), **Secondo** (I): the first, second. These terms indicate respectively the upper and lower (or leading and supporting) of a pair of instrumental parts.

Printing of music: *see* MUSIC PRINTING.

Prix de Rome (F): a prize awarded to French composers, painters, sculptors, engravers, and architects, enabling the recipients to spend four years at the Villa Medici in Rome. The prize is awarded by the French Government through the agency of the Académie des Beaux-Arts. Among the composers who have received the prize, BERLIOZ, GOUNOD, BIZET, and DEBUSSY are the most prominent.

Program music (Programme music): (1) in a restricted sense, the instrumental music of the 19th and early 20th centuries that aims at a cross-fertilization between music and verbal or visual imagery. The aesthetic underlying such works holds that music is the most direct, powerful, and universal means of communication, surpassing the word in the richness of its appeal to the imagination, and that music not embodying some form of "poetic" communication is of inferior value. The SYMPHONIC POEM (or tone poem) for orchestra is the most important genre of this music. (2) In a broader sense, music that seeks to represent specific ideas, persons, or objects. Almost anything that possesses motion or that—like emotion—can be translated into motion, can be imitated in music. Sounds, of course, may be imitated easily. Sometimes musical representation may be naturalistic, sometimes stylized, sometimes abstract or symbolical. The more abstract sorts of musical representation depend upon associative conventions such as the one that has been built up since the 16th century linking the portrayal of strong emotions with the use of chromatic HARMONIES. Although the broader definition will be adopted here because it is the more common of the two, such usage does not clarify the fluid boundaries between true program music and musical symbolism. Examples of symbolism that deal with notation rather than with music itself may be found in the *Augenmusik* (literally, eyemusic) of the turn of the 16th century: at a time when most note forms were void outlines, black notation was often employed for texts dealing with mourning. For an example of symbolism that affects the musical fabric itself, one might consider the practice observed in certain late BAROQUE sacred works of accompanying the RECITATIVES based on the words of Christ with string orchestra, while the other recitatives are accompanied only by keyboard and cello or bass.

The earliest programmatic genre was the Italian CACCIA of the 14th century, whose texts depict lively outdoor scenes. The vocal melodies imitate the sounds of hunting horns, alarms, and the general hurly-burly of such scenes. In the early 16th century Janequin composed a series of attractive program CHANSONS, including *Le Chant des Oiseaux, Les Cris de Paris,* and *La Guerre.* The last, commemorating the battle of Marignan (1515), began a vogue for battle pieces; the sounds of trumpets, of horses' hooves, of battle cries, etc., are imitated in engaging fashion. (Curiously, although the earliest programmatic genres are vocal, only a small portion of the vocal literature is customarily regarded as program music, regardless of how well the music may underline the text.)

During the 16th century it was the fashion among many composers to set certain words by appropriate musical figures. "Ascend," for example, would be set by a rising line; "run," by quick notes. This technique, known as WORD-PAINTING, was especially characteristic of the Italian MADRIGAL. Wordpainting continued to be practiced during the BAROQUE in all major European countries, particularly in Germany. Some of the most imaginative examples of its use are to be found in the CANTATAS and CHORALE PRELUDES of J. S. BACH. Although word-painting is a programmatic device, many of the pieces employing it are not ordinarily considered to be within the realm of program music because representation in these works is a matter of detail rather than a basic principle of construction.

Although true program music was written during both the Baroque and CLASSICAL eras (including Kuhnau's *Biblische Historien* and Bach's *Capriccio on the Departure of his beloved Brother*), it was not until the mid-19th century, with the works of BERLIOZ and especially LISZT that program music became a powerful force. ROMANTIC musicians generally regarded BEETHOVEN's *Pastoral Symphony*, which depicts different country scenes in each of its five movements, as the beginning point of the programmatic movement. However, Beethoven carefully specified that his work was an "expression of feeling rather than a painting." This attitude prevails also in most works with programmatic leanings by SCHUMANN and MENDELSSOHN (e.g., *The Hebrides Overture*); the structures of these works still conform with traditional norms. A detailed program—i.e., a verbal description of the music's content—is preserved in connection with WEBER's *Konzertstück* for piano and or-

chestra, but this work is not as heavily pictorial as Berlioz' *Symphonie Fantastique* and *Harold in Italy*. These led to such later works as Liszt's program SYMPHONIES, *Dante* and *Faust*.

Tone-painting was an important artistic goal for Liszt, the creator of the symphonic poem (or tone-poem). A composition of this genre is normally a one-movement orchestral work that originated as the musical expression of a literary or pictorial idea. As such, its form is flexible. The literary inspiration may be either a poem, story, or a well-known legend. Liszt's *Les Préludes* (based on Lamartine's *Méditations poétiques*) and DUKAS' *Sorcerer's Apprentice* are well-known examples of this type. The pictorial idea may derive from a painting, a particular geographic locality, or an image projected by the composer. Liszt's *Hunnenschlacht* (based on a painting by Kaulbach), SMETANA's *Moldau* (one of a cycle of six symphonic poems entitled *Má Vlast*, "My Fatherland"), and Debussy's *La Mer* are based on pictorial ideas. The symphonic poem reached a peak near the turn of the 20th century with the works of Richard STRAUSS and Debussy. Programmatic depiction is foreign to the thought of most modern composers, and the few tone-poems written after 1915 are mainly in a late Romantic rather than a modern idiom.

Prokofiev, Sergei Sergeyevich: *b.* Sonstkova, April 23, 1891; *d.* Moscow, March 5, 1953. One of the major Russian composers of the 20th century, Prokofiev displayed great talent when only a boy. He studied with his mother and with GLIÈRE before entering the St. Petersburg Conservatory at the age of thirteen; there he worked under RIMSKY-KORSAKOV, LIADOV, and TCHEREPNIN, among others. He won first prize as a pianist in his graduating year. The political unrest in the USSR caused Prokofiev to leave for the United States via Japan in 1918. Paris became his chief residence for the years 1920–33. Then, homesick for his native land, he returned to Russia late in 1933. There he was treated with honor for several years, although in 1948 his music, together with that of SHOSTAKOVICH, KHATCHATURIAN, and MIASKOVSKY, was denounced by the Central Committee of the Communist party.

Prokofiev has written in nearly all traditional genres: OPERA, BALLET, SYMPHONY, CONCERTO, SUITE, STRING QUARTET, piano SONATA, CHARACTER PIECE, song, and chorus. Although he was fond of DISSONANCE, especially during the 1920s, the main bases of his art are conservative. He adheres to a firm sense of tonality; triadic harmonies form the main element of his vocabulary; traditional forms are still to be encountered. Many of his best known works—*Peter and the Wolf, Lieutenant Kije,* the *Classical Symphony,* the suite from the opera *Love of Three Oranges,* etc.—are representative of the more conservative aspect of Prokofiev's art.

Prolation: (1) the relationship between semibreve and minim that is postulated as normal for a given piece of music written during the period *c.*1300–1600; (2) a wider sense of the term includes also the customary relationships between breve and semibreve for a given piece of music of the same period. *See* NOTATION (*History*).

Proper: the Introit, Gradual, Alleluia (or, in penitential seasons, Tract), Offertory, and Communion of the MASS. A substantial body of texts and music exists for each of these items, each setting being designed for specific use according to the liturgical calendar or to the special occasion prompting the particular Mass. The term may also refer to items of the OFFICE that vary in text and music according to liturgical occasion.

Provenzale, Francesco: *b.*

Naples, *c.*1627; *d.* Naples, September 6, 1704. Provenzale held several posts simultaneously: he was director of two conservatories, conductor at the Tesoro di San Gennaro, and associate conductor of the Royal Chapel. He helped develop the Neapolitan style of OPERA; he wrote also CANTATAS, ORATORIOS, MOTETS, and other sacred music.

Psalm: in the widest sense, a sacred song of praise; more specifically, one of the 150 prose-poems constituting the Book of Psalms of the Old Testament.

In liturgical usage, the psalms are traditionally sung rather than read. While no musical documents of either the First or Second Temple exist, the inscriptions heading several of the psalms are now interpreted as denoting the MELODY-type to which the particular psalm was to be sung. PSALMODY provided the basis for much of the earliest Christian liturgy.

The majority of texts employed in GREGORIAN CHANT are constituted either partly or entirely of psalm verses. In the OFFICE, entire psalms, each followed by the *Gloria Patri* (Lesser Doxology), are sung to simple melodic formulas known as PSALM TONES. In the MASS, only the Tract presents large portions of a given psalm. In the In-troit, Gradual, Alleluia, Offertory, and Communion, a single verse of a psalm is employed, amplified in various ways by later texts of appropriate subject.

Polyphonic settings of psalm texts began to appear during the RENAISSANCE. Works employing the psalm tones in simple chordal textures were written by the mid-15th century (e.g., by Binchois) and especially during the mid- and late-16th century in Italy. Elaborate MOTET settings were first created by BRUMEL and JOSQUIN, apparently shortly after 1500. This genre was continued by GOMBERT, LASSUS, and PALESTRINA, among others. BAROQUE composers set psalms both in the conservative motet style and in the progressive style employing both voice(s) and instruments. Psalm compositions equivalent to cantatas were written by VIVALDI, PERGOLESI, and HANDEL. Among the more important psalm settings by later composers are works of SCHUBERT, MENDELSSOHN, BRAHMS, LISZT, BRUCKNER, STRAVINSKY, and SCHOENBERG.

Psalmody: the manner or practice of singing PSALMS. In RESPONSORIAL psalmody, there is an alternation between soloist and CHORUS; in ANTIPHONAL psalmody, there is an alteration between two choruses (or between the two halves of one chorus). DIRECT psalmody refers to the singing of an entire psalm (or of several verses) without the addition of extraneous text.

Psalm tones: simple melodies employed for the chanting of PSALMS in the Roman Catholic liturgy. These consist of an Intonation (a short ascending figure), Tenor (a single note used for several syllables, the PITCH being the dominant of the CHURCH MODE being employed), Mediation (an ending for the half-verse), Tenor, and Termination (the final CADENCE). There is one psalm tone for each of the eight church modes, most of these tones being provided with alternative terminations (*differentiae,* differences). There is also an irregular *tonus peregrinus,* employed chiefly for the chanting of *In exitu Israel;* this tone uses in its second half a tenor different from that of the first half. The opening of an ANTIPHON (sometimes, a full antiphon) precedes the chanting of each psalm, while the full antiphon follows the *Gloria Patri* appended to the close of the psalm. The mode of the antiphon determines which of the various tones is to be employed for the chanting of the psalm, while the opening of the antiphon determines which of the alternative endings is to be used.

Psalter: a translation into the vernacular of the Book of Psalms — often in rhymed verse—intended for Protestant congregational and home devotional use. The Dutch *Souterliedekens* of 1540 were provided with melodies taken from popular secular songs. In 1562 a French Psalter was published (the Genevan Psalter) with translations begun many years previously by Marot and completed by Bèze and with music—some adapted, some newly composed — edited mainly by Bourgeois. These tunes were set polyphonically by several composers, the most important being GOUDIMEL, LE JEUNE, and SWEELINCK. Among the more widely used of the early English Psalters were those edited by Sternhold and Hopkins (1562) and Ravenscroft (1621). The two most important Psalters of the American colonists were the Ainsworth Psalter, first published in Amsterdam in 1612, and the Bay Psalm Book, published in Cambridge, Mass., in 1640.

Psaltery: a plucked string instrument with a shallow, trapezoidal body; the strings are stretched between the two converging sides. The psaltery was especially popular during the Middle Ages.

Puccini, Giacomo: *b.* Lucca, December 22, 1858; *d.* Brussels, November 29, 1924. Puccini's forbears were well-known local musicians as far back as the early 18th century; Giacomo was given music instruction as a boy so that he might continue this tradition. After study at the Istituto Musicale of Lucca with Angeloni, Puccini became an organist in a nearby town. In 1880 he entered the Milan Conservatory, where he studied with Antonio Bazzini and PONCHIELLI. His career as an OPERA composer began with a one-act work, *Le Villi,* produced in 1884. Puccini's first important success was *Manon Lescaut* (1893), followed by *La Bohème* (1896), *Tosca* (1900), and *Madama Butterfly* (1904). The last three are Puccini's most popular works. His last operas were *The Girl of the Golden West* (written for the New York Metropolitan Opera), *Il Trittico* (a set of one-act operas: *Il Tabarro, Suor Angelica,* and *Gianni Schicchi*), and *Turandot,* which was unfinished at the time of his death and was completed by Franco Alfano. Puccini was gifted with an excellent stage sense and a vein of emotion-arousing melody.

Punta d'arco (I): the tip of the bow.

Purcell, Henry: *b.* London(?), 1659; *d.* London, November 21, 1695; one of the greatest English composers.

Born to a family of musicians, Purcell became a chorister of the Chapel Royal (1669–73), receiving training under Henry Cooke and Pelham Humfrey, and studying later with BLOW. Beginning in 1677 he was awarded a series of appointments to high offices that were held concurrently: composer to the king's string orchestra (1677), organist of Westminster Abbey (1679), organist of the Chapel Royal (1682), and Keeper of the King's wind instruments (1683).

Purcell's style reveals an individual fusion of Italian and French traits together with traditional English elements. A study of his rich harmonies, liberally spiced with DISSONANCES, reveals increasing usage of the vocabulary of the developing tonal system. Purcell was active in every important field of composition current in England. His works include SERVICES, ANTHEMS (primarily verse anthems), both secular and sacred songs, CANTATAS, ODES, FANTASIAS and SONATAS for string ENSEMBLES, KEYBOARD music, and music for the stage, including the OPERA *Dido and Aeneas*. His extraordinary melodic gifts are well employed to evoke the sense of his texts.

Purfling: the beaded edges provided violins and other string instruments, both as decoration and as protection against chipping.

Q

Quadrille: an early 19th-century dance, first popular in France. The music, often adapted from popular operatic tunes and other well-known sources, was in five sections, alternating between 6/8 and 2/4 time. The dance was performed by two to four couples.

Quadruplet: a group of four equal notes or rests fitting into the time normally occupied by three equal values (or by some other number of values neither two nor eight).

Quantz, Johann Joachim: *b.* Oberscheden, January 30, 1697; *d.* Potsdam, July 12, 1773. Quantz studied with many teachers, among them FUX and GASPARINI. After traveling widely, he became flute instructor to Frederick the Great, and, in 1740, chamber musician and court composer. Quantz composed extensively for flute and wrote also a treatise on flute playing that contains valuable information on the performance practices of his time.

Quartal harmony: a harmonic style employed in certain 20th-century compositions in which the fourth (rather than the third) is the primary unit in chordal construction. Nonquartal harmony, on the other hand, avoids all use of the fourth as a structural INTERVAL — i.e., all fourths are

treated as DISSONANCE. A nonquartal style is to be found
in certain three-voice works
of the late 15th century, including CHANSONS by BUS-
NOIS.

Quarter note, Quarter rest:
♩ , 𝄽 , respectively; *see* NOTA-
TION.

Quarter tone: half of a half
step; among MICROTONES occurring in Western music, the
quarter tone is the most important.

Quartet: (1) a work for four
INSTRUMENTS or VOICES.
Among quartets in the present CHAMBER MUSIC reper-
toire, works for STRING QUAR-
TET (two violins, viola, and
cello) predominate; if a description does not indicate the
scoring of a quartet, the string
quartet is normally implied.
A piano, flute, oboe, or clarinet (etc.) quartet is usually
written for the specified instrument in conjunction with
violin, viola, and cello. Concerning the formal construction of 18th- and 19th-cen-
tury quartets, *see* SONATA. *See*
TRIO SONATA for works for
four instruments not classified
as quartets. (2) An ENSEM-
BLE of four performers.

Quasi (I): almost, as if.

Quatuor (F): QUARTET.

Quaver (Br.): eighth note,
eighth rest.

Querflöte (G): transverse flute
(i.e., the modern flute, in contradistinction to the RE-
CORDER).

Querstand (G): false relation.

Quinte (F): fifth. As a part
designation, occurring in
French BAROQUE music, the
term refers to the viola.

Quintet: (1) a work for five
INSTRUMENTS or VOICES. The
most common scoring for
STRING QUINTET is that em-
ploying two violins, two
violas, and a cello. A WOOD-
WIND quintet consists of flute,
oboe, clarinet, bassoon, and
French horn. *See also* SONATA;
CHAMBER MUSIC. (2) An EN-
SEMBLE of five performers.

Quintole: quintuplet.

Quinton: an 18th-century
French string instrument
similar to the violin, but with
five strings (tuned *g-d′-a′-
d″-g″*).

Quintuor (F): QUINTET.

Quintuplet: a group of five
equal notes or rests fitting
into the time occupied by
four (or, on a few occasions,
three) equal values.

Quodlibet (L): a composition
designed to show the wit and
ingenuity of the composer in
the simultaneous or consecutive mixing of snatches from
well-known tunes. (The quodlibet may also be a purely
literary work, built of an assemblage of prose or poetic
excerpts.) The simultaneous
quotation of preexistent material may, of course, be
traced to certain 13th-century
motets; these works, however,
are seldom considered as

quodlibets, nor are other later works which also employ pre-existent material as a structural skeleton. The quodlibet proper gained popularity during the late 15th century and examples of the genre have been created in each of the succeeding centuries. (Some RENAISSANCE quodlibets are known under the Spanish heading *ensalada*, some under the French heading *fricassée*.) The most famous example of a quodlibet is the final variation of BACH's *Goldberg Variations;* here Bach develops two German FOLK tunes.

R

Rachmaninov, Sergei Vasilievich: *b.* Oneg, April 1, 1873; *d.* Beverly Hills, March 28, 1943. Rachmaninov came of a musical family, and was sent first to the St. Petersburg Conservatory and then to the Moscow Conservatory, where his teachers included his cousin Siloti, Tanayev, and Arensky. Rachmaninov began touring as a pianist in 1895 and gradually established himself as one of the foremost pianists of his generation. He was also an excellent conductor, leading the Bolshoi Theatre Orchestra and the Moscow Philharmonic for two seasons each. He twice declined the conductorship of the Boston Philharmonic. After the Revolution of 1917 Rachmaninov left Russia permanently, settling first in Switzerland and, much later, in the United States. In Russia, England, and the United States he ranks among the most popular of the late ROMANTIC composers, his *Rhapsody on a Theme by Paganini,* two of his other four piano CONCERTOS, and isolated piano PRELUDES being well-known favorites. Rachmani-

nov wrote also three SYMPHO-
NIES, SYMPHONIC POEMS,
three OPERAS, some CHAMBER
MUSIC, a few choral works,
several sets of songs, and
many piano compositions. His
style, characterized by rich
sonorities, chromaticism, and
largely melancholy mood,
was much influenced by those
of TCHAIKOVSKY, LISZT, and
CHOPIN.

**Racket, Rackett, Ranket, Cer-
velas (F), Wurstfagott (G),
Sausage Bassoon:** an obsolete
double-reed WOODWIND of the
16th to 18th centuries. The
tube constituting the wind
column was doubled up on
itself five or more times so
that a comparatively long column was enclosed within a
stubby cylinder less than a
foot in height. A limited scale
was possible by fingering
holes pierced in the side.

Raddoppiamento (I): doubling: usually indicating the
reinforcing of the bass at the
lower octave.

Ragtime: an American style
of popular music in vogue for
a few decades around the turn
of the 20th century. Simple
rhythmic displacements and
SYNCOPATIONS p l a y e d a
prominent part in the style.
Some of these traits were
drawn upon by STRAVINSKY
in his *Ragtime* and *Piano
Rag-Music* and by other contemporary composers.

Rallentando (I): slowing down
(abbr.: *rall.*).

Rameau, Jean-Philippe: *bapt.*
Dijon, September 25, 1683;
d. Paris, September 12, 1764;
foremost French composer
and theorist of the late BA-
ROQUE.

Serving in Avignon, Cler-
mont-Ferrand, Dijon, Lyons,
and Paris, Rameau first
achieved fame as an organist,
keyboard composer, and theorist. In his *Traité de l'Harmonie* (1722), *Nouveau sys-
tème de musique théorique*
(1726), and later writings,
Rameau set forth the principles of CHORD BUILDING and
INVERSIONS that form the
cornerstone of tonal HAR-
MONY.

Rameau devoted the latter
part of his life chiefly to the
writing of stage works, first
in the service of La Pou-
plinière and then in that of
the king. The OPERAS *Hippo-
lyte et Aricie* (1733) and
Castor et Pollux (1737), the
opera-BALLETS *Les Indes
galantes* (1735) and *Les
Fêtes d'Hébé* (1739), and the
comic ballet *Platée* (1745),
are among the finest Baroque
works of their genre. Rameau
had a keen sense for musical
characterization, aided by a
rich melodic and harmonic
imagination; he was a master
of ORCHESTRATION.

Rank: a complete set of
ORGAN pipes of a single type.

Ranket: *see* RACKET.

Rasgado (S): a guitar direction calling for a rapid AR-

PEGGIO produced by sweeping the thumb across the strings.

Rattle: (1) a PERCUSSION INSTRUMENT in which a short wooden or metal rod is made to strike a revolving cogwheel through the pressure of a simple spring mechanism. (2) A family of percussion instruments, used especially in preliterate societies, which produce sound through the shaking together of several objects. Gourd rattles, now transformed into baby's toys, are among the most familiar of these instruments. The rattling receptacle may be made of various materials and in various shapes. Furthermore, there are strung and sliding rattles that do not have any enclosure proper.

Ravel, Maurice (Joseph): *b.* Ciboure, March 7, 1875; *d.* Paris, December 28, 1937; together with DEBUSSY, the leading French composer of the early 20th century.

Ravel's father, a mining engineer, was keenly interested in music, and Ravel was given excellent instruction, entering the Paris Conservatoire at fourteen. In later life he appeared both as a pianist and a conductor in performances of his own works, but never became noted as a performer.

As a composer, Ravel produced a few works in each of many genres: OPERA, BALLET, TONE POEM, CONCERTO, CHAMBER MUSIC, piano music, and songs. Like Debussy, Ravel was influenced by IMPRESSIONISM and by Russian music. In his music, he frequently sought to depict extramusical ideas similar to those that color much of Debussy's music, and he often used chordal combinations and textures akin to those of Debussy.

Admirers partial to each of the two composers often argued over questions of possible influence of one on the other; Ravel himself pointed out that his *Jeux d'eaux* appeared earlier than any of Debussy's more important piano works. Ravel's style differs from that of his older contemporary in several respects: his RHYTHMS and FORMS are more clearly organized, and he adheres more closely to diatonic harmonic progressions and well-established TONE CENTERS. A master in handling orchestral colors, Ravel orchestrated both keyboard pieces of his own (e.g., *Ma Mère l'Oye*) and of others (MUSSORGSKY's *Pictures at an Exhibition*). Ravel's *Boléro, La Valse,* and *Rapsodie espagnole,* together with the SUITES drawn from the ballet *Daphnis et Chloé* are his best-known orchestral works.

Re (Ray): in SOLMIZATION, either the second note of a

diatonic SCALE, or the note *d*.

Real: an adjective indicating the exact duplication of the INTERVALS of a MELODY when restated at another PITCH, either in the course of IMITATION (*see* FUGUE) or SEQUENCE.

Realization: the working out of compositional details left by the composer to the discretion of the performer. In the BAROQUE, the keyboard player in an ENSEMBLE work was normally provided only with a single voice-part, the bass, and was expected to provide complete harmonies following certain shorthand directions furnished by the composer (*see* FIGURED BASS). In Baroque performance practice, a soloist was often expected to embellish the main MELODY with various ORNAMENTS—some exceedingly elaborate.

Rebec: a bowed string instrument of the Middle Ages and RENAISSANCE with a pear-shaped body and three strings.

Recapitulation: *see* SONATA FORM.

Récit (F): (1) the swell ORGAN; (2) RECITATIVE.

Recital: a public performance by a soloist or small group. (A performance by an orchestra, chorus, or band would be termed a CONCERT.)

Recitative: a vocal style, preponderantly or exclusively syllabic with MELODY and RHYTHM patterned after stylized speech inflections proper to the text. Recitative is used especially in OPERAS, ORATORIOS, and CANTATAS for dialogue and narrative sections. The sparse, chordal ACCOMPANIMENT to recitative is normally provided by a KEYBOARD instrument, the BASS LINE sometimes being reinforced by a deep string instrument. Recitative was developed shortly before the turn of the 17th century by Florentine composers of opera. Despite the frequent use of repeated notes, many early recitatives have a reasonably lyrical quality. By the end of the 17th century, however, recitative was employed largely as a vehicle for rapid dialogue or narration, with minimal melodic interest and with comparatively irregular rhythmic patterns executed freely. This style is known as *recitativo secco* (dry). Exceptions to this style, recitatives that exhibit some degree of lyricism, more regular rhythms, and are accompanied orchestrally, fall under the heading, *recitativo accompagnato* (= *recitativo stromentato*).

Recorder: one of a family of WOODWIND instruments, classed as end-blown flutes.

Reed: a thin, flexible, sound-producing device set into vibration by a windstream.

There are cane and metal reeds; the term itself normally denotes the former. Cane reeds are used for many WOODWINDS: oboes, clarinets, bassoons, etc. (Because of the fragility of cane reeds, there have been experiments with plastic reeds for oboes and clarinets, though these entailed a certain loss in response and tone quality.) Metal reeds are employed in instruments such as the ACCORDION, HARMONICA, and HARMONIUM.

A cane reed is termed a *heterophonic reed*. It acts to initiate the sound, but, by itself, produces only a squawk; its size and shape have only limited influence on the pitch and tone color of the instrument. These qualities are determined mainly by the bore and length of the wind column with which it is coupled (*see* WOODWINDS: *Technique*).

Cane reeds are of two varieties, single and double. A *single reed* is sliced from the outer portion of cane of moderately large diameter. There is only a small curvature to the bark side of a ¾ inch wide reed; the under side is cut flat. An average-size reed may be 2½ inches high. The bark is scraped away from the upper section and the tip is made so thin that it is translucent. The reed is bound to a specially shaped mouth-piece, leaving only a tiny aperture at the top. Under pressure of a windstream this aperture closes and reopens with great rapidity.

A *double reed* is made of cane of smaller diameter. The higher the instrument, the smaller the diameter of the cane used for its reed. A slice of consistent thickness (i.e., curved, bottom and top) is taken, scored in the middle, and bent in half. The lower portions are trimmed symmetrically in width and the cane is soaked in water to make it flexible. By winding it with stout thread, the folded cane is either fastened to an oval metal tube or made to conform to a circular shape. This seals the two sides. The tip is then cut off and the upper portions scraped, as in a single reed. (The techniques and patterns of scraping vary, however, among different reeds.) The two leaves of cane form a tiny, somewhat elliptical aperture, which closes and opens rapidly under pressure of a windstream.

The tone of most modern woodwinds is dependent upon the damping of the reed by the lips. If the reed is permitted to vibrate freely, either by placing it within a bag (as in bagpipes) or within a windcap, dynamic nuances are no longer possible. The tone is usually more raucous, although the tone of the CROMORNE is not so.

Metal reeds are termed *idiophonic reeds.* They not only initiate the sound, but also determine its pitch and quality. If coupled with a pipe, the pipe acts only as a resonator. Most cane reeds and the metal reeds of organ reed stops are known as beating reeds. Either the single reed beats against a fixed slot, such as the clarinet mouthpiece, or the two leaves beat against each other. The metal reeds of harmonicas and accordions, however, are known as *free reeds.* Whereas the clarinet reed is tailored to the outside diameter of the mouthpiece, a free reed is shaped so that it will pass within and without the framework of a similarly shaped slot without striking it.

Reel: a folk dance in quick duple METER, executed by couples; variant forms of reels are found in countries of northern Europe and in the United States.

Refrain: a periodically recurrent section of text, text and music, or—by extension—music alone. (One meaning each of the terms, chorus and burden, is loosely synonymous with the term refrain.) The refrain principle is an ancient one; in our Western culture, it is to be found in a group of scriptural poems, the most famous being Psalm 136. The structure of RESPONSORIES and the early practice of singing an ANTIPHON before a PSALM and following each of its verses both reflect the refrain principle. Secular forms—such as the RONDEAU and VIRELAI—in which textual refrains governed also the musical structure were particularly prominent during the Middle Ages and RENAISSANCE. In the *chanson avec des refrains* and in certain 13th-century MOTETS, well-known refrains were quoted in new poetic context. The recurrent section of a RONDO is essentially an instrumental refrain, while certain RITORNELLI, as well as recurrent TUTTI sections of *concerto grosso* movements constitute still other applications of refrain principles.

Regal: a portable reed ORGAN of the RENAISSANCE and BAROQUE, with a nasal, penetrating tone. The instrument was employed by MONTEVERDI in his opera *Orfeo.*

Reger, Max: *b.* Brand, March 19, 1873; *d.* Leipzig, May 11, 1916. As a boy, Reger studied piano with his father, a schoolteacher, and organ with Lindner. His talent in composition was recognized by Riemann, with whom he also studied (1890–95). An eminent pianist and organist,

Reger held teaching posts at Wiesbaden, Munich, and Leipzig, and was conductor in Meiningen, Jena, and Leipzig.

Reger's music is much appreciated in Germany, but little elsewhere. Like BRAHMS, he was a champion of ABSO-LUTE MUSIC. (This, however, did not prevent him from writing descriptive music as well.) A master craftsman with an outstanding contrapuntal TECHNIQUE, Reger found his most natural outlet in BAROQUE forms—FUGUE, CHORALE PRELUDE, PASSACAGLIA, FANTASY, etc.—which he transformed through the use of ROMANTIC textures and chromatic harmonies. His music is often criticized as dense and prolix. His vast output includes some important organ music, together with some 250 songs, piano, chamber, choral, and orchestral music.

Register: (1) one or more sets of pipes (ranks) controlled by a single stop on an ORGAN. (2) A section of the vocal compass. *Head register* denotes the higher portion of the range, the singer having the sensation of resonance concentrated primarily in the head region; *chest register* denotes the lower portion of the range, with an awareness of resonance focused in the chest area. The two registers differ in timber. (3) A section of an instrumental compass, used in this sense especially when the particular section has a distinctive timber (e.g., the low register of a clarinet).

Registration: the selection of TONE COLOR in organ or harpsichord playing, this being effected by a choice of STOPS. Although composers of organ music of the past century and a half have generally been careful to indicate their desires in the matter of tone color by specifying particular stops to be employed, information of this nature is often incomplete or entirely lacking for music of earlier periods. In such instances the editor or performer must be guided by a knowledge of the resources of the instruments of the pertinent period and geographical area and by any contemporary descriptions of performance practice that may be available.

Reicha, Anton: *b.* Prague, February 26, 1770; *d.* Paris, May 28, 1836. Active in Bonn (where he knew BEE-THOVEN), Hamburg, Paris, and Vienna, Reicha settled in Paris in 1808, becoming a composition teacher at the Conservatoire in 1818. LISZT and GOUNOD were among his pupils. Reicha was named to the Institut de France in 1835. He composed four sets of WOODWIND quintets, as well as a great deal of other CHAMBER MUSIC, a few OPERAS, SYMPHONIES and other orchestral works, and some piano pieces; he also produced a piano method and textbooks on composition.

Reichardt, Johann Friedrich: *b.* Königsberg, November 25, 1752; *d.* Giebichenstein (Halle), June 27, 1814. Although introduced to music at an early age by his father, Reichardt did not receive thorough and systematic training. He traveled extensively and served as music director to Frederick the Great and Jerome Napoleon. Acquainted with many important German writers and philosophers, Reichardt was an influential composer of SINGSPIELE and songs. He created also a wide variety of instrumental music, wrote several books on music, and was an important music critic and editor.

Relative major, Relative minor: a pair of keys sharing the same KEY SIGNATURE. (The identity of tonal material suggested by the identical signatures is not fully preserved, however, in actual composition.) The TONE CENTER (tonic) of the relative major is a minor third above that of the relative minor.

Relative Pitch: (1) the relationship of one tone to another in terms of INTERVAL; (2) the ability to recognize fluently intervallic relationships. One of the main purposes of EAR TRAINING is to develop this latent ability.

Renaissance Music: the music of *c.*1420 to *c.*1600. During this period the intricate style of late MEDIEVAL MUSIC gave way to a simpler one with greater balance and unity. Forms grew longer, and the polyphonic MASS and MOTET reached their highest peak. Nonliturgical works—both delicate and vigorous, pious and earthy—were produced in abundance. Choral POLYPHONY (as opposed to polyphony for soloists) began during the Renaissance, as did the steady growth of instrumental music. Musicians from northern France and the Low Countries, often working in Italy, furnished the initial impetus to the musical Renaissance, which later enveloped all Europe. At the end of the period the trend toward greater emotional expression and the Venetian polychoral style led toward the BAROQUE.

The close intermingling of archaic and progressive traits in early 15th century music has resulted in differences of opinion regarding the most suitable dividing point between the Middle Ages and Renaissance. Depending upon the choice of trait taken to be the hallmark of the new period, scholars have marked the opening of the Renaissance c.1420 (as above), c.1450, and c.1475, corresponding with the early works of DUFAY, OCKEGHEM, and JOSQUIN, respectively.

In the music of Dufay and his contemporaries, there is a marked simplification of rhythmic structures in comparison to the extreme complexities current at the end of the 14th century. Simple rather than compound triple METER prevails, and all parts normally have the same rhythmical organization. Phrase structures are generally clearer, melodies more lyrical. The composition of complete MASS ORDINARIES assumes importance, with Dufay as the first great master of this form. The late medieval style dominated by the highest VOICE gives way to one in which two parts are of melodic importance. In secular music these two—the soprano and tenor—are complemented by an additional one, which serves to fill out the sonorities. Sacred music, at this time the more progressive in style, generally employs four-part texture. IMITATION appears particularly in CHANSON settings, but is not yet used systematically. The REFRAIN forms that had been the basis of medieval secular polyphony—RONDEAU, VIRELAI, and BALLADE—are retained; they

are expanded once more and the emphasis shifts from the ballade to the rondeau. Early Renaissance motets are frequently polytextual and often treat secular—sometimes political—subjects, as did their immediate, medieval predecessors. ISORHYTHM, an archaic trait, is normal among these works.

In the compositions of the next generation, headed by Ockeghem and BUSNOIS, imitation becomes more important and simple duple meter appears more frequently. The PITCH range used in composition is expanded, particularly on the low side; the characteristic medieval crossing of voice-parts occurs less frequently. The motet is once again a sacred form and generally remains so for the rest of its history. In Ockeghem's music the rhythmic flow is more continuous than in Dufay's; as a consequence, the phrase structure is not as clearly marked. Ockeghem frequently achieves a rhythmic climax toward the end of a piece through the use of faster values.

Renaissance rhythm is based on pulses of even strength. (Music of 1700–1900, on the other hand, is based on recurrent pulse patterns, the first pulse of each group being the strongest.) Musical STRESS was determined partly by coincidence with this even pulse and partly by the length of the individual note: a long note is naturally more prominent than a brief one. The lack of consistently enforced accent patterns permitted the Renaissance composer to create long melodic ARABESQUES with sensitively varied rhythmic configurations. In compositions in which linear interest is highest—as in those by Ockeghem—the stresses often occur at different times in different voices, thus making for a lively interplay between the voices. As dances and forms of popular origin increased in importance during the 16th century, the frequency and complexity of rhythmic interplay diminished, and more regular stress patterns prevailed. Nevertheless, the COUNTERPOINT of rhythm continued to be of importance until the very end of the period.

The Renaissance concept of TEMPO also differs from that of later periods. The rate of the pulse (tactus) was approximately that of the human pulse; there was therefore one basic tempo. The composer wishing quicker movement could either use smaller note-values or proportional symbols. A dash through the mensuration sign (see NOTATION) indicated the halving of time-values (proportio dupla); the number 3, a tripartition (proportio tripla); $\frac{3}{2}$, a reduction of values in the ratio 2:3 (proportio sesquialtera), and so forth.

The third generation of Renaissance composers brought the early part of the era to a peak. In addition to the incomparable Josquin des Prez, there was a host of excellent composers, including OBRECHT, LARUE, AGRICOLA, COMPÈRE, and MOUTON. In the hands of these men, the secular refrain forms achieved their final fulfillment and new forms of fresher content and structure emerged. Imitation became the primary form-producing element and duple meter was then the rule. Four-part TEXTURE was standard, but as many as six voices were often used. Passages using only high voices often adjoined others using low voices (or vice versa), producing effective contrasts. With the works of Josquin, the motet reached a peak equaled at the end of the 16th century with LASSUS and PALESTRINA, but never surpassed.

New currents arose in Italy toward the end of the 15th century in conjunction with the devotional lauda and the secular FROTTOLA. Both genres employ an unsophisticated, nearly syllabic musical style with similar or simultaneous rhythms in the various voices. (The poetic forms of the frottola, CAPITOLO, CANZONA, ODE, and STRAMBOTTA are comprised within the generic meaning of frottola.) In these repertoires there is usually a main melody, placed in the highest voice; its range is generally small and repeated notes are prominent. PHRASE structure is clear-cut. A more harmonic texture results. (Occasionally the same piece of music will serve both a frottola and a lauda text.) Of course, note-against-note writing had been employed in early polyphony, in the conductus of the High Middle Ages, in FAUXBOURDON of the early Renaissance, and in other compositions by Dufay's generation in order to highlight certain passages by means of contrast. In the 16th century note-against-note style began to find wider and wider application, although without threatening the greater importance of contrapuntal techniques, cultivated especially by northern composers such as GOMBERT, and brought to highest refinement in the sacred music of Palestrina. The early Italian MADRIGALS of the 1530s, exemplified in the works of VERDELOT, FESTA, and ARCADELT, inherited and refined *frottola* style. Both the lusty Parisian chanson, which began in the 1520s with such masters as JANEQUIN and SERMISY, and the more reflective psalter settings of the mid-16th century by GOUDIMEL and LE JEUNE make considerable use of chordal texture, which is prominent also in the earthy Italian villanelle of the late 16th century. Renaissance "chordal" writing came about more as a linear unfolding of concurrent melodic lines than as a series of vertically conceived chord progressions. The striking CHROMATICISM of the late Italian madrigal is most easily understood in these terms. Nevertheless, stemming from *frottola* style, there was a gradual trend toward a true harmonic idiom, with stylistic differentiation between the various parts, the musical structure being supported by a bass part that acts as a harmonic foundation rather than as another melody. This trend led to the monodic style of the early Baroque.

Among other important developments of the 16th century was the gradual emergence of instrumental writing. Though the Renaissance has been described in the past as the Golden Age of A CAPPELLA performance, unaccompanied singing was only one of several means of performance. Mixed vocal and instrumental ENSEMBLES were common throughout the period, as is shown by numerous paintings and written accounts. Individual voice-parts were usually created in such fashion that they could be performed vocally or instrumentally with equal ease. Idiomatic styles developed only in the lute and KEYBOARD repertoires. These began to grow steadily in importance during the 16th century, the latter culminating in the works of Cabezon and the English virginalists BYRD, BULL, and GIBBONS. The three main varieties of early keyboard music were pieces transcribed from the vocal repertoire, dances, and works with liturgical functions. By the end of the century, a number of free and imaginative forms had developed.

Two further stylistic developments were of importance, not only for their intrinsic value, but also as keys to the future. One was the Venetian development of music for several choruses. The first great master of this technique, which eventually led to the CONCERTATO style, was WILLAERT. The other trait was a heightened awareness of the text. One of the expressions of this awareness was word-painting (*see* PROGRAM MUSIC), a trait closely connected with the madrigal; its tech-

niques, often present in other forms, are described as madrigalisms. The heightened value of the text led also to increased concern for PROSODY, beginning with the early-16th-century settings of Horatian odes and culminating with the *vers mesurés* of Le Jeune. In these repertoires, the poetic meters are treated quantitatively, and the stressed syllables receive twice the musical duration of the weak ones. A third result of the increased awareness of text was the increased effort toward its expressive interpretation. On the one hand, expressiveness led to the sublime motets of Lassus, while on the other, it led to the recitative of the early Baroque.

Repeat: (1) a section of music identical with a previous one, normally the one immediately previous. The music for repeats is seldom written out a second time, but is indicated instead by certain signs. (2) The sign :‖, employed to indicate a repeat. A return to the beginning is implied unless a return to a central point is indicated by placing the sign ‖: at the point where the repeat is to begin. For terms governing repetition, *see* DA CAPO; DAL SEGNO.

Répétition (F): rehearsal; *répétition générale* (F), dress (final) rehearsal; *répétiteur* (F), operatic coach.

Replica (I): REPEAT; *senza replica*, without repeat(s).

Reprise (F): (1) recapitulation (*see* SONATA FORM); (2) a return of the opening section near the conclusion of a piece in BINARY FORM; (3) REPEAT.

Requiem, Requiem Mass, Messe des morts (F), **Messa per i defunti** (I), **Totenmesse** (G): (1) the MASS for the dead in the Roman Catholic rite. The term derives from the first word of the Introit, *Requiem aeternam dona eis, Domine* (Grant them eternal rest, O Lord). The chanted items of the Mass include, in order, this Introit, a Kyrie, Gradual, Tract, Sequence (the *Dies Irae*), Offertory, Sanctus, Agnus Dei, and Communion. The ritual PLAINSONG serves for most funeral rites, but POLYPHONIC Requiems—either elaborating the plainsong or independent of it—may be used if special pomp is desired. Most polyphonic settings omit one or more of the Gregorian items. In ritual (as opposed to concert) use, these omissions are rectified through the use of plainsong. The earliest surviving polyphonic Requiem is a late-15th-century work by OCKEGHEM, an apparently still earlier setting by DUFAY having been lost. In dealing with Requiems by composers of the mid-Renaissance, one must remember that the sequence of movements described above was not fixed until 1570 and that not all of the individual chants were the same both before and after that date. Among the more famous Requiems of later periods are those of MOZART, BERLIOZ, VERDI, DVOŘÁK, and FAURÉ; these are elaborate works for SOLO voices, CHORUS, and ORCHESTRA. (2) The term Requiem may also denote a work outside the Catholic rite that commemorates the dead. The outstanding work of this nature is BRAHMS' *German Requiem*, based on passages chosen from the German Bible.

Resolution: the progression from a dissonant INTERVAL to a less dissonant or consonant interval. In traditional HARMONY these progressions are not arbitrary, but follow a few standard norms. The interval of a minor seventh, for example, is expected to resolve inward, the upper note moving downward, the lower upward. If the composer wishes an outward resolution, he is expected to notate the same pair of sounds differently, so that they are read as forming an interval of an augmented sixth.

Resonance: vibrations created in a given body not by a player's actions (striking, scraping, blowing, etc.) or by a singer's vocal cords, but by transfer from another vibrating body. Both loudness and TONE COLOR are influenced by the nature of the resonance available to the original vibrating medium. One of the main functions of the body of a musical instrument is to provide resonance. In singing, this function is provided for by the head and chest cavities. *See also* ACOUSTICS.

Respighi, Ottorino: *b.* Bologna, July 9, 1879; *d.* Rome, April 18, 1936. Respighi was trained at the Liceo Musicale of Bologna, studying further with RIMSKY-KORSAKOV and BRUCH after embarking on a career as a performer. Respighi was earlier active as a violist, violinist, pianist, and conductor. Respighi taught composition at the Academia di St. Cecilia in Rome. His rich, post-Romantic harmonies and songful melodies enjoyed considerable vogue during the first half of this century. Among his most famous works are the SYMPHONIC POEMS *The Birds, The Fountains of Rome,* and *The Pines of Rome.* Respighi wrote a few OPERAS, BALLETS, other orchestral works (including CONCERTOS), choral and CHAMBER compositions, and songs.

Respond: (1) RESPONSORY; (2) RESPONSE (infrequent usage).

Response: standard congrega-

tional or choral replies to the utterances of the priest in the Anglican and Episcopalian rites.

Responsorial: an adjective describing a method of performing liturgical music (e.g., PLAINSONG) in which there is alternation between a soloist and either the CHOIR or the congregation.

Responsory, Responsorium (L), **Respond:** responsorial CHANTS of the Roman Catholic rite, appearing as part of the OFFICE.

Rest: a symbol indicating a certain length of silence, either for the music as a whole or for an individual part. (Symbols for rests are identified in Appendix E—Musical Symbols.)

Resultant tones: *see* COMBINATION TONES.

Retardation: a NONHARMONIC TONE sustained from the previous BEAT (at which time it was a consonance), resolving upward. The retardation is rhythmically similar to the suspension, which resolves downward.

Retrograde: a restatement of a series of notes that reverses their original order (i.e., it proceeds from the last note to the first). Synonymous terms are *cancrizans, crab, al rovescio,* and *per recte et retro.* Retrograde motion has been used in a variety of contexts from the 14th to the 20th centuries. Sometimes it is used only in a single voice, sometimes in an entire polyphonic complex. Works using retrograde motion that were written before the 20th century (e.g., MACHAUT's *Ma fin est mon commencement*, some of the CANONS of BACH's *Musical Offering*, the minuet of HAYDN's Sonata No. 4 for violin and piano, the last movement of BEETHOVEN's *Hammerclavier Sonata*, Op. 106) retain in the retrograde statement the time-values of the original. In the TWELVE-TONE technique, however, retrograde is used as a purely structural device; adherence to the rhythm of the first (or any other) statement of the set is unusual.

Retrograde inversion: a restatement of a series of notes that not only reverses their original order but also reverses the direction of each melodic step. (Every ascending melodic INTERVAL is replaced by a like descending interval, and vice versa.) Special examples of retrograde inversion occur in works designed by composers to be read either upright or turned upside down. The *Interlude* that concludes HINDEMITH's *Ludus Tonalis* is the retrograde inversion of the one at the opening, using, however, different ACCIDENTALS. Retrograde inversion is a standard structural device of the TWELVE-TONE technique.

Rhapsody: the title of several 19th- and 20th-century compositions; these are nearly all instrumental works in one MOVEMENT, of a nationalistic, epic, or rhetorical nature. Among the most famous are a few of the twenty Hungarian Rhapsodies by LISZT and the two Rhapsodies for piano by BRAHMS. (Brahms also wrote a Rhapsody for Alto, male chorus, and orchestra on three stanzas of a poem by Goethe.) The title does not denote any particular structural format.

Rhythm: the durational organization of music, comprehending the ebb and flow of movement. Although rhythm is a fluid element, concerned primarily with the governance of motion, it must frequently be discussed in somewhat static terms, dealing with the time-values of individual notes and the presence or absence of accents that may mark off temporal groups. (In particular, the correction of mistakes in rhythm in performance often focuses attention on isolated notes.) Rhythm may exist as an element independent of PITCH. As such, it is most clearly expressed by PERCUSSION INSTRUMENTS of indefinite pitch. Usually, however, rhythm is an essential property of MELODY, which cannot exist without it. Since harmonic progressions are also subject to temporal organization, one may also speak of *harmonic rhythm,* the rate of change of the basic harmonies of a piece. (Basic CHORDS may each be prolonged over several measures, creating a slow harmonic rhythm, or they may change with each beat, producing a fast harmonic rhythm.) The rhythmic styles observable in the music most familiar to the average listener constitute only a portion of the total stylistic spectrum. Other styles of great interest and variety are observable in music of non-European cultures, in much late MEDIEVAL and RENAISSANCE music, and in certain present-day styles.

It is possible to classify rhythmic styles according to three broad categories: (1) those in which there is no fixed musical unit of time; (2) those in which all time-values derive as multiples or fractions of a fixed unit, but which lack regular accent patterns; (3) those in which time-values are derived as in (2), and which also feature recurrent ACCENT patterns.

The first of these styles occurs among many non-European cultures. The proportions between the time-values of individual notes can be extremely complex, so much so that they can neither be readily classified by the human ear nor easily set down in present notation. Such form of rhythmic freedom is present also in segments of MODERN MUSIC not dependent upon the traditional forms of musical NOTATION. Included within this category is both music in which the composer entrusts to the performer a greater role in shaping the musical gesture and music in which the composer bypasses the performer and shapes his sound material himself, either directly through ELECTRONIC synthesis and recording, or indirectly through COMPUTER-generated statistical profiles that are converted and synthesized. Passages employing rhythm without fixed time units may occur also within works of stricter rhythmic organization, when there is a deliberate loosening of the TIME structure, as in a *rubato, accelerando,* or *ritardando.* The second category of rhythmic style, measuring time-values in terms of a fixed unit, but without regard for larger shapes of recurrent lengths, occurs in much liturgical CHANT, certain RECITATIVES and CADENZAS, and in some modern music. The third category, comprising music with recurrent accent patterns (METER), includes most music from 1600 to the present. Terminology distinguishing between these three styles is not standardized. *Free rhythm* may indicate either of the first two styles, and *measured rhythm* either of the last two. The last is sometimes known as *metrical rhythm;* it has also been called *accentual rhythm.*

The rhythmic idiom proper to most familiar music is very highly organized. The composer will combine long and short notes in such fashion that the listener will consciously or subconsciously perceive a pattern of even pulses. A long note will be perceived not as an indivisible unit, but as a complex unit comprised of several pulses. Short notes will not be perceived as separate entities, but as subsections of a single pulse. Melodic and harmonic progressions, as well as subtle accentuations, will lead the listener to group a small series of pulses into a larger unit—the measure—and to accord a sense of primacy to the note occurring at the beginning of this measure. Indeed, all pulses and even the subdivisions of these pulses fall into a strict hierarchy of importance, the exact nature of the hierarchy being dependent upon the number of pulses constituting a measure (*see* METER.) That number is expected to remain constant throughout a long section or an entire work. Under normal circumstances long notes will occur at the beginning of a measure rather than

in the middle or at the end. And, on a more minute level of organization, they will occur at the beginning of a pulse rather than in the middle or at the end. Furthermore, the idiom of familiar music is such that a composer will normally develop a few related rhythmic patterns within a given section rather than a large number of unrelated patterns. The composer with an extraordinary rhythmic sense is able to envisage the possibilities for development inherent in any given rhythmic idea; he is able to conduct this development in a convincing manner.

Rhythmic modes: a set of rhythmic patterns—similar to poetic feet—that governed much of the music created between 1160 and 1300. The 13th-century theorists usually distinguished between six such patterns. The foot of the first consists of a long value followed by a short; the second, a short followed by a long; the third, a long followed by two unequal shorter values; etc. The time-values may be expressed in the modern equivalents shown on the next page. Normally more than one MODE is employed among the several voice-parts of a polyphonic complex, but change of mode within a given part is rare. A composer may obtain some variety by subdividing a given portion

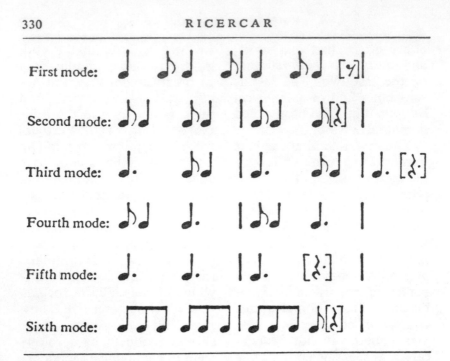

First mode:

Second mode:

Third mode:

Fourth mode:

Fifth mode:

Sixth mode:

of a foot into two or more time-values. The values constituting a foot might sometimes be fused into one larger value, or an individual value might be replaced by its equivalent rest. Most ORGANA and CONDUCTI, all early MOTETS, and a sizable segment of secular MONOPHONY employed modal rhythm. *See also* MEDIEVAL MUSIC.

Ricercar (I): (1) a contrapuntal, instrumental work of the 16th to 18th centuries, based on the imitative development of one or more subjects. One of the forerunners of the FUGUE, the ricercar is usually distinguishable from the latter on the following bases: the ricercar normally develops several subjects rather than one, and these generally exhibit less sharply defined tonality and less incisive rhythms than do characteristic fugue subjects. Consistency in terminology was not, however, maintained by BAROQUE composers. There are certain fugues which reflect elements of ricercar style, while a few works labeled ricercars are considered by some as fugues. During the late Baroque, the ricercar was often used as a vehicle for the display of technical command over numerous contrapuntal devices. (2) An instrumental study of the 16th and early 17th centuries, usually in a homophonic style.

Richter, Franz Xaver: *b.*

Holleschau, December 1, 1709; *d.* Strasbourg, September 12, 1789. In 1747 Richter joined the Mannheim orchestra, where he remained until 1769, when he became music director at the Strasbourg Cathedral. He is known primarily for his contribution to the early development of the SYMPHONY.

Ricochet, Jeté (F): a BOWING technique utilizing the upper section of the bow; the bow is bounced against the string in one main movement which provides the momentum for a group of tiny rebounds, each producing a light articulation.

Riegger, Wallingford: *b.* Albany, Georgia, April 29, 1885; *d.* New York City, April 2, 1961. After study at the Institute of Musical Art and the Berlin Hochschule, Riegger began his career as a conductor in Germany. He soon returned to the United States and taught at various schools. Riegger's later style is based on a free use of the serial technique combined with traditional melodic and rhythmic elements. His works include four SYMPHONIES and other orchestral music, CHAMBER MUSIC, songs, piano pieces, and music for modern dance.

Rigaudon (F): a Provençal dance of the 17th century in quick duple METER. Music

for this dance was used in French operatic BALLETS and in instrumental SUITES (as an optional MOVEMENT).

Rigo (I): staff.

Rimsky-Korsakov, Nikolai Andreyevich: *b.* Tikhvin, March 18, 1844; *d.* Lubensk, June 21, 1908; outstanding Russian nationalistic composer, one of the Mighty FIVE.

Rimsky-Korsakov began a career as a naval officer, but resigned in 1873. Despite the meagerness of his musical training—chiefly in piano—he was appointed professor of composition and orchestration at the St. Petersburg Conservatory in 1871. He worked diligently to improve his command of theory and became a master orchestrator. In his mature years Rimsky-Korsakov was one of the dominant figures in Russian music. He was an influential teacher (among his pupils were ARENSKY, GLAZUNOV, IPPOLITOV-IVANOV, LIADOV, STEINBERG, and STRAVINSKY), an advisor to the Belaiev publishing firm, and a conductor of some importance. He directed several concerts of Russian music in major European centers and succeeded GRIEG as a corresponding member of the French Academy.

Rimsky-Korsakov's general musical outlook was conservative, but his music does contain occasional examples of novel melodic patterns and bold handling of dissonance. Though he collected and published FOLK tunes and used them in his music—as in the *Russian Easter Overture*—Rimsky-Korsakov was less militantly nationalistic than BALAKIREV. His orchestral music—including the SUITE *Scheherezade,* the *Capriccio espagnol,* and two SYMPHONIES—is imaginative and colorful. He wrote 15 OPERAS, most of them during his last decade; the best known are *Sadko, The Golden Cockerel,* and *The Legend of the Invisible City of Kitezh.* Symphonic suites were arranged from four operas. In addition, Rimsky-Korsakov wrote a number of chamber, choral, and piano compositions.

Rinforzando (I), abbreviated *rf, rfz:* (1) a pronounced accent, often at a point where one might not expect such a STRESS; (2) a brief, sharp CRESCENDO (increase in loudness).

Ripieno (I): the full orchestral complement employed in a CONCERTO, in distinction to the soloist(s) or a group of reduced size. A composer scoring a passage for the latter would indicate *senza ripieni.* The term *ripieno* is used especially with reference to the *concerto grosso.*

Ripresa (I): REPEAT; the word is sometimes used in the sense of recapitulation or refrain.

Risoluto (I): resolutely.

Ritardando (I): a progressive slackening of pace.

Ritenuto (I): (1) a synonym for RITARDANDO; (2) a pace slower than that which prevailed previously.

Ritornello (I): (1) in BAROQUE operatic ARIAS, a recurrent instrumental section used as an introduction, interlude, and conclusion. While the first and last statements of the *ritornello* would be in the TONIC key, intermediate ones would often be in related keys. (2) The TUTTI section of a *concerto grosso* movement, functioning as in (1). (3) An instrumental REFRAIN occurring after each verse of certain 17th-century German songs. (4) The concluding section of a 14th-century MADRIGAL or CACCIA. This section normally displays poetic and rhythmic structures that contrast with those of the main body of the work.

Rococo: a musical style of the period 1710–75, being distinguished by a lightness of TEXTURE, a certain ornateness of MELODY, and an elegant sentimentality. The style embodies elements of both BAROQUE and CLASSICAL styles and is often referred to as the *style galant.* It is represented especially by the works of COUPERIN, DAQUIN, and TELE-

MANN and finds its sharpest contemporaneous opposite in the concentrated polyphony of J. S. BACH. (Bach's SUITES, however, show that this master did not remain entirely aloof from the *style galant*.)

Rode, Jacques Pierre Joseph: *b.* Bordeaux, February 26, 1774; *d.* Château-Bourbon, November 25, 1830. One of the prominent violinists of his generation, Rode wrote CONCERTOS, CAPRICES, ETUDES, and other works for the violin.

Rodgers, Richard: *b.* New York City, June 28, 1902. One of the most successful composers of musical comedies, Rodgers studied at Columbia University and at the Institute of Musical Art. He worked together with Lorenz Hart for some 18 years and then with Oscar Hammerstein II. Among his best known shows are *A Connecticut Yankee, Babes in Arms, Pal Joey, Oklahoma, Carousel, South Pacific,* and *The King and I.*

Roll: a series of very rapid drum beats.

Romance, Romanze (G), Romanza (I): a title employed during the CLASSIC and ROMANTIC periods for both vocal and instrumental works (or movements thereof), these being of small or moderate size. Most are of lyrical nature, some of narrative.

Romanesca (S): a Spanish song of the mid-16th century by the title *O guardame las vacas.* A stylized simplification of the bass was used as the foundation for many instrumental and vocal variations of the late RENAISSANCE and early BAROQUE.

Romantic music: the music of *c.*1820 to *c.*1910. The Romantic composers enlarged the CLASSICAL genres of SONATA, SYMPHONY, and OPERA, and contributed to a brilliant flowering of ACCOMPANIED song and instrumental miniatures. During this period program music came into its own, and there was a proliferation of clearly delineated national styles. An increased awareness of instrumental idioms and virtuosity prevailed, together with a heightened feeling for TONE COLOR and a concomitant growth of the ORCHESTRA. Sharp contrasts existed side by side, the miniature with the monumental, the intimate with the spectacular. Among the greatest masters of the period are SCHUBERT, BERLIOZ, MENDELSSOHN, SCHUMANN, CHOPIN, LISZT, WAGNER, VERDI, and BRAHMS.

The term Romantic was coined by German writers of the late 18th century, who, in their desire to shun that which they considered prosaic and shallow, turned to the romances and other cultural forms of the Middle Ages. This search for the exotic, the individual, the distant and unattainable, characterizes much of musical Romanticism. The concept of the composer as a solitary genius and of the musical work as the liberation of an inner compulsion via sudden inspiration is primarily of Romantic origin. During the 18th century the composer was regarded as a craftsman, working for a particular patron and turning out products for immediate consumption and approval. Then, as now, the masters stood apart from the hacks by virtue of their superior imagination as well as their superior craft. However, the composer did not consciously seek individuality for its own sake, and imagination was not singled out for special homage. During the 19th century, composers such as Wagner insisted on the uniqueness of their musical style and often preferred not to acknowledge the relationships that bound their music with those of others.

The concern for the musical past is another important characteristic of the Romantic musicians. Before the 19th century, a work was rarely kept before the public eye for as much as fifty years. As musical styles changed, older pieces were either remodeled or dropped. It is true that both MOZART and BEETHOVEN knew some of BACH's keyboard works and that Bach's CANTATAS were used by some of his successors at St. Thomas in Leipzig. However, Bach was a shadowy figure in the early 19th century, and Mendelssohn's performance of the *St. Matthew Passion* in 1829 was an important milestone that awakened the minds of many to the greatness of earlier music. Though some Romantic composers, Berlioz, for example, vigorously rejected the musical past, the Romantics not only preserved the best music of their predecessors but enlarged their heritage by delving into works that had previously been forgotten. They systematized the study of music history, which became of consistent rather than sporadic concern.

The emphasis on individuality and expressiveness naturally affected details of composition. In the preceding era, moderation, economy of means, and balance were stressed. The gifted Classical composer was able to achieve individuality through nuance of detail. He could base the major part of a musical structure on a relatively modest harmonic vocabulary and plumb the possibilities offered by such a vocabulary; when richer, more distant harmonies were introduced, these had fresh impact. In seeking greater expressiveness, the Romantic composer drew on the outer reaches of his harmonic vocabulary more consistently. This resulted not merely in increased lyricism; in many works a larger framework was needed in order that the primary tonal landmarks should not be submerged by the overall richness of detail. Beginning with Beethoven, composers began increasingly to experiment with ways in which they could avoid the prompt definition of a tonality by opening with a series of harmonies other than the TONIC and postponing the first clear dominant-tonic CADENCE.

The vigor and clarity of Classical music stem from themes with strong rhythms and clear tonalities. The development section of the SONATA FORM—the most prominent of the Classical forms— often derives its sense of drama through the dissection of a theme into constituent motives. Lyrical Romantic themes are not as well suited to this sort of treatment. Consequently, in the hands of Romantic composers such as Schubert, sonata form becomes looser and more expansive. In place of the finely calculated coherence and balance of a Classical score, there is greater discursiveness and richer harmonic and tonal color. In order to achieve unity among the separate movements of the expanded sonata and symphony, several composers, including Berlioz, FRANCK, and BRUCKNER, interrelated various sections through the use of the same or similar themes. (In this they followed an example set by Beethoven.) Thematic recall occurs also in Romantic opera, not only in the works of Wagner and his followers, but also in some by Verdi; in this medium it serves primarily a symbolic purpose.

One of the most natural outlets for Romantic subjectiveness was PROGRAM MUSIC. The expression of extramusical ideas led to the SYMPHONIC POEMS of Liszt and others and affected even the composition of symphonies. Moreover, the Romantics sought to find a programmatic key to the music of the Classical period; in this quest they would often invent their own interpretations of the "meaning of the music." The nickname *Moonlight Sonata,* for example, was not devised by Beethoven, but by a later musician.

Other typically Romantic forms were the abundant vocal and instrumental miniatures. The LIED, which had been of comparatively minor concern in the Classical era, suddenly became a central means of expression. An incredibly rich repertoire of song masterpieces was created by Schubert, Schumann, Brahms, WOLF, and Richard STRAUSS. Other fine works were created by lesser composers and by masters not normally thought of as vocal composers (as, for example, Liszt). As a rule, the quality of these works derives not only from the lyric expressiveness of the vocal line, but also from the imaginative nature of the piano accompaniment.

The instrumental counterpart of the *lied* was the character piece for piano, a genre that comprised much of the Romantic keyboard literature. The repertoire begins with Beethoven's *Bagatelles* and includes, for example, Schubert's *Moments musicaux* and *Impromptus*, Mendelssohn's *Songs without Words*, Chopin's *Preludes* and *Nocturnes*, Schumann's *Papillons*, *Kinderszenen*, *Carnaval*, *Noveletten*, and *Bunte Blätter*, Brahms' *Intermezzos*, *Ballades*, *Capriccios*, and *Rhapsodies*, and Liszt's *Années de Pèlerinage*. Some of these fully capture a mood within a handful of measures; often the briefer ones are performed as part of a set. Many such sets, including *Papillons* and *Carnaval*, are so closely knit that their component pieces cannot be played individually without considerable loss of musical meaning. The more extensive character pieces may set forth a contrast between two moods.

In opposition to these works are the operas and virtuoso instrumental works designed to dazzle the new mass audience that replaced the select gatherings of earlier periods. In Italian opera, the emphasis on vocal display continued, often at the expense of the accompaniment and of the narrative elements of the drama. In French grand opera, the emphasis was placed on spectacle, with magnificent sets, extravagant BALLETS, and mass scenes. A love of spectacle appears also in Wagner, although it is subordinated in his works to a cogent musicodramatic conception. A great part of the atmosphere of the Wagnerian music-drama derives from the role of the orchestra, which goes beyond mere accompaniment and portrays the essence of the text's emotions. Wagnerian opera, the Romantic lied, the solo CHARACTER PIECE, and orchestral program music all illustrate in some fashion the Romantic's belief in the fusion of the arts, in particular, in the merging of music and poetry.

Despite the wealth of vocal music, the Romantic era is primarily of INSTRUMENTAL orientation. Instrumental techniques were expanded with amazing rapidity, and the increased demands of composers were reflected in corresponding developments in instrument making. New mechanisms were invented for most of the WOODWINDS and BRASS, permitting greater technical versatility. The quest for greater tonal brilliance led to the alteration of old violins and to new methods of piano construction. The piano became a competitor of the orchestra. The orchestra itself grew rapidly in size, due chiefly to the expansion of the woodwind and brass choirs. The lesser members of various families, such as the piccolo and English horn, were used more frequently. In previous eras, writing for orchestra normally followed certain conventional patterns determined chiefly by the portions of the instrumental ranges that were considered most characteristic. In Romantic music, the upper and lower portions of the various instrumental ranges were explored more often for the sake of their individual colors. Sensitivity to tone color is one of the important Romantic traits. Orchestration became a consummate art in the hands of Berlioz, RIMSKY-KORSAKOV, and others.

The virtuoso took on new importance. Skilled performers had, of course, always been acclaimed. However, with the growth of public concerts in large halls, they reached a wider and wider audience. In the Romantic era, the functions of creator and interpreter were filled in increasing extent by different persons, and this trend has continued to the present day.

Nationalism, a potent force on the political scene, was mirrored in the arts. Local musical traditions were consciously nurtured, leading to specifically Russian, Bohemian, Norwegian, Spanish, and other national schools. The Russians—led by MUSSORGSKY, BORODIN, and Rimsky-Korsakov—and the Czechs—led by SMETANA and DVOŘÁK—produced works of wider and more lasting significance than their counterparts elsewhere. Even in France, Italy, and Germany, the countries with the richest musical traditions, awareness of national idioms increased sharply. The composer, lacking the personal contact with his audience that he had enjoyed previously, often sought to establish his relationship to society through an awareness

of national idioms. Interest in
FOLK SONG and in folklike
qualities grew rapidly. The
importance of folk-influence
on the works of Brahms,
Liszt, and Chopin is considerable. An awareness of local
color also made it possible
for composers to write realis-
tically in styles of countries
other than their own, resulting in such works as BIZET's
Carmen and TCHAIKOVSKY's
Capriccio italien.

As the 19th century wore
on, the harmonic vocabulary
of the Romantic composer
became increasingly rich.
CHORDS based on notes foreign to the scale of the piece,
and chords enriched with any
of a variety of sevenths,
sixths, or ninths were used in
ever greater numbers. Modulations were more rapid and
startling. Eventually, the tonal
structure, which depends
upon the definition of and
adherence to a main center,
was undermined. Wagner's
Tristan und Isolde, which
conveys the essence of the
passionate by means of chromaticism, represents the first
and probably greatest peak
in this movement. Completed
in 1859, the opera exerted
strong influence on many late
Romantics, who returned
more and more frequently to
this kind of idiom. From the
eventual feeling of surfeit of
harmonic richness and the

gradual emancipation from
the vocabulary of tonality
there arose the currents leading to MODERN MUSIC.

Romanza (I), **Romanze** (G):
romance.

Rondeau (F): (1) a French
musico-poetic refrain form of
the 13th to 16th centuries. It
is customary to indicate the
structure of single stanzas as
follows: *AB aA ab AB.* In
this schema, REFRAIN sections
are represented by capital
letters, while lower-case letters indicate fresh text cast in
the pattern of the corresponding refrain section. Identical
letters—regardless of type
font—indicate identity of music. The individual sections
may comprise 1–3 lines of
poetry, the *A* section being
either equal to or one line
longer than the *B* section. (2)
An instrumental form of the
late French BAROQUE based
on the alternation between a
refrain and two or more different episodes, known as
couplets. See RONDO.

Rondo: one of a family of
instrumental forms based on
an alternation between a recurrent section and one or
more contrasting episodes.
Various repetition patterns
are possible within this general format. Each episode
may be different (*see* RON-
DEAU, sense 2), or the initial
episode may return as the
last. The pattern *A B A C*

A B A is a frequent one. In some movements, the *C* section, rather than being independent, develops musical ideas presented in previous sections. The flanking *A B A* groups therefore take on the character of the exposition and recapitulation of SONATA FORM, this character being emphasized by presenting the initial *B* in the DOMINANT key, the final *B* in the TONIC. Such structures are often referred to as *rondo-sonata* or *sonata-rondo* forms. The shorter pattern, *A B A C A,* is sometimes designated either as a *second* or a *modified* rondo form. Occasionally the composer may wish to vary the regularity of the recurrence of the *A* section and may fashion a work that may be represented by the schema: *A B A C B A.*

Root: the tone on which a CHORD is founded.

Rore, Cipriano de: *b*. Antwerp(?), 1516; *d*. Parma, 1565. Rore was trained in Antwerp and Venice (under WILLAERT); he worked in Ferrara, Parma, and Venice. Outstanding as a madrigalist, Rore contributed also CHANSONS, MOTETS, MASSES, a PASSION, and some instrumental music. A highly expressive composer, Rore helped further the development of CHROMATICISM in the madrigal.

Rosalia: an unimaginative, real sequence (*see* SEQUENCE, sense 1).

Rose: an ornamental openwork carving forming part of the circular sound-role of a string instrument.

Rosenmüller, Johann: *b*. Ölsnitz, Germany, *c*.1620; *d*. Wolfenbüttel, Germany, September 10, 1684. The most important of Rosenmüller's posts was that of ducal music director at Wolfenbüttel. He wrote a wide variety of music, including MASSES, MOTETS, SONATAS, instrumental CANZONAS, and dance SUITES.

Rosin (Resin): a solid substance—prepared from gum of turpentine—that is wiped against the hair of a bow in order that the bow, when drawn, should maintain the proper degree of friction against the string.

Rossi, Luigi: *b*. Torremaggiore, 1598(?); *d*. Rome, February 19, 1653. Rossi was active chiefly in Rome, although he visited Florence, Paris (twice), and Provence. His chief importance lies in his contribution to the early BAROQUE chamber CANTATA. He helped further the growing distinction between RECITATIVE, ARIOSO, and ARIA styles. He wrote about 250 cantatas, together with ORATORIOS, OPERAS (including *Orfeo*, the first Italian opera written specifically for a Paris production), MOTETS, and other vocal works.

Rossini, Gioacchino Antonio: *b.* Pesaro, February 29, 1792; *d.* Paris, November 13, 1868; one of the most important Italian operatic composers.

As a boy Rossini became proficient on several instruments and was an accomplished singer. He studied with Padre Mattei at the Bologna *Liceo Musicale,* but broke off his studies to write *La Cambiale di matrimonio,* produced in Venice in 1810. From 1810 to 1823, he composed a series of OPERAS for various Venetian, Neapolitan, and Roman theaters. Among these were the serious operas *Tancredi, Otello,* and *La donna del lago,* and the comic gems *La Scala di Seta, L'Italiana in Algeri, La Cenerentola, La Gazza Ladra,* and *The Barber of Seville* (1816), one of the greatest of all comic operas. Irked by the cool reception accorded to *Semiramide* in 1823, Rossini went first to London and, in 1824, to Paris. He reworked two operas for the Parisian public and brought out *Le Comte Ory,* a comic opera, and his famous grand opera, *William Tell* (1829). A contract to write another five operas for the French court was broken following the 1830 revolution. At this point, having written about 40 operas in two decades—together with 16 CANTATAS, CHAMBER MUSIC, and other works—Rossini abruptly curtailed his creative activity. He spent the years 1836–55 in Italy and then returned to Paris for the remainder of his life. His wit and hospitality—he became a gourmet cook—made his home an attractive meeting place for many artists. His last works include a *Stabat Mater* (1842), the *Petite Messe solennelle* (1864), and a number of songs and piano pieces which Rossini nicknamed *Sins of Old Age.* In general, his work is marked by lilting MELODY, piquant RHYTHM, and clear, though colorful ORCHESTRATION. Some of the vocal coloraturas provide a stern test of the singer's technique. A master at depicting the comic, Rossini is keenly aware of its frequent undertone of pathos.

Rota (L): ROUND.

Roulade (F): a highly ornate vocal passage in an operatic ARIA of the CLASSICAL or ROMANTIC period, consisting of rapid runs, turns, and the like.

Round: a circular (or perpetual) CANON; that is, a vocal piece in which the several voices sing the same MELODY in overlapping succession, each voice repeating the melody upon its conclusion until the performers agree to stop.

Roussel, Albert: *b.* Tourcoing,

April 5, 1869; d. Royan, August 23, 1937. After a brief career in the French navy, Roussel completed his musical education at the Schola Cantorum under D'INDY, later becoming a teacher at that institution. As a composer, Roussel is best known for his four SYMPHONIES and the SUITE from the BALLET *The Spider's Feast*. He wrote, in addition, various stage works, orchestral suites, SYMPHONIC POEMS, CHAMBER and KEYBOARD music, songs and choral works. Each of the important stylistic trends of early 20th-century French music is to be observed in Roussel's work: the post-Romanticism of FRANCK and d'Indy, IMPRESSIONISM, and NEOCLASSICISM. He used both Oriental TONE COLORS and JAZZ idioms.

Rovescio, Al (I): (1) RETROGRADE MOTION; (2) INVERTED MOTION.

Row (Tone row): the succession of PITCHES used to provide the structural basis of a TWELVE-TONE composition.

Rubato (Tempo rubato): (1) in normal usage, a departure in performance from the strict observance of the relationship between time-values called for by the NOTATION; that is, a flexibility of RHYTHM in which important notes are lengthened slightly at the expense of notes deemed less important. Although rhythmic flexibility of this nature existed in the late 16th century and in the 17th century, the term itself is of 18th-century origin. In the late 18th century this rhythmic flexibility concerned MELODY alone, the ACCOMPANIMENT being maintained in strict time. In the 19th century, however, *rubato* often affected the entire musical fabric; this interpretation is largely prevalent today. (2) It has been suggested that the term *rubato* was used briefly (e.g., by CHOPIN) to indicate alteration of normal dynamic values, rather than of rhythm.

Rubinstein, Anton Gregoryevich: b. Vekhvotinets (Podolia), November 28, 1829; d. Peterhof, November 20, 1894. Rubinstein studied piano with Alexander Villoing and toured Europe frequently (and once the United States) from the age of ten. He founded the St. Petersburg Conservatory, which he directed (1862–67, 1887–91). His compositions, which reveal the influence of German ROMANTICISM more than Russian nationalism, were highly successful. They include OPERAS, SYMPHONIES, piano CONCERTOS, CHAMBER MUSIC, piano pieces, and songs.

Rückpositiv (G): (1) a set of ORGAN pipes which, in old German instruments, were located behind the organist, between him and the nave; (2) the manual KEYBOARD governing these pipes.

Ruggiero (I): a BASS LINE that underlies numerous sets of VARIATIONS of the period c.1650–1750. Apparently the name was taken from the opening of a stanza of Ariosto's *Orlando furioso*.

Russian bassoon: a late-18th-century wind instrument related to the bass horn and serpent (*see* BRASS INSTRUMENTS).

Rust, Friedrich Wilhelm: b. Wörlitz, July 6, 1739; d. Dessau, March 28, 1796. Music director to Leopold III of Anhalt-Dessau; he wrote many instrumental works and some incidental music for stage plays.

Rutini, Giovanni Maria: b. Florence, April 25, 1723, d. Florence, December 7, 1797. Rutini was active in Italy, Germany, Czechoslovakia, and Russia as both composer and conductor; he is known principally for his contribution to Italian KEYBOARD literature.

S

Sackbut: trombone (16th–17th-century English term).

Saint-Saëns, (Charles) Camille: b. Paris, October 9, 1835; d. Algiers, December 16, 1921. A man of many gifts, Saint-Saëns was an outstanding pianist and organist, one of the most important French composers of his day, a minor poet, dramatist, essayist, an amateur scientist, and a music editor. He completed his musical training under HALÉVY at the Paris Conservatoire. He was organist at the Madeleine (1857–77). His early musical style was much influenced by LISZT and WAGNER, and he remained conservative in face of the enormous changes that took place during his lifetime. Saint-Saëns composed a large quantity and variety of music, including OPERAS and incidental music (one still hears excerpts from *Samson and Delilah*), songs, choral and keyboard works. His most popular works include the SYMPHONIC POEM *Danse macabre* and the *Carnival of Animals*, together with the third of his SYMPHONIES and several of his CONCERTOS (for piano, for violin, and for cello).

Saite (G): string; *Saiteninstrument*, string instrument.

Salieri, Antonio: *b.* Legnago (Verona), August 18, 1750; *d.* Vienna, May 7, 1825. Salieri studied with his brother, then at the St. Mark's singing school in Venice, and with Florian Gassmann. He became Gassmann's deputy in Vienna in 1770 and his successor as court composer and conductor in 1774. He was appointed music director in 1788. Salieri was a renowned teacher, BEETHOVEN, SCHUBERT, and LISZT being among his pupils. He composed more than three dozen OPERAS, as well as CANTATAS, MASSES, TE DEUMS and other sacred music, SYMPHONIES,

CONCERTOS, and other instrumental works.

Salmo (I): PSALM.

Saltando: *see* SAUTILLÉ.

Saltarello (I): a term for a few different dances, primarily of Italian origin. The 19th-century saltarello (imitated by MENDELSSOHN in the last movement of the *Italian Symphony*) is in quick, bouncing 6/8 rhythm. In the late RENAISSANCE, the saltarello—a lively dance in triple METER—often followed after a statelier dance in duple meter. Medieval pieces labeled saltarelli are in various meters; they were apparently in slower TEMPO than later dances of the same name.

Saltato: *see* SAUTILLÉ.

Sammartini (San Martini), Giovanni Battista: *b.* Milan, 1701(?); *d.* Milan, January 15, 1775. Organist at several Milanese churches, Sammartini was music director at the Convent of Santa Maria Maddalena (1730–70). GLUCK was his greatest pupil. A prolific composer, Sammartini influenced the development of the early classical SYMPHONY. He wrote—in addition to more than 80 symphonies—CONCERTOS, a large quantity of CHAMBER MUSIC, keyboard SONATAS, sacred music (including an ORATORIO), stage works, and CANTATAS.

Sanctus (L): the fourth section of the MASS ORDINARY.

Saraband, Sarabande (F, G): a dance which, during the 17th and 18th centuries, was in stately triple METER, often with a stress on the second beat of the measure. During the mid- and late BAROQUE, the sarabande was one of the four standard movements of the SUITE. The dance was apparently introduced to Europe from the Orient via Spain. According to 16th-century Spanish writers, the early sarabande was wild and lascivious, but these qualities soon disappeared.

Sarasate y Navascuez, Pablo Martín Melitón: *b.* Pamplona, March 10, 1844; *d.* Biarritz, September 20, 1908. After completing his training at the Paris Conservatoire, Sarasate soon became one of the famous violin virtuosi of his day. LALO wrote his *Symphonie Espagnole*, BRUCH, his *Scottish Fantasy*, for Sarasate. The violinist himself wrote various works for his instrument, the best known being *Zigeunerweisen*.

Sardana: a national dance of Catalonia, usually accompanied by pipe and tabor, the music normally being in quick 6/8 time.

Sarrusophone: a family of metal, double-reed WOODWIND instruments.

Satie, Erik Alfred Leslie: *b.* Honfleur, May 17, 1866; *d.* Paris, July 1, 1925. After study at the Paris Conservatoire, which he found repellent, Satie worked as a cabaret pianist and composed sporadically. At forty he felt the need for a firmer technical command and studied with D'INDY and ROUSSEL. Satie's style represents a rebellion especially against the heavy emotionalism of the German Romantic SYMPHONY and Wagnerian OPERA but also against the mysticism of French IMPRESSIONISM. He sought clarity and simplicity instead. His music has a wry humor and forthrightness that derive in part from cabaret traditions. His work includes numerous piano pieces and songs, three BALLETS and other stage music, the symphonic drama *Socrate,* and a MASS. Satie deeply influenced the trends of 20th-century French music.

Satz (G): a MOVEMENT (e.g., of a SONATA, SUITE), setting or composition.

Sautillé (F), **Saltando** (I), **Saltato** (I), **Spiccato** (I): a BOWING technique for rapid detached notes; the middle portion of the bow is made to bounce against the string.

Saxhorn: a family of BRASS INSTRUMENTS with wide conical bores.

Saxophone: a family of metal,

single-reed WOODWIND instruments of conical bore.

Scale: the consecutive arrangement of the basic melodic material of a composition (the tones of its MODE) from low to high or vice versa. Some scales have both an ascending and a descending form, which vary either in content or in NOTATION. Scales and scale segments may furnish either thematic or transitional material in a composition. They are used in the technical training of almost all performers, instrumental and vocal.

Traditional theoretic instruction and analysis is founded on three main scales: major, minor, and chromatic. The C major scale consists of the notes *c, d, e, f, g, a, b, c* —the white keys of the piano. The interval pattern thus formed consists of two whole steps, a half step, three whole steps, and a half step; this pattern may begin on any of the twelve different notes of the octave. The PITCH content of each of the resultant forms (in other words, the particular combination of white and black keys on the piano) is individual. The sharps or flats used in the scale basic to the main portion of a composition are indicated at the beginning of each staff by a KEY SIGNATURE.

The minor scale has three forms: natural, harmonic, and melodic. The natural minor scale of A consists of the notes *a, b, c, d, e, f, g,* and *a.* The interval pattern— which may also begin on any of the twelve different notes of the OCTAVE—consists of a whole step, half step, two whole steps, half step, and two whole steps. It is possible also to derive a natural minor scale from the major scale beginning with the same tone by lowering the third, sixth, and seventh degrees of the major scale. The customary sharps or flats of the natural minor scales' are also indicated by key signatures.

The lowered seventh of the natural minor is often replaced in composition by a raised seventh, particularly at CADENCES. The harmonic minor scale accords theoretical recognition to this fact. However, the resultant alteration creates an INTERVAL of an augmented second between the sixth and seventh degrees. The melodic minor arose in composition partly as a means of avoiding this interval, judged clumsy in previous centuries. The ascending form of this scale raises both the sixth and seventh degrees, while the descending form is identical with the natural minor.

The degrees of major and

minor scales may be designated either by their numerical position or by equivalent terms.

1. Tonic
2. Supertonic
3. Mediant
4. Subdominant
5. Dominant
6. Submediant
7. Leading tone
8. Tonic

A chromatic scale consists of a succession of half steps, including each of the twelve different tones of the octave. Partly to avoid unnecessary ACCIDENTALS, it is customary to notate an ascending chromatic scale with sharps and a descending one with flats. A chromatic scale may occur as an ornamental form in music based on the conventions of the major-minor system or it may represent an abstraction of music built on different principles (TWELVE-TONE music), in which each of the tones is—at least in theory— of equal importance. In the latter event, it is sometimes known as a *duodecuple* or *dodecuple scale*.

Scale (Scaling): the ratio between the diameter and the height of an ORGAN pipe.

Scarlatti, Alessandro: *b*. Palermo, May 2, 1660; *d*. Naples, October 24, 1725; the most important OPERA composer of the Neapolitan school.

Alessandro Scarlatti studied with CARISSIMI in Rome. He served there as music director to Queen Christina of Sweden (1680–84), before going to Naples as music director to the Spanish Viceroy (1684–1702). The next seven years were spent in Florence and Rome; Scarlatti then returned to Naples as music director to the Austrian viceroy. He was associated with several Neapolitan conservatories.

Scarlatti and his peers helped shape Italian operatic tradition through the development of the ARIA DA CAPO. He also helped crystallize contrasting styles of recitative and the form of the tripartite Italian OVERTURE. Among his 115 operas—less than half of which survive—*Tigrane* and *Griselda* were most popular. His facile melodic and harmonic imagination found still greater scope in the realm of the secular CANTATA; he composed well over 600 works in this genre, the great majority for voice and CONTINUO. His output includes also MASSES, ORATORIOS, and other sacred music, MADRIGALS, SERENATAS, CONCERTOS, harpsichord music, and miscellaneous CHAMBER MUSIC.

Scarlatti, (Giuseppe) Domenico: *b*. Naples, October 26, 1685; *d*. Madrid, July 23, 1757; an outstanding harpsichord composer. Domenico's early training and career were guided by his father, Alessandro. His first major posts were in Rome, where he served Queen Maria Casimira of Poland (1709–14) and was assistant music director and then music director at St. Peter's (1713–19). In 1720, D. Scarlatti went to Lisbon as music director to King João V and teacher to Princess Maria Barbara. He accompanied the princess to Spain upon her marriage to Prince Ferdinand and spent the rest of his life in her service. He was knighted by King João in 1738.

Like HAYDN, Domenico Scarlatti achieved his full powers rather late in life. After fifty, he created a vast repertoire of harpsichord SONATAS, which opened new vistas in KEYBOARD style. Some are lyrical, but more are gay, often with catchy rhythms that recall dance and guitar patterns. The melodic and harmonic patterns range imaginatively beyond the bounds of conventional figurations; the textures are chordal or quasi-polyphonic. An *L* followed by a number indicates the position of a sonata in the edition by Longo; a *K* number indicates its place in the roughly chronological list by Ralph Kirkpatrick.

Scena (I): (1) an operatic MOVEMENT of dramatic rather than reflective nature, for solo voice or voices. Often the *scena* is less symmetrical and less repetitive in its organization than the ARIA proper. (2) A work similar to (1), but intended for CONCERT rather than stage presentation. The term was further extended by Spohr to include an instrumental work (a violin CONCERTO) in similar style. (3) The stage itself and its appurtenances.

Schalmei (G): SHAWM.

Scheidt, Samuel: *b.* Halle, November 1587; *d.* Halle, March 24, 1654. A student of SWEELINCK, Scheidt was court organist (1609) and then music director (1619) in his native town. Among his numerous organ works, the *Tabulatura nova* (1624) is of particular importance. It contains some of the earliest contrapuntal elaborations of CHORALE tunes (i.e., chorale FANTASIES), together with VARIATIONS, fantasies, and dance pieces. Scheidt also issued a volume of harmonized chorales. His large output includes choral works, concerted works for voices and instruments, and instrumental CHAMBER MUSIC; the majority of his sacred works are based on chorales, but he wrote also MASSES, MAGNIFICATS, PSALMS, and pieces with Biblical texts.

Schein, Johann Hermann: *b.* Grünhain (Saxony), January 20, 1586; *d.* Leipzig, November 19, 1630. After serving as music director to Duke Johann Ernst of Weimar, Schein became cantor at St. Thomas in Leipzig in 1616. His style, like that of SCHÜTZ and M. PRAETORIUS, was deeply influenced by Italian techniques (MONODY and CONCERTATO style); he was the first to set CHORALE tunes in monodic fashion. He wrote a wide variety of sacred music (both German and Latin), sacred and secular MADRIGALS, LIEDER, and instrumental SUITES. The latter include some of the earliest examples of the "variation-suite," their several movements being derived from a common theme.

Schellen (G): small bells, jingles.

Schellentrommel (G): tambourine.

Scherzando (I): playful.

Scherzo (I): a work of light, humorous, or vigorous nature.

(1) The term most frequently refers to a movement —usually the third—of a SONATA, SYMPHONY, or CHAMBER work. Such movements were used in place of the earlier MINUET, from which they were derived during the late 18th century. A scherzo is therefore in triple METER and normally consists of three main subdivisions— scherzo, trio, scherzo—each in rounded BINARY FORM. The scherzo is more rapid and forceful than the minuet and often uses prominently the element of rhythmic surprise. A consistent distinction in terminology between minuet and scherzo styles was not, however, maintained during the late 18th century.

(2) In the 19th century both CHOPIN and BRAHMS wrote independent works for piano entitled scherzos, expanding greatly on the earlier classical framework. In order to obtain the desired element of contrast, they each included sections of more lyrical nature than was previously customary.

(3) In the 17th and early 18th centuries, the term was used for a variety of lighthearted vocal, instrumental, and mixed compositions by such composers as MONTEVERDI, Baggio Marini, SCHENK, STEFFANI, and BACH.

Schlag (G): BEAT; *Schlaginstrumente, Schlagzeug,* PERCUSSION INSTRUMENTS.

Schmetternd (G): a French horn direction calling for a harsh, blaring tone.

Schneller (G): a late-18th-century ornament progressing with great rapidity from the main tone to the note above and back.

Schobert, Johann: *b.* Silesia, *c.*1740; *d.* Paris, August 28,

1787. Chamber musician to the prince de Conti from 1760, Schobert influenced the development of the early CLASSICAL SONATA style in France. His works include KEYBOARD sonatas with and without optional violin accompaniments, keyboard TRIOS and CONCERTOS, as well as a few SYMPHONIES.

Schoenberg, Arnold: *b.* Vienna, September 13, 1874; *d.* Los Angeles, July 13, 1951; one of the dominant composers of the 20th century.

As a student in the Vienna Realschule, Schoenberg learned to play the violin and cello. His musical education was curtailed by the death of his father when he was sixteen; nevertheless, he managed a brief period of COUNTERPOINT study with Alexander von Zemlinsky, two years his senior. He obtained odd jobs as a conductor and arranger, both in Vienna and Berlin, before meeting Richard STRAUSS, who helped him obtain a teaching post at the Stern Conservatory in Berlin. Except for various tours, Schoenberg moved between Berlin and Vienna, attracting the support of Gustav MAHLER in Vienna and teaching briefly at the Vienna Academy. In 1925 Schoenberg went once more to Berlin, where he held a master class in composition at the Prussian

Academy of Arts until ousted by the Nazi regime in 1933. He emigrated to the United States. After a year in Boston, he taught at the University of Southern California and the University of California at Los Angeles. He became an American citizen in 1941. Schoenberg's influence as a teacher was profound; among his pupils were Alban BERG, Anton von WEBERN, and Egon Wellesz.

Schoenberg's earliest masterpieces, *Verklärte Nacht* (1899), *Pelleas und Melisande* (1905), and the *Gurrelieder* (1900–11) display the rich harmonic and melodic vocabulary of late ROMANTICISM. However, Schoenberg soon joined the expressionistic movement pervading all arts at that time and, in fact, produced a number of worthwhile expressionistic paintings. Having reached the limits of traditional tonality, he began to investigate new harmonic possibilities, using CHORDS built of fourths and irregular combinations. The late Romantics often introduced one DISSONANCE while resolving another; the next logical step was to dispense with this token resolution. Taking this step, Schoenberg developed a terse, atonal style with great rhythmic fluidity. The works of 1908–15 include two sets of Piano Pieces,

Op. 11 and 19, the song cycles *Das Buch der hängenden Gärten* (Op. 15) and *Pierrot Lunaire* (Op. 21), and the monodrama *Erwartung* (Op. 17). Bitter controversy attended the new technical features and unfamiliar TONE COLORS of these works—especially the *Sprechstimme* of *Pierrot Lunaire*, midway between a speaking and singing voice.

Shortly after the First World War, Schoenberg began to form his theories concerning TWELVE-TONE composition, marking the beginning of a new creative period. As he progressed from works such as the *Serenade*, Op. 24, and the *Piano Suite*, Op. 25, to the *Woodwind Quintet*, Op. 26, and the *Variations for Orchestra*, Op. 31, Schoenberg's handling of the serial technique became considerably freer. Among the masterpieces of his American period are his fourth *String Quartet*, Op. 37, the *Violin Concerto*, Op. 36, the *Piano Concerto*, Op. 42, and the *Ode to Napoleon*, Op. 41. His OPERA, *Moses und Aron*, remained unfinished.

Schottische: a mid-19th-century dance similar to a slow POLKA.

Schubert, Franz Peter: *b.* Lichtenthal, January 31, 1797; *d.* Vienna, November 19, 1828; one of the greatest lyrical masters of all time.

Schubert was taught violin by his father, a schoolmaster, and piano by his brother, Ignaz. He studied further with the local choirmaster, Holzer, and was admitted to the Imperial Choir in Vienna in 1808. The school connected with the choir provided Schubert with theory lessons under Wenzel Ruzicka and SALIERI. After leaving the choir in 1813, Schubert prepared for a teaching career and indeed taught at his father's school (1814–17). However, his preoccupation with composition was such that he felt impelled to quit. From 1817 to his death, he led essentially a Bohemian existence in Vienna. He was employed by Count Johann Esterházy as a music teacher for two summers (1818, 1824) spent in Hungary. Applications for various posts at Laibach, Vienna, and Hamburg were unsuccessful. Often in poverty, Schubert depended on the generosity of his friends and on the meager receipts from the sale of his works. His health began to weaken in 1823, leaving him easy prey to a fatal attack of typhus.

As a youth, Schubert was stirred by many influences: the BALLADES of ZUMSTEEG; the operas of ROSSINI; the SYMPHONIES, SONATAS, and quartets of HAYDN, MOZART, and the young BEETHOVEN.

He composed his first song when fourteen and reached full maturity in this realm with *Gretchen am Spinnrade,* written at age seventeen. Gifted with an amazingly fecund imagination, Schubert created over 600 songs during his brief lifetime, together with about 400 other compositions. Yet he worked critically, revising pieces such as *Die Forelle* and *Erlkönig* as many as four times. Deeply perceptive, Schubert was able to create both melodies of unsurpassed beauty and accompaniments that capture the poetic essence with remarkable economy of means. In this he was aided by an exceptionally keen instinct for harmonic coloration. Schubert was the first master of the Romantic LIED; many of his best-loved works have in effect become FOLK SONGS. Although some of his songs and instrumental works are highly dramatic, and although his 14 stage works (operas, SINGSPIELE, and melodramas) contain some beautiful music, Schubert did not have the theatrical sense of a WEBER or ROSSINI and never achieved success with his stage works.

Schubert's skill as a miniaturist is reflected in the instrumental realm by numerous collections of LÄNDLER and WALTZES, as well as by charming *Moments musicaux* and Impromptus of modest size. Comparatively few of his instrumental works pose difficult technical problems for the performer, and Schubert wrote only one CONCERTO, that for violin. (Since he played before friends rather than for a concert public, there were no economic reasons for Schubert to develop a technically brilliant idiom.) The lyric nature of his musical thought resulted in themes that are more expansive than those of Haydn, Mozart, and Beethoven, and often with richer harmonic coloration. These traits encouraged a looser treatment of development, and more frequent exceptions to the tonal norms of classical SONATA FORM. Schubert's early large instrumental works appear conservative when one considers that they were written after Beethoven had completed the masterpieces of his middle period; although Schubert revered Beethoven, he was sometimes disturbed by the Rabelasian element in the older master and based his work on more reserved CLASSICAL models. However, in the works of his last 8 years —which include the last 3 of his 15 STRING QUARTETS, his string quintet and piano quintet, the last 5 of his 15 piano sonatas, and the *Unfinished* and "Great" C Major Symphonies, as well as the MASSES in Ab and Eb (the last of 7)

—he achieved a new synthesis utilizing his individual melodic gifts, his ROMANTIC feeling for sonority, and traditional forms. Each of these works ranks among the finest of its kind.　　　　,

Schuman, William Howard: *b.* New York City, August 4, 1910. After training for a business career, Schuman abruptly changed to the study of music. He received degrees from Teachers College (Columbia University) and studied also under Roy Harris. He was a teacher at Sarah Lawrence College (1935–45) and president of the Juilliard School of Music (1945–62), before being appointed president of Lincoln Center in 1962. Schuman's works include seven SYMPHONIES, two CONCERTOS, orchestral OVERTURES, band music, four STRING QUARTETS and other CHAMBER MUSIC, choral works, songs, and piano pieces. His style features expansive melody, vigorous rhythms, and forms based on the extensive development of thematic material.

Schumann, Robert: *b.* Zwickau, June 8, 1810, *d.* Endenich, July 29, 1856; outstanding German ROMANTIC composer and critic.

Schumann's boyhood literary and musical interests were encouraged by his father, a writer and bookseller. He began to study law, but quit in 1830 to devote himself intensively to music; his teachers were Friedrich Wieck (piano) and Heinrich Dorn (theory). In an effort to improve his technique, Schumann experimented with a device that crippled the fourth finger of his right hand, ending his hopes of a career as a concert pianist. In 1833, Schumann, together with Wieck and some others, began plans for a music journal, the *Neue Zeitschrift für Musik,* which he served as sole editor (1835–44). Schumann married Clara Wieck—an outstanding pianist—in 1840, much against her father's wishes. In that year he received an honorary doctorate from the University of Jena. In 1843, MENDELSSOHN invited Schumann to join the faculty of the newly established Leipzig Conservatory. In the autumn of 1844, Schumann resigned both this post and his editorship and went to Dresden as a private teacher. He became the conductor of the *Liedertafel* in 1847 and organized the *Chorgesang-Verein* in 1848. In 1850, Schumann was appointed music director by the town of Düsseldorf. Mental illness, which had threatened previously, forced his resignation in 1853. His last two years were spent in an asylum.

Schumann's early works

consist entirely of piano compositions. His major works in this area include three SONATAS and the *Études symphoniques*. His numerous CHARACTER PIECES are more typical of his genius. He issued well over a dozen sets of these, among them *Papillons, Carnaval, Kinderszenen, Kreisleriana, Waldszenen*, and *Bunte Blätter*. The ability to capture a mood within a few measures enabled Schumann to become a worthy successor to SCHUBERT as a song composer. Beginning in 1840, he poured out many song cycles —including *Myrthen, Frauenliebe und Leben*, and *Dichterliebe*—and a few separate songs. Although Schumann displays a wonderful gift for vocal lyricism, the balance between voice and piano maintained by Schubert shifts subtly in favor of the piano; much care is lavished on the details of the accompaniment.

In the realm of orchestral music Schumann contributed four SYMPHONIES, a piano CONCERTO, violin concerto, and cello concerto, as well as a number of miscellaneous works. By virtue of their melodic and harmonic inspiration these are among the finer Romantic works of their kind even though Schumann does not excel in the handling of FORM or ORCHESTRATION. Schumann's CHAMBER MUSIC, which includes three STRING QUARTETS, a piano quintet, a piano quartet, and three piano trios, is surpassed among Romantic works only by the masterpieces of BRAHMS. One of the least-known segments of Schumann's output is that comprised of choral works, both with and without ACCOMPANIMENT. Among these, *Paradise and the Peri* is perhaps the most outstanding. Schumann's sole OPERA, *Genoveva*, was unsuccessful, though apparently deserving of a better fate. In the use of continuous scenes and recurrent motives, Schumann foreshadowed the music drama of WAGNER.

As a critic, Schumann exerted a profound influence on the contemporary scene. He was the first to write about the genius of CHOPIN and Brahms; he recognized the greatness of BACH and of BEETHOVEN's last works; he fought vigorously against the empty posturing of lesser men.

Schütz, Heinrich: *b.* Köstritz, October 8, 1585; *d.* Dresden, November 6, 1672; the greatest of early BAROQUE German composers.

Trained as a choirboy at Cassel, Schütz studied with Giovanni GABRIELI in Venice from 1609 to 1612. As a mature master he returned (in 1628) to work with MONTEVERDI. After service as court organist at Cassel, Schütz became music director to the elector of Saxony in 1617. He held this Dresden post for the remainder of his life, though spending long periods in Copenhagen during the Thirty Years' War.

MOTETS, vocal pieces in monodic style, PASSIONS, and ORATORIOS form the bulk of Schütz's output. He also wrote a collection of MADRIGALS, as well as a BALLET and OPERA (both lost), but no independent instrumental music. His art represents the fusion of Italian training and German heritage. Polychoral writing, chromaticism, and pictorial representation of key words are Italianate traits appearing in the *Psalmen Davids* (1619), *Cantiones Sacrae* (1625), and *Symphoniae Sacrae* (1629, 1647, 1650). Italianate too is the dramatic interpretation of sacred texts rather than their symbolic representation by means of CHORALE melodies. Germanic is his mastery of POLYPHONY and the avoidance of a too-facile reliance on FIGURED BASS. Even when figured bass is used prominently, as in the *Kleine geistliche Konzerte* (1636, 1639), there is polyphonic interplay between the bass line and the vocal melody. In later life, for his Passions, Schütz returned to an A CAPPELLA style with unaccompanied vocal

RECITATIVE. His *Sieben Worte am Kreuz* (*c*.1645) and *Historia von der Geburth Gottes* (1664) are among his greatest masterpieces.

Scordatura (I): an abnormal tuning of a stringed instrument, employed either to facilitate unusual technical problems, to obtain different TONE COLOR, or to deepen slightly the range of the instrument. CHORDS that might be impossible or very difficult to play under normal tuning may be made convenient by means of scordatura.

Score: NOTATION that gives in proper vertical alignment a number of different vocal or instrumental parts meant to be performed simultaneously. A score thus presents the full musical fabric of a choral, chamber, or orchestral work. (Although keyboard music is in the broad sense notated in score, the term is not commonly used in this connection.) The various instrumentalists normally perform from individual parts, while the score is employed by conductors and by students or scholars studying the work. Choral singers usually perform from scores.

In a score each different INSTRUMENT or VOICE is generally indicated on a separate staff, though two parts intended for the same variety of instrument or voice may be coupled on a single staff. The visual arrangement reflects a loose classification of performing range from high to low. In an orchestral score the arrangement is somewhat more complex because the instruments are first grouped according to family and then classified according to range within the proper family. The WOODWINDS are placed on top, followed by the BRASS and PERCUSSION, while the STRINGS appear at the bottom. Additional forces—harp, piano, voices, or soloists—are inserted between the percussion and string parts. The first page of a small orchestral score provides a staff for each instrument used during the piece, but later pages use staves only for those instruments playing at the given moment.

Frequently a score may be reduced to two staves to permit performance on the piano. Such notation is termed a *piano score* or *piano reduction*. *Vocal score* normally indicates music in which the vocal parts are notated on individual staves while the instrumental parts are given in reduction so that they may be performed on the piano for rehearsal purposes. Naturally, in arranging an orchestral work for piano, it is often necessary to give only the most important lines, omitting less essential details.

Early medieval compositions were notated in score fashion. However, in the later Middle Ages, choirbook notation was adopted for final copies, each part being notated on a different section of a pair of facing pages or— less frequently—of a single page. This form of notation for polyphonic music was employed almost exclusively until the end of the 15th century, and persisted throughout the 16th century. During the latter century it became increasingly common to notate the individual parts in separate part books. Score writing again became accepted practice at the end of the 16th century, and has remained so since.

Scoring: *see* ORCHESTRATION.
Scotch snap: *see* LOMBARDIC RHYTHM.
Scriabin, Alexander Nikolayevich: *b.* Moscow, January 6, 1872; *d.* Moscow, April 27, 1915. Scriabin completed his training at the Moscow Conservatory. He was a competent pianist and toured frequently, performing particularly his own works. These took the music of CHOPIN, LISZT, and WAGNER as a point of departure rather than the nationalistic music of other Russian composers. Scriabin quickly became absorbed in

harmonic experiments which he related to his mystical religious speculations. He created a "mystic chord" of seven notes arranged in fourths (an augmented, diminished, augmented, and three perfect fourths, in that order). His experimentation climaxed in his last work, *Prometheus, or The Poem of Fire,* which attempted a synthesis of the arts through the use of a color organ, which was to project changing colors on a screen. (This color organ was used in only one performance.) Scriabin's work includes several sets of piano PRELUDES, SONATAS, SYMPHONIC POEMS, two SYMPHONIES, and a piano CONCERTO.

Second: any INTERVAL written by means of consecutive alphabet letters (e.g., *c♯-d, c-d, c-d♯*). There are two customary sizes of second, major (synonyms: whole tone, whole step) and minor (synonym: half step). The first two notes of *Frère Jacques* form a major second, the first two of the *Londonderry Air,* a minor second.

Segno (I): a sign, 𝄋 , used to mark the beginning or end of a section to be repeated.

Segue (I): (1) a direction to continue from one MOVEMENT to the next without pause (synonym: *Attacca*); (2) a direction to continue a pattern that is written out in full one or more times but which is abbreviated in subsequent presentations.

Seguidilla: a dance of southern Spain in fast triple METER, more rapid than the somewhat similar BOLERO.

Semibreve: a whole note.

Semiquaver: a sixteenth note.

Semitone: a half STEP.

Sempre (I): always.

Senfl, Ludwig: *b.* Zürich, *c.*1490; *d.* Munich, *c.*1543. A pupil of ISAAC, Senfl was a singer at the court of Maximilian I and, in 1517, succeeded Isaac as chamber composer. In 1523 Senfl began service with the Bavarian court chapel at Munich, apparently remaining there until his death. A highly gifted and versatile composer, Senfl wrote polyphonic LIEDER, MASSES, MOTETS, MAGNIFICATS, and settings of Lutheran CHORALES.

Sennet: a direction in Elizabethan plays calling for the interpolation of instrumental music, often in the nature of a fanfare.

Senza (I): without.

Septet, Septuor (F): a work for seven INSTRUMENTS or VOICES.

Septuplet, Septimole, Septolet (F): a group of seven equal values to be performed in the time normally allowed to either four or six.

Sequence: (1) the repetition of a musical pattern within the same VOICE or voices at either a higher or lower PITCH level. Often multiple repetition is involved; indeed some restrict the use of the term to instances in which the repeated pattern appears three or more times. The most obvious sequences are those in which the entire musical complex—MELODY, RHYTHM, and COUNTERPOINT or HARMONY —is duplicated at a different pitch, quite frequently a second lower or higher than the preceding statement. If each INTERVAL of the original statement is preserved exactly in the subsequent statements, flats or sharps not part of the original key will be introduced and the sequence will result in change of key. Such sequences are termed *real* or *modulatory*. Unimaginative real sequences are often referred to by the disparaging term *rosalia*. If the composer wishes to remain in the same key while using a sequence, he will avoid the introduction of new flats and sharps, thus changing certain intervals in quality (e.g., from major to minor, or vice versa) in successive statements. Such a sequence is termed *tonal* or *diatonic*. The composer is not bound to duplicate the entire musical complex in sequential construction. He may limit himself to the duplication of a single melodic-rhythmic

pattern; purely rhythmic or harmonic sequences are also possible.

(2) A MEDIEVAL CHANT; the original function of a work of this genre was that of a concluding trope to an ALLELUIA. Of the enormous repertory of sequences, all but *Victimae paschali laudes, Veni sancte spiritus, Lauda Sion,* and *Dies irae* were outlawed from Catholic ritual by the Council of Trent; the *Stabat Mater* was readmitted in 1727.

Serenade: (1) a work in several MOVEMENTS, normally of light character, written for instrumental ENSEMBLE, and intended for evening entertainment. Many serenades written for wind instruments were meant for outdoor use. The genre originated in the mid-18th century and drew upon elements of both the SUITE (i.e., MINUETS and MARCHES) and the SYMPHONY (movements in SONATA FORM). The serenade shares many features of the DIVERTIMENTO and CASSATION. (2) A song offered as a token of love.

Serenata (I): (1) SERENADE; (2) a CANTATA or short OPERA of the early 18th century, written to honor a patron.

Series (Serial music): *see* TWELVE-TONE MUSIC.

Sermisy, Claudin de: *b.* *c.*1495; *d.* Paris, September

13, 1562. A choirboy at the Sainte-Chapelle, Sermisy became a singer in the Royal Chapel by 1515. He was appointed assistant director of that group before 1532. Sermisy is best known for his CHANSONS, which are in a mainly syllabic and chordal style, using vivacious rhythms. He composed also a number of MASSES and MOTETS, together with one PASSION.

Serpent: an obsolete, curved, wooden instrument employing a BRASS INSTRUMENT mouthpiece.

Service: a polyphonic setting of the Anglican versions of the canticles (forming part of the Morning and Evening Prayer) and of certain movements of the MASS ORDINARY (forming part of the Communion Service). The texts of these works are in English even though they retain as titles the Latin incipits of their counterparts in the Catholic rite. The stylistic distinction among 16th-century Services between simple, rather chordal settings and more elaborate ones in polyphonic or antiphonal style is mirrored by the terms *Short* and *Great Service,* respectively. A *Full Service,* on the other hand, is one that provides music for both Morning and Evening Prayer as well as for Communion. The finest Services were written dur-

ing the late 16th and 17th centuries, including works by TALLIS and BYRD. Later Services were composed by PURCELL, ATTWOOD, S. WESLEY, and SULLIVAN, among others.

Sessions, Roger: *b.* Brooklyn, N.Y., December 28, 1896. After graduating from Harvard and Yale Universities, Sessions completed his studies under Ernest BLOCH. A series of fellowships enabled him to spend much of 1926–33 in Florence, Rome, and Berlin. Over the decades he has proved one of the most influential American teachers of composition. He believes in both the self-sufficiency and the expressiveness of musical ideas. His style leans toward an atonal, chromatic, and contrapuntal idiom. Sessions' works include five SYMPHONIES, two CONCERTOS, two STRING QUARTETS, SONATAS, a MASS, the OPERA *Montezuma,* and other stage music. He has also written books on music.

Sestetto (I): SEXTET.

Set: (1) the succession of PITCHES used to provide the structural basis of a TWELVE-TONE composition; (2) an ORGAN rank.

Settimino (I): SEPTET.

Seventh: any INTERVAL written by skipping five alphabet letters (e.g., *a♯-g, a-g, a-g♯*). Humming the first and third notes of *Over the Rainbow* or *Bali Hai* will illustrate the sound of a major seventh.

Seventh chords: a family of CHORDS combining a *triad* with a note a seventh above the root. The main varieties are: (1) dominant seventh, a major triad with a minor seventh above the root; (2) major seventh, a major triad with a major seventh above the root; (3) minor seventh, a minor triad with a minor seventh above the root; (4) half-diminished seventh, a diminished triad with a minor seventh above the root; (5) diminished seventh, a diminished triad with a diminished seventh above the root. These chords are important in chromatic HARMONY and often figure prominently in MODU-LATION.

Sextet: a work for six INSTRU-MENTS or VOICES.

Sextuor (F): SEXTET.

Sextuplet, Sextolet (F): a group of six equal values to be performed in the time normally allowed to four.

Sforzando (I), **Sforzato** (I): a strong ACCENT.

Shake: TRILL.

Shanty: a work song of English and American sailors.

Shape notes: a system of NO-TATION employing different shapes (triangle, diamond, rectangle, oval) for note heads in order to make note names more readily recognizable and sight-singing simpler. These note forms, known also as *buckwheat notes,* were used in American hymn books of the 19th century.

Sharp: (1) the sign ♯, which calls for a PITCH a half step higher than that represented by an alphabet letter alone (e.g., *a♯* is a half step higher than *a*); (2) the raised pitch designated by means of the ♯; (3) an out-of-tune pitch an indeterminate distance higher than required, caused either by improper tuning or faulty performance.

Shawm: one of a group of early double-reed WOODWIND instruments, predecessors of the oboe.

Shofar: an ancient Jewish instrument made of a ram's horn, used in the ritual celebration of the New Year.

Short octave: the lowest OC-TAVE of certain 16th- and

Seventh chords

Major   Dominant   Minor   Half-   Diminished
Diminished

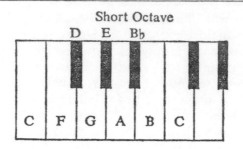

Short Octave

17th-century KEYBOARD instruments, which omitted the PITCHES for sharps and flats other than B♭ and disposed of the keys for C, D, and E in the unusual fashion indicated above.

Shostakovich, Dmitri Dmitriyevich: *b.* St. Petersburg, September 25, 1906. Shostakovich was trained at the St. Petersburg Conservatory under GLAZUNOV and STEINBERG. His *First Symphony* brought him early fame in 1926. The twelve SYMPHONIES that followed are of uneven quality; the Fifth and Seventh are the best known. Despite the fact that several symphonies are dedicated to important events in Soviet history, Shostakovich came under severe censure at various times in his career, in 1930, 1936 and in 1948. His OPERA, *Lady Macbeth of Mzensk,* was attacked as the negation of the principles of Soviet art. Shostakovich extends basically the paths of late ROMANTICISM; MAHLER and FRANCK deeply influenced his style. In addition to his symphonies, he has written ten STRING QUARTETS, CONCERTOS, piano music, songs, choral pieces, and BALLETS.

Si: the note B.

Sibelius, Jean: *b.* Tavastehus, December 8, 1865; *d.* Järvenpää, September 22, 1957. The greatest Finnish composer and one of the last ROMANTIC symphonists, Sibelius was trained at the Helsinki Conservatory. A government grant permitted him to study further in Berlin and in Vienna (under Fuchs and GOLDMARK). His first important works were a series of TONE POEMS on Finnish subjects, including *Finlandia* and *The Swan of Tuonela.* Other major compositions include seven SYMPHONIES and a violin CONCERTO. Sibelius also wrote an OPERA, incidental music, a variety of CHAMBER and KEYBOARD MUSIC, songs, and choral works. His creative activity ceased after 1929.

Siciliano (I): an instrumental

or vocal piece or movement in slow compound duple ME-TER (6/8 or 12/8), with dotted RHYTHM, similar to the PASTORALE. The genre derived from a Sicilian dance type and was cultivated primarily during the 17th and 18th centuries.

Sight reading (Sight singing): the ability to play or sing a piece not previously performed by the musician in question. A well-trained musician is expected to read well enough at first sight to produce a reasonable impression of a work of average difficulty. This skill demands practice—i.e., the habitual perusal of new repertory—a good rhythmic sense, and an awareness of a wide variety of musical idioms. (This awareness permits the ready recognition of standard melodic and harmonic formulae, enabling the performer to read at a glance a comparatively large number of notes.) The instinctive recognition of all INTERVALS, both common and rare, is basic to all sight reading. Beyond this, the problems posed by the voice and by each of the different instruments vary. The singer must instantly correlate a recognition of interval with a foreknowledge of the physical reaction required of the vocal chords to produce the desired interval. The keyboard artist requires a tactile sense of interval distance that must be especially keen since he normally must play several notes at once and these may involve progressions that vary simultaneously in distance, direction, or both. The violinist and other string players require also a tactile sense of interval distance as well as an awareness of the proper moment to shift position or to change from one string to another. *See also* SOLMIZA-TION.

Signature: *see* KEY SIGNATURE or TIME SIGNATURE.

Simile (I): similarly; this direction indicates that the performer is to continue the mode of performance prescribed for the measures immediately preceding; this may involve the continuation of patterns of PHRASING, PEDAL-ING, ARPEGGIATING, BOWING, etc., that are specified initially by means of appropriate symbols, these being discontinued after the pattern has been made clear.

Sin' al fine (I); **Sin' al segno** (I): until the end; until the sign.

Sinfonia (I): (1) SYMPHONY. (2) In the 17th and 18th centuries, an introductory MOVE-MENT or set of movements for orchestra; such music might preface a SUITE, CAN-TATA, or Italian OPERA. (3) The title of the introductory movement of BACH's second *Partita* (for harpsichord) and of a set of fifteen keyboard works that are known more familiarly as *Three-Part Inventions.* (4) As used sometimes by early 18th-century composers (e.g., MARTINI), a synonym for CONCERTO.

Sinfonia concertante (I): a work sharing features of the SYMPHONY and CONCERTO; usually a small group of solo instruments is featured (but sometimes only one). The most famous of these works is by MOZART.

Sinfonietta (I): a short SYMPHONY.

Sinfonische Dichtung (G): SYMPHONIC POEM.

Singspiel (G): a German comic OPERA of the 18th or early 19th centuries, employing spoken dialogue. The genre derived from the English ballad opera, and the musical style of most early examples was relatively simple. The two finest, most highly developed of such works are MOZART's *Abduction from the Seraglio* and *Magic Flute.*

Sinistra (I): left hand.

Sistema (I): staff.

Sistrum: an ancient Egyptian rattle, employing small metal jingles strung on rods within a pear-shaped frame.

Six, Les (F): "the Six," a name coined by H. Collet to denote a group of six French composers—Arthur HONEG-

GER, Darius MILHAUD, François POULENC, Georges Auric, Germaine Tailleferre, and Louis Durey—active after World War I and influenced by the ideas of Erik SATIE.

Six-four chord: the second inversion of a TRIAD (*see* CHORD).

Sixteenth note, sixteenth rest:

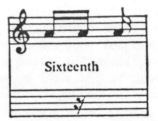

Sixteenth

Sixth: any INTERVAL written by skipping four alphabet letters (e.g., $b\sharp$-g, b-g, b-$g\sharp$, bb-$g\sharp$). Humming the first two notes of *My Bonnie Lies Over the Ocean* will recall the sound of a major sixth; the first and third notes of BEETHOVEN's *Moonlight Sonata* form a minor sixth.

Sixth chords: a group of CHORDS, some unrelated, which may be classed as follows: (1) First INVERSIONS of TRIADS. The Neapolitan sixth is the first inversion of a major triad based on the lowered second degree of the scale; it is sometimes described as a major $_3^6$ chord whose lowest note is the fourth degree of the scale. (2) Added sixth chords. These consist of major or minor triads combined with a major sixth above the root. The added sixth originated as a variant of the subdominant chord when used in a plagal cadence. This limitation is no longer observed. The chord often appears at the end of arrangements of popular songs. (3) Augmented sixth chords. These employ the interval of an augmented sixth together with different internal configurations. The simplest of these consists of a root, major third, and augmented sixth; it is known variously as an *augmented sixth*, an *augmented six-three*, and an *Italian sixth*. An *augmented six-five-three* (= augmented six-five), or *German sixth*, consists of a major triad combined with an augmented sixth above the root; its sound is the same as that of a dominant seventh chord, its function different. There is also an *augmented six-four-three* (= augmented six-four), known as a *French sixth*. The augmented sixth in these chords is treated as a DIS-SONANCE and normally resolves outward.

Slaatt, Slaater: a Norwegian folk composition, usually in the character of a march.

Slide: (1) the movable section of a trombone or slide trumpet. A comparatively gross movement of the slide will produce a distinct alteration of PITCH; a very tiny back-and-forth movement will produce a VIBRATO. (2) A tuning device on BRASS IN-STRUMENTS, permitting fine adjustments of pitch. (3) In string playing, the shifting of the hand along a string, producing a change of position and a slight *portamento* (3) A 17th- and 18th-century ORNAMENT consisting of a pair of notes leading upward quickly and in stepwise fashion to the main note.

Slur: a horizontal arc placed above or below a group of notes to call for LEGATO performance, no tone ceasing before the beginning of the next. (Sometimes a slur may indicate a group of notes comprising a musical thought or a meaningful subsection thereof.) A slur combined with dots above or below the individual notes indicates

Sixth chords

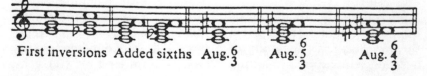

First inversions Added sixths Aug. $\frac{6}{3}$ Aug. $\frac{6}{5}$ Aug. $\frac{6}{4}$

PORTATO, i.e., semi-detached performance.

Smetana, Bedřich: *b.* Leitomischl, March 2, 1824; *d.* Prague, May 12, 1884. Smetana, the first great Czech nationalistic composer, completed his training in Prague under Josef Proksch. He became a concert pianist and teacher, and, in 1856, conductor at Göteborg (Sweden). He resigned this post and returned to Prague in 1861, attracted by the foundation of a national opera there. He wrote nine OPERAS (the last incomplete) for this theater, of which the second, *The Bartered Bride*, and *Libussa* are his masterpieces. Though afflicted by deafness in 1874, Smetana continued to compose, producing, among other works, his STRING QUARTET, *From My Life*, and his cycle of SYMPHONIC POEMS, *My Country* (*Má Vlast*). The most famous of the latter is *The Moldau*. Smetana's output includes also three early symphonic poems, songs and choruses, piano music, and a few CHAMBER works. Although he rarely drew upon actual FOLK tunes, much of his music is permeated by their spirit.

Smorzando (I): dying away.

Soggetto (I): SUBJECT; often the more specific meaning of a brief, slow-moving FUGUE subject is intended. A *soggetto cavato* is a RENAISSANCE subject constructed by equating the vowels of a name or a group of words with notes having corresponding vowels following the system of SOLMIZATION. For example, from the name *Hercules, dux Ferrariae* (Hercules, duke of Ferrara), Josquin constructed a subject proceeding *re, ut, re, ut, re, fa, mi, re* (d, c, d, c, d, f, e, d), which he used as the basis for a MASS.

Sol: either the fifth note of the SCALE or the note G.

Soler, Antonio: *b.* Olot, December 3, 1729; *d.* Monastery of the Escorial, December 20, 1783. Music director and organist at the monastery of the Escorial, Soler was a pupil of D. SCARLATTI. He was a prolific composer, writing a large quantity and variety of church music, CHAMBER MUSIC, CONCERTOS for two organs, songs for stage works, and miscellaneous works for organ and harpsichord. His many harpsichord SONATAS, while revealing the influence of his teacher, show a highly original style.

Sol-fa (Tonic Sol-fa): *see* SOLMIZATION.

Solfeggio (I), **Solfège** (F): (1) a method of teaching SIGHT SINGING evolved from SOLMIZATION; (2) an exercise designed or adapted for instruction under (1); (3) general instruction in musicianship.

Solmization: a method for simplifying SIGHT SINGING developed by Guido d'Arezzo in the early 11th century. Employing a hymn to St. John the Baptist in which the first note of each of the first six lines forms part of a musical acrostic that rises stepwise from *c-a*, Guido instructed that the pupil associate the syllables set by these notes—i.e., *ut, re, mi, fa, sol*, and *la* —with their relative pitch position in this chant. In Guido's system, this six-note group (HEXACHORD) could be based on the written notes *c, f,* or *g*. By changing from one of these hexachords to another, it was possible to use solmization syllables for CHANTS of extended range; the act of changing from one hexachord to another is known as mutation. Only one half step exists in Guido's hexachord, that between the syllables *mi* and *fa*. Thus any half step had to be represented by these two syllables. As MEDIEVAL and RENAISSANCE composers began using ACCIDENTALS other than *bb* (the only accidental in Guido's system), hexachords on degrees other than *c, f,* and *g* were employed in solmization. In certain tours de force of the late Renaissance, hexachords were formed on every degree of the chromatic OCTAVE. In the system of SOLFEGGIO that evolved from solmization, the guttural syllable *ut*, unconducive to good vocal tone, is normally replaced by *do*, and the system is expanded by the addition of the syllable *si* (or, later, *ti*), representing the seventh degree of the major SCALE. There are two main systems of solfeggio. In that employed in France and Italy, the syllable *do* represents the note *c*, regardless of the tonal structure of the work. In the English and American system (Tonic SOL-FA), the syllable *do* represents the first degree of the scale, whatever note that may be. The two systems are referred to respectively by the terms fixed *do* and movable *do*.

Solo: (1) a work for a single performer or for a principal performer and ACCOMPANIMENT; (2) a passage in an ENSEMBLE, orchestral, or choral work that features a single performer, placing the others in supporting roles.

Solovox: an electronic KEYBOARD instrument with a range of three octaves. The instrument is normally mounted parallel to the right-hand portion of a piano keyboard and is used to provide a variety of TONE COLORS for the MELODY, the ACCOMPANIMENT being played on the piano.

Sonata (I): a term designating a number of different instrumental forms from the late 15th century to the present. The word is derived from the Italian *suonare*, to sound, and was first used in contradistinction to CANTATA, from *cantare*, to sing.

(1) The term usually refers to a CLASSICAL, ROMANTIC, or MODERN work, intended for one or two instruments and generally consisting of three or four large sections called MOVEMENTS. The same kind of work, written for three instruments, is called a trio; for four instruments, a quartet; for five instruments, a quintet; and so forth. A SYMPHONY is the same form written for ORCHESTRA, and so is a CONCERTO, which is conceived for one or more SOLO instruments and orchestra. The main segment of the sonata repertoire in current use is constituted of works by HAYDN, MOZART, BEETHOVEN, and SCHUBERT. The genre is somewhat less prominent in the works of later composers, although great examples have been contributed by SCHUMANN, MENDELSSOHN, LISZT, and BRAHMS, among others.

In most three- and four-movement sonatas, the first and last movements of a sonata are fast and energetic. SONATA FORM may be employed for both, or the last may be a RONDO. The second movement is usually slow and is often in TERNARY FORM. In four-movement sonatas, a MINUET or SCHERZO is generally employed between the slow movement and the finale. However, the history of the form is one of continual change; neither the number of movements nor their make-up remained constant. Beethoven wrote several magnificent two-movement sonatas, while the Liszt Piano Sonata is in a single movement. On the other hand, Brahms' Third Piano Sonata contains five movements. Beethoven's *Moonlight Sonata* consists of three movements with the TEMPO progression, slow, medium, fast. In several sonatas the first movement is a THEME and VARIATIONS. Normally the movements are self-contained units separated by pauses. In many instances, however, the composer may indicate that one movement is to flow into the next without pause. Usually the only readily describable interrelationship between movements is one of key. However, late Romantic composers such as FRANCK wrote sonatas and symphonies employing deliberate thematic interrelationships between movements. The term for such technique is *cyclical* (cyclic).

(2) The term is applied to a repertoire of some 555 harpsichord pieces by Domenico SCARLATTI, both in surviving manuscript copies and in present usage. (In an early selection, published during Scarlatti's lifetime, the pieces were entitled *Essercizi,* Exercises.) The pieces consist of single movements, often in BINARY FORM, that exploit brilliantly the resources of the harpsichord. Many of the later ones were intended to be performed in groups of two or three.

(3) A *trio sonata* is a Baroque work written for two solo instruments and CONTINUO. During this period, the term *solo sonata,* normally designated a work for a solo instrument and continuo. (Examples of sonatas for one instrument, such as the Bach Sonatas for Solo Violin, were then comparatively rare.) Each type may be classified according to its form. A *sonata da camera* (chamber sonata) consists of a PRELUDE (SINFONIA) followed by a series of dance movements; in other words, it is similar to a SUITE. A *sonata da chiesa* (church sonata), on the other hand, normally consists of four movements in a slow-fast-slow-fast sequence. Imitative style is frequent in the fast movements.

(4) In the RENAISSANCE, the term occurs in a literary source as early as 1486. The oldest surviving use as a specific title occurs in a lute book of 1561; there it designates a pair of dances based on related material. Later the term was approximately synonymous with CANZONA, an imitative instrumental form derived from the French CHANSON.

Sonata form (Sonata allegro): a form comprising two asymmetrical sections, the first consisting of an exposition, the second of a development and a recapitulation. (Some prefer to classify the form as *ternary;* while such practice describes accurately certain 19th-century movements, it ignores the origin of the form and conveys a distorted impression of the central portion of the form's evolution.) This form is one of the most important of the CLASSICAL and ROMANTIC forms (*see* SONATA). Since it may be employed in both slow and quick movements, the term *Sonata allegro* is not always apt.

The exposition is normally built around two main key areas, the first section being in the TONIC, the second in the DOMINANT (or, if the MOVEMENT is in minor, the relative major). In some movements three key areas may be used. Usually the thematic materials in each key are individual. However, there are also examples (e.g., by HAYDN) in which the opening theme is the main basis of both key areas; contrasting material may be of very minor import or lacking. If the TEMPO is rapid, the first theme group is likely to be vigorous, the second, lyrical. A theme may be conceived as an integral whole or as a logical grouping of two or more ideas. The transition passage between the two main areas is called a *bridge*. Large movements in sonata form may contain an introduction or a postlude to the exposition, the latter being termed a CODETTA.

The nature of the development section is quite variable. In early examples of sonata form, the section is apt to be quite brief and may consist of little more than a restatement on the dominant of the material that opens the movement. Gradually the section increased in importance. It came to equal and even surpass the exposition and the recapitulation in length. Since in many late Classical and Romantic works the development section provided not only tonal contrast but also an intensification of motivic pace through the dissection and regrouping of thematic materials, the section came to constitute a dramatic high-

point of the form. In other works, including some by SCHUBERT, the development became more of a leisurely and colorful digression.

The recapitulation is basically a repetition of the exposition with one important difference: the second theme group is in the tonic key. Most sonata forms end with a coda. Originally this section was quite short, but in the works of BEETHOVEN and later composers, it was greatly expanded, often functioning as a second development and bringing the work to a final dramatic climax.

Sonata form evolved as an expansion of rounded BINARY FORM. In early sonatas, CHAMBER WORKS, and SYMPHONIES of small dimensions, each of the two basic divisions was repeated. In a later stage, only the exposition was repeated, and then composers dropped even this repetition. In general concert practice, indicated repetitions are often ignored.

Sonatina (I), **Sonatine** (F): a short SONATA in one, two or three MOVEMENTS, usually without technical difficulty.

Song: in the broadest sense, a vocal work or a work in vocal style. This extremely vague form of usage may be made somewhat more precise by stripping away the less frequent connotations of the word. Apart from entirely incorrect usage, the word song is rarely used as a simile to denote instrumental music in vocal style. Furthermore, song is seldom used to denote vocal works for choral performance. Next, liturgical CHANT is normally excluded from among the connotations of song. A more restricted definition of song would thus be a setting of a nonliturgical poem for one or more solo VOICES, either accompanied or not. Within the vast repertoire thus comprised, it is possible to distinguish between FOLK SONG and ART SONG. Often the various groups that are included within the category of art song are designated by terms that possess more specific meanings indicative of language (LIED, CHANSON, MÉLODIE, CANZONETTA, etc.), form (RONDEAU, BALLADE, ARIA DA CAPO, etc.), or subject matter (AUBADE, LAUDA, etc.). In a given context the word song may be used as a variant of a more precise term and thus momentarily acquire more precise meaning.

The earliest surviving songs are a handful of Greek works, mostly fragmentary, from later antiquity and the Christian era. The general melodic outlines are ascertainable, but there is still disagreement regarding details of these outlines and rhythm. Settings of CLASSICAL and early MEDIEVAL Latin poetry (including a lament on the death of Charlemagne and works by Goliards) survive in staffless NEUMES which cannot be deciphered. The songs of the troubadours and trouvères of the 11th to 13th centuries constitute the earliest sizable repertoire of secular song transcribable. Except for a few late examples, these songs are notated as unaccompanied melodies, mostly without indication of RHYTHM. Verbal and pictorial evidence indicates that instrumental ACCOMPANIMENT was provided frequently, but we do not know whether the instrumentalist played more than a PRELUDE or POSTLUDE, and, if so, whether he merely doubled the vocal line or provided a simple harmonic foundation. While the texts deal principally with stereotyped themes of courtly love, one segment comprises devotional songs to the Virgin. Both secular and sacred forms were cultivated by the slightly later MINNESINGERS, while the Spanish *cantigas* and the Italian *laude* are entirely devotional. It is not customary to treat other musical genres of the Early and High Middle Ages under the heading song, although this is not necessarily a technical differentiation. HYMNS, CONDUCTI (for one or more voice-parts), MOTETS, etc., would fit under this heading; indeed some late-13th-century motets incorporate trouvère chansons into their structure.

Adam de la HALLE (d. 1287) is among the earliest composers of polyphonic song, providing charming settings of brief refrain forms, but this genre does not achieve major importance until the advent of MACHAUT in the 14th century. During this century polyphonic song became the norm (although monophonic song did not die out) and works of great charm and considerable intricacy were created in both France—ballades, rondeaux, and VIRELAIS—and Italy—BALLATE, CACCE, and MADRIGALS. Only rarely did medieval or RENAISSANCE composers specify the media for their compositions; most works of the 13th to 16th centuries may be performed by a wide number of vocal and instrumental combinations. Melodic lines of angular, disjunct style and those of subsidiary interest suggest instrumental rather than vocal performance. On this basis we conclude that much 14th-century song was normally performed by one or two SOLO singers, accompanied by one or more instru-

ments. This means of performance continued through the 15th and 16th centuries, although the rapid growth of IMITATION in the mid-15th century and the resultant stylistic integration of the various parts led to the composition of polyphonic songs suitable for performance by vocal soloists alone. Such performance is suitable also for many 16th-century songs of more harmonic idiom. During this century the French chanson and the Italian madrigal provided the main channels for secular artistic endeavor, but there was a wealth of other song in Spain, England, the Netherlands, and Germany, as well as numerous popular genres, including the FROTTOLA of the early decades, the *villanella, villanesca, air de cour*, etc. The earliest repertoire specifically intended (rather than transcribed) for voice and instrument—vihuela or lute—was created during the 16th century.

A momentous stylistic change occurred at the end of the 16th century with the development of the declamatory style of MONODY and the concomitant use of FIGURED BASS. (*See* BAROQUE music.) The new style of RECITATIVE was used for some late madrigals and formed the basis for new developments in CAN-

TATAS and OPERAS. This style was adopted and transformed by German composers, who made numerous contributions to song literature in the early 17th century. Although a large number of songs of simple style were written during the 17th and 18th centuries, the more consequential means of expression for major composers was normally furnished by composite forms, such as opera. (Toward the end of this period, several composers—including MOZART and BEETHOVEN—wrote separate arias for concert purposes.) While both Mozart and Beethoven wrote some fine songs for voice and piano, the songs of SCHUBERT, written during the second and third decades of the 19th century, mark both the beginning of intense interest in the song on the part of ROMANTIC composers and a high point of the song repertoire. The impetus provided by Schubert was carried forward in Germany and Austria by SCHUMANN, BRAHMS, WOLF, MAHLER, and R. STRAUSS and spread through Europe in works by DUPARC, FAURÉ, DEBUSSY, MUSSORGSKY, and others. Romantic song is a highly personal art, the composer seeking to reveal the essence of the poetry not merely through the expressive beauty of the vocal line, but also through the meaningful background provided by the piano part. Given the nature of the present concert repertoire, reference to art song may sometimes denote primarily the repertoire of 19th- and early 20th-century song. Song continued to provide an important medium for both conservative and progressive composers of the 20th century. In the works of SCHOENBERG, WEBERN, and others influenced by them, the predominantly smooth, flowing vocal style associated with traditional song literature was discarded in favor of a more disjunct style with distended leaps and irregular rhythms.

Song cycle: a set of songs by one composer, often based on poems by one poet. Customarily a song cycle is conceived as a unit, although the performance of individual songs from a cycle is by no means rare. BEETHOVEN's *An die ferne Geliebte* is the earliest song cycle; SCHUBERT's *Die schöne Müllerin* and *Winterreise* and SCHUMANN's *Dichterliebe* and *Frauenliebe und Leben* are other outstanding examples of the genre.

Song form: a vague term for small forms—both instrumental and vocal—in two or three sections. The terms *binary* (or *two-part*) *song form* and *ternary* (or *three-part*) *song* *form* are more specific, but their use is nevertheless discouraged because there is little ground to associate such structures purely with vocal literature or to postulate a vocal derivation for instrumental works in small binary and ternary forms.

Sopra (I): above; the term is used as a KEYBOARD direction to indicate the positioning or passing of one hand above the other.

Sopranino: a designation for the smallest and highest of a family of instruments.

Soprano: (1) a female VOICE of high range, or a boy's voice of identical range; (2) a variety of CLEF; (3) the highest or next highest of a family of instruments (e.g., soprano saxophone); (4) the highest voice-part of a composition (instrumental or vocal).

Sordino (I): (1) MUTE; *con sordino, senza sordino,* with, without the mute, respectively; (2) the felt dampers of the piano; *senza sordini,* with the dampers raised (i.e., by means of the right-hand pedal).

Sordun: a member of a small family of obsolete double-reed WOODWIND instruments of comparatively low range (i.e., predecessors of the BASSOON).

Sostenuto (I): sustained, oftentimes majestic or ponderous.

Sotto (I): under. *See also* SOPRA.

Sotto voce (I): softly.

Soundboard: a thin wooden board extended over the body of a string instrument (e.g., piano, dulcimer, zither) to serve as a resonator.

Sound holes: holes cut in the soundboard or table of a string instrument to permit greater freedom of vibration.

Sourdine (F): *see* SORDINO.

Sousa, John Philip: b. Washington, D.C., November 6, 1854; d. Reading, Pa., March 6, 1932. As a youth Sousa learned violin and a variety of wind instruments. He played in the Marine Band at thirteen, and led a vaudeville orchestra at eighteen. He was appointed leader of the Marine Band in 1880 and organized his own band in 1892. In addition to the MARCHES which earned him the nickname, the March King, Sousa wrote WALTZES, songs, SUITES for orchestra and for band, and light OPERAS.

Sousaphone: a tuba with a wide, circular body (*see* BRASS INSTRUMENTS).

Speech song: *see* SPRECH-GESANG.

Spiccato (I): *see* SAUTILLÉ.

Spinet: (1) a small HARPSI-CHORD with one KEYBOARD; (2) a 19th-century square PIANO; (3) the smallest form of upright piano of modern manufacture.

Spiritual: a religious song of the American Negro, usually based on a Biblical story. Pentatonic or other modes often underlie the simple melodic style of spirituals; SYNCOPATION is a frequent rhythmic trait. The harmonizations derive in style from the four-part harmonizations of HYMNS.

Spohr, Ludwig (= Louis): *b.* Brunswick, April 5, 1784; *d.* Kassel, October 22, 1859. As one of the leading violinists and conductors of his generation, Spohr made numerous tours through various European cities from London to St. Petersburg. In 1822 he was appointed music director at Kassel. Spohr's musical thought and style of composition was basically conservative, but he nevertheless was an early champion of WAGNER. He wrote a large quantity of music including several OPERAS, ORATORIOS, a MASS and other sacred music, choral music, songs, SYMPHONIES, CONCERTOS, STRING QUARTETS and other CHAMBER MUSIC, and piano works.

Spontini, Gasparo Luigi Pacifico: *b.* Majolati, November 14, 1774; *d.* Majolati, January 24, 1851. A prominent OPERA composer of his time, Spontini completed his training at the Conservatorio della Pietà de' Turchini in Naples. He was active at the Neapoli-

tan court, in various Italian cities, and in Paris, where he became composer to Empress Josephine in 1803. In 1807 and 1809 he scored his two major triumphs with the OPERAS *La Vestale* and *Fernando Cortez*, which reinforced Napoleonic tastes for elaborate productions. From 1820 to 1841, Spontini was court composer and music director to Friedrich Wilhelm III in Berlin. There he produced *Nurmahal, Alcidor,* and *Agnes von Hohenstaufen.*

Sprechgesang (G): speech song, a style of vocal performance intermediate between speaking and singing. The composer prescribes both rhythm and vocal inflection, utilizing careful gradations over a range far wider than that of normal speech; musical tone itself is not desired of the performer. This style was first employed by SCHOENBERG and was used also by BERG.

Sprechstimme (G): speaking voice, the designation for a vocal part to be performed as SPRECHGESANG.

Staccato (I): detached. The performer is directed to release the tone promptly instead of prolonging it for the full written value. (The remainder of the value is absorbed by an unwritten REST.) The present indication for staccato is a dot placed under or over the note; a particularly sharp staccato is indicated by a similarly placed wedge. In the late 18th century, however, the wedge indicated a normal staccato, and the dot a less pronounced one.

Staff: a set of lines (now normally five) used in NOTATION for graphing the relative height of a tone.

Stamitz, Johann Wenzel Anton: *b.* Deutsch-Brod, June 19, 1717; *d.* Mannheim, March 27, 1757. Named CHAMBER MUSIC director to the elector of Mannheim, Stamitz soon made the electoral orchestra one of the most famous in Europe. He was influential both as a teacher and composer, playing a major role in the development of the early Classical symphonic style. He was among those who developed stylistic contrast between THEMES, used more flexible DYNAMICS, and employed a greater number of WOODWINDS, dropping the theretofore omnipresent CONTINUO. A prolific composer, he wrote SYMPHONIES, CONCERTOS, chamber music, SONATAS for violin solo, and some sacred music. His son Carl Stamitz (1745–1801) was a noted viola virtuoso and the music director of the University of Jena. His second son, Anton Thadäus (1754–1809), was

a prominent violinist and teacher in Paris. Both sons composed symphonies, concertos, and chamber music.

Ständchen (G): SERENADE.

Stave: alternative spelling of STAFF.

Steffani, Agostino: *b.* Castelfranco, July 25, 1654; *d.* Frankfort, February 12, 1728. Diplomat, composer, and priest, Steffani was widely traveled. He studied music in Munich under Johann Caspar Kerll and in Rome under Ercole Bernabei. As a musician, he was active principally in Munich, Hanover, and Düsseldorf. His music combines features drawn from Italian, German, and French styles in a manner foreshadowing that of HANDEL. He wrote OPERAS, CHAMBER CANTATAS and duets, sacred music of various sorts, and trio SONATAS.

Steg (G): the bridge of a string instrument.

Step: the INTERVAL of a second. A whole-step is a major second, a half-step a minor second.

Stile antico (I), **Stile moderno** (I): terms that distinguish between the two chief styles of the late 16th and early 17th centuries. *Stile antico* (or *prima prattica*) refers to the contrapuntal style of late-16th-century composers such as PALESTRINA and to the related style of sacred music that evolved during the 17th and early 18th centuries. Although the latter was conceived as a continuation of Palestrina style, significant changes of stylistic detail crept in, both with regard to the treatment of melodic lines and with regard to strictness of DISSONANCE treatment. *Stile moderno* (or *seconda prattica*) denotes the harmonic style of the early 17th century, with freer dissonance treatment, freer treatment of melodic leaps, and the harmonic support of the BASSO CONTINUO.

Stile rappresentativo (I): the early-17th-century style of RECITATIVE in which the composer based his MELODY on the stylization of natural speech inflections, seeking thereby to produce a more dramatic effect.

Still, William Grant: *b.* Woodville, Miss., May 11, 1895. Still completed his musical studies under CHADWICK and VARÈSE. The foremost Negro composer of his day, Still has sought to fuse Negro musical traditions with those of European symphonic music. He has written a wide variety of orchestral music, including four SYMPHONIES (among them, the *Afro-American Symphony*), OPERAS and BALLETS, and some vocal and CHAMBER works.

Stimme (G): VOICE or voice-part (i.e., a term applicable both to vocal and instrumental music).

Stockhausen, Karlheinz: *b.* Mödrath, August 22, 1928. After study with Frank MARTIN, MESSIAEN, and BOULEZ, Stockhausen quickly became one of the leading avantgarde musicians of Germany. He is associated with the Studio for Electronic Music of the Cologne Radio Station and is co-editor of *Die Reihe*, a journal devoted to modern music. His compositions include CHAMBER works, piano pieces, and a few orchestral scores. In general these extend the paths of WEBERN, bringing almost all musical elements under serial control (*see* TWELVE-TONE MUSIC). He has also written ELECTRONIC MUSIC, and, in *Gesang der Jünglinge*, combines vocal and electronic sounds.

Stop: (1) on the ORGAN, a small lever (ivory tablet) or draw-knob which controls the admission of air to a set of pipes of the same basic construction; (2) a set of organ pipes; (3) the draw-knob governing a set of jacks on an older HARPSICHORD; (4) either a set of harpsichord jacks together with the set of strings they govern, or a mechanism for altering the tone of a harpsichord; (5) to stop a string means to adjust the vibrating length by pressing the string against a finger-board or against a fret; (6) double, triple, and quadruple stops (or *stopping*) refer to the simultaneous or nearly simultaneous playing of two, three, or four tones on a bowed string instrument; (7) stopping on the French horn involves the insertion of the right hand into the bell, raising the PITCH and altering the TONE COLOR.

Stradella, Alessandro, *b.* Rome, October 1(?), 1644; *d.* Genoa, February 25, 1682. Stradella, reputedly a student of Bernabei, was active in Rome, Venice, Florence, Turin, and Genoa as a violinist, singer, teacher, and composer. His OPERAS and ORATORIOS stand at the peak of middle BAROQUE Italian achievements in these genres; in them he furthered the expansion in form of the ARIA. Other vocal works include CANTATAS, MADRIGALS, and MOTETS. His *Sinfonie a più stromenti* (*c.*1682) contain some of the first examples of the separation between SOLO and TUTTI parts that marked the nascent CONCERTO GROSSO.

Strauss, Johann, Sr.: *b.* Vienna, March 14, 1804; *d.* Vienna, September 25, 1849. After serving in orchestras led by Pamer and by Lanner, Strauss formed a small orchestra of his own in 1826. His success earned him the nickname "The Father of the Waltz." In addition to more than 150 WALTZES, the elder Strauss composed GALOPS, QUADRILLES, POLKAS, and MARCHES.

Strauss, Johann, Jr.: *b.* Vienna, October 25, 1825; *d.* Vienna, June 3, 1899. "The Waltz King" formed a small dance orchestra in 1844, despite his father's objections to a career in music, and won almost instantaneous success. He combined his group with that of his father after the latter's death in 1849 and toured Austria, Germany, Poland, and Russia. In 1872 he visited the United States. The charm of his *Blue Danube Waltz;* the *Emperor Waltz; Tales of the Vienna Woods; Wine, Woman, and Song;* and many others were appreciated by such different men as WAGNER and BRAHMS. In the 1870s Strauss turned to the composition of OPERETTAS and won great success with such work as *The Bat, The Gipsy Baron, A Night in Venice,* and more than a dozen others.

Strauss, Richard: *b.* Munich, June 11, 1864; *d.* Garmisch, September 8, 1949; important composer of TONE POEMS and OPERAS.

The son of a horn player, Strauss studied piano and violin as a child; he composed his first piece when six. He began a noteworthy conducting career as an assistant to Hans von Bülow. From 1885 to 1924, Strauss directed orchestras in Munich, Weimar, Berlin, and Vienna; he toured both Europe and the United States. Having achieved financial success, he retired from the podium. Under Hitler, Strauss became president of the *Reichsmusikkammer*, but soon resigned.

Most of Strauss's best works were written during the period 1885–1912. His later ones, while showing technical mastery and a warm, lyrical vein, are of uneven merit. In his youthful piano and CHAMBER MUSIC, Strauss followed the path of BRAHMS. He soon abandoned this style and, influenced by Alexander Ritter, turned to the descriptive vein of LISZT and WAGNER. Beginning with *Aus Italien* (1887), he composed several tone poems, the most famous being *Death and Transfiguration, Don Juan, Till Eulenspiegel's Merry Pranks, Thus Spake Zarathustra*, and *Don Quixote*. In these, he used his imaginative verve and mastery of ORCHESTRATION to achieve more realistic depiction than was envisaged by Liszt. The orchestral resources are huge and the individual instruments are often used in atypical fashion. *Guntram*, the

first of Strauss's operas, was completed in 1894; he reached a peak in this medium with *Salome* (1905), *Elektra* (1909), and *Der Rosenkavalier* (1911) — the last two with librettos by von Hofmannsthal. In accordance with Wagnerian principles, Strauss employs a rich orchestral texture and avoids small, closed forms. LEITMOTIVES are used systematically. *Salome* and *Elektra* shocked the public by their emphasis on the macabre. The music exhibits expressive melodic leaps, a masterly use of DISSONANCE, and chromatic HARMONY that continues the *Tristan* vein. *Der Rosenkavalier* is a charming work, as are many of the later Strauss operas, e.g., *Ariadne* and *Arabella*. Among Strauss's approximately 150 songs are some of the finest examples of the late Romantic LIED. He wrote also piano and chamber music, CONCERTOS, and BALLETS.

Stravinsky, Igor: *b.* Oranienbaum, June 17, 1882; *d.* New York City, April 6, 1971; one of the greatest and most influential modern composers.

Stravinsky's father, a prominent singer, wished his son to become a lawyer, but provided him with a musical education nonetheless. After matriculating at the University of St. Petersburg, Stravinsky was encouraged to a career in music by RIMSKY-KORSAKOV, with whom he later studied. His early works —a SYMPHONY, a SONG CYCLE, and an orchestral FANTASY— were successful, but are only rarely heard now. He achieved international fame through three BALLETS commissioned by Diaghilev and first produced in Paris: *The Fire Bird* (1910), *Petrushka* (1911), and *The Rite of Spring* (1913). Stravinsky lived mainly in Switzerland (1914–18), and in Paris (1920–39). However, he toured frequently both as pianist and conductor. He came to the United States in 1939 to give the Charles Eliot Norton Lectures at Harvard and remained here, becoming a citizen in 1945. Articulate and witty, he has written an autobiography (*Chronicles of my Life*) and essays (*Poetics of Music*).

The subject matter and rich ORCHESTRATION of Stravinsky's first three ballets reveal the importance of his Russian heritage. Each work is more daring than its predecessor and the seething primitivism of *The Rite of Spring* provoked a near riot at its première. (These ballets are best known in the form of orchestral SUITES.) A dynamic rhythmic drive, often with asymmetrical features,

is characteristic both of these scores and later works. Stravinsky uses rhythmic groups of irregular size, calls for displacement of ACCENTS, and combines different METERS simultaneously. An interest in JAZZ led to the composition of *Ragtime for 11 Instruments* and *Piano-Rag Music*, followed much later by the *Ebony Concerto* for clarinet and swing band. With regard to tonal structure and harmony, Stravinsky avoids the chromatic richness of his predecessors and uses primarily a diatonic idiom with clearly established TONE CENTERS. He makes effective use of dissonant chords and POLYTONALITY.

After 1914, Stravinsky's style began to change markedly. He came to write for smaller groups and to place greater stress on control of FORM. *The Soldier's Tale*, the ballets *The Wedding* and *Pulcinella*, short piano pieces, songs, and CHAMBER MUSIC were composed before 1923. Later works, beginning with the *Octet* (1923) and including the OPERA *The Rake's Progress* (1951), are usually dubbed "neoclassical." These works are characterized by a certain emotional restraint as well as by masterly craft; several allude to or quote music of older masters. Among the more important are the *Symphony of Psalms* (for chorus and orchestra), the opera-ORATORIO *Oedipus Rex*, the ballet *Apollon Musagète*, a MASS, the *Symphony in C*, the *Symphony in Three Movements*, the *Dumbarton Oaks Concerto*, and the *Basel Concerto*. In the 1950s Stravinsky began to employ the TWELVE-TONE technique in sections of several compositions, including the *Canticum Sacrum*, the *Septet*, *Threnodies*, and the ballet *Agon*.

Streichinstrumente (G): string instruments.

Stretto (I): (1) two or more statements of a fugal subject appearing in overlapping rather than successive fashion; (2) a quickened TEMPO used toward the end of a piece.

Stringendo (I): a gradual acceleration of TEMPO.

String quartet: (1) an ENSEMBLE consisting of two violins, viola, and cello; (2) a work written for such an ensemble. The development of the string quartet parallels that of the SONATA from 1750 on, inasmuch as the two genres are basically related in structure. HAYDN, MOZART, BEETHOVEN, and SCHUBERT each wrote numerous string quartets, many of these being among their finest works. Even though composers of the later 19th and 20th centuries wrote fewer quartets, the medium has remained an important mode of expression until the present day. MENDELSSOHN, SCHUMANN, BRAHMS, DVOŘÁK, FRANCK, DEBUSSY, RAVEL, SCHOENBERG, BERG, WEBERN, STRAVINSKY, SESSIONS, and CARTER, among others, have contributed important quartets.

Strings: (1) the string instruments of the orchestra—i.e., two groups of VIOLINS, and one each of violas, cellos, and double basses; (2) lengths of gut or metal wire, tautly stretched, that may be bowed, plucked, rubbed, or struck in order to produce sound on string instruments. *See illustration page 421.*

Strophic: an adjective describing a setting of a text in which all stanzas are set to the same music. This kind of setting is common among FOLK SONGS and HYMNS.

Strumento, Stromento (I): instrument. *Strumenti a corde,* string instruments; *strumenti d'arco,* bowed string instruments; *strumenti a fiato,* wind instruments; *strumenti di legno,* woodwinds; *strumenti d'ottone (strumenti di metallo),* brass; *strumenti a percossa,* percussion; *strumenti da tasto,* keyboard instruments.

Stück (G): piece.

Study: *see* ETUDE.

Style: the complex of characteristic and unusual traits in the MELODY, HARMONY, RHYTHM, FORM, and treatment of medium of a given work or group of works. The study of style involves not only the investigation of the numerous details which together account for the individuality and effect of a work, but also the examination of the relationship between the techniques employed in the given work and others of either the same composer, the same period, the same genre, the same medium, or the same nationality of composer.

Style galant (F): *see* ROCOCO.

Subdominant: the fourth degree of the SCALE, or the CHORD built thereon.

Subito (I): immediately.

Subject: a theme—a musical idea of moderate length, as opposed to a brief motive— that either underlies an entire musical structure or provides one of its prominent bases. Prominence may be achieved either through position (e.g., statement at the beginning or at the point at which a new tonality is firmly established), repetition, or development.

Submediant: the sixth degree of the scale, or the CHORD built thereon.

Suite: a set of related pieces. There are three basic sorts: those made up of dances, those made up of excerpts from stage works, and those based on a story or idea.

In BAROQUE usage, a suite normally designated a set of dances in one key. Other terms used for similar purpose were *partie* and *partita, overture (French Overture), sonata da camera, lesson,* and *ordre.* Some of these terms are interchangeable; only a few are distinctive. *Ordre,* for example, is the title for François COUPERIN's suites, which are lengthy collections containing primarily dance movements, some having fanciful descriptive titles.

The four basic MOVEMENTS of a Baroque suite are the ALLEMANDE, COURANTE, SARABANDE, and GIGUE. A consistent order was not followed throughout the period; that given is the one used by BACH. Optional movements, such as the MINUET, GAVOTTE, BOURRÉE, PASSEPIED, etc., could be inserted between the Sarabande and Gigue. Often the set was prefaced by some introductory movement. In general, the dance movements were no more intended for dancing than a CHOPIN or BRAHMS waltz; they were rather stylizations—usually in BINARY FORM—derived from dances that in some instances were already out of fashion. The paired dance movements of the late 16th century (PAVANE and GALLIARD, PASSAMEZZO and SALTARELLO) were the ancestors of the Baroque suite. The

DIVERTIMENTO, CASSATION, and SERENADE may be viewed as its progeny. In rare cases, the title, suite, might be employed as a synonym for SONATA (as in some suites by HANDEL).

Since the late 19th century, the term has been applied to concert arrangements of incidental music for plays (e.g., the two *L'Arlésienne Suites* by BIZET, the *Peer Gynt Suite* by GRIEG) and films (*Louisiana Story* by Virgil Thomson), music accompanying BALLET (e.g., TCHAIKOVSKY's *Nutcracker Suite*, STRAVINSKY's *Firebird Suite*), and OPERA. By extension, the term has been applied also to multi-movement pieces based on one idea or story (e.g., RIMSKY-KORSAKOV's *Scheherezade*, ALBENIZ's *Iberia*, MILHAUD's *Suite Française*).

Suivez (F): (1) continue to the next section without pause; (2) follow the rhythmic modifications made by the soloist.

Sul ponticello (I): bow near the bridge of a string instrument.

Sul tasto (I): bow near the fingerboard of a string instrument.

Sullivan, Arthur Seymour: b. London, May 13, 1842; d. London, November 22, 1900. As a boy Sullivan was a chorister at the Chapel Royal and then studied at the Royal Academy of Music and the Leipzig Conservatory. He was an organist and taught composition at the Royal Academy of Music. After writing the CANTATA *Kenilworth,* an OVERTURE, STRING QUARTETS, and other music, he began composing comic OPERAS. His association with the librettist W. S. Gilbert began in 1871; their first success, *Trial by Jury,* was produced in 1875. There then followed *H.M.S. Pinafore, The Pirates of Penzance, Patience, Iolanthe, Princess Ida, The Mikado, Ruddigore, The Yeomen of the Guard,* and *The Gondoliers;* the tunefulness and technical mastery of these works has won them lasting popularity. Sullivan was knighted in 1883; he wrote also a grand opera, *Ivanhoe,* CANTATAS, BALLETS, church music, songs, and piano compositions.

Supertonic: the second degree of the SCALE, or the CHORD founded thereon.

Suppé, Franz von (Francesco Ezechiele Ermenegildo Cavaliere Suppe-Demelli): b. Spalato, April 18, 1819; d. Vienna, May 21, 1895. Studied at the Vienna Conservatory. Beginning in 1846 he produced a series of more than 30 OPERETTAS and numerous other stage pieces that for a time rivaled the successes of OFFENBACH. The most famous of these is *Poet and Peasant.*

Suspension: a NONHARMONIC TONE occurring on a strong BEAT, produced by sustaining one tone of the previous consonant INTERVAL while the other tone moves in such a fashion that a DISSONANCE is created. This dissonance is normally resolved by the downward, stepwise motion of the note that had been sustained; if there is an upward resolution, the nonharmonic tone is often classed as a RETARDATION.

Sustaining pedal: see PIANO.

Sweelinck, Jan Pieterszoon: *b.* Deventer, May 1562; *d.* Amsterdam, October 16, 1621. Organist at the Old Church in Amsterdam beginning 1580 (possibly still earlier), Sweelinck achieved great fame as a performer and teacher. In his keyboard FANTASIAS, he contributed to the development of imitative forms based on a single theme. He was also a master of the VARIATION and TOCCATA. His vocal works include CHANSONS, PSALMS, and MOTETS.

Swell (Swell box): a shuttered chamber enclosing the pipes of an ORGAN division; the opening of the shutters increases the volume of sound reaching the listener, while the closing of the shutters decreases that volume.

Swell (Swell organ): see ORGAN.

Sympathetic strings (Sympathetic vibration): see ACOUSTICS.

Symphonia: (1) Latin for SYMPHONY (*see also* SINFONIA); (2) the title of a few early BAROQUE works for voices and instruments; (3) an early term for several instruments: double-headed drums, each head producing a different PITCH (7th century), the hurdy-gurdy (14th century), the bagpipe, and certain small keyboard instruments (around the 1600s); (4) ancient Greek term for UNISON and also for CONSONANCE.

Symphonic poem: an orchestral work in one MOVEMENT; normally the symphonic poem arises from the composer's desire to express certain extramusical ideas, although it is possible that in a few instances the music itself was created prior to the program with which it became associated. The genre is proper to the late 19th and early 20th centuries. *See also* PROGRAM MUSIC.

Symphonie (F, G): SYMPHONY.

Symphonie concertante (F): *see* SINFONIA CONCERTANTE.

Symphony, Symphonie (F, G), **Sinfonie** (G), **Sinfonia** (I): (1) for early uses of this term, *see* SINFONIA and SYMPHONIA. (2) Under present usage, the term indicates an orchestral work, often in four MOVEMENTS, having the architectural features of a SONATA. The modern symphony began to emerge c.1725–40, the most important of its several ancestors being the three-movement Italian operatic OVERTURE (the *sinfonia avanti l'opera*). There is an extremely rich, though little known repertoire of symphonies by Italian, German, Austrian, French, and English composers of the mid-18th century. In these works—especially those written after 1750—the original three-movement norm gave way to a four-movement norm, the inner parts gradually achieved greater individuality and independence, echoes of BAROQUE style (including the use of the CONTINUO) became fewer, and the ORCHESTRATION became fuller. The genre grew rapidly in importance with the works of HAYDN and a high point of symphonic composition was reached during the years 1785–1825 with the mature symphonies of Haydn and MOZART and those of BEETHOVEN. The genre continued to be of importance during the ROMANTIC era, reaching a second peak with the works of BRAHMS. Other symphonic composers of importance during this period are SCHUBERT, MENDELSSOHN, SCHUMANN, BRUCKNER, DVOŘÁK, TCHAIKOVSKY, and MAHLER. During this period, the musical ideas became somewhat less incisive and more lyrical, the orchestration increasingly rich. The programmatic tendency incipient in Beethoven's *Pastorale Symphony* was explored further by Mendelssohn and especially by BERLIOZ and LISZT. The admixture of orchestra and voices employed in Beethoven's *Ninth Symphony* was employed also by Berlioz, Liszt, and Mahler. (3) The *Symphony of Psalms* by STRAVINSKY is a work for ORCHESTRA and VOICES in the manner of a CANTATA.

Syncopation: a rhythmic pattern that displaces normal metrical stresses by emphasizing either BEATS or subdivisions of beats that would ordinarily be unstressed. This transfer of emphasis may be achieved by accenting notes which under usual circumstances would be regarded as weak, by introducing RESTS

at the points normally regarded as strong, or by tying notes across the strong beats so that no attack is heard at these points. The listener's sense of syncopation arises from the awareness that the expected stress pattern is momentarily being avoided.

System: (1) a group of staves constituting a musical unit in a SCORE. (Score is taken here to include KEYBOARD music— i.e., two-stave piano music and three-stave organ music.) (2) A single STAFF.

Szymanowski, Karol: *b*. Timoshovka (Ukraine), October 6, 1882; *d*. Lausanne, March 28, 1937. Szymanowski studied privately in Warsaw under M. Zawirski and Sigismund Noskowski. He was strongly influenced by the music of CHOPIN, R. STRAUSS, SCRIABIN, and DEBUSSY. In the 1920s Szymanowski became deeply interested in the Polish FOLK idiom. He served briefly as director of the Warsaw Conservatory. His compositions include OPERAS, BALLETS, SYMPHONIES, CONCERTOS, CHAMBER MUSIC, and many songs and keyboard pieces.

T

Tablature: (1) a system of NOTATION that indicates PITCHES by numbers or letters rather than notes. There were several such systems during the RENAISSANCE and BAROQUE periods. Most were designed either for keyboard or for plucked string instruments (lute, guitar, etc.).

In German organ tablatures of *c*.1450–1550, the pitches of the lower parts are indicated by their corresponding letters, while those of the highest part are given in normal STAFF notation. After 1550, letters might be used for all parts; late examples of this kind of notation were familiar to BACH.

In Spanish keyboard tablature, each voice-part is represented on a horizontal line. Numbers from 1-7 are placed on these lines to indicate the diatonic pitches from *f* to *e′;* these are modified by additional symbols when pitches in higher or lower octaves are required.

Horizontal lines in lute tablatures represent the strings of the instrument. Italian and Spanish tablatures place numbers on these lines in order to indicate finger placement on the respective strings. French tablatures employ letters in similar fashion. The number 0 and the letter *a* correspond to an unstopped string; the numbers 1, 2, 3 and the letters *b, c, d* correspond to strings stopped at the first, second and third frets respectively. German lute tablature dispenses with horizontal lines and uses a more complicated system of numbers and letters to indicate finger placement.

In modern guitar and ukelele tablatures, a stylized representation of the top of the instrument is given. The vertical lines indicate the strings, the horizontal ones, the FRETS. The placement of fingers is indicated by dots placed on the proper strings.

(2) In the 16th and 17th centuries, the term had also the sense, keyboard score.

(3) The set of rules governing the art of the MEISTERSINGERS.

Table: the upper surface of the body of a string instrument.

Tabor: a small double-headed drum, beaten with one stick, and used to accompany a pipe (a small, three-holed recorder). Known in the Middle Ages, this combination is still used to accompany traditional folk dances.

Tacet (L): a direction inserted into an individual part indicating that the performer concerned is not involved either in the entire movement or in a long section thereof.

Tactus (L): BEAT; the term was used by RENAISSANCE writers to describe the regular measurement of time using up and down motions of the hand or fingers.

Taille (F): (1) a tenor or other interior voice-part; (2) the viola; (3) the oboe da caccia.

Tallis, Thomas: *b.* unknown *c.*1505; *d.* Greenwich, November 23, 1585. Gentleman of the Chapel Royal from 1540 until his death, Tallis was the outstanding English composer of the generation before BYRD. In 1575 he and

BYRD were granted a monopoly by Queen Elizabeth I for the printing of music and music paper. Tallis composed a wide variety of sacred music with both Latin and English texts (MASSES, MOTETS, LAMENTATIONS, ANTHEMS, SERVICES, etc.), together with secular vocal, keyboard, and instrumental ENSEMBLE music.

Talon (F): the heel of a BOW (the lowest portion, held by the player).

Tambour (F): DRUM; *tambour militaire*, snare drum; *tambour de basque*, tambourine.

Tambourin (F): (1) a deep TABOR; (2) TAMBOURINE; (3) an old Provençal dance. *Tambourin de Béarn*, a ZITHER with strings tuned to the TONIC and DOMINANT, played together with a RECORDER to accompany dancing.

Tambourine, Tamburin (G), **Tamburino** (I): a shallow, single-headed DRUM with pairs of metal jingles inserted into the frame.

Tamburo (I): DRUM; *tamburo militare*, snare drum; *tamburo rullante*, tenor drum.

Tampon (F): a two-headed drumstick, grasped in the middle and rotated in alternate directions to produce a roll on the bass drum.

Tam-tam: gong.

Tangent: *see* CLAVICHORD.

Tango: an Argentinian dance in slow duple METER, with syncopated rhythms; the dance became popular in Europe and North America about 1910.

Tanto (I): so much.

Tanz (G): dance.

Tarantella: a south Italian dance in brisk 6/8 time; according to legends, the dance was caused by or was a cure for the poisonous bite of the tarantula.

Tardo (I): slow; *tardando,* becoming slower.

Tarogato: a Hungarian WOODWIND instrument now employing a single reed. (Earlier forms made use of a double reed.) The instrument is used in WAGNER's *Tristan und Isolde.*

Tartini, Giuseppe: *b.* Pirano, April 8, 1692; *d.* Padua, February 26, 1770. A great violin virtuoso, Tartini's chief post was as violinist and conductor at St. Antonio in Padua. He was an important teacher and wrote many theoretical works as well as treatises on violin playing. His compositions include numerous violin CONCERTOS and SONATAS, as well as SYMPHONIES, CHAMBER MUSIC, and some sacred music.

Tastiera (I): the fingerboard of a string instrument.

Tasto (I): (1) TASTIERA; (2) FRET; (3) a key of a KEYBOARD instrument. In a FIGURED BASS, the direction *tasto solo* indicates that no harmonies are to be added above the bass notes; the performer is to play only the notes written.

Taverner, John: *b. c.*1495; *d.* Boston (Lincolnshire), October 25, 1545. A leading composer of sacred music, Taverner wrote MASSES, MAGNIFICATS, and MOTETS. Instrumental transcriptions of the *In nomine* section of his Mass *Gloria tibi Trinitas* prompted a vogue for instrumental works based on the *Gloria tibi Trinitas* melody and entitled *In nomine.* For a brief period Taverner was master of the Choristers at Cardinals' College (now Christ Church), Oxford.

Tchaikovsky, Peter Ilyich: *b.* Votkinsk, May 7, 1840; *d.* St. Petersburg, November 6, 1893; outstanding Russian ROMANTIC composer. (Other spellings of the name include Chaikovskii, Tchaikowsky, Tschaikowsky, etc.)

After studying law and serving briefly as a government clerk, Tchaikovsky entered Anton RUBINSTEIN'S Conservatory in St. Petersburg in 1861. Five years later he became a harmony teacher in the newly established Moscow Conservatory. He was able to retire from teaching in 1877 through the generosity of Nadezhda von Meck, who provided him with an annuity until the end of 1890.

Tchaikovsky traveled widely in Europe and visited the United States. He died of cholera.

Tchaikovsky's music is suffused with a rich romanticism that has won it great popularity. A highly gifted melodist, Tchaikovsky himself was aware of his weakness in handling FORM. His early works (e.g., the first three SYMPHONIES) reveal an interest in FOLK materials, but Tchaikovsky did not share the militant nationalism of the FIVE.

Of his 11 OPERAS, *Eugene Onegin* and *The Queen of Spades* are best known. *Swan Lake, Sleeping Beauty,* and *The Nutcracker* are staples of the traditional BALLET repertoire. His orchestral works include six numbered symphonies and one entitled *Manfred,* four SUITES (besides those drawn from his operas and ballets), the FANTASY *Francesca da Rimini,* the *Capriccio Italien,* the *1812 Overture,* and the OVERTURE-fantasy *Romeo and Juliet.* Tchaikovsky's *Violin Concerto* and the first of his three piano CONCERTOS (the last incomplete) are standard virtuoso items. He wrote about 100 songs, a similar quantity of piano music, some CHAMBER MUSIC—including three STRING QUARTETS—and a few choral works. The quality of Tchaikovsky's compositions is somewhat uneven.

Tcherepnin, Alexander Niko-layevich: *b.* St. Petersburg, January 20, 1899. The son of a prominent conductor and composer (Nicolai Tcherepnin, 1873–1945), Tcherepnin has been active as a pianist and composer not only in Russia, but in many areas of Western Europe, China, Japan, and the United States. He has written OPERAS, BALLETS, incidental music, SYMPHONIES, CONCERTOS, CHAMBER MUSIC, piano pieces, songs, and CANTATAS; his idiom is essentially conservative, and he often uses Oriental tonal devices.

Te: in English and American usage, the seventh degree of the major SCALE, equivalent to the Italian *si*.

Te Deum (L): a Latin HYMN of praise, employed in the Roman Catholic liturgy at Matins on important feasts of joyous nature and, in translation (We praise thee, God), in the Anglican liturgy during Morning Prayer. The Lutheran equivalent is *Herr Gott, dich loben wir*. Numerous polyphonic settings of the text have been composed from the 16th century on; among the more famous are compositions by PURCELL, LULLY, HANDEL, BERLIOZ, BRUCKNER, DVOŘÁK, and VERDI.

Telemann, Georg Philipp: *b.* Magdeburg, March 14, 1681; *d.* Hamburg, June 25, 1767. Almost entirely self-taught as a musician, Telemann entered the University of Leipzig in 1701 as a law student, but turned to a career in music in 1704 as organist at the Neukirche. He held posts of increasing importance at Sorau (1704), Eisenach (1708), Frankfurt (1712), and Hamburg (1721). His style was more progressive than that of BACH and he enjoyed greater repute among his contemporaries as a composer. Telemann produced an extraordinary amount of music. He was an important composer of OPERAS, CANTATAS, PASSIONS, ORATORIOS, orchestral SUITES, CONCERTOS, trio SONATAS and other CHAMBER MUSIC, and KEYBOARD music.

Tema (I): THEME.

Temperament: *see* TUNING (sense 1).

Temple block: *see* CHINESE BLOCK.

Tempo (I): the basic rate of speed of a composition. Tempo is calculated according to the underlying pulse (unit of time) rather than according to the speed of individual notes. Fast notes may occur in slow tempi if the composer uses particularly small note-values, while notes of moderate speed may occur in fast tempi if the composer uses large note-values. (The lyric quality of many Mozartean themes in fast movements comes about partly in the latter fashion.)

Tempo may be indicated either by flexible terminology or by fixing the number of BEATS per minute by means of a METRONOME. Much terminology is in Italian. *Largo, lento,* and *adagio* indicate slow tempi; *andante, moderato,* and *allegretto,* medium tempi; and *allegro, vivace,* and *presto,* fast tempi. The terms within each group are arranged in order of increasing speed according to normal usage. However, distinctions within these groups cannot be made with consistency. (In this respect the fixed tempo boundaries indicated on many metronomes are misleading.) An *andante* in one piece may be the equivalent of a *moderato* in another. Not only does usage vary among composers—and even within the output of a single composer —but interpretations of a particular term in a given composition vary among different performers. Moreover, a given tempo for a particular work may arouse different reactions by different listeners. Even when the composer indicates the desired number of beats per minute for a composition, the performer's motion sense may produce a conviction strong enough to override the composer's direction.

Tempo designations began to appear during the late 17th century but were not used consistently before the mid-18th century. (For example, most—but not all—tempo indications appearing in modern publications of BACH's and HANDEL's music represent the editor's suggestions and not the composer's directions.) As national feelings were awakened in Europe, composers began increasingly to write tempo indications in their native languages rather than in Italian.

Tempo giusto (I): (1) in strict time; (2) at a fitting speed.

Teneramente (I): tenderly.

Tenor: (1) a male VOICE of high range; (2) a variety of CLEF; (3) one of a family of instruments, lower (larger) than alto and higher (smaller) than baritone or bass; (4) an obsolete English term for viola; (5) the next-to-lowest voice-part of a four-part work; (6) in ORGANA and MOTETS of the 12th and 13th centuries, the lowest part of the composition, based on a preexistent melody; (7) the RECITATION tone of a psalm-tone, known also as the *dominant* or *tuba*.

Tenorhorn (G): a BRASS INSTRUMENT of the saxhorn

family, similar to the baritone.

Tenth: an INTERVAL of an octave and a third; in traditional harmonic theory the tenth is treated as the equivalent of a third.

Tenuto (I): a direction to hold a note or CHORD for its full written value; the direction occurs when the musical context is such that the written value might be replaced in performance by a shorter value and a brief REST.

Ternary form (Three-part form): a musical structure consisting of three elements, the outer two being similar or identical; frequently this structural pattern is represented by the letters *A B A* (or *A B A'* in the event that the last section is a variation of the first). The *B* section is contrasting, both in content and in key. Each of the three sections may be subdivided. Many MINUETS, SCHERZOS, band MARCHES, BAROQUE and CLASSICAL operatic ARIAS, and ROMANTIC CHARACTER PIECES (Nocturnes, Novellettes, Intermezzi, etc.) are in ternary form, as well as numerous slow movements of SONATAS, SYMPHONIES, CONCERTOS, and CHAMBER MUSIC. In the Baroque ARIA DA CAPO and similar movements of Baroque concertos, it was common practice for the soloist to improvise florid embellishments to the final section.

Terzetto (I), **Terzett** (G): an operatic movement or other piece for three SOLO vocalists.

Tessitura (I): (1) the portion of the total range of a voice-part that is most characteristic of that part, disregarding the very high or very low notes that are used only occasionally; (2) the most characteristic portion of a singer's total range. If a particular passage for soprano VOICE uses only the lowest third of the soprano compass, that passage is described as being of low tessitura. If the voice of a specific soprano is at its best in the upper portion of the soprano range, the singer is described as having a high tessitura. The use of the term is extended also to describe instrumental parts.

Testo (I): the part of the narrator in ORATORIOS, PASSIONS, etc.

Tetrachord: a SCALE segment, normally consisting of four notes, spanning the interval of a fourth.

Texture: the disposition of the horizontal (or linear) and vertical elements in music. The former, which arise from the progression of one tone to the next, may be indicated by the terms MELODY, line, voice, voice-part, or part. The latter, which ensue from the relationships between tones sounded simultaneously, may be indicated by the terms HARMONY, CHORD, TRIAD, or

INTERVAL. There are four main classes of textures: monophonic, heterophonic, polyphonic, and homophonic.

Monophony consists of unaccompanied melody; it comprises most liturgical CHANT and much music of non-European peoples. In Europe itself, monophony remained of importance in amateur circles throughout the Middle Ages and RENAISSANCE; the repertoires of the TROUBADOURS, TROUVÈRES, MINNESINGERS, and MEISTERSINGERS were primarily monophonic, as were the early *laude* and the *Cantigas de Santa Maria*. FOLK SONG is monophonic (although not performed as such in accompanied arrangements). *Heterophony* arises when two or more persons or groups perform simultaneously different versions of the same melody. It is frequent in China, Japan, and Java, and in some sections of Africa.

Polyphony refers to a style in which two or more melodic lines are combined. These lines may employ common material, as in canon and other imitative forms, by having this material enter the various voices at different times. Or, the material assigned each voice may be highly individual. In the latter event, the various lines may be either of equal or unequal melodic value. Generally, there is a tendency to make the highest part the most important or lyrical, although exceptions to this are numerous. (In much MEDIEVAL and Renaissance music the part labeled *tenor*—either the lowest or an interior part —is of basic structural or melodic importance.) Often the term polyphony tends to imply that the various lines are of comparable importance. The independence of motion of the different parts may also vary greatly. At one extreme, this independence may be limited only by very loose melodic or harmonic conventions. At the other, one part may parallel another in strict fashion or submit to strict contrapuntal or harmonic laws that govern the vertical coincidence of parts. Under normal usage, the term polyphony implies the avoidance of the simultaneous use of parallel rhythmic or melodic contours, irrespective of the nature of the interdependence among the different voices.

Homophony refers to a style in which attention is focused on a primary melody, supported by chordal ACCOMPANIMENT. The manner in which this accompaniment is worked out may vary greatly. In a keyboard work, for example, the number of tones sounded simultaneously may change with great frequency, and linear interest may further be kept to a minimum through the liberal use of wide skips in the accompaniment. In other common solutions the tones of the chords may be played in consecutive fashion in repetitive patterns, which, though they have the continuity of a line, lack in melodic interest. On the other hand, the composer may choose to develop also secondary melodic motives that do not usurp the focus of attention. A concern for part-writing is in fact mandatory in most ENSEMBLE writing. Most art music from the 12th through the 16th centuries is essentially polyphonic. Both homophonic and polyphonic textures are important in the music of the 17th and early 18th centuries, while homophony is predominant in later music. However, comparatively few works are purely polyphonic or purely homophonic.

Theme: (1) a self-contained idea, either borrowed or newly invented, usually having a simple repetition pattern, used as the basis for a set of VARIATIONS; (2) a characteristic idea or group of ideas that figure prominently in the structure of a work or a movement thereof. The term is used loosely to designate any prominent and easily remembered MELODY within a large work.

Theorbo: a LUTE of the 17th century having, in addition to the normal complement of strings, a set of bass strings running outside the fingerboard. *See illustration, p. 167.*

Theory: in the current sense, a curriculum concerned with the materials of music and with basic musical skills other than performance. The most elementary stages of theory deal with NOTATION, the classification of INTERVALS, and the structure of SCALES and CHORDS. The student is then expected to learn the norms of traditional chord progression and the traditional rules of voice-leading in both HARMONY and COUNTERPOINT. The disciplines of EAR TRAINING and SIGHT SINGING help the student to notate music that has been heard and to obtain—either through actual singing or through the imagination—an impression of notated music without the aid of instrumental realization. Auxiliary skills, such as ORCHESTRATION, are provided in more advanced stages of theoretic training. Analysis of MELODY, RHYTHM, harmonic structure, and FORM also falls within the domain of theory. Narrow usage of the term theory precludes composition, despite the fact that one of the goals of theory is to provide a basis for musical creativity. Whereas in earlier centuries, theoretic training was usually directly applicable to composition, the gap between such training and the contemporary idiom has widened steadily during the 20th century.

In earlier centuries, theory had a still broader sense which included not only analytical and practical skills, but also the discipline of ACOUSTICS and the pertinent subsections of aesthetics and metaphysics.

Theremin: an ELECTRONIC INSTRUMENT producing one sound at a time; progression from one main tone to the next is not effected by sharply distinguished step or skip, but through a continuous gliding from PITCH to pitch. The instrument, invented before 1924 by L. Theremin, operates through the amplification of the frequency difference between two oscillating currents. This difference is controlled by motions of the hand toward or away from an antenna.

Third: any INTERVAL notated by skipping one alphabet letter (e.g., *d♯-f, d-f, d-f♯, d♭-f♯*). Humming the first two notes of *The Marines' Hymn* or *Old Black Joe* will illustrate the sound of a major third; the opening of Brahms' *Lullaby* or *Greensleeves* will recall a minor third.

Thirty-second note, rest:

Thomas, (Charles Louis) Ambroise: *b.* Metz, August 5, 1811; *d.* Paris, February 12, 1896. Thomas concluded his studies at the Paris Conservatoire with the winning of the Prix de Rome in 1832. Upon his return from his Italian stay he turned to a career as an OPERA composer, achieving considerable success thanks to a melodious style. His best known operas are *Mignon* and *Hamlet*. In 1852 he was appointed composition teacher at the Conservatoire, becoming director in 1871. He wrote also some sacred works, songs, CHAMBER MUSIC, and piano pieces.

Thompson, Randall: *b.* New York City, April 21, 1899. Thompson studied at Harvard University and worked further under BLOCH. From 1922 to 1925 he was a Fellow of the American Academy in Rome. He has since taught at several major American schools, most recently at Harvard. Thompson has written a few works in each of a wide variety of traditional genres, including three SYMPHONIES and a STRING QUARTET; he is especially successful as a choral composer (e.g., *Alleluia* and *Testament of Freedom*).

Thomson, Virgil: *b*. Kansas City, Mo., November 25, 1896. Before graduating from Harvard University, Thomson studied for a year with Boulanger in Paris. He returned to Paris (1925–32). From 1940 to 1954, Thomson was an influential critic for the *New York Herald Tribune*. The majority of his best-known works employ a simple DIATONIC style, reminiscent of American FOLK music and HYMNS; however, Thomson has also written in a dissonant, polytonal style and has used TWELVE-TONE techniques with freedom. He has written two OPERAS (*Four Saints in Three Acts* and *The Mother of Us All*), a BALLET, some fine film music, and a variety of orchestral, choral, solo vocal, ensemble, and keyboard music.

Thorough bass: FIGURED BASS.

Through-composed: a setting of a STROPHIC text in which different music is provided for each stanza of the poem; the term is a clumsy translation of the German *Durchkomponiert*.

Tie: a horizontal arc connecting two successive notes of the same PITCH, directing that the second be treated as a prolongation of the first rather than as a separate entity.

Tiento (S), **Tento** (P): a title employed for 16th-century keyboard compositions in imitative style, similar to the RICERCAR.

Tierce (F): (1) third; (2) an ORGAN stop sounding two octaves and a third higher than written. *Tierce de Picardie, see* PICARDY THIRD.

Timbale (F), **Timballo** (I): TIMPANI (kettledrum).

Timbre (F): TONE COLOR.

Time signature: a symbol used to indicate metrical organization. Usually this symbol consists of two numbers placed one over the other. The bottom number stands for a note value, the numbers 1, 2, 4, 8, and 16 representing whole notes, halves, quarters, eighths, and sixteenths, respectively. The top number indicates how many of these notes are to constitute a measure. Often the bottom number of a time signature indicates the note variety equivalent to the basic pulse of the music; this, however, is by no means invariable. In pieces with fast TEMPOS, the actual unit of time may be a note larger than the one indicated by the time signature, while in slow pieces, the unit of time may be smaller. The unit of time for pieces with 9/8 and 12/8 time-signatures is normally the dotted quarter-note, which serves also fast pieces in 6/8.

Many MARCHES—including the *Washington Post* and *Semper Fidelis*—are written in 6/8, with two beats to the bar. In a fast waltz, an entire measure of 3/4 time may be treated as a single unit. On the other hand, a slow movement with a 2/4 time-signature may employ the eighth note as the basic unit of time.

A symmetrical ordering of pulses is implied by all standard signatures (i.e., those with top numbers of 2, 3, 4, 6, 9, or 12). The signature 9/8, for example, indicates that the measure is to contain the equivalent of nine eighth-notes, grouped in threes. If the composer desires an asymmetrical grouping of the same values—as happens in some MODERN MUSIC — he may specify a signature such as $\frac{4+2+3}{8}$. The signatures, C (= 4/4, otherwise known as COMMON TIME) and ₵ (= 2/2, otherwise known as ALLA BREVE) are remnants of an earlier system of indicating rhythmic organization. In most music proper to the Western tradition a time-signature is placed at the beginning of the composition (or movement) and at every later point where a change in rhythmic organization occurs. Time signatures are not used, however, in the notation of free rhythms such as occur in GREGORIAN CHANT on the one hand, and in certain mid-20th-century works on the other.

Timpani (Kettledrums): large, single-headed DRUMS of definite PITCH, with bowl-shaped metal bodies and a mechanism to adjust the tension of the drumheads.

Tirasse (F): organ coupler.

Toccata (I): (1) a title (derived from *toccare,* to touch) employed for KEYBOARD pieces of the mid-16th to 20th centuries. Rhapsodic and virtuoso elements are prominent in many of the more familiar toccatas, and these traits, though not universally present, are regarded as characteristic of the genre. It is thus possible to speak of some works—e.g., certain BACH *Preludes*—as being in toccata style. The earliest toccatas are homophonic, alternating chordal and scale passages. Before the end of the 16th century Merulo developed a form based on the alternation of homophonic and fugal sections. Both sorts were developed further during the BAROQUE. The Italian composers, such as A. SCARLATTI and PASQUINI, developed the earlier type into brilliant showpieces, often of insignificant musical content. The north German composers, on the other hand, preferred the type incorporating fugal sections, this type reaching its apogee in the works of J. S. Bach. The toccata may be used also as an introductory movement before a FUGUE. A third type of toccata, in the style of a dignified prelude and serving a liturgical function, was cultivated by early Baroque composers such as FRESCOBALDI. Only sporadic examples of toccatas were written after the peak reached during the Baroque.

(2) The title for short movements in fanfare style, written for BRASS INSTRUMENTS (or fuller ensembles) in the early 17th century.

Toch, Ernst: *b.* Vienna, December 7, 1887; *d.* Santa Monica, October 1, 1964. Toch turned to a career in music after studying medicine and philosophy. He was active in various German cities until 1933, when he emigrated to the United States. He taught at the University of Southern California and at various other American schools. Toch has written OPERAS, film music, SYMPHONIES, CONCERTOS, miscellaneous orchestral and band music, CHAMBER works, piano pieces, songs, and choral music. His idiom emphasizes melodic flow and is basically tonal, although there are works incorporating TWELVE-TONE procedures.

Toëschi, Carlo Giuseppe: *b.* Padua, *c.*1722; *d.* Munich, April 12, 1788. A pupil of J. A. STAMITZ, Toëschi succeeded his teacher as concert master of the Mannheim orchestra. He remained with the court following its transfer to Munich and became music director in 1780. He wrote over 60 SYMPHONIES, an equal quantity of CHAMBER MUSIC, and BALLET music for OPERAS.

Tomaschek (Tomášek), Johann Wenzel (Jan Václav): *b.* Skutsch, April 17, 1774; *d.* Prague, April 3, 1850. Tomaschek was one of the more esteemed pianists, teachers, and composers of his day. His works include SONATAS and other pieces for piano, CHAMBER MUSIC, songs, a SYMPHONY, a CONCERTO, three OPERAS, and some sacred music.

Tombeau (F): a title employed by French composers for works written in honor of dead persons. Several such works were composed during the 17th century, and the title was revived during the 20th century by RAVEL (*Le Tombeau de Couperin*).

Tomkins, Thomas: *b.* St. David's, 1572; *d.* Martin Hussingtree, June 1656. A student of BYRD, Tomkins was organist of Worcester Cathedral *c.*1596–1646 and one of the organists at the Chapel Royal from 1621. A versatile composer, Tomkins wrote ANTHEMS, SERVICES, MADRIGALS, KEYBOARD works, and instrumental FANTASIAS.

Tom-tom: a DRUM of indefinite PITCH used by the American Indians and certain Oriental peoples. Imitations are sometimes found in dance bands. The term is sometimes used incorrectly for drums made of hollowed logs, known properly as *slit drums.*

Tonada (S): song.

Tonadilla (S): a Spanish OPERETTA.

Tonal: (1) a statement of a SEQUENCE or a FUGUE subject that is modified either in INTERVAL (e.g., a fourth changed to a fifth) or interval quality (a major third changed to a minor third), often to avoid premature change of key; (2) a style of composition in which the harmonic idiom is that of the major-minor system or is clearly derived therefrom. In some instances the use of this adjective is extended to apply to other compositions using a more modern harmonic idiom while still employing readily perceivable tone centers.

Tonality: (1) in the most comprehensive meaning, a sense of tonal gravity. The musical styles denoted are such that the listener consciously or subconsciously perceives that:

(a) the main musical impulses arise from and flow toward one or a limited number of tone centers, these tones thus acquiring greater importance than the remainder; (b) these tone centers themselves vary in importance and function, the main center serving as the point of ultimate repose (*see* FORM). In this sense, tonality may be observed in music based on the CHURCH MODES, in music based on the major and minor modes, and in much MODERN MUSIC that has broken away from the conventions of major and minor. (Much of the latter music is often—though incorrectly—referred to as *atonal.*) To a large extent, tonality is an objective quality dependent merely upon musical construction. However, there is also a limited area in which tonality is a subjective quality, dependent upon the listener's perceptivity and familiarity with a given idiom. Those who regularly listen to and perform music in contemporary idioms acquire the ability to perceive tone centers whose existence passes unnoticed by those who do not have a thorough familiarity with those idioms.

(2) In a more restricted meaning, the melodic, harmonic, and rhythmic vocabulary of the major-minor

system. The basic PITCH materials of major and minor are discussed under SCALE. Some of the conventions of this system are as follows. MELODY normally unfolds against a harmonic background, whether real or imaginary. (The frequency of broken CHORDS in melodic writing—e.g., in *The Star Spangled Banner* and in BEETHOVEN's *Eroica Symphony* —is one illustration of this trait.) The most important tonal center is established by the tonic chord. This is contrasted with a second important center established by the DOMINANT chord (based on the fifth degree), the subdominant chord constituting a possible third center. Each chord has but a few functions, these serving ultimately to circumscribe the TONIC. There is a powerful drive toward the tonic from the half-step below, the leading tone (seventh degree). The basic harmonic drives are reinforced by symmetrical rhythms, which help the informed listener to anticipate many progressions toward the tonal center. The composer may introduce tones foreign to the key for ornamental purposes, or, in an extended movement or work, he may introduce such notes in order to establish new keys — momentarily cancel-

ling the sense of tonal gravity that accrues to the main tone center. The various keys are related to each other in a fixed hierarchy. For any given key there are certain others that are considered as being "close" (i.e., those sharing the greatest amount of tonal material in common), while the remainder are considered as "distant" (with relatively little tonal material in common). The composer normally is expected to evolve a course between closely related keys, though he may often surprise the listener by an imaginative excursion to distant keys. Regardless of the freedom that may be employed in modulating from one key to another, a return to the original tonic is an inevitable expectation of the major-minor system.

(3) In the most limited sense, a synonym for *key*.

Tondichtung (G): SYMPHONIC POEM.

Tone: (1) a musical sound; the normal equivalent in British usage is note; (2) the quality of sound produced by an instrumentalist or vocalist. (3) short for whole tone (*see* WHOLE STEP); (4) one of the recitation formulas used in GREGORIAN CHANT.

Tone cluster: a group of neighboring notes, sounded together, thus producing a strong DISSONANCE. Tone clusters generally appear in works for piano or other keyboard instruments; they may be played with the fist, forearm, or elbow, rather than with the fingers.

Tone color: the quality of sound that permits one to distinguish between sounds of the same PITCH and intensity performed on different instruments or by different voices. Major principles determining this quality are discussed under ACOUSTICS.

Tone Poem: SYMPHONIC POEM.

Tone row: an ordering of pitches governing a TWELVE-TONE composition.

Tonguing: the use of the tongue for purposes of articulation in wind playing. *See* WOODWINDS; *technique.*

Tonic: (1) the main tone center of a composition, the first degree of the SCALE; (2) the CHORD founded thereon.

Tonic sol-fa: *see* SOLMIZATION.

Tonkunst (G): music.

Tonleiter (G): SCALE.

Tonreihe (G): TONE ROW.

Tonsatz, Tonstück (G): composition.

Tonus peregrinus (L): *see* PSALM TONES.

Tordion (F): *see* TOURDION.

Torelli, Giuseppe: *b.* Verona, April 22, 1658; *d.* Bologna, February 8, 1709. Famed as a violinist, Torelli's chief places of residence were Bo-

logna (1686–95, 1701–9), Ansbach (1697–99), and Vienna (1695, 1699–1701). Together with CORELLI, he played a vital role in the early development of the CONCERTO GROSSO. He was also among the first—perhaps actually the first—to write solo CONCERTOS for the violin. Other works include SINFONIAS, trio SONATAS, and other string CHAMBER MUSIC.

Totenmesse (G): REQUIEM Mass.

Touch: the manner in which a KEYBOARD performer strikes the keys of his instrument. Although the basic principles of piano, organ, harpsichord, and clavichord technique are similar, the finer details vary considerably because each instrument responds to key pressure in a different fashion. A tremendously refined control over striking speed and weight is required in order to obtain the fullest range of tonal nuance available on the piano. Because the mind is unable to calculate these fine gradations from a purely objective standpoint, the pianist's approach to these problems is generally indirect, involving the carriage of the fingers, hand, and arm both before and after striking, as well as the projection of emotional attitudes. Such subtleties are inappropriate to organ playing since the tone of that instrument is not affected by changes in striking speed. The organ, on the other hand, poses problems in legato playing and in release that are in some sense more acute than the equivalent problems on the piano. The harpsichord requires a slightly firmer touch than does the piano or organ.

Touche (F): (1) the key of a KEYBOARD instrument; (2) the FINGERBOARD of a string instrument; (3) a FRET; (4) obsolete synonym for TOCCATA.

Tract: an item of the PROPER of the MASS employed during Lent and Ember Days and as part of the REQUIEM Mass. On other occasions it is replaced by the ALLELUIA. The melodies are thought to belong to the earliest stratum of GREGORIAN CHANT.

Traetta, Tommaso Michele Francesco Saverio: *b*. Bitonto, March 30, 1727; *d*. Venice, April 6, 1779. A pupil of DURANTE, and one of the leading OPERA composers of his generation, Traetta was active in Naples, Parma, Vienna, Venice, St. Petersburg, and London. In addition to more than 40 operas (which anticipate some of GLUCK's "reform" features), he wrote an ORATORIO, a STABAT MATER and other sacred music, and separate ARIAS and duets.

Tranquillo (I): tranquil, calm.

Transcription: (1) a synonym for arrangement; (2) with regard to music written before 1650, the converting of an older form of NOTATION into a modern form.

Transition: (1) a passage that serves primarily a connective rather than a thematic function; (2) a change of key.

Transposing instruments: wind instruments that use a NOTATION not indicative of actual PITCH. (Nothing more than a convention of notation is involved.) A musician able to play one wind instrument is normally expected to be familiar with others of the same family. The convention referred to dictates that a given written symbol calls for the identical mode of playing (e.g., FINGERING) within a family of instruments regardless of the actual sound produced on a specific instrument. Thus, the note written c' calls for the same fingering on the oboe, the *oboe d'amore*, and the English horn. This fingering, however, produces c' on the oboe, a on the *oboe d'amore*, and f on the English horn. If the composer wishes the *oboe d'amore* to sound c', he must write eb'; if he wishes the English horn to sound c', he must write g'. If the composer did not transpose the music, then the player would have to learn a different set of fingerings or lip responses for each instrument of the family; his technical facility on the less-used instruments would be seriously impaired.

Transposing instruments are classed according to the sound produced when playing written *c*. Clarinet in B♭ means that the note written and fingered *c′* sounds *b♭*. From the above data, one can see that the *oboe d'amore* is an *A* instrument, while the English horn is an *F* instrument. Other important transposing instruments are the trumpet (and cornet) and French horn.

Some 18th- and early-19th-century music is written for particular forms of transposing instruments no longer used because of subsequent improvements in the technical capacities of the family as a whole. The player reading from such parts must be able to transpose the music to the proper level for the instrument he is playing. *See* TRANSPOSITION.

Transposition: the transference of a piece of music from its notated key to another. In this process all INTERVAL relationships present in the original are retained in the transposed version. The average listener will not be able to tell the difference between the two versions unless he is made aware of the change in PITCH level between the two. Sometimes transposition must be done at sight, while at other times a written transposition may be prepared in advance. No given key for a song is equally comfortable for singers with different ranges; therefore many songs with keyboard ACCOMPANIMENT are published in three keys, high, medium, and low. If the version at hand does not suit a particular singer, the accompanist is expected to be able to transpose his part at sight to a key more comfortable for the singer. A conductor must be able to transpose mentally those parts in a SCORE that are written for TRANSPOSING INSTRUMENTS. The conventions governing the use of these instruments have not remained constant during the past centuries, and the players of these instruments must be able to transpose parts written for species of instruments now largely obsolete. A part for French Horn is *E♭*, for example, must be transposed by the modern performer, who uses a horn in *F*.

Transverse flute: 18th-century term used to distinguish the flute from the RECORDER. The term flute then generally implied the latter rather than the former.

Traps: the various accessories

associated with drum playing in modern dance bands.

Trauermarsch (G): funeral march.

Trautonium: an ELECTRONIC INSTRUMENT producing one sound at a time, invented by F. Trautwein in 1930.

Traversa (I), **Traversière** (F), **Traverso** (I), **Traversflöte** (G): TRANSVERSE FLUTE.

Treble: (1) a child's VOICE of high range (the adult female equivalent is normally termed soprano); (2) a variety of CLEF; (3) the highest or one of the highest of a family of instruments; (4) the uppermost part of a composition.

Tre corde (I), **Tutte le corde** (I): a piano direction ordering the release of the soft (i.e., left-hand) pedal. *See* UNA CORDA.

Tremolo: (1) an extremely rapid repetition of a single note or an equally rapid alternation between two notes. The former kind of tremolo is characteristic of bowed string TECHNIQUE, being produced by tiny up and down strokes of the bow in quivering fashion. The effect is sometimes imitated on the piano by alternating notes an octave apart. (Flutter TONGUING is perhaps the closest approach to this sort of tremolo that is possible on wind instruments.) In string playing, the tremolo alternat-

ing between two notes is known as a fingered tremolo; the two notes involved are normally members of one chord. This effect is obtainable on other orchestral instruments and is also part of standard piano technique. On this instrument the effect may be enriched by alternating a group of two notes with a third.

(2) A wavering in the PITCH of a vocal tone that is wider than a VIBRATO. The vocal tremolo is usually a sign either of poor taste or poor control. (*See also* TRILLO.)

(3) A term used by Leopold Mozart as a synonym for vibrato.

Tremulant: an organ device that seeks to produce pulsations similar to those of a VIBRATO by alternately increasing and decreasing the wind pressure.

Trepak: a Russian dance in fast duple METER.

Triad: a CHORD of three tones, comprised of a chain of two thirds.

Triangle: a PERCUSSION INSTRUMENT of indefinite PITCH, made of a steel bar bent to form an equilateral triangle. The instrument is struck with a steel rod, and, in order that it may sound freely, is played suspended from a cord or hook.

Trill (Shake: Brit.): an ornament consisting of a rapid alternation between one note and another a second above it (occasionally, in MODERN MUSIC, a second below). The ornamental figure may be written out in full, leaving no doubt regarding its realization, or it may be indicated in abbreviated form by writing the main note and placing above it either *tr*, ᴧᴧᴧ, or both in succession. The number of notes in a trill depends largely on the length of the written note; there may be only a single alternation if this note is of very brief duration. Whether the unwritten note is to be a sharp, natural, or flat depends on the KEY SIGNATURE unless an ACCIDENTAL appears in conjunction with the symbol. In music of the 17th and 18th centuries the trill begins with the upper of the two notes unless this note immediately precedes the trill. In later music the trill begins with the main note. In all periods a composer may specify that the trill is to be preceded by an upper or lower APPOGGIATURA or that it is to be concluded with a TURN.

Trillo (I): in early-17th-century Italian vocal practice, an ORNAMENT consisting of a series of increasingly rapid reiterations of a tone written as a single note of moderate or long value.

Trio: (1) a work or movement for three INSTRUMENTS or VOICES. (In the latter event, the possible presence of an instrumental accompaniment is not taken into consideration in using the term.) The most common combinations found among instrumental trios are the piano trio—consisting of piano, violin, and cello—and the string trio—consisting of violin, viola, and cello. Regarding the customary structures of instrumental trios, *see* SONATA. (2) A composition written in three voice-parts, whether performed by one instrument (e.g., the *Trio Sonatas* for organ by BACH) or several. The customary scoring of a trio sonata is for four instruments. (3) The middle section of a MINUET or SCHERZO, as well as of certain other TERNARY FORMS (especially MARCHES). (4) A group of three performers.

Triplet: a group of three equal values (notes or rests) performed in the time of two or four. In some passages two of these values are combined into one larger value. A triplet is normally indicated by a *3* in italics.

Tritone: the INTERVAL of an augmented fourth, which contains three WHOLE STEPS.

Tromba (I): trumpet; *tromba da tirarsi*, slide trumpet.

Tromba marina (I), **Trum-**

scheit (G), **Marine trumpet,** **Nonnengeige** (G), **Trompette marine** (F): a bowed string instrument with a slender, tapering body about six feet long and only one visible string. Different PITCHES were obtained by touching rather than STOPPING this string, thus producing harmonics. These tones were reinforced and supplemented by the vibration of many sympathetic strings concealed within the body. The instrument was used from the 15th to the early 18th centuries.

Trombone: one of a small group of lower-pitched BRASS INSTRUMENTS.

Trommel (G): DRUM; *Grosse Trommel,* bass drum; *Kleine Trommel,* snare drum.

Trompete (G), **Trompette** (F): trumpet.

Trope: (1) an addition of words, music, or both, either before, in the course of, or after a liturgical CHANT. See MEDIEVAL MUSIC. (2) A form of TWELVE-TONE organization proposed in the 20th century by Josef Hauer. In this sense, a trope consists of two 6-note segments with no repeated notes or notes in common. In Hauer's theory, the trope is defined by the musical content of each of the two segments and not by the ordering of the notes (i.e., their intervallic relationship).

Troppo (I): too much.

Troubadours, Trouvères: MEDIEVAL poet-musicians who wrote in Provençal and Old French, respectively.

Trumpet: one of a family of higher-pitched BRASS INSTRUMENTS.

Tschaikowsky: *see* TCHAIKOVSKY.

Tuba: (1) one of a group of lower-pitched BRASS INSTRUMENTS; (2) the reciting note (dominant, tenor) of a PSALM TONE.

Tubular bells: *see* CHIMES.

Tucket: a fanfare of trumpets and drums of the Elizabethan period.

Tuning: (1) a method of calculating the PITCH relationships between the various INTERVALS of a musical system. Given a pitch standard for a single note, one must be able to calculate the correct pitches for the remaining notes. Various methods of determining relative pitches have been employed in Western music.

Just intonation is one of the two "natural" methods of establishing pitch relationships between the intervals of our tonal system. The initial pitch standard is furnished by the full-length vibration of a string. Stopping the string at the halfway point doubles the frequency of vibration and produces the octave. If a third of the string is dampened, the remaining segment vibrates 3/2 as quickly as the full string and produces the fifth; if a fourth of the string is dampened, the remaining segment produces the fourth, while if a fifth of the string is dampened, the remainder produces the major third. Other intervals may be calculated by combining the ratios of these basic intervals; these ratios must be multiplied (or divided), not added. A major seventh, for example, is produced by combining a fifth and a major third ($3/2 \times 5/4 = 15/8$). A major sixth may be established by combining a major third and a fourth ($5/4 \times 4/3 = 5/3$), though a slightly more complicated process is often used. A major second is obtained by combining two fifths and lowering the result by an octave ($3/2 \times 3/2 \div 2 = 9/8$).

While the individual intervals produced in just intonation may sound "purer" than those in the present system of equal temperament (see below), there are serious drawbacks to the system as a whole. The interval ratios do not always remain constant within the system of just intonation. If, for example, the ratio of the major third, c-e, is 5/4 and the ratio of the major second, c-d, is 9/8, then the ratio of the major second, d-e, is not also 9/8 but 10/9 ($5/4 \div 9/8$). Furthermore, not all fifths are pure; in a system calculated from the base, c, the fifth, d-a, would have a ratio of 40/27 instead of the ratio 3/2. Because of these discrepancies modulation is extremely awkward, if not impossible, within this system.

Pythagorean tuning, the second of the "natural" methods of tuning, is based on our ability to distinguish when a perfect fifth is in tune

1:1 9:8 5:4 4:3 3:2 5:3 15:8 2:1

1:1 9:8 81:64 4:3 3:2 27:16 243:128 2:1

(i.e., when a ratio of 3/2 exists). The various tones of the scale are obtained by proceeding around a spiral of fifths, producing the results above.

Although the Pythagorean system is reasonably satisfactory for diatonic melodies, difficulties are encountered when chromatic notes are introduced. Enharmonic notes (e.g., *b♯* and *c,* or *c♯* and *d♭*), which are identical in pitch in our present system of tuning, are nearly a quarter of a tone apart in the Pythagorean system. (*See* COMMA.)

The term *temperament* denotes various compromise systems of tuning and occasionally the two natural systems of tuning as well. *Meantone temperament,* which was known by the beginning of the 16th century, is based on a fifth with a ratio slightly less than 3/2. The third of just intonation is expanded by two octaves and this interval is divided into four equal fifths. Meantone tuning works well in simple keys, but is poor in keys with more than three sharps or flats.

In *equal temperament,* the system presently used, the octave is divided into twelve halfsteps of equal size. Thus, no one key is favored at the expense of others, and accidentals and modulations may be employed freely. It should be noted that, except for the octave, none of the intervals in equal temperament is identical with its counterpart in just or Pythagorean tuning. However, our ears have become adjusted to these compromises. A very close approximation of equal temperament was suggested by Vincenzo Galilei in 1581, and the system itself was described by Mersenne in 1635. However, equal temperament was not universally adopted throughout Europe until the mid-19th century. Other musical cultures employ different tunings.

(2) The act of adjusting the pitch of an instrument to bring it into accord with a preestablished standard. This standard is usually furnished by a TUNING FORK or tuning bar. In string instruments, pitch is regulated by adjusting the tension of the strings. In wind instruments, the length of the wind column is adjusted, either by moving the reed or mouthpiece in or out, or by working a tuning slide.

Present standards of pitch are of comparatively recent origin; several standards existed during the 17th and 18th centuries. (Lack of data prevents the drawing of conclusions regarding pitch in earlier periods.)

The three main varieties of

BAROQUE and CLASSICAL pitch standards are generally known as chamber pitch (*Kammerton*), choir pitch (*Chorton*), and cornett pitch (*Cornettton*); they governed instrumental ensemble music, organ and choir music, and brass band music, respectively. Thus, a note written *c* would vary in pitch according to the standard employed. Furthermore, the standards themselves varied in different places and at different times. The choir pitch used in a North German organ might be as much as a whole step higher than that in a Prague organ; both would be higher than present standard pitch. Chamber pitch, on the other hand, was generally a half-step lower than present standard pitch. In other words, the orchestral works of BACH, HANDEL, HAYDN, and MOZART generally sounded a half-step lower than they do now. Cornett pitch, of less importance, was, like choir pitch, higher than present standard pitch.

The standard represented by chamber pitch rose steadily in the early 19th century. In 1858 the Paris Academy recommended that the pitch of the *a* above *middle c* be fixed at 435 vibrations per second; international recognition of this standard was given at a Vienna conference in 1889. Within recent years the standard was raised slightly, and now the same note is fixed at 440 vibrations per second.

Tuning fork: a small, slender, two-pronged steel fork that is used to provide a standard for the judging of PITCH accuracy in VOICES or INSTRUMENTS. (*See* TUNING, sense 2.)

Turca, Alla (I): in Turkish style. This designation was used for works written around the turn of the 19th century that purported to give the flavor of Turkish military music with its many PERCUSSION INSTRUMENTS.

Turina, Joaquin: *b.* Seville, December 9, 1882; *d.* Madrid, January 14, 1949. Prominent among Spanish nationalistic composers, Turina completed his studies in Paris under D'INDY and Moritz Moszkowski. His style, which exhibits both ROMANTIC and IMPRESSIONISTIC traits, was influenced by ALBÉNIZ and DE FALLA. Turina wrote SYMPHONIC POEMS, CHAMBER and KEYBOARD MUSIC, songs, OPERAS, and incidental music.

Turn: an ORNAMENT that weaves about a main tone, first from above, then from below. This decorative figure may be written out in full or be represented by a sign, as shown on page 408. The in-

verted turn is a similar ornament, starting, however, from
underneath.

Tutte le corde (I): *see* TRE
CORDE.

Tutti (I): passages in orchestral works, especially in CON-
CERTOS, where the full OR-
CHESTRA is employed rather
than limited accompanying
or soloistic groups.

**Twelve-tone music, Twelve-
note music (Brit.)** (Serial music, Dodecaphony): modern
compositions based on a
TONE ROW. This row, set, or
series is a succession of the
twelve PITCHES of the octave
in an order chosen by the
composer. The material subsequently used in the composition itself is derived from
the continuous repetition of
the series in changing rhythmic guise; hence the term
serial technique. The tones
of the row may be used successively to furnish MELODY,
or simultaneously to furnish
HARMONY. A composer may
base the melody of a work
on one statement of his row,
while using another statement
of the row for harmony. Or
he may employ selected tones
of his row for the melody,
while using the remaining
tones in proper rhythmic
place for the harmony. In
strict style each statement of
the row must be complete; a
tone may be reiterated but
may not otherwise recur
within a single statement of
the row; no extraneous material is employed. Different
composers treat the TECH-
NIQUE with various degrees
of freedom; sometimes serial
and tonal techniques may be
combined.

The serial technique is
more flexible than might appear at first glance. A tone
row may be used in its original form, in INVERSION, in
RETROGRADE, and in retro-
grade inversion. Any one of
these four forms may be
transposed to begin with any
one of the twelve pitches of
the OCTAVE. Each of the notes
of a row may be employed

in any octave register desired by the composer. Usually great rhythmic freedom prevails, although more recent serial techniques seek to control the succession of note-values and dynamic levels according to preselected patterns, in manner similar to that which establishes control over INTERVAL content.

The twelve-tone technique was developed shortly after 1920 by Arnold SCHOENBERG. BERG and WEBERN were among its first outstanding adherents; other composers, including STRAVINSKY, have employed it occasionally. The technique is associated with irregular pitch contours, expressive melodic leaps, fluid rhythms, and a lack of emphasis on tonal centers. However, it permits a considerable range of style since it is concerned primarily with a form of musical organization.

Tye, Christopher: *b. c.*1500; *d.* 1573. An important composer of sacred music, Tye wrote MASSES, MOTETS, ANTHEMS, and SERVICES, together with some instrumental ENSEMBLE music. He was master of the choristers at Ely Cathedral (1541–61).

Tympani: alternative spelling for TIMPANI.

Tympanon (Gr): (1) an obsolete term for large DRUMS; (2) a medieval term for DULCIMER.

U

Übung (G): study.

Ukulele: a small, four-stringed Hawaiian guitar. Ukulele music is written in a TABLATURE notation in which four vertical lines represent the strings of the instrument, a series of horizontal lines, the frets.

Dots indicate finger placement.

Una corda (I): "one string," a PIANO direction ordering the use of the soft (i.e., left) pedal. The direction to release the pedal is *tre corde* (or *tutte le corde*), "three strings" (or "all the strings"). The terminology refers to the fact that all except the lowest two dozen notes of the piano are provided with three strings each. In the grand piano, the action of the soft pedal shifts the entire keyboard to the right so that the hammer does not hit all three. (In piano of the late 18th and early 19th centuries, use of the soft pedal resulted in the hammer hitting only one string and in a noticeable change in TONE COLOR.) In upright pianos, the bank of hammers is shifted closer to the strings.

Ungherese, All' (I): in Hungarian style. The term does not distinguish between the gypsy idiom and the Hungarian folk idiom proper. A poor spelling, *all' ungarese,* is also found.

Unison: (1) an INTERVAL formed when two parts employ the same sound; (2) in unison denotes the performance of a passage by more than one INSTRUMENT or VOICE, regardless of whether the doubling is at the identical PITCH or one or more octaves higher or lower.

Unterwerk (G): Choir ORGAN.

Upbeat: (1) the last beat of a measure, signaled in conducting by an upward motion of the hand or BATON; (2) one or more notes that: (a) occur in the last portion of a measure and (b) function as the beginning of a PHRASE or motive.

Up-bow: the motion in which the BOWING arm comes toward or across the body, pushing the bow across the string.

Ussachevsky, Vladimir: *b.* Hailar, Manchuria, November 3, 1911. Trained at the Eastman School of Music, and a faculty member of Columbia University, Ussachevsky has composed a few works for traditional media. He is best known, however, for his efforts at furthering ELECTRONIC MUSIC and for his compositions for tape recorder.

Ut (L): (1) the first PITCH of a HEXACHORD; (2) the note *c* in French usage.

V

Valse (F): WALTZ.

Valve: a mechanism used in BRASS INSTRUMENTS to shunt the airstream through an additional section of tubing.

Vamp: an improvised introduction or ACCOMPANIMENT to a popular song, utilizing a simple (and generally repetitive) harmonic and rhythmic scheme.

Varèse, Edgar: b. Paris, December 22, 1885; d. New York City, November 6, 1965. Trained by D'INDY, ROUSSEL, and WIDOR, Varèse was active in Paris and Berlin as a choral conductor. He came to the United States in 1915 and devoted himself to the promotion of MODERN MUSIC, being responsible for first American performances of music by SCHOENBERG, WEBERN, BERG, and others. The idiom of his early works reflects both ROMANTIC and IMPRESSIONISTIC traits, but after World War I Varèse began to use a wider vocabulary of sounds in a dissonant and often athematic context. He used standard, percussion, and electronic instruments in great variety and number in unusual combinations. Complex rhythmic constructions often constitute the most important structural element of the music. In the 1950s Varèse began to write ELECTRONIC MUSIC. Although few of his works have gained wide circulation (*Ionisation, Density 21.5, Intégrales*), Varèse is regarded as one of the important figures of his generation by many progressive composers of the mid-20th century.

Variation: (1) a basic principle of musical construction, involving the modification of familiar material. It is generally implied that both the material to be modified and the modification occur within the same work, but variation technique may also be applied to the quotation of material drawn from outside sources—e.g., a familiar tune, PLAINSONG, etc. (In this sense, works labeled as *paraphrases, arrangements,* and *transcriptions* fall within the category of variation.) (2) the modification discussed above (i.e., a passage rather than the process itself). *See also* VARIATIONS.

The means of variation are numerous. A MELODY may be altered simply by surrounding the chief notes with ornamental figuration. If the chief notes retain their original rhythmic positions, the relationship between variation and original is immediately clear to the listener. As the ORNAMENTED configuration becomes richer and as more of the chief notes are shifted to slightly different rhythmic positions, variation presents increasingly subtle possibilities. The simplest sort of rhythmic variation may be obtained merely by shifting values occurring on the BEAT to offbeats. Or, variation may involve a change of METER—e.g., from duple to triple—or of MODE—i.e., from major to minor. The original melody may be presented unchanged but surrounded by new HARMONIES or new COUNTERPOINTS. Or the melody itself may be partially or entirely abandoned in favor of new melodic material constructed over the harmonies of the original. Specific passages may combine two or more of these techniques. In the freest sort of variation not even the structure of the original may be retained, the relationship between model and variation depending upon the use of characteristic motives common to both.

Variations: (1) a generic designation for musical works which consist of a series of modifications of given material. (2) a shortened form of THEME and variations, the most familiar of the specific categories included within the generic meaning of the term. Other works comprehended within that meaning are DIFERENCIA, STROPHIC bass, GROUND, DIVISION, BASSO OSTINATO, CHACONNE, PASSACAGLIA, etc.; certain PARTITAS, RHAPSODIES, GLOSAS, and early SUITES; BACH's *Musical Offering* and R. STRAUSS's TONE POEM *Don Quixote*. A set of variations may constitute an independent work or may occur as a section within a large instrumental or vocal work.

One may distinguish between two main classes of variations according to the nature of the material furnishing the basis for variation. In one class the material consists of a brief harmonic progression that may or may not be associated with a repetitive bass line. In the passacaglia and chaconne, the two best-known genres of this class, the germ material is often either four or eight measures in length and in triple meter; the material is not musically self-sufficient, but is designed so that the end of one statement fuses naturally with the beginning of the next. The continuous history of this class of variation begins with 16th-century dance forms such as the romanesca and passamezzo. The class was developed extensively during the BAROQUE, reaching a peak in such diverse works of Bach as the organ *Passacaglia in c minor*, the *Chaconne* from the *Partita in d minor* for solo violin, and the *Crucifixus* of the *B minor Mass* (based on a movement from Cantata 12). Its use declined rapidly after the mid-18th century; nevertheless later examples of magnificence—such as the last movement of BRAHMS' Fourth Symphony—are to be found.

In the other class of variations, the germ material (or theme) consists of a MELODY together with its concomitant HARMONIES. This theme, which may be either newly composed or borrowed from another work, usually possesses a simple, repetitive structure and constitutes a unit, which, however small, is capable of standing alone. Although many examples of this class of variations were written during the 16th and 17th centuries, the class assumed major artistic significance only in the mid-18th

century with such works as Bach's Goldberg Variations. From that point on, the form grew in importance in the works of HAYDN, MOZART, BEETHOVEN, and Brahms. The form continued to be of interest during the first half of the 20th century, although its use waned steadily. The evolution of this class is one directed toward increasing freedom of treatment. In most early variations, there was fairly strict adherence to both the melody and the harmony of the theme, the most important variation technique being melodic ORNAMENTATION. During the 18th and 19th centuries, the dependence on the melodic outline of the theme grew less and less. In many Beethoven variations the relationship between variation and theme is principally that of similar or identical harmonic progression, while even this tie is weakened in certain variations by Brahms. In still more advanced, "free" variations by SCHUMANN, D'INDY, and R. STRAUSS, only the recall of prominent motives links specific variations with the theme serving as a point of departure.

Variazione (I): VARIATION.

Varsovienne (F): a dance of Polish origin, popular around 1850–70, in slow triple METER, with dotted rhythms.

Vaudeville: (1) a topical, often satirical French song of the turn of the 18th century, usually set to a popular tune. By extension, the term has been applied to other sorts of popular songs. (2) A French term for musical comedies and similar variety shows from the 18th century on.

Vaughan Williams, Ralph: *b.* Down Ampney, October 12, 1872; *d.* London, August 26, 1958. Vaughan Williams studied at the Royal College of Music under Charles Parry and Charles Stanford and also under BRUCH in Berlin and RAVEL in Paris. He taught at the Royal College immediately after World War I and was active as a conductor and as a member of the English Folk-Song Society. Intensely interested in his national heritage, Vaughan Williams furthered the nationalistic awakening among 20th-century English composers. He arranged FOLK SONGS and his melodic writing was influenced by them. His major works include nine SYMPHONIES, two CONCERTOS, the *Fantasia on a Theme by Tallis* and other orchestral works, CHAMBER MUSIC, numerous sacred and secular choral works, six OPERAS and other stage music, and many songs.

Vecchi, Orazio: *b.* Modena, December 1550; *d.* Modena, February 19, 1605. Choir director at Cathedrals of Reggio and Modena and also to the duke of Modena, Vecchi composed MASSES, MOTETS, CANZONETTE, and MADRIGALS. His best known work is the "madrigal opera," *L'Amfiparnaso,* a set of 15 pieces, dramatic in nature but not intended to be staged.

Venetian Swell: a device to control volume on an ORGAN.

Vent (F): wind.

Ventil (G), **Ventile** (I): valve.

Veracini, Francesco Maria: *b.* Florence, February 1, 1690; *d.* near Pisa, *c.*1750. One of the most famous violin virtuosos of his time, Veracini traveled widely, playing in Venice, London, Dresden and Prague, among major musical centers. He was an important composer of SONATAS and CONCERTOS for violin, writing also SYMPHONIES for string orchestra, OPERAS, and CANTATAS.

Verdelot, Phillipe: *d. c.*1540. One of the earliest madrigalists, Verdelot was a Frenchman active in Venice and Florence. His sacred music includes a book of MOTETS and one MASS.

Verdi, Giuseppe: *b.* Le Roncole, October 10, 1813; *d.* Milan, January 27, 1901; the greatest Italian OPERA composer.

The son of an innkeeper,

Verdi received his first music lessons from the village organist, whom he succeeded when still a boy. He studied also with Provesi at nearby Busseto and acted as assistant conductor for the Busseto Philharmonic. In 1832, Verdi applied for admission to the Milan Conservatory, but was refused. He studied instead with Lavigna, a member of the La Scala staff. The years 1834–38 were spent chiefly at Busseto, where Verdi wrote his first opera, *Oberto, conte di San Bonifacio.* The success of this work and of his third opera, *Nabucco,* firmly launched his career as an independent composer. In all, Verdi wrote 26 operas, including more than a half dozen outstanding masterpieces. With the exception of the "Manzoni *Requiem,*" completed in 1874, and his last work, *Four Sacred Pieces,* his few other works are incidental. Verdi wrote only one wholly instrumental work, a STRING QUARTET with numerous operatic traits.

Verdi's creative life may be divided into four periods. The first includes the fifteen operas produced between 1838 and 1850; among these are *I Lombardi, Ernani, Macbeth,* and *Luisa Miller.* The second period (considered by some as the culmination of the first), includes his first three masterpieces, *Rigoletto* (1851), *Il Trovatore* (1853), and *La Traviata* (1853). The third period includes the two grand operas written for Paris, *Les Vêpres siciliennes* and *Don Carlos,* together with *Simone Boccanegra, Un ballo in maschera, La forza del destino,* and *Aida,* commissioned for the 1871 ceremonies marking the opening of the Suez Canal. The fourth period is comprised of Verdi's two finest works, *Otello* (1887) and *Falstaff* (1893).

Verdi was aware of international developments in opera and respected the achievements of WAGNER. Unlike the latter, he was no revolutionary. His art is founded on the centuries-old tradition of Italian opera and, more specifically, on the achievements of ROSSINI, DONIZETTI, and BELLINI. Verdi had strong nationalistic feelings and held that each composer should create within the idiom natural to his country. For an Italian, this meant emphasis on vocal MELODY and clarity of FORM. Vocal ensembles were accepted as a matter of course and handled skillfully. The CHORUS also has a notable role in many Verdi operas. Many of his most famous melodies are constructed over rather plain HARMONIES; the ORCHESTRATION of his early works rarely exceeds the conventional. Because of these traits his works were scorned by many Germans of Wagner's convictions. Verdi's greatness rests, however, not merely on his melodic gifts. He had an instinct for dramatic situations and an ability to capture them in his music; he had a deep interest in human problems and conflicts—as opposed to abstract symbolism —and was able to create moving musical characterizations. As he matured, his technique became more refined. His harmonies became richer and subtler, his orchestration more imaginative. He occasionally used recurrent musical motives for dramatic effect, as in *La forza del destino,* but such devices are not basic to his technique. In *Otello* and in *Falstaff—* Verdi's only comedy except for his unsuccessful second opera, *Un giorno di Regno—* there is a continuous undercurrent of orchestral music, fusing the individual vocal sections into larger formal units.

Verismo (I): a late-19th-century operatic movement seeking to depict contemporary life in "realistic" terms. Among the best known examples are MASCAGNI's *Cavalleria Rusticana* and LEONCAVALLO's *Pagliacci.* The subject matter of works such as these concerns the emotional crises of "ordinary" people. The musical style abandons the pretty tunes and virtuoso ARIAS of traditional Italian opera in favor of terser, less symmetrical melodies. A more lyrical style is displayed in the works of PUCCINI, which stem from this movement.

Verschiebung (G): soft pedal.

Verse: a SOLO section of certain GREGORIAN CHANTS that employs as text the verse of a PSALM, CANTICLE, or—occasionally—another Scriptural text.

Verset: a short piece for organ, based on a PLAINSONG; in the Catholic rite this instrumental piece may replace the normal vocal performance of the plainsong. During the 16th to 18th centuries many composers wrote organ settings for the even-numbered verses of PSALMS, CANTICLES, and the MAGNIFICAT, the odd-numbered verses being performed in plainsong.

Vespers: the evening services of the Roman Catholic and Anglican Churches. In the Roman Catholic rite, Vespers is the only one of the several Hours of Divine Service in which polyphonic music is admitted. (*See* OFFICE.)

Vibraphone: a member of the XYLOPHONE family, with metal bars and tuned, tubular resonators.

Vibrato: a rapid and minute

fluctuation of PITCH, employed to give warmth to tones of moderate or long length. On string instruments, vibrato is produced by a shaking motion of the hand, which moves the finger stopping a string a sufficient distance back and forth to produce a tonal fluctuation. As late as the mid-18th century the use of string vibrato was restricted to passages of particular importance. Nowadays most performers employ vibrato throughout, technical demands permitting. On wind instruments, vibrato is usually produced by tiny fluctuations in breath pressure. In addition, a trombonist may obtain a broad vibrato—used chiefly in popular music—through rapid, tiny, back-and-forth motions of the slide. A vibrato is possible also on the clavichord, being produced by a series of reiterated pressures on a key being held down. The result is a change of tension that affects pitch; the technique is commonly known under the German term, *Bebung*. Effects similar to vibrato are possible also on the ORGAN, vibraphone (*see* XYLOPHONE, sense 2), and ELECTRONIC keyboard instruments. Singers may produce a vibrato through variation of breath pressure. The fluctuation of pitch observable in a good vibrato—whether vocal or instrumental—is expected to be very small; a coarse vibrato is deemed to be in poor taste.

Vicentino, Nicola: *b.* Vicenza, 1511; *d.* Rome, 1572. Both theorist and composer, Vicentino is known for his interest in chromaticism and in MICROTONES. He served the Cardinal Ippolito d'Este and published four books of MADRIGALS, only the first surviving.

Victoria, Tomás Luis de: *b.* Ávila, 1548(?); *d.* Madrid, August 27, 1611. Victoria entered the Collegium Germanicum in Rome in 1565 to prepare for the priesthood and to further his musical studies. From 1569 to 1584 he held various posts at Roman churches and seminaries, succeeding his friend PALESTRINA as choir director at the Collegium Germanicum in 1571. Victoria returned to Spain as chaplain to Empress Maria and spent his last years as music director at the Convent of the Descalzas Reales, Madrid. Victoria was one of the great masters of the late RENAISSANCE. His MASSES, MAGNIFICATS, MOTETS, REQUIEMS, PSALMS, etc., are highly expressive, often mystical. He wrote no secular music. Victoria's technique is similar to that of Palestrina, although more varied, including more melodic leaps and more frequent harmonic passages.

Vielle (F): (1) a medieval fiddle with four strings for melody playing and one drone string; (2) a short form of *vielle à roue*, a term used in the 17th and 18th centuries for the HURDY-GURDY (*see* sense 2 of that term).

Viertel (G): quarter note.

Vieuxtemps, Henri: *b.* Verviers, February 17, 1820; *d.* Mustapha, June 6, 1881. After preliminary study with his father and Lecloux, Vieuxtemps studied briefly with Charles (= Auguste) de Bériot. He began to tour Europe—and later the United States—as a violinist by the age of thirteen. He taught at the St. Petersburg Conservatory and was soloist to the tsar (1846–51), and professor of violin at the Brussels Conservatory (1871–73). One of the outstanding performers of his day, Vieuxtemps wrote chiefly for his own instrument, including seven violin CONCERTOS, works for violin and piano, and CADENZAS to BEETHOVEN's *Violin Concerto.*

Vif (F): lively.

Vihuela (S): (1) short form for *vihuela de mano,* a Spanish instrument of the 16th century shaped like a large guitar (i.e., with a waisted body and flat back). Some forms had six courses of strings tuned in the manner of a LUTE. (Seven-course forms with different tunings also existed.) Music for this instrument was written in TABLATURE. (2) *Vihuela de arco,* viol; *vihuela de braço,* violin. (3) A generic term for string instruments.

Villa-Lobos, Heitor: *b.* Rio de Janeiro, March 5, 1887; *d.* Rio de Janeiro, November 17, 1959. Villa-Lobos obtained the rudiments of music from his father and studied briefly at the National Institute of Music in Rio. Deeply interested in the folk music of his country, he made several trips to the interior of Brazil to collect FOLK SONGS. These exercised a powerful influence on his music. A government grant in 1923 made possible a trip to Europe. In 1932 he was appointed superintendent of music education in Rio; his innovations vitalized public music programs throughout Brazil. The greatest among Latin American composers, Villa-Lobos was incredibly prolific, though his works are of uneven quality. His compositions include OPERAS, BALLETS, SYMPHONIES, SYMPHONIC POEMS, CONCERTOS, CHAMBER and piano music, songs, choruses, and an ORATORIO. His style is basically tonal, although often charged with DISSONANCE; there is a large sweep to much of his work that is romantic in spirit. The color palette is rich and often unusual for its time. For example, his *Bachianas Brasileiras* Nos. 1, 2, 5 are scored for eight cellos, the last two employing voice also.

Villancico (S): (1) a Spanish musico-poetic refrain form of the 15th and 16th centuries with a structure similar to or identical with that of the VIRELAI. There are examples both for ensembles of either three or four VOICES and for SOLO voice with vihuela accompaniment. (2) A Spanish work of the 17th or 18th century, written for vocal soloists, CHORUS, and orchestra, in the pattern of a CANTATA (i.e., in several movements, some using solo voice(s), others for chorus). The texts were on sacred subjects, frequently pertaining to Christmas. (3) In modern Spanish usage, a Christmas carol.

Villanella (I), **Villanesca** (I), **Villota** (I): (1) three terms of the 16th and early 17th centuries (the first two being nearly interchangeable) for light, dancelike partsongs in popular vein intended for sophisticated, aristocratic audiences. The most common scoring of the villanella is for three VOICES, while the villota is usually for four. The latter,

which was known in the early 16th century, often reveals elements drawn from street songs and delights in the use of nonsense syllables. All are primarily chordal and display a coarseness in the handling of parallel motion that would not have been acceptable in more polished forms. (2) The first two of these terms have been adopted by 19th- and early-20th-century composers for pieces in rustic style, both instrumental and vocal.

Viol: one of a family of bowed string instruments having three principal sizes, treble, tenor, and bass. Smaller sizes, as well as a double bass, were also known. Widely used during the 16th and 17th century, the viols outwardly resemble members of the VIOLIN FAMILY. Nevertheless, there are important differences in detail: the viols have sloping rather than rounded shoulders, flat rather than convex backs, six strings rather than four, sound-holes in a c- rather than f-shape, deeper ribs, a less arched bridge, and frets. Because the instruments were played resting on the knees or held between them, they were known under the generic heading *viola da gamba.* In the 18th century, this term designated the bass viol, the only member of the family still in frequent use. The stick of the viol bow curves slightly out from the hair and is held from below. The strings are tuned in fourths except for a third in the middle. The instruments produce a lighter, less richly colored sound than do violins. As a family, they reached a peak of popularity in 17th-century England; a good "chest of viols" included two each of the main sizes. The bass viol was used extensively to reinforce the BASS LINE of the CONTINUO; it possesses also a significant accompanied SOLO repertoire, including works by MARAIS, Karl Abel, and BACH.

Viola: the second highest member of the VIOLIN FAMILY, slightly larger than the violin and tuned a fifth lower.

Viola da braccio (I): (1) in the 17th century, a generic name for string instruments held against the shoulder ("in the arm"); (2) in the 16th and 17th centuries, a generic term for the VIOLIN FAMILY, including those members of the family (e.g., the cello) that were not held "in the arm"; (3) in the early 18th century, a term for the VIOLA.

Viola da gamba: see VIOL.

Viola d'amore (I): (1) in 17th-century usage, a violin or treble viol having wire strings; (2) in later usage, a string instrument akin to the treble viol, but having below the six or seven strings an additional set of strings not touched by the bow. The latter provide resonance through sympathetic vibration (see ACOUSTICS). The viola d'amore is held as a modern viola. It is used rarely, but appears in scores by BACH, HAYDN, MEYERBEER, R. STRAUSS, PUCCINI, and HINDEMITH.

Viola pomposa (I): an 18th-century bowed string instrument that was apparently a large viola with five strings. Parts were written for the instrument by TELEMANN and GRAUN, among others. BACH neither invented the instrument nor wrote for it, stories to the contrary notwithstanding. *Violino pomposo* seems to have been an alternate name for the same instrument.

Viole (F, G): VIOL.

Violin family: at present, a group of four instruments: violin, viola, violoncello (cello), and double bass (bass fiddle, bass viol, contrabass). Before the 19th century the term violin referred to the entire family, which then included instruments of other sizes now discarded (such as the violino piccolo, tenor violin, and violoncello piccolo).

The violin has a body length of approximately 14 inches, the viola about 16 inches, the cello about 30 inches, and the double bass

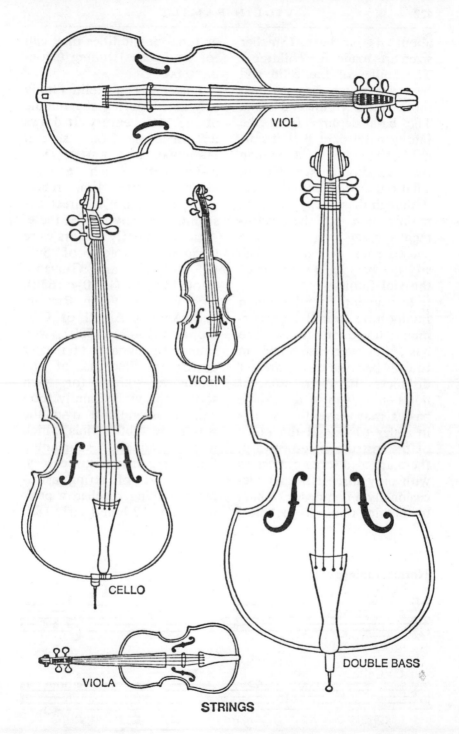

VIOL

VIOLIN

CELLO

VIOLA

DOUBLE BASS

STRINGS

about 44 inches. (Smaller sizes are made for children.) The bodies of the cello and bass are much deeper than those of the violin and viola. The bass departs from the family pattern in that it normally has sloping rather than rounded shoulders and often a flat rather than convex back. Although these departures are mainly due to the instrument's great size, they have caused some writers to classify the bass as a member of the viol family.

Instruments of the violin family have four strings, normally tuned in fifths. The bass, however, is tuned in fourths because of the greater distances between adjacent notes on a given string. (Some basses may have five strings in order to extend the range of the instrument downward; there are also some old basses with only three strings.) Occasionally a composer seeking to obtain unusual technical or tonal possibilities may call for an unusual tuning (SCORDATURA).

History. The violin family originated during the middle of the 16th century. It draws its features from several MEDIEVAL and RENAISSANCE instruments (such as the vielle, violetta, lira, rebec, etc.), but is not a direct descendant of any one of these. Among the early makers were Gasparo Bertolotti of Salò (1540–1609) and Giovanni Paolo Maggini (1580–c.1632), who were active in Brescia, and Andrea Amati of Cremona (c.1505–c.1580), who founded a dynasty of master craftsmen. Because of the BAROQUE liking for rich sound, the violin family soon gained ascendance over the softer and subtler viols, which were gradually supplanted during the late 17th century.

The art of string-instrument making reached a peak in the late 17th and early 18th

Normal tunings of:

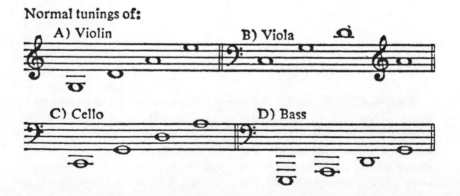

A) Violin   B) Viola

C) Cello   D) Bass

centuries. Nicolo Amati (1596–1684)—a grandson of Andrea; Antonio Stradivari (1644–1737)—one of Nicolo's pupils; Giuseppe Guarneri del Gesù (1687–1744), and the Tyrolean Jacob Stainer (1621–1683) are the most famous members of families of violin makers. Guarneri's father, also named Giuseppe; his uncle Pietro; and his grandfather Andrea, all made fine instruments. Although these craftsmen are famous mainly for their violins, most made other string instruments as well. Stradivari's violas and cellos are highly prized, as are his lutes, guitars, and viols.

Each fine instrument has its own tonal character. This individuality results from the differences of vibrational response between pieces of wood (even among woods of the same variety), different varnishes, and especially different dimensions. Cellos may vary as much as two inches in body length, while violas may vary by nearly four inches. Although variations among violins are smaller, they are significant. Highly-arched Stainers are less brilliant than flatter "Strads."

Superb instruments have been produced in the years after 1740, but the early peak has not been surpassed. Yet many of the early instruments —including almost all of the violins—have been altered during the past 150 years. The transfer of concerts from noblemen's chambers to large concert halls demanded a matching increase in dynamic power. In the violin, the neck and FINGERBOARD were tilted back, requiring a higher bridge; a chin-rest was added. The neck was lengthened and gut strings were discarded in favor of strings made of steel or of nylon wound with metal. These are put under greater tension than formerly and the inside supports of the instruments have therefore been strengthened. Gut strings are still used for the cello and bass; often they are wound with metal.

BOW construction has been changed sharply. In the 17th century there was a very gentle convexity to the upper portion, particularly at the tip. In the modern bow the tip has a sharp rise and the overall shape is plano-concave. The bow is made of horsehair attached to a rod of Pernambuco wood in such fashion that the tension of the hair can be adjusted.

Technique. Instruments of the violin family are normally played by drawing a bow— placed between the bridge and fingerboard—over one or more strings. The bow hair is rubbed with ROSIN (resin) so that it should grip properly. Since the bridge is curved, the player governs the choice of string by changing the angle of elevation of the bow. Two notes may be played at one time by having the bow touch two strings. The technique is known as *double-stopping*. *Triple-stops* can be produced by greater bow pressure, but only two of the three notes can be sustained. The bridge conducts the strings' vibrations to the body. (They are spread over the entire surface with the aid of the bass-bar, a narrow strip of wood glued inside the body, running perpendicular to the left foot of the bridge.) If the normal vibrations of the bridge are restricted by a MUTE—often a triple-pronged, clamplike device— a special, subdued tone quality results.

Nuances of bow technique permit the string player to obtain great subtlety of articulation and considerable tonal variety. A smooth *legato* is secured by playing several notes with one uninterrupted bow stroke. Or the bow may be lifted after each note, or skip along the string; or the bow direction may be reversed after each note or group of notes. A rapid, tiny, back-and-forth movement of the bow produces an effect known as a *tremolo*. Placing the bow close to the bridge (*sul ponticello*) results in a strange, glassy tone, while placing the bow near or above the fingerboard (*sul taste*) results in a rather colorless tone. Sometimes the composer may direct that the player strike the string with the wood of the bow (*col legno*). The bow may be temporarily discarded and the strings plucked (*pizzicato*). *Coll' arco* signals the return to playing with the bow.

The fingers of the hand supporting the instrument govern pitch by firmly stopping a given string against the fingerboard, thus determining its vibrating length. (A tiny oscillation in this length, produced by a shaking motion of the hand, results in a tonal variation known as VIBRATO.) At the top of the fingerboard, an average handspan will control the INTERVAL of a fifth (only a fourth on the double bass). Extended range is obtained not only by changing from lower strings to higher ones, but by shifting the entire hand to a higher position on the fingerboard, each position beginning a tone higher than the previous one. Since a perceptible variation of TONE COLOR results when the same note is played on different strings, the art of FINGERING can be very subtle. A light rather than firm stopping of the string will produce harmonies with flutelike tones.

Music. Apart from KEY-

BOARD instruments, the violin enjoys the greatest of all SOLO instrumental literatures; that belonging to the cello is a distant second. Only a small proportion of this literature is for unaccompanied violin or cello, as, for example, in the SONATAS for each of these instruments by BACH or in compositions of the mid-20th century. There is an extraordinarily rich literature for violin and keyboard, with examples from all periods and all of the main nations, and the violin is often used as a solo instrument either in a CONCERTO or as an OBBLIGATO part to a Baroque movement for vocal solo. The same is true, to a more limited extent, of cello music. The viola is less fortunate because, as a middle-range instrument, it was overshadowed during the Baroque and CLASSICAL periods. During the 19th century the viola gradually received more attention in CHAMBER MUSIC and this interest has slowly spread to its orchestral and solo possibilities. Although there have been a few outstanding bass virtuosos, the literature for that instrument is negligible. The greatest corpus of chamber music is written for STRING QUARTET, consisting of two violins, viola, and cello; this repertoire dates from c.1750. Numerous other combinations of string instruments have also been used. The violin family constitutes the backbone of the ORCHESTRA; normally there are two violin parts and one part for each of the other string instruments, each part being played by a group of players. Many works have been written for string orchestra, without the use of winds.

Violine (G): VIOLIN.

Violino (I), **Violon** (F): (1) in modern usage, VIOLIN; (2) in 16th-century usage, a generic term for the members of the VIOL and violin families; (3) in 17th-century usage, *violon* was a generic term for the members of the violin family.

Violino piccolo (I): a small violin, tuned a third or fourth higher than the standard instrument, used c.1600–1750. BACH wrote solo parts for the violino piccolo in the *Brandenburg Concerto No. 1* and in Cantata 140.

Violino pomposa (I): see VIOLA POMPOSA.

Violon (F): see VIOLINO.

Violoncello: the bass member of the VIOLIN FAMILY, held between the knees.

Violoncello piccolo (I): a small-sized cello preferred by BACH for solo parts because it was better adapted to rapid passage work than the contemporary German cello of standard size.

Violone (I): (1) the double bass viol (a six-stringed instrument); (2) in 18th-century usage, the term was applied also to a double bass violin.

Viotti, Giovanni Battista: *b.* Fontanetto da Po, May 12, 1755; *d.* London, March 3, 1824. Following a highly successful European tour as a violinist, Viotti settled in Paris in 1782, where he became court musician to Marie Antoinette and joint director of the Italian opera. He was forced to flee France in 1792, going to England and then Germany, returning to France, 1819–22. Viotti contributed significantly to the advancement of violin technique and wrote 29 concertos for his instrument. Other works include string ENSEMBLE music, violin and piano SONATAS, solo piano sonatas and two *symphonies concertantes.*

Virelai (F): a French musicopoetic refrain form of the 13th to 16th centuries. The structure consists of a refrain —often divisible into two segments—a couplet comprised of equal halves, a tierce (patterned after the poetic structure of the refrain and employing the refrain's music), and finally the return of the refrain. The individual sections may comprise 2–5 lines of poetry. If there are several stanzas to the poem, the immediate repetition of the refrain is avoided by telescoping the final refrain of one stanza with the initial refrain of the next. In the 15th cen-tury, a one-stanza form of virelai was known as a *bergerette.* Similar or identical forms were known in other countries under the terms *ballata, villancico,* and *zajal;* the form was also employed in several CANTIGAS and LAUDE.

Virginal, Virginals, Pair of Virginals: a KEYBOARD instrument of the HARPSICHORD family (the plural forms of the term are misleading), used in Germany, the Netherlands, and, above all, in 16th- and 17th-century England. In modern usage, the term refers to small instruments of rectangular shape, but in English usage of the 16th and 17th century it was applied indiscriminately to instruments of rectangular, trapezoidal, or wing shape. A particularly rich literature was created for the instrument by such masters as BYRD, BULL, and GIBBONS.

Virtuoso: a performer of extraordinary technical capabilities. The term may also have a negative connotation, denoting a performer whose musical insight and knowledge is far inferior to his technique.

Vitali, Giovanni Battista: *b.* Cremona, *c.*1644; *d.* Modena, October 12, 1692. A pupil of the Bolognese composer Maurizio Cazzati, Vitali's most important posts were as assistant music director

(1674) and music director (1684) to the duke of Modena. Although active in several fields of composition, his chief importance lies in his CHAMBER MUSIC for strings. His trio SONATAS and dance movements provided influential models for his contemporaries and immediate successors.

Vitry, Philippe de: *b.* Vitry, October 31, 1291; *d.* Meaux, June 9, 1361; a churchman famed as a poet, composer, and musical theorist. In his treatise *Ars nova*, Vitry codified the new notational practices of the 14th century that reflected changed treatment of RHYTHM. A handful of isorhythmic MOTETS by Vitry survive.

Vivace (I): lively, fast; *vivacissimo*, very lively.

Vivaldi, Antonio: *b.* Venice, *c.*1675; *d.* Vienna, July 1741; leading BAROQUE CONCERTO composer.

Antonio received his first musical instruction from his father, Giovanni Battista, and studied later with Giovanni Legrenzi. He became a candidate for the priesthood in 1693 and took Holy Orders before 1703. From the latter date until 1740 Vivaldi was a teacher at the music school of the Convent of the Pietà in Venice. However, he was often absent for long periods; he traveled much and served the Landgrave of Hesse-Darmstadt for four years in Mantua. In 1740 Vivaldi went to Vienna, where he died impoverished.

Most of the large body of Vivaldi's vocal music—comprising about 40 OPERAS, secular CANTATAS, SERENADES, and church music—is now forgotten. His present fame rests on his 454 CONCERTOS, together with his SINFONIAS and CHAMBER MUSIC. Vivaldi played a vital role in the development of the solo concerto. In particular, the rhythmic incisiveness of his themes and their clear-cut structure influenced many Baroque composers. J. S. BACH greatly admired Vivaldi's concertos and used some written for violin as models for transcriptions.

Vivo (I): lively.

Vocalise: a textless composition for solo VOICE, either accompanied or unaccompanied.

Voce (I): voice; *colla voce,* a direction to an accompanist to adapt his playing to the rhythmic freedom employed by the singer; *mezza voce,* rather softly; *sotto voce,* very subdued in tone.

Vogler, Georg Joseph (Abbé): *b.* Würzburg, June 15, 1749; *d.* Darmstadt, May 6, 1814. The son of a violin maker, Vogler studied law and theology, took Holy Orders in 1773, and was made chamberlain to the pope and

Knight of the Golden Spur. He completed his musical training under MARTINI and Vallotti. He held court posts at Mannheim (later moving to Munich) and then Stockholm, and traveled extensively. He founded several schools and wrote about his teaching theories. WEBER and MEYERBEER were among his pupils. An organist, Vogler developed several new ideas on organ building. He was a prolific composer, writing OPERAS, a large variety of sacred music, CHAMBER MUSIC, organ and piano pieces, and piano CONCERTOS.

Voice: man's most direct and personal means of musical expression. The vocal mechanism consists of the lungs, which act as a bellows, the vocal cords, which act as a double reed, and the various cavities of the upper body and head (lungs, throat, mouth, nose, sinuses), which act as resonators.

In general, singing requires a greater breath supply, kept under a greater and better controlled pressure, than speaking. If, however, this controlled pressure—or breath support—is obtained through the constriction of the throat muscles, the effect on both the vocal tone and the physical mechanism itself will be harmful. In ordinary breathing, the vocal cords are relaxed and wide apart. In speaking and singing, they are brought into close proximity; the air pushing by them causes them to vibrate, producing a tone. The more relaxed the vocal cords are, the lower the tone; the tighter they are, the higher the tone. The loudness of the tone varies according to the degree of breath pressure. The vocal sounds produced vary according to the shape of the mouth's resonating cavity, which is controlled by the position of the tongue. The principles of vocal technique are subtler than those of instrumental techniques because they depend to a greater extent on inner sensation rather than on outwardly visible movement.

The vocal range of the individual depends partly on physical constitution and partly on training. One who sings infrequently may find the octave-and-a-fifth range of the *Star Spangled Banner* taxing. A trained singer, on the other hand, usually has a compass of about two OCTAVES; exceptional individuals have attained compasses of three octaves. The male range may be extended upward by the use of falsetto. This is an artificial way of singing in which the vocal cords vibrate only on the edges rather than en masse. The resultant tone quality is thinner than normal. The high parts of early choral polyphony were often sung falsetto by male altos when boy choristers were unavailable. Now, however, falsetto is little used; the technique survives in some English choral groups and is occasionally used by soloists for particularly high notes lying outside their normal range.

In choral organizations it is customary to distinguish between four vocal ranges: *soprano, alto* (the customary, shortened form of contralto), *tenor*, and *bass*. The first two indicate high and low women's voices, respectively; the last two, high and low men's voices. A *mezzo-soprano* (often known as a *mezzo*) is a woman with an intermediate vocal range; her male counterpart is known as a *baritone*. The average vocal ranges may be described as follows:

The actual range used in choral writing is apt to be somewhat less than that given, while the range of an extensive operatic part is often greater.

Voices are classed not only according to range, but also according to TONE COLOR. A *dramatic soprano*, for example, has a strong voice used for powerful dramatic effect; such a voice is required for Wagnerian heroines. A *lyric soprano*, on the other hand, has a lighter and more agile voice, capable of sustaining more delicate lines and possessing greater purity of tone. Midway between the two is the *lirico spinto*, a voice combining some of the power of the dramatic soprano with the finesse of the lyric. A soprano with a particularly high range and great agility is generally known as a *coloratura soprano* (or merely COLORATURA); a more suitable, though less familiar designation is *soprano leggiero*. Distinctions between tenor voices parallel those drawn between so-

Vocal ranges of:

A) Soprano B) Alto C) Tenor D) Bass

pranos. There is the *dramatic tenor* (*tenore robusto*) and the *lyric tenor* (*tenore di grazia*). Among singers of the German school, the former is known also as a *Heldentenor* (heroic tenor). A tenor with a particularly light voice and a range corresponding to that of a contralto is known as a *countertenor*; such voices are rare. The countertenor is particularly useful in the performance of early music. A bass with a deep and powerful voice is termed a *basso profondo*, whereas one with a lighter voice is known as a *basso cantante*. Russian basses are famous for the depth of their voices.

Range indicates mainly the extremes of a voice or vocal part. Of greater importance is that section of the range which is used consistently in a vocal part or which is comfortable for the voice. This section is known as the *tessitura*. It is the tessitura rather than the range that determines the suitability of a part for a given singer. A bass or contralto, for example, might be capable of occasional high notes, but would probably be uncomfortable in a piece of high tessitura. A tenor or soprano, on the other hand, would probably be uncomfortable in a piece of low tessitura, even if the notes remained within the extremes

of the vocal range. (*See also* REGISTER.)

Although vocal music normally has text, the voice may also be used without text, for the sake of its tone color. That is, the voice may be treated as an instrument. The technique of singing on a vowel—rather than with text —is known as *vocalization*. Vocalises—pieces intended for this method of performance—are often written as technical exercises; compositions employing this technique include DEBUSSY's *Sirènes*, RAVEL's *Vocalise en forme d'Habanera*, VAUGHN WILLIAMS' *Flos Campi*, and VILLA-LOBOS' *Bachianas Brasileiras, No. 5*. The technique was apparently used extentively during the Middle Ages and RENAISSANCE.

When text and MELODY are combined, the demands of dramatic expression may conflict with those of vocal tone production. In the late 17th and 18th centuries it was customary—especially among Italian operatic singers—to emphasize sheer vocal beauty and brilliance. The resultant style, which is still of importance, is termed *bel canto* (literally, beautiful singing). In the 19th century the ROMANTICS favored a more dramatic style. The voice might be distorted by combining the vocal tone with either a whisper, sob, laugh, or cry of rage; this was done to enhance the effectiveness of the text. The modern artist should command both styles.

The attributes of desirable vocal tone have varied according to period and civilization. They continue to vary. The man who views singing as the embodiment of a spirit, the man who uses singing to enter a trance, and the man who enjoys a vocal concert as one of the finer graces of life obviously have vastly different conceptions of vocal tone. In the first two instances, the voice is often meant to be disguised—unnatural. The tone quality of Oriental singing is usually far more nasal than that of Western singing. It is thought that this style influenced the singing of early Christian CHANT; some traces are still to be observed in certain Catholic churches. Even within the more limited sphere of Western music, singing styles vary from country to country. Divergences of style among the numerous singers of "hit songs" of the present day are particularly noticeable.

Voice, Voice-part: any one of the several melodic strands forming a polyphonic web. These terms are applicable to both instrumental and vocal music. They are used chiefly in the discussion of works of contrapuntal texture—especially FUGUES; however, they may be used also in the discussion of works of primarily homophonic texture provided that the number of notes (and RESTS) used simultaneously remains fairly constant and there is a logical progression from each note to the following one on the same relative level.

Voice leading, Part writing (Brit.): the progression of each of the several voices of a work from one tone to the next with proper regard for the relationship between the various voices. The composer is expected to work out the voice leading of a composition to conform with the melodic and harmonic usage of his given style and to produce for each voice the most interesting melodic line possible within the stylistic context. The theorist examines voice leading in order to determine some of the hallmarks of a given style and to ascertain the composer's skillfulness within the style.

Volkslied (G): a FOLK SONG or a popular song in folk style.

Volles Werk (G): full ORGAN.

Volta (I): (1) a dance of the late 16th and early 17th centuries in fast 6/8 time; (2) *see* PRIMA VOLTA, SECONDA VOLTA.

Volti (I): turn (the page);

volti subito, turn quickly (a warning to be prepared to resume playing quickly).

Voluntary: an English composition for organ designed to introduce or conclude services. The earliest of these, appearing in the mid-16th century, are short works in imitative style. After 1600, voluntaries were written in a number of different styles corresponding to those of various other contemporary genres (e.g., TOCCATA, ARIA, etc.). Often voluntaries were improvised.

Vorspiel (G): PRELUDE, operatic OVERTURE.

Vuota (I): empty; *corda vuota*, opening string; *misura vuota*, a measure of silence.

W

Wagenseil, Georg Christoph: *b*. Vienna, January 15, 1715; *d*. Vienna, March 1, 1777. A court composer in Vienna, Wagenseil contributed to the development of the early classical SYMPHONY. He wrote also CONCERTOS, a dozen OPERAS, three ORATORIOS, and some CHAMBER MUSIC.

Wagner, (Wilhelm) Richard: *b*. Leipzig, May 22, 1813; *d*. Venice, February 13, 1883; the greatest German operatic composer.

Wagner was largely a self-taught musician. Composition was learned in snatches, his early instrumental works being quite insignificant. Wagner's interest in the theater derived perhaps from his step-father (possibly his true father), the actor Ludwig Geyer. He achieved stature not merely by virtue of his considerable literary and musical talents, but also through a fierce determination and an egocentric outlook that brooked no ethical bounds.

Wagner began his career in 1833 as a chorusmaster at Würzburg, where his brother Albert was stage manager. The following year he became conductor at Magdeburg, going to Königsberg in 1836 and Riga in 1837. During these years he wrote the librettos and music to *Die Feen* and *Das Liebesverbot* and began *Rienzi, der Letzte der Tribunen*. In 1839 Wagner went to Paris in an attempt to have *Rienzi* performed there. Failing, he managed a precarious living doing hack work. Successful performances in Dresden of *Rienzi* in 1842 led to a court appointment, first as conductor and later as music director. *The Flying Dutchman* was produced in 1843 and *Tannhäuser* in 1845. Unable to obtain immediate performance of *Lohengrin* (produced in 1850 by LISZT at Weimar), Wagner became enmeshed in radical politics and had to flee Saxony with the failure of the May 1849 revolt. He was aided during the next decade by many friends, especially Liszt, whose music influenced Wagner's. These years were spent primarily in Switzerland, although Wagner also fulfilled conducting engagements in London and Paris. He issued several essays on his operatic philosophies and began writing his mature masterpieces. The first two

OPERAS of *The Ring of the Nibelung, Das Rheingold* and *Die Walküre*, were completed in 1854 and 1856; *Tristan und Isolde* was finished in 1859. In 1860 Wagner was permitted to reenter Germany except for Saxony, where he was barred until 1862. The personal patronage of King Ludwig of Bavaria relieved Wagner of his most pressing financial difficulties in 1864. *Die Meistersinger von Nürnberg* was completed in 1867 and *Siegfried* (the third part of the *Ring*) a few years later. In 1872 the city of Bayreuth offered Wagner a site for a special theater; the completion of the building in 1876 was marked by a full performance of the *Ring*, including *Götterdämmerung* (*The Twilight of the Gods*), finished two years before. Wagner's last work was *Parsifal*, completed in 1882.

Wagner sought a new fusion of music and drama in a form uniting all arts, a *Gesamtkunstwerk*. Being both librettist and composer, he was in a unique position to achieve this aim. Primary emphasis was placed on dramatic continuity. Wagner created continuous scenes of large format, which he unified by means of varied rather than literal repetition. The alternation of RECITATIVE and ARIA, the use of small closed forms, vocal display for its own sake, and other operatic conventions hindering dramatic continuity were dispensed with. Wagner's vocal lines are comparatively terse and declamatory. The music itself is often propelled forward by a surging chromaticism, which, in *Tristan,* goes to the very bounds of the tonal system, if not beyond. The musical enrichment and interpretation of the drama is entrusted chiefly to the orchestra, the most important symbolic device being the LEITMOTIV. Wagner's mastery of ORCHESTRATION—including his enlargement of the brass section—is another central feature of his work. The flexibility of his technique is shown by *Die Meistersinger,* which, in its diatonic style and use of closed forms and ensembles, departs from several of Wagner's stated theories.

Wait: (1) a street musician, formerly a wind player employed by a king, nobleman, or by a town; (2) a piece of music performed by a group of waits; (3) a synonym for SHAWM.

Waldhorn (G): the French horn; in 19th-century usage, a distinction was sometimes made between the *Waldhorn* (a valveless horn) and the *Ventilhorn* (a horn with valves).

Waldteufel, Emil: *b.* Strasbourg, December 9, 1837; *d.* Paris, February 16, 1915. One of the best-known WALTZ composers of his time, Waldteufel was trained at the Paris and Strasbourg Conservatories. The success of his first works determined his further career and led to rewarding tours of major European cities. Among the most famous of his waltzes are *The Skaters, Estudiantina,* and *Dolores.*

Walther, Johann Gottfried: *b.* Erfurt, September 18, 1684; *d.* Weimar, March 23, 1748. A pupil of J. Bernhard Bach, Walther served as town organist at Weimar beginning in 1707 and as court musician beginning in 1720. His CHORALE variations rank among his most important compositions. Although respected as a composer, he is best remembered as the compiler of the first music lexicon to include biography, bibliography and terms, the *Musikalisches Lexikon oder Musikalische Bibliothek,* Leipzig, 1732. He wrote also a composition textbook.

Walton, William Turner: *b.* Oldham, March 29, 1902. The son of a music teacher, Walton studied at Christ Church, Oxford. He won early prominence through *Façade,* a witty setting of poems by Edith Sitwell for speaking voice and instruments. His music derives essentially from the ROMANTIC tradition. Prominent among his works are the OPERA *Troilus and Cressida,* the ORATORIO *Belshazzar's Feast,* a viola CONCERTO, a violin concerto, and two STRING QUARTETS. He wrote some fine film music.

Waltz: a dance in triple ME-TER that developed from the Ländler (or *Deutscher Tanz*) of the late 18th century. A waltz may be either slow, medium, or fast, the most characteristic TEMPO being moderately fast. Many of the famous waltzes intended for dancing were written by Viennese composers, among the more important being Joseph Lanner; Johann STRAUSS, Sr.; Johann STRAUSS, Jr. (nicknamed The Waltz King), and Josef STRAUSS. The characteristic harmonic accompaniment of the waltz consists of a low note on the first beat and light chords on the second and third beats. Waltz rhythms also stirred the imagination of more versatile composers, such as BERLIOZ, WEBER, CHOPIN, BRAHMS, TCHAIKOVSKY, R. STRAUSS, and RAVEL, who wrote waltzes intended wholly or primarily for concert performance rather than for dancing.

Walze (G): the crescendo pedal of an organ.

Walzer (G): WALTZ.

Weber, Carl Maria (Friedrich Ernst) von: *b.* Eutin, November 18, 1786; *d.* London,

June 5, 1826; the "founder" of German ROMANTIC OPERA.

Weber's father, an army officer and musical amateur, served as musical director to a traveling troupe. Because of this itinerant mode of life, Carl Maria studied briefly with a large number of teachers and obtained an early knowledge of the theater. He became a concert pianist while yet a boy and his first published compositions were for piano. Weber's later works for that instrument are in a facile virtuoso vein suited to the tastes for Romantic music. Other instrumental works include some CHAMBER MUSIC, CONCERTOS for various instruments, and two SYMPHONIES. From the age of thirteen much of his attention was devoted to opera. He held conducting posts at Breslau, Prague, and Dresden. After writing a few minor operas, including *Peter Schmell* and *Abu Hassan,* Weber began work on his masterpiece, *Der Freischütz,* in 1817, completing it about a year before its premiere in 1821. The opera was an instantaneous success. Its colorful ORCHESTRATION and the effective setting of a tale with a strange mixture of the supernatural and romance affected many works written in the following decades. Weber's last two major operas, *Euryanthe* and *Oberon,* show similar traits. Other vocal works by Weber include a few MASSES and CANTATAS, several choral works, and songs.

Webern, Anton, (von): *b.* Vienna, December 3, 1883; *d.* Mittersill, September 15, 1945; an outstanding serial composer.

Webern received a Ph.D. in musicology from the University of Vienna in 1906 after study with Guido Adler. From 1904 to 1910, he studied composition with SCHOENBERG. He was active for various periods as a conductor, chiefly in Prague, Vienna, and in Germany. After World War I he devoted himself mainly to composition and teaching.

Though Webern's output is relatively small—comprising only 31 opus numbers—his style has strongly influenced later generations of serial composers. His music contains fewer elements reminiscent of tonal practice and more purely serial elements than does that of BERG and Schoenberg. He presents highly refined musical ideas with utmost brevity and economy of means, several of his pieces lasting less than a minute each. Webern displays an acute sense of TONE COLOR, often tracing a line by means of one or a few notes played by each of several different instruments. Dynamics are controlled in great detail.

Contrapuntal techniques such as CANON are prominent in several works. Webern does not use large forces. Much of his music is for CHAMBER ENSEMBLE; there are also songs, choral works, piano pieces, and works for chamber orchestra.

Weelkes, Thomas: *b. c.*1575; *d.* London, November 30, 1623. Organist at Winchester College and then at Chichester Cathedral. Weelkes is known for his many fine MADRIGALS. He wrote also much church music, as well as works for instrumental ENSEMBLE.

Weill, Kurt: *b.* Dessau, March 2, 1900; *d.* New York, April 3, 1950. Among Weill's several teachers were HUMPERDINCK and BUSONI. Though he wrote assorted CHAMBER MUSIC, piano pieces, songs, choral, and orchestral works, he is known chiefly for a few of his stage works, including *The Three-Penny Opera, Down in the Valley,* and *Mahagonny*. He wrote the scores for several successful musical comedies.

Whole note, Whole rest: (i.e., a rest hanging below a line— usually the fourth).

Whole

Whole step (Whole tone, Major second): an INTERVAL containing two half steps. Any two keys (black or white) separated by one intervening key on the piano form a whole step. Its sound may be illustrated by humming the first two notes of *Frère Jacques*.

Widor, Charles-Marie Jean Albert: *b.* Lyons, February 21, 1844; *d.* Paris, March 12, 1937. The son of an organist, Widor completed his studies under Nicholas Lemmens and François Fétis. He became organist at St.-Sulpice in Paris and taught at the Paris Conservatories. Albert Schweitzer was one of his pupils. He composed ten large-scale organ works entitled symphonies, CHAMBER and orchestral music, songs, sacred music, and OPERAS.

Wiegenlied (G): cradle song.

Wieniawski, Henryk (Henri): *b.* Lublin, July 10, 1835; *d.* Moscow, April 12, 1880. One of the outstanding violinists of his generation, Wieniawski was trained at the Paris Conservatoire. He toured widely and taught for a few years each at the St. Petersburg and Brussels Conservatories. He composed for his instrument, writing CONCERTOS and shorter works suitable for the salons of the ROMANTIC era.

Wilbye, John: *b.* Diss, March 1574; *d.* Colchester, September 1638. Wilbye spent most of his life in the service of Sir Thomas Kytson. His two volumes of MADRIGALS rank high among English works of this genre. Also extant are a few sacred pieces.

Willaert, Adrian: *b.* Bruges(?), *c.*1485; *d.* Venice, December 7, 1562. A student of Mouton in Paris, Willaert went to Italy as a young man, seeing service with the Este family. From December 12, 1527, he was music director of St. Mark's in Venice. Willaert's music represents a gradual blending of Netherlandish contrapuntal and Italian harmonic idioms. One of the great masters of the polyphonic MADRIGAL, Willaert also composed CHANSONS, MOTETS, PSALMS, and MASSES. He was also an important instrumental composer, especially in the field of the RICERCAR and CANZONA. At St. Mark's, prompted by the existence of two choir lofts, he developed the practice of writing for two antiphonal CHOIRS, a feature that was to become characteristic of Venetian music for some time. Among his pupils were Andrea GABRIELI, RORE, and Gioseffo Zarlino.

Wind machine: a mechanism used to imitate the sound of wind, called for occasionally in orchestral scores (e.g., in R. STRAUSS's *Don Quixote*). The sound is produced by friction. Silk is stretched over the surface of a barrel-like frame that is placed in a cradle; when the frame is rotated by means of a handle, the cloth rubs against a hard face of wood or cardboard. The speed with which the framework is turned regulates the pitch of "the wind."

Wolf: in general, a disagreeable sound produced either by an improper tuning of an instrument, by design problems in the construction of an instrument, or by musical problems occurring within a given system of TUNING. The term may, for example, describe the sounds produced by a pair of imperfectly tuned organ pipes, certain weak tones on bowed string instruments, or the conflict between enharmonic PITCHES in systems other than equal temperament.

Wolf, Hugo: *b.* Windischgraz, March 13, 1860; *d.* Vienna, February 22, 1903; outstanding late ROMANTIC song composer.

Wolf received his first musical training from his father, an amateur musician. He entered the Vienna Conservatory in 1875 but was expelled in 1877 because of a quarrel with the director. Wolf supported himself at first by giving piano lessons. From 1883 to 1887 he was critic for the *Wiener Salonblatt.* An unstable person of violent opinions and an ardent admirer of WAGNER, Wolf poured abuse on BRAHMS and others whose principles were opposed to Wagner's. A large proportion of his finest music was composed during two brief periods, 1888–91 and 1895–97. These periods of intense activity alternated with periods of infertility and despondency. In 1897 Wolf suffered a mental breakdown; his remaining years were spent in an asylum.

Wolf's songs—about 300 in number—rank with those of SCHUBERT, SCHUMANN, and Brahms. He also wrote *Der Corregidor* (an OPERA), the *Italienische Serenade* (one version for STRING QUARTET, another for orchestra), *Penthesilea* (a SYMPHONIC POEM), a string quartet, and some choral works. Wolf was particularly sensitive to his song texts and drew on some of the finest German poets—Goethe, Mörike, and Eichendorff—and German translations of Spanish and Italian poems—including three by Michelangelo. The nature of the individual poem is closely reflected in its setting. The lighthearted texts are often coupled with folklike melodies and diatonic harmonies. The more serious ones, representative of the larger part of Wolf's production, are usually set by terse declamatory melodies in a style closely related to that of Wagner and by chromatic harmonies. The piano is given a vital role in the establishment of mood.

Woodwinds: instruments that are played by blowing across a mouth-hole or into a whistle mouthpiece or reed, thus causing an enclosed column of air to vibrate. While most woodwinds are made of wood, some are made of either bamboo or other reedy materials, earthenware, metal, or plastic. The orchestral woodwinds comprise members of the flute, oboe, clarinet, and bassoon families. Other important families are the saxophones and recorders.

The *flute* is now a cylindrical tube, about 26½ inches in length and ¾ inch in diameter. Its head is closed by a parabolic stopper; the player blows across a side hole a few inches from this end. The instrument has a range of three OCTAVES, its lowest note normally being *middle c*. The lowest octave is rather husky and breathy in sound; the middle is clear and pure, and the highest penetrating and somewhat shrill. While older instruments were turned from wood, present instruments, made in three joints, are generally made of silver. (In rare instances gold or platinum may be used.) Other

members of the flute family are the *piccolo*, a tiny flute sounding an octave higher; the *alto flute* (sometimes called a bass flute), a fourth lower than the normal flute; and the *bass* (or contrabass) flute, an octave lower than normal. The last instrument is very rarely used.

The *oboe* consists of a conical tube, about 23½ inches in length, with an upper outside diameter of ¾ of an inch and a lower outside diameter of about 2 inches. The oboe is also made in three joints; the lowest, called the *bell*, flares gently. A double REED is inserted into the upper end. The instrument has a range of just under three octaves, beginning a second lower than the flute. The oboe has a nasal, somewhat melancholy sound. The lowest notes are difficult to play softly; the upper ones tend to be thin. Normally, the instrument body is made of one of a few, hard, black, woods, but recently some fine instruments have been made of plastic, eliminating problems of cracking that occur in wood. The keys are made of metal, plated with silver. Other instruments of the oboe family are the *English horn*, an instrument with a pear-shaped bell, pitched a fifth lower than the oboe; the *oboe d'amore*, similar to the Eng-

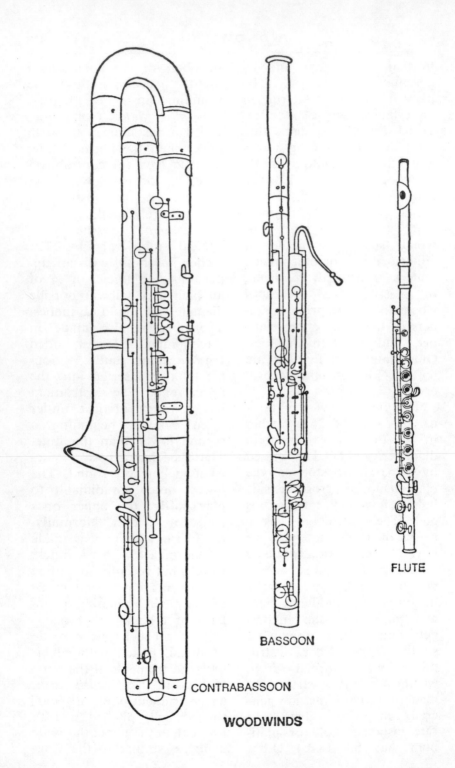

CONTRABASSOON

BASSOON

FLUTE

WOODWINDS

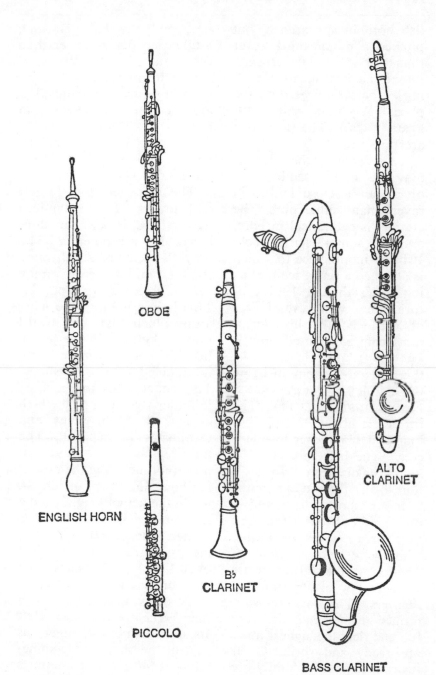

OBOE

ENGLISH HORN

PICCOLO

B♭
CLARINET

BASS CLARINET

ALTO
CLARINET

lish horn in appearance, but pitched a minor third lower than the oboe; and the *Heckelphone*, an instrument sounding an octave lower than the oboe. (*See* TRANSPOSING INSTRUMENTS.) The last two are rarely used.

To a novice, the *clarinet* may at first resemble the oboe, but a close look will reveal many differences. The clarinet is cylindrical in bore, and has a more flaring bell. It has a mouthpiece to which is attached a single reed. During the 18th and 19th centuries there were several sizes of clarinets; the instrument most commonly used now is known as a clarinet in *B*♭, the next most common being the clarinet in *A* (*see* TRANSPOSING INSTRUMENTS). The former is about 23½ inches long and 1¼ inches in diameter. (The bell flares to 2⅞ inches in diameter.) In addition to the three main joints, it has a short barrel and a mouthpiece. It has a range of over three octaves, beginning with the *e* below *middle c′*. The tone of the clarinet varies considerably in its different registers. The low register, termed *chalumeau*, is very full and rich; the highest notes are reedy and shrill. Other instruments of the family are the small *E*♭ clarinet, pitched a fourth above the *B*♭ clarinet; the alto clarinet in *E*♭, a fifth lower than the *B*♭ clari-

net; and the bass clarinet, pitched an octave lower than the standard instrument. These instruments are common in symphonic bands, but are used only infrequently in orchestras. There is also a double-bass (contrabass) clarinet, two octaves lower than the *B*♭ clarinet.

The *bassoon*, the largest and lowest of the standard woodwinds, is another double-reed instrument. The player's breath passes through the reed into a narrow piping called a crook (or bocal). This is inserted into the wing joint, which leads downward into the butt (or double-joint); here the conical wind column is doubled into a *U*-shape. The outlet leads to the long joint, an ascending pipe which adjoins the wing joint and terminates in the bell. The total length of the wind column (not including the crook) is about 85 inches in length, while the actual height of the instrument is about 52½ inches. The outside diameter increases gradually from just over 1 inch to 2 inches. The bassoon has a range of over three octaves, beginning with the *b*♭ below the bass clef. Its sound is not as pungent as that of the oboe, but is somewhat reedier and sometimes buzzy. The uppermost register has an unusual, thin quality. Still larger than the bassoon is the contrabassoon (double bassoon), pitched an octave lower.

The *saxophones* are a family of seven metal instruments, invented by Adolphe Sax in the 1840s. They are conical, with a mouthpiece and single reed similar to that of the clarinet. The family comprises the *sopranino* in *Eb*, the *soprano* in *Bb*, the *alto* in *Eb*, the *tenor* in *Bb*, the *baritone* in *Eb*, the *bass* in *Bb*, and the *contrabass* in *Eb* (*see* TRANSPOSING INSTRUMENTS). The *alto, tenor,* and *baritone saxophones* are used regularly in dance bands and in symphonic and marching bands; the alto saxophone is occasionally employed in orchestral scores. The highest and lowest saxophones are rarely used. The tone quality is capable of much variation; the jazz style is often powerful and strident, the symphonic style, restrained and smooth.

A little-known counterpart to the saxophones are the *Sarrusophones,* a family of nine conical, metal instruments with double reeds invented by Sarrus about 1856. They are used in French military bands, and the contrabass sarrusophone is sometimes used in French orchestras instead of the contrabassoon.

The *recorders* are among the few modern woodwinds that are entirely or largely without a key mechanism. These instruments are vertical flutes, the orchestral flutes being of the transverse variety. The player's breath passes through a flue and is split against a sharp edge incised in the front of the instrument, a few inches from the top. Part of the airstream is diverted outside the instrument; part remains within the wind column, which is shaped in a contracting cone. There are four main sizes of recorders: *soprano* (descant), *alto* (treble), *tenor,* and *bass;* the lowest note of each is, respectively, the *c* above *middle c*, the *f* above *middle c, middle c*, and the *f* below *middle c*. These instruments have ranges of just over two octaves each, except for the bass recorder, whose range is slightly smaller. Larger and deeper bass recorders have been built, as well as small sopranino recorders.

Technique. The basic principles of woodwind playing are similar for all instruments, even though the embouchure—the position of the lip muscles—varies according to the instrument. Each woodwind has a number of holes in its tube. As each additional hole is closed by the player's finger (proceeding successively downward from the top), a lower pitch is obtained. These pitches form a segment of a major SCALE.

Intermediate pitches needed for a chromatic passage may be had by cross-FINGERING. This technique involves the uncovering of the next lowest or third lowest of a series of covered holes. It may entail two disadvantages: pitch may be somewhat inaccurate, and tone quality may be inferior. To avoid these faults, modern woodwinds are fitted out with spring-actuated key mechanisms. These permit the instrument maker to drill a greater number of holes into the instrument than could normally be covered by the fingers, thus avoiding the necessity for cross-fingering. Keys also permit the acoustically correct positioning of the holes when such positioning would require difficult or impossible finger stretches without keys. Specific key mechanisms vary from instrument to instrument, even though their basic principles are few in number. Often one key has partial or complete control over the closing of several holes. Extended range is obtained by overblowing. That is, a tightening of the lip muscles and an increase of breath pressure will produce a high note (harmonic) rather than the low one (fundamental) normally obtained through a given fingering. Often OVERBLOWING is aided by opening a tiny hole near the top of the instru-

ment. All instruments except the clarinet overblow first at the octave (second harmonic); the clarinet overblows at the twelfth (third harmonic) (*see* ACOUSTICS). By increasing the pressure still further, higher harmonics may be obtained.

Articulation — phrasing — depends on the continuity or interruption of the breath, which can be controlled by the tongue. In order to obtain a precise beginning to a tone, the player releases his breath by forming the letter *t*, as in *ta* or *too*. If a series of detached notes is desired, this process is repeated for each note. If a series of connected notes (*legato*) is desired, the breath stream remains uninterrupted for the duration of the series. Double-TONGUING (*ta-ka, ta-ka, ta-ka*, etc.) and triple-tonguing (*ta-ka-ta, ta-ka-ta,* or *ta-ta-ka, ta-ta-ka,* etc.) may be employed in passages too rapid for single tonguing. An unusual tone quality may be produced by flutter-tonguing, produced by a motion similar to that required by a heavily rolled "r."

History. Ancestors of flutes and oboes were known to ancient civilizations of the Near and Far East; their primitive counterparts are found today in widely scattered areas. The single reed instruments (clarinets) are of slightly more recent origin. In

Europe, in the Middle Ages, the woodwinds were often used outdoors for military or other processions and for dancing. The modern instruments began to evolve during the second half of the 17th century. Jean Hotteterre and Michel Philidor are credited with developing the oboe from its predecessor, the SHAWM. Differences between the two instruments involve a narrower and more exact bore, smaller fingerholes, and a narrower, lip-controlled reed as characteristic of the newer instrument. The flute was also remodeled during this period, possibly by the same men. It retained its cylindrical head, but adopted a narrowing conical bore, which was used until the mid-19th century, at which time the flute again became cylindrical. The clarinet was developed near the end of the 17th century by J. C. Denner, who apparently based his work on a folk instrument. The creation of the various complex key mechanisms was the work of several 19th-century instrument makers. Among the most important were Theobald Boehm (1794–1881) and Adolphe Sax (1814–94). In addition, the improvements of Auguste Buffet, Guillaume and Frédéric Triébert, and Wilhelm Heckel (who contributed especially to the development of the bassoon) were significant.

Music. The woodwinds are essentially ENSEMBLE instruments. Music for a single instrument, such as BACH's *Sonatas for Solo Flute,* is rare. A woodwind may be used in SOLO capacity, either in a CONCERTO for one or more solo instruments (and orchestra) or as the solo part of an accompaniment to a vocal ARIA in a CANTATA, ORATORIO, MASS, PASSION, or OPERA. The greater part of this repertoire was created during the BAROQUE era. There is also a modest, but steadily growing repertoire of woodwind CHAMBER MUSIC that includes trio SONATAS and other Baroque works for mixed groups, and SERENADES, DIVERTIMENTI, and NOTTURNI of the CLASSICAL period. (The latter are also often for mixed groups.) The term *woodwind quintet* normally denotes an ensemble consisting of flute, oboe, clarinet, bassoon, and French horn (a BRASS INSTRUMENT). The recorder was used prominently during the Baroque—Bach's Second and Fourth Brandenburg Concertos, for example, contain solo parts for recorder —and the instrument is also appropriate for the performance of much MEDIEVAL and RENAISSANCE music. However, little music was written for recorder after 1800. A major part of the woodwind repertoire consists of orchestral parts. Style in ORCHESTRATION has, of course, changed greatly over the past three centuries. In the Baroque, oboes, bassoons, and flutes were each used to provide swathes of color. In Classical scores, these swathes were usually broken into short snatches, bringing about greater variety and contrast of color. During the 19th century, composers became increasingly conscious of tone color and individual instru-mental idioms. It was then that the clarinet first achieved orchestral prominence. In some 20th-century works, instruments are employed in atypical rather than idiomatic fashion. During the present century, music for concert band—providing another segment of the woodwind repertoire—has slowly risen in quality. The band is becoming less dependent upon MARCHES and transcriptions of music written for other media.

Word painting: *see* PROGRAM MUSIC.

X

Xylophone: (1) a family of instruments consisting of wooden bars of graded sizes, supported at two nodes, and struck by sticks, clubs, or globular beaters. Primitive instruments of this family may consist of nothing more than a few bars placed across the legs or across a wooden trough. As late as the mid-19th century European virtuosi used small bundles of straw as supports for the wooden bars. Modern instruments have a fixed frame of wood or metal, the bars resting on strips of felt or rubber. If without resonators, the instrument may be placed on a table, or it may have a stand that places it at a comfortable playing height. Forms of xylophones with tubular metal resonators, one hung below each bar, are being used more and more. The bars themselves are arranged in two interlaced rows, somewhat in the fashion of a piano keyboard. The longer the bar, the deeper the tone. Some degree of tonal variation may be obtained by using beaters with heads of different degrees of hardness. (2) The term is also used loosely to describe other instruments of similar format, whether the bars are made of wood (as in the MARIMBA), metal (as in the VIBRAPHONE), or stone. The latter two varieties are more properly classed as *metallophones* and *lithophones*, respectively. The marimba has a lower range than the xylophone and is characterized by the use of gourd or wooden resonators. The vibraphone has bars of a metal alloy and tubular metal resonators with circular discs at the upper ends. By means of a motor these discs may be rotated on their axes, thus alternately opening and closing the resonators and producing thereby the effect of a vibrato. The speed of this vibrato is determined by the speed with which the discs rotate, this being subject to a motor control. The GLOCKENSPIEL is a portable metallophone used especially in marching bands.

Z

Zampogna (I): (1) BAGPIPE; (2) SHAWM; (3) HURDY-GURDY.
Zarzuela (S): a Spanish OPERA with spoken dialogue. The genre, traceable to the mid-17th century, was espe-

cially popular during the late 19th and early 20th centuries. The works of this latter period fall into two main classes: the light, comic *zarzuelitas (genero chico)* in one act and the serious, dramatic *zarzuelas grande* in three acts.

Zilafone (I): XYLOPHONE.

Zingarese, Alla (I): in gypsy style.

Zink (G): the cornett, an obsolete, wooden, wind instrument (*see* BRASS INSTRUMENTS).

Zither: (1) a generic designation for a large family of string instruments having neither a neck or yoke, the strings being stretched from one end of the body to the other. The body itself may have the form of a round stick (as in the *vina* or *sitar* of India), a lath, a tube, or a shallow box (as in the psaltery, dulcimer, piano, harpsichord, clavichord, etc.). The body may serve as a resonator or it may require one or more attached resonators. (2) A specific term for an instrument classifiable as a *board zither*, with a flat, wooden sound box and 30 or more strings. The four or five strings closest to the player serve for the melody; they run above frets and are played with a PLECTRUM. The remainder serve for the accompaniment and are plucked with the fingers. (3) A *chord zither* is a related instrument with a mechanism that governs the simultaneous shortening of several strings, facilitating the playing of a few simple CHORDS. (4) a German term for CITTERN.

Zoppa, Alla (I): designation for a rhythm employing a short note on the BEAT, followed by one three times as long, after the beat; synonym for SCOTCH SNAP.

Zukunfstmusik (G): "Music of the Future," a designation used in the late 19th century with reference to the music of WAGNER.

Zumsteeg, Johann Rudolf: *b.* Sachsenflur, January 10, 1760; *d.* Stuttgart, January 27, 1802. A director of the Stuttgart Opera from 1792, Zumsteeg wrote eight OPERAS, together with several church CANTATAS and assorted instrumental music. He is best remembered, however, as the precursor of SCHUBERT in the composition of BALLADES for solo voice and piano.

Zurückhaltend (G): holding back.

Zwischenspiel (G): (1) interlude; (2) episode.

FOR REFERENCE

Do Not Take From This Room